Kimchi and IT
nformation echnology

Tradition and Transformation in Korea

Choong Soon Kim

ILCHOKAK

Copyright © 2007 Choong Soon Kim
Published by ILCHOKAK

ILCHOKAK Publishing Co., Ltd.
1-335 Sinmunno 2-ga, Jongno-gu, Seoul, Korea 110-062
Tel 82-2-733-5430
Fax 82-2-738-5857

All rights reserved. No part of this book may be reproduced in any form or any means without the written permission of publisher.

First published 2007
Printed in Seoul, Korea
ISBN 978-89-337-0528-5 03300

한국국제교류재단

The Korea Foundation has provided financial assistance for the undertaking of this publication project.

The National Library of Korea Cataloging-in-Publication Data

Kimchi and IT / Kim Choong Soon. -- Seoul, Ilchokak, 2007
p. ;   cm

Includes bibliography
ISBN 978-89-337-0528-5 03300 : ₩30,000

911-KDC4
951.9-DDC21   CIP2007003586

Acknowledgments

Since this book is a synthesis of my previous research and the work of other scholars, I am indebted to numerous individuals and organizations. Nevertheless, because it is difficult to acknowledge all of them here, I have been ruthlessly selective in listing their names and parsimoniously brief in mentioning their roles.

In preparing for this project, I drew an overall picture of Korea and its culture in 1993 when I was writing a section on Korea for the *Encyclopedia of World Cultures* under the auspices and with the support of the Human Relations Area Files at Yale University (Kim 1993:144-149). Several chapters of this book are a synthesis of my previous fieldwork and subsequent publications thereafter, especially chapter 2 (Nascent Modernization in the Midst of the 'Broken Calm'), chapter 3 (Political Evolution and Revolution in Contemporary Korea), and chapter 9 (Economic Development, Industrialization, and Environmental Conservation). Harumi Befu's (1971) introductory book on Japan has been a valuable guide in organizing this volume.

Publication of this book has been partially supported by a publication grant to the publisher from the Korea Foundation, to which I am immensely indebted. Also, I have built upon insights garnered through research made possible by various funding sources, and I am grateful for their support. They are the Asia Foundation (1963-1965); Committee on Korean Studies, Association on Asian Studies (1988); Institute for Far Eastern Studies, Kyungnam University (1988); a National Science Foundation grant for travel (1988); two Alma and Hal Reagan Faculty Development Grants (1993, 1998); the Rockefeller Foundation's Scholar-in-Residence Award (1991-1992); two Senior Fulbright Research and Lecturing Grants (1988-1989, 1993-1994); a Smithsonian Institution Travel Grant (1978); the U.S. Department of Health, Education, and Welfare (1974, 1978); E. Hunter Welles (2000); the Wenner-Gren Foundation for Anthropological Research (1988); and numerous Faculty Research Grants from the University of Tennessee at Martin (1981, 1982, 1984, 1986, 1988, 1991-1992, 1996).

I owe special gratitude to Kyung-Koo Han [Han Kyung-Koo], a fellow anthropologist and personal friend, who has been a staunch advocate for this project, and offered me many valuable suggestions and comments for revision of an earlier draft. His constructive criticism improved this book. Samuel Gerald Collins, a fellow anthropologist and a Koreanist, read this manuscript during his tenure in Korea as a senior Fulbright scholar. I owe special thanks to Kyungjin Cho [Cho Kyungjin], who filled in the roughest spots after reading the first draft of the manuscript word by word, making it a readable book. Sarah M. Nelson and Chong-pil Choe [Choe Chong-pil], both of whom are archaeologists and experts in Korea, also read the draft version and offered valuable comments and suggestions.

In its enthusiastic support and expeditious evaluation, Ilchokak Publisging Co., Ltd. was essential to this project. I am particularly indebted to K.E. Duffin, Lisa Eveleigh, and Lee Minjeong for their meticulous editing. Um Hyesun has been a highly capable assistant in researching relevant materials.

I owe many thanks to my family: my wife, Sang Boon; my two sons, John and Drew; my two daughters-in-law, Karen and Nancy; and my grandchildren, Matthew, Ryan, Jack, Luke, and Caroline. They have been inspirational.

Contents

Acknowledgments — V

INTRODUCTION — 1

Korea as an Obscure Nation · 1
Is Korea the Land of the "Morning Calm?" · 3
Contents of the Book · 6
Through an Anthropological Lens · 9
Romanization · 12

CHAPTER 1 — Cultural Origins and Historical Background — 15

The Origins of Korean Ethnicity · 16
Prehistory of Korea · 19
Early History · 24
Contemporary Koreans' Renewed Interest in the Three Kingdoms · 25
The Three Kingdoms · 27
The Cultural Legacy of the Three Kingdoms Period · 33
Goryeo Dynasty · 34
Joseon Dynasty · 38

CHAPTER 2 — Nascent Modernization in the Midst of "Broken Calm" — 47

Modernization as a Complex Process · 50
Transformation of Joseon Society in the Midst of Japanese Domination · 52
Japanese Colonization and the Independence Movement · 57
Korean Modernization in Retrospect: "Development without Development" · 67
Recent Korean Modernization Since the Mid-1960s · 68
Role of a Mandatory Draft in Recent Korean Modernization · 70

CHAPTER 3   **Political Evolution and Revolution in Contemporary Korea** ——————— 73

    The Post-War Power Vacuum · 76
    The General Election and the Birth of the Republic of Korea · 82
    The Fratricidal Korean War · 84
    Evolution and Revolution of Korean Politics · 90
    Democratic Development · 97
    Regionalism vs. "Generationalism" in Contemporary Korean Politics · 99
    Structure and Organization of the Current Korean Government · 104
    Current Inter-Korean Relations · 105

CHAPTER 4   **Kinship, Marriage, and Family** ——————— 109

    Kinship is the Key · 112
    Marriage · 112
    How Does One Marry? : Ceremonial Aspects of Korean Marriage · 124
    Family · 131
    Achievement of Korean Women · 135
    Kin Group Organization and Kinship System · 137

CHAPTER 5   **Traditional Rural Life and the Current Exodus** ——————— 143

    Maeul as the Center of Social Life in Rural Korea · 144
    The Social Structure of Korean Villages · 148
    Transformation of Rural Korean Villages · 155
    Massive Exodus of Rural Peasants to Urban and Industrial Zones · 167
    The Changing Paradigm of Korea's Rural Villages · 171

CHAPTER 6   **Religion and Belief** ——————— 179

    Inclusiveness and Syncretism · 180
    Korean Native Beliefs · 183
    Foreign-born Religions in Korea · 190
    New Religions · 213

CHAPTER 7   **Class, Mobility, and Education** —————— 219

    Historical Survey of Korean Social Classes · 220
    Joseon Social Classes with Yangban · 221
    Ranking of Occupational Prestige · 224
    Recent Social Classes · 225
    Education for Korean Upward Mobility · 226
    Education in Contemporary Korea · 232
    Korean Enthusiasm for Overseas Education · 236
    The Korean Obsession with Education and the "Three 'Nots' Policy" · 240
    Challenges for Korean Education · 246

CHAPTER 8   **Ethos** —————————————————— 249

    Historical Circumstance and the Korean Ethos · 252
    Contradictory Patterns · 259
    Diminishing Traditional Patterns · 271
    Persisting Patterns · 275

CHAPTER 9   **Economic Development, Industrialization, and Environmental Conservation** —————— 281

    Economic Development and Industrialization · 281
    Motivating Forces of Korean Development: What Makes Korea Tick? · 292
    Environmental Conservation · 301
    Environmental Alteration and the Restoration Movement · 304
    Restoration Projects · 308

EPILOGUE   **Korea's Place in the World: The "Hermit Kingdom" No More?** ———————— 317

    From "Mendicant" to Foreign Aid Donor · 317
    The Challenge of Continuing Economic Development and Industrialization · 319
    Improving the Quality of Life · 333
    Can an Anthropologist Go Home Again? · 337

Notes · 341
Selected Bibliography Cited · 391
List of Abbreviations · 415
Index · 417

INTRODUCTION

Korea as an Obscure Nation

In the late 1960s, when I was conducting anthropological fieldwork on pulpwood harvesting industrial workers in the American rural South, a woodworker wanted to know my ethnic identity. He asked me, "Are you Chinese?" When I answered "no," he persisted "Are you Japanese?" When I said "no" again, he seemed frustrated. "What the hell are you, then?" That I was Korean never occurred to him.

Michael Breen (204:ix), a British journalist who has covered North and South Korea for several newspapers, tells a shocking story: "A relative of mine once asked me, 'Korea? That's part of Vietnam, isn't it?'" Unfortunately, such ignorance about Korea is not rare. It was even common among academics until recently. In the mid-1980s, for instance, a college level textbook on Asia published by a major publisher in the United States treated Korea along with Tibet in a single chapter under the title "Land of Mystery and Isolation" (Tweddell and Kimball 1985:245-262).

When foreigners were asked to free-associate about Korea — to complete the sentence "when I think of Korea, I think of ⋯ the words that tumbled out included divided, violent, riots, police, military, grim, war, corruption, tariffs, Olympics, World Cup, freezing, MASH,[1] cars, ships, computer chips, financial crisis" (Breen 2004:16). Even

1

someone familiar with the industrial products manufactured by Samsung, LG, and Hyundai does not always connect them with Korea. Foreigners' images of Korea can be vary slightly by their age, sex, political persuasion, education, and contact with Korea and Koreans.

Korea has a prehistory that stretches over half a million years (Nelson 1993:26). It has also been an independent kingdom for much of its millennia-long history, and has maintained a homogeneous culture with an exceptional continuity (Henderson 1968:13). Nevertheless, Korea has been obscure to the outside world, for a long time. Perhaps the isolationist policy developed by Daewongun's regent from 1864 to 1873, in response to foreign intrusion contributed to the image of Korea as the "Hermit Kingdom"[2] — "isolated" and "secluded."

Although Korea has maintained a distinct culture, it has often been assumed that its culture and tradition are merely pale imitations of those of China and Japan. As Sarah M. Nelson (1993:5) has pointed out, "Korea is not and was not a mere off-shoot of China. Nor is Korea a clone of Japan." As a result, in schools throughout the world, Korean studies are given secondary status, if not ignored outright.[3]

Because of its geographic location, Korea has long been considered very important strategically to Asian and Russian powers. Yet Korea has been overlooked in the past and still is today. In the thirteenth century, Korea was the Mongols' military base in their attempt to subjugate Japan. It was Korea's strategic importance that drew Japan into the Russo-Japanese War (1904-1905). Korea again became a hot spot during the Cold War era, although it was clear that American strategic planners had very limited knowledge of Korea. Even Gen. John Hodge, the former Commanding General of the U.S. Armed Forces in Korea, "instructed his officers that Korea was an enemy of the United States" and therefore "subject to the provisions and the terms of the surrender" (Cumings 1981:126). Hodge's lack of knowledge about Korea created political chaos in postwar Korea and led to further confusion regarding the role of the United States in the Korean peninsula (Henderson 1968:121).

After World War II, U.S. involvement in Korean affairs was deep and its impact profound. The American military government ruled Korea for three years following World War II. It played a major role during the Korean War (1950-1953), in which some 33,000 young Americans lost their lives. After the war, America gave over $1.3 billion in aid to Korea. Nevertheless, there have been very few experts on Korea in the United States. David Steinberg, an expert on Korea and former director of the Asia Foundation, surmises that "fewer than half a dozen U.S. academicians could be considered 'experts' on Korea" (Steinberg 1989:xiii).[4] Despite intensive contact between the two countries for the past half a century, Steinberg's earlier assessment remains largely unchanged. Even during the most critical situations, such as North Korea's nuclear weapons test in October 2006, and ongoing negotiations between Korea and the United States to sign a Free Trade Agreement (FTA) in April 2007, few experts on Korea have been available.

A more serious problem than lack of interest was the distorted image held by world-class intellectuals such as George Kennan, a well-known writer and intimate friend of former President Theodore Roosevelt. Kennan was the source of the worst image of Korea yet known to the Western world, blasting Koreans as "the rotten product of a decayed Oriental civilization"[5] and suggesting that Japan's takeover of all Korean affairs would be logical, for as a people, Koreans were inferior to the Japanese (Choy 1979:66; Cumings 1997:129-30; Grajdanzev 1944:34-36; Kim 2000:2-4).[6]

Since Korea has been so grossly misunderstood at times, and it is still necessary, periodically, to counteract the legacy of such incomprehension. The best way to do so is by closely examining the real Korea.

Is Korea the Land of the "Morning Calm?"

Korea is located in the middle of the Far East, adjacent to China and Japan. Although Korea is a peninsula, it is separated from the Asian continent by two mighty rivers, the Amnokgang (Yalu), which flows to

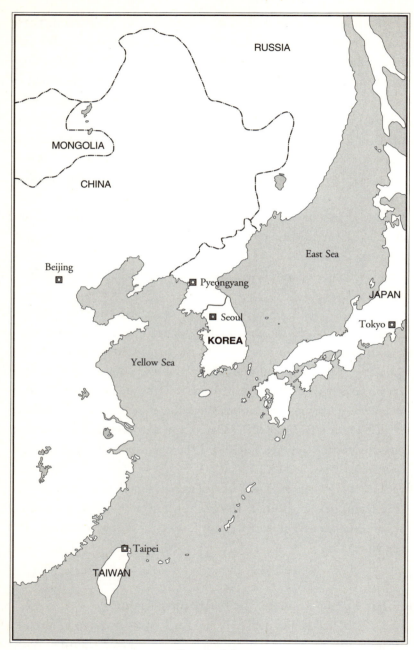
Korea in Asia

the Hwanghae(Yellow Sea) from the Baekdusan, and the Dumangang (Tumen). The long northern border of the Korean peninsula abuts the vast expanse of China, including Manchuria, an area almost forty-three times the size of Korea. The vast Russo-Siberian landmass, with which Korea shares a sixteen-kilometer border, defies comparison with Korea if only because of its sheer size. Across the East Sea sits Japan, almost 70 percent larger than Korea.[7] Thus surrounded, the peninsula has always been vulnerable to attacks from neighboring countries, which are bigger, stronger, and sometimes hostile.

The name "Korea" comes from the Goryeo (Koryŏ) dynasty (918-1392), but Koreans themselves have long used the term "Joseon (Chosŏn)," which originates from the name of the first Korean state of Gojoseon (2333-108 B.C.).[8] The literal meaning of Joseon, the Korean version of the Chinese phrase *chao-hsien*, may be roughly translated as "morning calm and freshness." From this, Korea acquired the epithet, "the land of the morning calm." Percival Lowell (1855-1916), an American astronomer and author of several books on East Asia, was the first to use the translation "Land of the Morning Calm" for the title of his 1886 book on *Joseon*. Lowell was also the counselor to the 1883 Special Mission from Korea to the United States (Pobingsa).

Those familiar with the geopolitical history of Korea may wonder if Korea has ever been calm. Historical evidence indicates that Koreans, instead of resting peacefully, have often awakened to the clattering of horses' hooves or the artillery fire of foreign invaders. It is perhaps more appropriate to call Korea "the land of broken calm," the subtitle of Shannon McCune's (1966) book on Korea. Nevertheless, Korea has been united since the seventh century and has maintained its identity and cultural uniformity with a common language while enduring the depredations of foreign intruders as well as internal wars. Since 1945, however, the Korean peninsula has been divided into north and south along the thirty-eighth parallel. Presently, over 70 million people live on the peninsula.[9] Even in the past century, Korea had to endure Japanese colonization as well as the devastating Korean War. Despite these adversities, Korea has managed to transform itself from one of the poorest nations to one of the largest economies in the world, a radical transformation indeed.

Korea's recent visibility in the world community, heightened by its phenomenal economic growth and increase in international trade as well as its role as host to the 1988 Summer Olympic Games and the 2002 FIFA World Cup (co-hosted with Japan), has generated a growing worldwide interest in Korea. Who are the Koreans entering our lives as employers, business associates, and partners? Who are the Koreans that enroll in our colleges and universities? Who are the Koreans that make our ships, cars, and cell-phones? What makes Koreans different from the Chinese and Japanese? Where have they come from, and where are they going? Most importantly, what makes Korea tick?

Contents of the Book

My desire to write this book came about when I was unable to find an adequate textbook on Korea after being assigned to teach a survey course on East Asia at the University of Tennessee at Martin in 1971. Colleagues who had similar teaching assignments shared the same difficulty. As representative of Anthropologists for Korean Studies (AKS), an interest group in the American Anthropological Association, I assembled an *ad hoc* committee to edit a book to address this need. The committee worked on the project until the mid-1990s, but its members were so overwhelmed by their respective commitments that the volume never crystallized. I believe that demand for such a text still exists, and the need to complete this book has always been in the back of my mind.

In the meantime, demand for a comprehensive introduction to Korea has also come from overseas Korean descendants — Korean Americans, Korean Canadians, and others — eager to learn about their ethnic heritage. Additional impetus comes from the non-academic fields of business and industry. As overseas direct investment has grown, Korean business and industrial circles have realized they need a book in English that can introduce Korea and its culture to the native people who work for overseas Korean firms. When I was a chief advisor to the chairman of PMX Industries, Inc., a Korean direct investment firm in Cedar Rapids, Iowa, I had to resort to my lecture notes to teach workers about Korea.

Also, another motivation for writing this book is the recent growing popularity of Korean pop culture. The "Korean pop-culture wave" or "*Hallyu,*" the Korean version of the Chinese phrase "*Hanliu,*"[10] has generated much interest in Korea and its culture. This pop-culture term was coined in response to the public's enthusiasm for Korean movies and television soap operas as well as musical performances by Korean singers and dancers in Japan, China, Taiwan, and other Southeast Asian countries in the early 2000s. The number of foreign visitors to Korea reached an all-time high of 6 million in 2005, when this wave was at its peak. Bae Yongjoon, a Korean actor who played a major role in one of the most popular TV soap operas, *Gyeoul Yeonga* (Winter Sonata), generated $4 billion.[11] The smash-hit TV soap opera series *Daejanggeum* (Jewel in the Palace) and the actress Lee Youngae, who plays the female protagonist, have been so popular in China, Hong Kong, Taiwan, and other Southeast Asian countries that the networks are offering reruns.[12]

As for the current international popularity of Korean pop culture, Ogawa Junko, a Japanese television producer with the Japanese NHK network, states that it has not come about simply because the actors and actresses in those movies and dramas are handsome, attractive, and beautiful, but because the Japanese viewing audience is attracted by Korean culture itself.[13] This insight seems sound, because since the beginning of *Hallyu*, more and more foreigners are becoming interested in learning about Korean culture.

When I was no longer teaching in the classroom and advising business and industrial firms, I encountered a more personal use for this book: I needed a way to teach my grandchildren who were born and still live in the United States about Korea and its culture. When you are developing a textbook for your own grandchildren, you realize how important it is to select the most essential subjects and present them effectively, to sustain interest. Many overseas Korean parents and grandparents share my situation and sentiments.

With such a multi-dimensional inquiry in mind, I have organized this book into ten chapters. Chapter 1, in an effort to trace the racial and cultural origins of Koreans, introduces the prehistory of Korea based on recent archaeological findings and summarizes its ancient history from the early kingdoms to the recent dynasties. Chapter 2 surveys the most turbulent history of Korea, the modern era beginning in the nineteenth century, which can aptly be described as a time of "broken calm" instead of "morning calm." During this period, Korea had to endure Japanese invasion, Western intrusion, World War II, the partition of the peninsula, and the Korean War.

Chapter 3 describes the evolutionary and revolutionary process of Korean political institutions. This chapter includes autocratic rule, military control, and the recent civilian government, in the context of hegemonic struggles between and among regions and age groups, especially those who were born in the 1960s and went to college in the 1980s. Traditional Korean marriage, family, and kinship patterns as well as the effects of modern trends are discussed in Chapter 4. Chapter 5 describes Korea's rural village life and the changes resulting from urbanization, industrialization, and the New Village Movement (*Saemaeul Undong*), along with the role of a mandatory military draft system and its impact on Korean modernization and rural development. Addressing Korean religious beliefs, Chapter 6 explores Korea's indigenous beliefs systems, including ancestor worship, village gods, and Shamanism as well as foreign-born religions such as Buddhism, Christianity, and Taoism. Since the Korean view of religion is inclusive, Koreans often combine several religious systems into one, creating new religions such as "Cheondogyo" (Religion of the Heavenly Way) among others.

Chapter 7 addresses Korean class, mobility, and education. Because traditional Korean social classes were largely ascribed and hereditary, social mobility was limited. However, as Korean society gradually adopted an open-class system, education became a major means for improving class affiliation and attaining new status. This chapter discusses the resulting obsession with education that characterizes contemporary Koreans. The many sacrifices made for education not only impose a heavy burden on parents financially, but also hinder traditional family life. Chapter 8 examines the origins of the Korean ethos and how it has changed in response to Korea's economic development and hosting of various world events such as the 1988 Summer Olympic Games and the 2002 FIFA World Cup. Chapter 9 summarizes Korean economic development and industrialization, and offers an anthropological interpretation of Korea's success. Korea's rapid industrialization has accelerated its economic advancement, but has also brought about various environmental hazards. This chapter discusses Korea's environmental problem as a major challenge, if not threat, and efforts to maintain a balanced ecosystem; it also introduces two major environmental restoration projects. It describes how the Demilitarized Zone (DMZ), which was devised to prevent inter-Korean acts of hostility and remains inaccessible to the public, has become a safe haven for ecological studies. In the epilogue, I relate my personal sentiments about Korean's accomplishments and future prospects, and the need for Koreans to address the importance of the humanities for quality of life and environmental issues.

Through an Anthropological Lens

This book is not intended only for professional anthropologists or Korea specialists, and has been written for a broad audience. Nevertheless, I admit that I have not been completely free from my disciplinary bias as an anthropologist. Consequently, I have emphasized the overarching relationships among components of culture such as kinship, marriage and family, social structure. Also, even though this book deals with one society, it makes historical comparisons between traditional and modern Korea to trace the sources of the most recent changes.

This book adopts several features of anthropological works.

Following anthropological tradition, generalizations about the subjects are not a prominent feature. Instead, I have made an effort to delineate local realities (Fernandez 1982:xx).[14] Indeed, the views of the so-called natives or inculture persons are important as Magorah Maruyama (1969:229-280) has stated: "Inculture persons are full of hypotheses of their own. These are inculture-relevant hypotheses, and are often of the sort that cannot be dreamed up by outsiders."

I realize that giving my viewpoint as a native Korean may allow subjective feelings to hinder objectivity. However, such subjectivity can be minimized because I have taken many advantages of my dual identity as both insider and outsider: I am, in a sense, an insider who was born, raised, and partly educated in Korea for twenty-seven years, but I am also an outsider who has been absent from Korea for a prolonged period of time — living, teaching, and doing research in the United States for many years — and thus I have acquired reflexivity — a "sense of distancing from self" (Fernandez 1980:27-39).[15] Reflexivity has been an asset to my way of thinking, and results from my life and work in other cultures (Kim 1977, 1987, 1990, 2002).

Relating my own perceptions about Korea and its culture on the basis of my own field experience helps in gauging how far Korea has shifted from tradition to modernity, a process mirrored by my own journey from the premodern to the ultramodern. I believe that readers may find some knowledge of my background useful in interpreting the subjects I have included in the book, although a good many anthropologists have typically avoided talking about themselves. Miles Richardson (1975:53), an anthropologist and a good friend of mine, has indicated that traditionally "anthropologists have published little on their social background and their place in American society." As anthropologists Lamont Lindstrom and Peter Stromberg (1999:9) have indicated, "When anthropologists talk, people expect to hear about others — not about themselves."

Margaret Mead (1972) might have been exceptional in incorporating into her work her own insights and experiences from childhood and personal experiences in various cultures, including Samoa, Bali, and

New Guinea. She makes the case for anthropology as an intimate interpersonal understanding in her celebrated book *Blackberry Winter* (1972). Recently, anthropologists have begun to describe their own backgrounds in discussing their field experiences. Notably, a growing number of feminist anthropologists, whose origins are non-Western and who have done their fieldwork at home, and anthropologists whose origins encompass both Western and non-Western worlds have been very candid in discussing their backgrounds.[16]

By relating my life history as this book unfolds, I can enhance a reader's understanding of Korean history, especially the Japanese colonial period (1919-1945) and the Korean War (1950-1953). Although much has been written on these periods, in the interest of objectivity most historical documents deal with "his story," not "my story." My story may lack objectivity in comparison with "his story," but the validity of life history as a major research method is well documented in the anthropological literature (Kim 1998; Langness 1965). Life histories are "useful for examining the patterning of general values, foci of cultural interests, and perceptions of social and natural relationships ⋯ and very frequently a chief anthropological concern is the patterning of people's beliefs and conceptualizations of past events, rather than the truth or falseness of these accounts" (Pelto 1970:99). My aim in relating my life history is to reflect the sentiments of many Koreans of my generation who struggled to survive under colonial rule, war, and poverty. I hope that this book is in part an ethnohistory of an encapsulated modern Korean society.[17]

In my lifetime, I have had many extreme experiences. Cumulatively, these experiences constitute a long journey — temporally, from the premodern to the ultramodern; and spatially, from East to West. The village in which I was born consisted of a single patrilineal clan of *yangban* (noble class) that had lived there since the Joseon dynasty. Kinship rules dominated in village life. I was born the last son of a landlord who lost his fortune due to the 1949 Land Reform. When I left the village in the mid-1960s, it did not even have electricity or a single telephone. When I returned (which actually felt more like "going," not "returning") three decades later, the village had been transformed into to an ultramodern place equipped with personal computers and Internet access. Via the Internet, the villagers could reach virtually anyone, anywhere in the world. I cannot think of any generation of human beings other than my own that has gone through such a drastic change and cultural transformation in so short a time.

During my stay in the United States, I conducted anthropological fieldwork with various groups of rural whites and rural African Americans in the American South, Native Americans in twenty-two states, Southern and Midwestern industrial workers who work for "foreign bosses," and Japanese entrepreneurs, business and industrial managers in the American South. At the same time, in order not to lose my ties with Korea, I did fieldwork there as well from the early 1980s, studying the Korean families dispersed by the partition of the peninsula, and Korean business and industrial organizations.

In this late stage of my academic career, after I returned to Korea in 2001 to assume the presidency of Korea Digital University, a completely on-line university, I began studying contemporary Korean society for this book. In sum, it is a synthesis of my previous work on Korea, coupled with my participation in and observation of Korea as an actual resident.

Following anthropological tradition, this book relies more on qualitative information rather than quantified statistics. Using quantitative data with elaborate statistics not only hinders the understanding of readers, but such data may not even warrant credulity. Francis L.K. Hsu's (1977:206) "pebble analogy" captures the sentiments of many anthropologists: "Some of our scientific investigations are not unlike counting, classifying and 'computerizing' pebbles on the beach to determine the causes of rising and ebbing of tides."

Romanization
In this book, Korean terms, including the names of persons, dynasties,

and places, except for Seoul, are romanized according to new Korean Romanization system, which was developed by The National Institute of the Korean Language in July 2000. However, there are so many exceptions to the new system, because so many Korean authors, including myself, have established their own romanizations for their names and published elsewhere before the new system has been introduced. I do not have any choice but to respect their preferences in citing their names and their publications in this book. Also, even now, many articles and books published in the West still use the conventional McCune-Reischauer system in romanizing Korean terms.[18] When I quote their works on Korea in this book, I have to quote them as they are, instead of translating their works from the McCune-Reischauer system into the new Korean Romanization system. This will confuse many readers. There is an episode regarding such a confusion resulting from two different ways of romanization: a foreign traveler came to Busan (romanization in accordance with the new Korean system), and asked directions to go to Pusan(romanization of McCune-Reischauer system).

Also, I have to warn readers about another possible confusion regarding the order of Korean and Japanese names. Following Korean and Japanese usage, when I refer to Koreans and Japanese, I give their family names first before their personal names, except for Syngman Rhee. However, when the publications of Korean and Japanese authors are in English, I follow the Western practice of personal name before family name. As a result, in some cases a person's name may appear in two different ways in the book. Readers can assume that if any Korean author's last name appears first his publication is in Korean. The same principle has been applied in the bibliography: Korean and Japanese authors whose works were written in their native languages are listed by their family names without placing a comma before their personal names. Otherwise, I follow the Western practice.

Most of the materials included in this book are on South Korea because I have been unable to access the North. Except for some less reliable secondary sources and piecemeal information, I have not been able to consult any thoughtful anthropological scholarship on fieldwork in North Korea. Because of such limitations, this work cannot treat both Koreas equally. If one day I gain access to the North, I would be willing to revise this book. In the meantime, I have made every effort to avoid misleading readers by making unsupported assumptions about North Korea or by presenting a distorted image of the North. The official name of South Korea is the Republic of Korea (ROK) and the official name of North Korea is the Democratic People's Republic of Korea (DPRK). Throughout this book, however, the informal designations Korea or South Korea for ROK and North Korea for DPRK have been adopted for easier reading, but they are not intended to have either a positive or negative connotation. I do not want to undermine or discredit the integrity of either regime.

CHAPTER 1

Cultural Origins and Historical Background

Every once in a while I was asked by American colleagues at the university where I used to teach whether I could identify the nationality of East Asians — Chinese, Japanese, or Koreans — just by looking at them. In order to spark a lively conversation, I used to say, "Although I might not be able to provide any definite way of discerning them, I think I might be able to tell fairly well when I see an East Asian." This is analogous to an astute remark made by former U.S. Justice Potter Stewart when he was asked to distinguish between "art" and "obscenity." Stewart answered, "Although I couldn't rightfully define obscenity, I know it when I see it."[1]

If I can indeed discern whether someone is Chinese, Japanese, or Korean, such ability is not based on scientific findings, but on my personal feelings, instinct, and experience in associating with East Asians. Nevertheless, I have to confess that it is difficult to judge by appearance alone, for some Koreans have features more similar to Chinese than to fellow Koreans. For instance, Francis L.K. Hsu (1909-1999), a Manchurian-born anthropologist and my former mentor, used to comment to me, "You and I look more alike than any other fellow Chinese and I. Your ancestors and my ancestors might have belonged to the same tribe." It was a casual remark, yet it provokes curiosity about the origins of East Asians in general, and Koreans in particular.

In spite of the complexity of determining nationality by appearance, East Asians do seem to belong to different physical groups. Sarah M. Nelson (1993:6) states that "Koreans as a people can be distinguished as a physical type, different from the Japanese and Chinese. Physical comparison of many kinds, including blood types and fingerprints, show the Koreans to be related to their neighbors, but possessing their own distinctive patterns of gene frequencies."

The Origins of Korean Ethnicity

It is widely understood that the population of the Korean peninsula is more homogeneous culturally, physically, and linguistically than most large groups of people elsewhere in the world. This suggests a shared ethnic origin, but whether contemporary Koreans are the descendants of early inhabitants of the peninsula remains an unanswered question.

We do not know whether Paleolithic (300,000-350,000 B.P.) foragers on the peninsula metamorphosed into villagers, whether a new group of pottery producers migrated from the north, bringing with them an advanced foraging technology, or whether pottery came from China or Japan by diffusion (Kown 1990:4-12). A major population influx may have occurred during the Neolithic (6000-2000 B.C.) when people who originated in the Lake Baikal region of the north moved into the peninsula. Subsequently, they may have been expelled or assimilated by the Tungus group, who introduced bronze metallurgy and agriculture (Kim 1963:5-8, 1973). However there is no direct evidence to support the migration theory (Choe 1991:7-43; Nelson 1993:265).

To trace the racial origins of the Neolithic inhabitants of the Korean peninsula, some archaeologists, such as Se-jin Na(1963:9-29), have studied physical traits of present-day Koreans, including cranium index, epicanthic fold, and skin color, for comparison. However, Chong Pil Choe (1991:42) indicates that "the division of the populations of any species into biological 'race' tends to be arbitrary, but when it comes to human races, the situation is a quagmire. The population of H. [Homo] sapiens is not on its way to speciation. There are no nonadaptive physical traits. A phenotype is the result of the dynamic interaction of several genes and the environment. Therefore, particular physical traits cannot delineate the boundaries between ethnic groups." In fact, there is no such thing as a racially pure human group. During the Goryeo dynasty (918-1392), many Jurchen migrated into the Goryeo domain, and to these people, all of whom were assimilated into the Korean population, Goryeo gave land, dwellings, and a means of livelihood (Eckert et al. 1990:78).[2]

From a physical and archeological standpoint, there is not enough evidence to reach solid conclusions about the origins of Koreans in the peninsula. As Nelson (1993:267) states, many of the hypotheses and propositions regarding Korean ethnic origins are now considered fairy tales. Reality was probably far more complex. New traits were introduced to the Korean peninsula gradually and proliferated into many strands over thousands of years (Choe 1991:7-43; Nelson 1993:267).

In tracing Korean ethnic identity, aspects of culture including the Korean language and traditions may shed light on Korean ethnicity, although some Chinese cultural influences are prominent and profound as Hi-seung Lee (1963:13-16) has shown. As Nelson (1993:6) indicates, "The Korean language is a prime example of both the distinctiveness of the peninsula from nearby lands and the relative homogeneity within." Korean is spoken as the primary language of the entire population, and dialect differences are minor throughout the length of the peninsula. As languages, Korean and Chinese are entirely different and unrelated, even though the Korean vocabulary has been enriched by Chinese loan words.[3] Nevertheless, one can see an affinity between the Korean and Japanese languages. They are comparable in grammatical structures (Befu 1971:17; Miller 1980), but vocabulary similarities appear to be largely based on the identity of Chinese loan words.[4]

Other ethnographic evidence can shed light on the origins of Korean ethnicity and its continuity. Anthropologists have recently traced a particularly potent symbol of personal and group identity by describing and analyzing certain foods (Wilk 1999:244-255). Some archaeologists use beverages such as beer to denote ethnic identity (Farnsworth 2000:18; Wilkie and Farnsworth 1999:283-320). *Kimchi*, pickled cabbage and radish, invariably seasoned with spices and condiments, is a food that can be used in tracing Korean ethnic identity (Kim 2002:xvii). Several scholars surmise that even in the "Early Villages" period (6000-2000 B.C.) inhabitants used large storage vessels called *onggi* (Sayers: 1987:58-63) as *kimchi* pots (Nelson 1993: 263). *Kimchi* has long been a popular Korean food and its export overseas has become a thriving business.

There are several other ethnographic clues to Korean identity, all of which have been corroborated by archaeological findings (Nelson (1993:262-263):

> Koguryo [Goguryeo] wall murals depict clothing, hairstyles, dwellings and even kitchens that were little changed into this century. Straw sandals and the *chige*, a device for carrying loads on the back, are represented in Silla and Kaya pottery, along with shoes with upturned toes. ··· Royal burials continued to be made under the largest mounds through the end of Yi [Joseon] dynasty. Continuous traditions since the Three Kingdoms period are quite clear ··· *ondol* floor goes back to that time [Wŏnsamguk time]. A large town of semi-subterranean dwellings in Cholla Namdo shows that houses built above the ground were not instantly adopted everywhere, and Chinese records (especially the *Wei Ji*) relate to this point as well.

A major difficulty is trying to understand synchronic East Asian entities of the past by using today's concept of the modern nation-state. Lothar von Falkenhausen (1987)[5] has raised this crucial question: "What territory do we mean?" Before the modern-day name "Korea" came into being, there had been many different names over time for the country whose sphere of interaction stretched from the eastern border of the Mongols via Manchuria, a northern part of China proper, into central Japan. Most importantly, the world of "Korea," whatever its boundaries in previous eras, intermingled with that of its neighbors. Any single prehistoric and/or historic event invariably involved a large part of East Asia. The prehistoric inhabitants of East Asia did not have the same concept of territory that we have. There were no immigration officers, nor did people carry passports. Even the word "Asia" is irrelevant, for people were in the region long before the word was introduced.[6]

Prehistory of Korea

In searching for the ethnic and cultural origins of Koreans, a brief survey of Korean prehistory is in order. In fact, recent archaeological findings indicate that the Korean peninsula was inhabited by lower Paleolithic[7] people between 300,000 to 350,000 years ago (Bae 2002). Findings from Jeongok-ri and more than 100 other Paleolithic sites uncovered since the 1980s reveal various stone tools employed by Paleolithic people to hunt animals and utilize the vegetal resources of the deciduous forest. The early dwellers in the peninsula appear to have exploited marine resources as well. Shelters for dwellings indicate that these early inhabitants lived in small foraging groups consisting of extended families. Their largest social unit seems to have been the band.

Following the Paleolithic period, the early history of the Korean peninsula continued through the Mesolithic, Neolithic, Bronze Age, Iron Age, and formation of the early kingdoms. In analyzing the evolutionary stages of Korean prehistory, some scholars argue that the ancestors of contemporary Koreans are not the original inhabitants from the Paleolithic period but latecomers who arrived on the peninsula during the Neolithic period.[8] At present, however, there is no scientific evidence for or against this hypothesis.

Before the Paleolithic archeological period transitioned to the Neolithic period, a relatively short Mesolithic period[9] occurred in some

Paleolithic stone tools

parts of the Old World. During this time, humans acquired a wide variety of food sources, and thus the Mesolithic is known for the advent of "broad spectrum food collecting." In the past, some historians have expressed skepticism about the existence of a Mesolithic period in Korea (Eckert et al. 1990:3). However, archaeological findings in Gosan-ri and Hahwagye-ri, which predate 10000 B.P., indicate evidence of a Mesolithic presence on the peninsula, and a settled village life (Choe and Bale 2002:95-121).

Sedantary life, however, did not begin until the Neolithic period, approximately 6000-2000 B.C. (Nelson 1992). It was characterized by

Julmun (or "Combware"), a type of incised pottery whose exterior is decorated with geometric patterns. While some archaeologists such as Nelson (1993) and G.L.Barnes (1993) identify this pottery as "Julmun," other Korean archaeologists and their associates label it "Bitsalmunui" (Choe and Bale 2002:95-121). It is called combware because of the appearance of the geometric patterns on its exterior. "Julmun" or "Bitsalmunui" have frequently been used as general terms to describe the first 4,000 years or so of settled villages in Korea, analogous to the use of the term "Jōmon" in Japan's chronology (Nelson 1993:59).

The combined data on flora and fauna, artifacts, including stone hoes, stone sickles, and pottery, and dwellings, indicate that the Neolithic inhabitants of Korea practiced horticulture, had stable residences, and possessed the ability to store food. There is some speculation regarding their social organization and belief systems, but no archaeological findings substantiate any of these assumptions. However, the Korean Neolithic period differs from the Western Neolithic. "The stone-bronze-iron age sequence was created for European prehistory, where pottery, ground stone tool-making technology, sedentism, and agriculture are elements of the Neolithic cultural complex" (Choe and Bale 2002:96). Nevertheless, the Korean case does not follow the same sequence. According to Chong Pil Choe and Martin T. Bale (2002:96, 103), "A great deal of Korean research is based on the stylistic variation of pottery," because in Korea "sedentary village life was established in some areas by 6000 B.C., about 3,000 years before cultivation appeared." During the Neolithic period, however, the present national boundaries were wholly irrelevant, and networks of trade and other interaction were probably limited to the region (Nelson 1993:109).

Often referred to as the dawn of civilization,[10] the Bronze Age in the Korean peninsula may have begun around the fifteenth century B.C., although a great majority of researchers use a later date.[11] The cultural achievements of Korea in the Bronze Age were not as sophisticated as those of the Xia and Shang dynasties of China, a comparable era.[12] Nevertheless, the essential characteristics of Bronze

Age culture, including the use of bronze metallurgy, the emergence of craft specialists, and social inequality, along with intensive agriculture such as rice cultivation, were displayed.[13]

Most often, the Bronze Age is characterized by the use of bronze metallurgy, but some archaeologists, Chong Pil Choe for one, believe that the Korean Bronze Age can best be characterized by the appearance of dolmens.[14] Some burial objects removed from dolmen tombs are made of bronze. Dolmens can be seen in great numbers in virtually every part of the country and appear in two basic forms of construction: table-style and board-style.[15] Because so much labor had to be mobilized to erect them, the size of the dolmen capstone implies the presence of social stratification and a ruling elite.[16]

The ceramics from this period, Mumun pottery, and various lithics including polished stone artifacts and the semi-lunar knife, provide evidence of intensive agriculture. In addition, sites have revealed bronze artifacts such as daggers, mirrors, buttons, belt hooks, and horse trappings, especially in the north. The manufacture of bronze weapons and implements was widespread throughout the peninsula by the fourth century B.C.[17]

The quality of polished stone and bronze implements suggests that they were the products of specialists. Differences in house size and contents of burial sites are strong evidence that high-status individuals existed. Craft specialization is further implied by the presence of local bronze metallurgy, including the rise of smiths and miners of raw material. As agriculture intensified, surpluses were stored, and the specialization of labor into peasant, artisan, and bondman emerged. Consequently, Bronze Age inhabitants of the peninsula were able to create the earliest form or prototype of state structure. Some historians call these states "walled-town states" based on written documents such as *Samguksagi* (History of the Three Kingdoms) by Kim Busik (1075-1151), and *Samgungnyusa* (Memorabilia of the Three Kingdoms) written by the monk Ilyeon (1206-1289) (Eckert et al. 1990:11; Lee 1984:12-13).[18]

The state of Buyeo arose in the Sungari River basin as a walled-town state north of the peninsula, Yemaek developed along the middle reaches of the Amnokgang (Yalu), and Gojoseon (Old Joseon) arose around 1000 B.C. in the basin between the Liao and Daedonggang. The most advanced of these states was Gojoseon. South of the Hangang, there were three walled-town states with a widely disseminated iron culture, Jinhan, Mahan, and Byeonhan, known collectively as Samhan (Three Han).

The Gojoseon was a confederate kingdom whose founding is the subject of The Dangun legend. This tale, which dates to 2333 B.C. according to *Samgungnyusa*, belongs to the tradition of cultural heroes and miraculous births: "A common version of the story begins with a female bear and a tigress who lived together in a cave, both aspiring to become human. Hwan-in, the chief god, gave them mugwort [*ssuk* in Korean] and garlic to eat, and instructed them to stay in the dark and not see the sun for 100 days. The tigress became restless and failed at the task, but the she-bear persevered and became human, married the son of Hwan-in, and bore a son name Tangun Wanggom [Tan'gun Wanggŏm]" (Nelson 1993:155). Dangun, the originator of millet cultivation (a gift from his deity), set up a kingdom in Pyeongyang and named the country Joseon, meaning "morning calm and freshness." Since the legendary story is about forest-dwelling peoples instead of steppe nomads, Dangun seems to be indigenous to Korea.[19]

According to old Chinese documents[20] and archaeological evidence, Gojoseon in its later years had an organized, centralized bureaucracy with the power to mobilize both labor and armies, even in some of the remoter regions. However, by the end of the fourth century B.C. it had experienced a gradual decline due largely to pressure from the Chinese state of Yen. Yen eventually invaded the Liao-tung peninsula, and the region became a commandery (equivalent to 'province') of the Yen domain. It later fell under the domination of the Ch'in empire and then of the Han dynasty of China.

During this period, refugees migrated eastward. A leader among these refugees, Wiman, overthrew the Gojoseon king between 194 and 180 B.C. Judging by his dress and topknot hairstyle, Wiman was not a man of Yen but rather of Gojoseon in terms of "nationality" (Lee

1984:16-17). Apparently, he had been a Joseon immigrant to Yen China, and brought back Chinese political, economic, and cultural influence to his new kingdom, but retained the name "Joseon." He placed Joseon people in high government positions, and under Wiman, Joseon grew strong economically and militarily, and expanded its territory in all directions. However, the Han invasion proved more powerful, and the kingdom fell in 108 B.C. Eventually, Han China established the three commanderies of Lolang, Chen-fan, and Lint'un in the former Wiman territories. Nevertheless, the Han were expelled soon after by another kingdom, Goguryeo.

Early History
The prehistory of the Korean peninsula has been reconstructed mostly from various anthropological sources, especially archaeological findings from recent excavations and some piecemeal ethnographic information. When it comes to the Three Kingdoms period, there are some written documents, notably *Samguksagi* (History of the Three Kingdoms) and *Samgungnyusa* (Memorabilia of the Three Kingdoms). For historians, these are precious sources that complement archaeological findings. Nevertheless, on many occasions, written documents from long ago carry intentional and unintentional biases.

Some of these biases and errors come from the Confucian and Buddhist beliefs of their authors. Although most of those documents have come down to us in their original form, "they were written many centuries after the events they record, and each has a point of view which guided the selection of topics to be included," as Nelson (1993:206) points out. She states, "I have noted differences of reading when relating the ancient writings to the archaeological record" (Nelson 1993:9).

Nelson (1993:9) has also pointed out that "Japanese sources, more nearly contemporaneous with the Three Kingdoms, tend to ascribe a secondary status to Korea, a stance which may have arisen from motives other than historical accuracy." Since 2002 under the so-called Northeast Asia Project (Dongbuk Gongjeong in Korean), the Chinese government has launched a major campaign to make the history of Goguryeo (37 B.C.-668) and Balhae (698-926) part of China's regional history. This is meant to convey that Goguryeo was a local ethnic government under Chinese rule that existed in the northeastern region. To promote such a proposition, the Chinese government has sponsored "various research projects" on the subject.[21] Many Koreans have expressed concern about the ultimate motives of this Chinese project, which would distort the early history of Korea — the Three Kingdoms period in general and the history of Goguryeo in particular.

Contemporary Koreans' Renewed Interest in the Three Kingdoms

Since 2006, Koreans have paid more attention to the history of the Three Kingdoms than that of any other dynastic period. Before this proliferation of interest, Koreans tended to focus on the histories of more recent dynasties, either the Goryeo (918-1392) or the Joseon (1392-1910). One of the most popular TV soap operas that helped generate the "Korean pop culture wave (*Hallyu*)," *Daejanggeum* (Jewel in the Palace), which depicts the story of a legendary girl who became the first female supreme royal physician of her time, was set in the Joseon dynasty. From 2001 to 2005, only one TV drama out of fifteen series telecast by the three major Korean TV networks (KBS, MBC, and SBS) dealt with the Silla dynasty (57 B.C.-935), the rest being set in either the Joseon or the Goryeo. Suddenly, beginning in 2006, all but one TV series of the three major networks focused on the Goguryeo and Balhae dynasties, indicating a rising interest in the Three Kingdoms.

Contemporary Koreans' fascination with the Three Kingdoms, particularly Goguryeo, probably results from several factors. First, China's Northeast Asian Project, especially the fear that it might alter the early history of Korea, has generated much interest in Goguryeo.[22] Characterized by the image of warriors on horseback confronting nomadic northern tribes as well as the powerful Chinese Sui and T'ang dynasties, Goguryeo symbolizes bravery and has become a source of national pride for Koreans, because it represents the thwarting of a bigger and stronger nation like China. Consciously or unconsciously, such feelings now coexist with a growing anti-American sentiment among the younger generation of Koreans. Second, contemporary Koreans see a striking resemblance between the time of the Three Kingdoms when the peninsula was divided into three regions, and present-day Korea, which is divided into north and south. Third, interestingly enough, some essential aspects of contemporary Korean culture appear to have roots in the Three Kingdoms period. The male-dominated system of family relations, deeply influenced by Confucianism, is now evolving, though at a snail's pace, is a case in point. Of course, the coexistence of these three factors with growing interest in the Three Kingdoms may simply be coincidence.

If this book is to be an anthropological interpretation written by an anthropologist, what role should history play in the discussion? Clifford Geertz (1995:165-166), a renowned cultural anthropologist, provides a good answer by quoting Kierkegaard: "It is difficult to know what to do with the past. You can't live in it, no matter how much you may fantasize doing so, or how gravely nostalgic you grow when remembering it. You can't foretell the future from it, however suggestive, promising, or ominous it may seem; things in the offering frequently don't arrive, thing unhinted at frequently do ⋯ the only one that comes to much as usable truth is Kierkegaard's 'Life is lived forward but it is understood backward.'" A brief survey of early Korean history will serve such a purpose, enabling us to better understand contemporary Korea.

I do not pretend to be an historian, nor do I intend to introduce Korean history in detail chronologically and methodically as historians do. Therefore, my descriptions of Korean history will be ruthlessly brief because the book's focus is on aspects of contemporary Korean culture whose historical connections and roots I will trace.

The Three Kingdoms

The Three Kingdoms included Goguryeo, Baekje, and Silla, which were true states formed during the first century.[23] Goguryeo, which was located in the far north, was the first state to organize, followed by Baekje, and finally Silla.

Goguryeo

Goguryeo was founded in 37 B.C. by Jumong. Jumong was known to be from Buyeo, a walled-town state in the Sungari River basin. Goguryeo people were engaged in agriculture (Choi 1971:21; Hatada 1969:8; Nelson 1993:207; Osgood 1951:171), but their land was not fertile enough for intensive farming.

Goguryeo was under constant threat from invading Chinese forces and also from nomadic tribes in the northern frontier. In response, the Goguryeo people became warrior horsemen, and established military dominance over Baekje and Silla in the earlier years. The height of Goguryeo's power came under King Gwanggaeto, who ruled from 391 to 413. His impressive military record is carved in the memorial stele standing at his tomb in modern T'ung-kou by the Manchurian side of the Yalu River. Under King Gwanggaeto's leadership, the Liao-tung peninsula became Goguryeo territory.

The Sui dynasty (589-618) launched unsuccessful attacks against Goguryeo in 598 and 612, and the consequent failure of these military raids contributed to the collapse of Sui in 618, facilitating the rise of the T'ang dynasty (618-907). The T'ang sent expeditions against Goguryeo in 645 and 647 that also failed because of Goguryeo's strong defense system.[24]

Archaeological findings from Goguryeo include stone tombs with wall paintings as well as cities and forts surrounded by stone walls. Written documents also indicate that Goguryeo was a stratified society with a wealthy and powerful elite capable of mobilizing a large labor force to build tombs for the upper class and other public works projects. Scenes from tomb murals show brightly colored hunting scenes, and other murals show husbands and wives together, implying

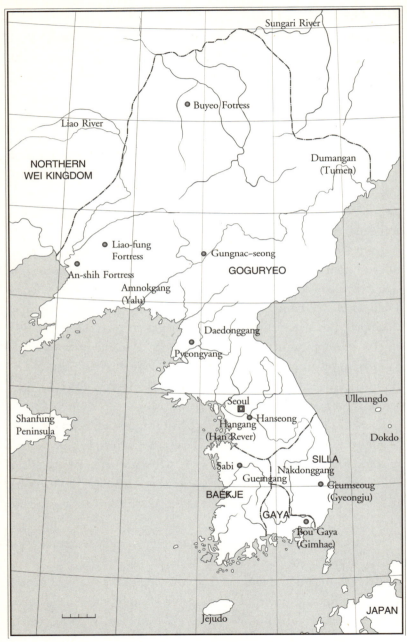

Goguryeo at the height of its expansion in the fifth century

that women enjoyed considerable equality. Dress and house styles from this time show some continuity with those of historic Korea.

The only writing system at the time was comprised of Chinese characters, which the elite learned in order to function effectively. In 372, Goguryeo established a National Confucian Academy or "university." The Goguryeo elite emulated the Chinese model while maintaining their native Korean culture and tradition (Nelson 1993:211). Buddhism was introduced to Goguryeo from northern China and was officially recognized in 372. Nevertheless, native shamanistic religious practices continued to co-exist with Buddhism.

For a northern frontier state, Goguryeo's cultural accomplishments were considerable. Contemporary Koreans, however, tend to think of Goguryeo mainly as a strong kingdom whose military stopped Chinese aggression and even expanded its territory toward China. Goguryeo did in fact conquer a total of sixty-four fortresses, including 1,400 villages in China (Lee 1984:38), extending its domain to include most of China's Manchuria. For that reason, Goguryeo has become a symbol of Korean pride in successfully standing up to a bigger country.

Baekje

According to *Samguksaki*, Baekje was founded in 18 B.C. when Onjo and his brother Biryu, sons of Jumong, the founder of Goguryeo, moved south. Onjo built his headquarters on the Hangang, southeast of Seoul. Since Baekje was founded in one of Korea's most productive rice-growing areas, its economy was basically agrarian.

Cultural artifacts from the early Baekje have been poorly preserved and little has been recorded. Not much was left after the armies of T'ang and Silla plundered and burned the state. Tombs were looted and abandoned, cities razed, and temples destroyed.[25] What remains are temple foundations and pagodas near Buyeo, Baekje's last capital, and Gongju, further north of the capital. Recently, however, some sites have been revealing new information about this era.

Archaeological findings and written documents indicate that the Baekje court was literate in Chinese at least by the fourth century, and probably earlier. Buddhism was introduced to Baekje in 384. The tomb of King Muryeong (501-523) in particular shows that the king and queen wore gold crowns and bronze shoes, providing evidence of the luxurious lifestyle of Baekje's elite.

Baekje dwellings were heated by the *ondol* system, still widely used in contemporary Korea. Warm flues from the kitchen run under the stone floors to all areas of the house; thus the kitchen's cooking heat is used to warm sitting and sleeping areas. The *ondol* is a unique Korean heating system, and differs from that of the Chinese and Japanese. Korea's long tradition of having warm winter floors has prolonged the Korean preference for sitting on the floor which contrasts with the Chinese preference for stiff-backed chairs and high tables. Bruce Cumings (1997:35) reports that "Ice may form in a water jug on the table, while a person sleeps comfortably on a toasty warm *ondol*." The *ondol* system must have encouraged Koreans to be closer to nature, to the earth.

Baekje could be characterized as one of the most "internationalized" kingdoms because of its relations with southern China and western Japan. Baekje imported Buddhism, literacy, and many art forms from China, incorporating them into its own unique culture, and then exporting them to Japan. Baekje art became the basis for the art of the Asuka period (552-645) of Japan (Hatada 1969:20; Cumings 1997:33-34). After Baekje became literate in Chinese in the fourth century, Baekje scholars were sent to the Yamato court in Japan to teach the Chinese classics (Nelson 1993:221). The crown prince of Baekje was sent to Japan in 393, cementing relations with that country. The contents included in the Fujinoki tomb near Nara demonstrate close stylistic ties with Baekje, further evidence of the cultural bonds between Baekje and Japan (Nelson 1993:221).

Although Baekje was successful in its foreign relations with China and Japan, its relations with Goguryeo were antagonistic. King Gwanggaeto and King Jangsu (413-491) of Goguryeo attacked the Baekje fortresses along their common border near the Hangang, capturing some. Baekje had difficulty fending off Goguryeo's attacks, although at times it mounted successful counterattacks. In 551, for instance, through an alliance made with Silla, Baekje was successful in driving back Goguryeo's forces. Two years later, however, when Silla gained sole control over the region, Goguryeo became Baekje's mortal enemy.

Militarily, the people of Baekje might not have been as strong as the Goguryeo people, but they created a unique and elaborate culture of their own by importing some Chinese cultural traits and making them their own. In turn they exported their own culture to Japan, which preserved Baekje culture well until recently. Perhaps Baekje should be remembered for its effort to "internationalize" if not "globalize" its culture.

Silla

In 57 B.C., the six villages of Saro or Seorabeol held a council meeting in the Gyeongju plain. Three leaders were chosen from the Park, Seok, and Kim clans, and they ruled the kingdom on a rotating basis. From the fourth century on, kingship became hereditary within the Kim clan. In the third century, Silla was invaded by a Goguryeo tribe that lived on the upper Hangang. Beginning in the fourth century, Silla was able to control the area around the Nakdonggang, and it conquered the Gaya kingdom. Silla's expansion was possible largely due to its geographic location, which was at a relatively safe distance from the Chinese border. As an indication of its power as a state, Silla had a social stratification system in which the hand of distinction rested on the "quality of bone" (*Golpum*): the "holy bone" (*Seonggol*) being the highest group and *Jingol* the next, followed by three lesser ranks.

The archaeological remains of Silla are numerous and include forts, shrines, Buddhist temples, pagodas, a palace, and even an astronomical observatory (Cheomseongdae).[26] Silla was also equipped with high-quality iron weapons, including long swords, arrowheads, horse fittings, and armor. Sword hilts often had elaborate pommels. Silla was famous for its youthful warrior society *Hwarang* (Flower of Youth), which was organized by the monk Wongwang.[27]

Silla culture was best preserved in elite tombs, and there are 155 well-preserved Silla tombs in the capital of Gyeongju alone. Burial goods include gold crowns, gold earrings, belts with dangling pendants, gold bracelets, and gold rings, which were found on every finger of one ruler. In fact, Silla was referred to as the "gold-glittering nation" in the ninth century, known to the Arabs as "el Sila" (McCune 1976:3). Silla might have had direct contact with the West by sea as well as through the "silk road" (Nelson 1993:24).

Chinese thought and customs began to influence Silla a century before Buddhism was introduced and accepted. Some stone monuments with Chinese inscriptions are clear evidence of the fact that Silla was literate in the fifth century. A truncated brick pagoda only three stories high resembles the Large Wild Goose Pagoda in Xian (formerly Ch'angan), capital of the T'ang dynasty. The capital of Silla was laid out in imitation of Xian as was Nara in Japan. The largest and most important of the Silla temples was Hwangnyongsa, erected in 553, which lasted until in the Mongolian invasion of 1238. The famous Bulguksa remains intact today.

The Three Kingdoms were not seeking a symbiotic coexistence but attacked each other frequently, alone or in alliance with one another. Finally, allying itself with T'ang China, Silla conquered the lower Hangang basin, by the Yellow Sea. Silla then defeated Baekje in 660 and Goguryeo in 668, finally becoming the sole ruler of the peninsula as United Silla.

After the defeat of Baekje and Goguryeo, the Chinese tried to establish an administration to govern the peninsula, including Silla. Silla responded to this aggression by helping Goguryeo's resistance movement in the north and by moving against T'ang troops in the south. By 671, Silla had taken the old Baekje capital, and in 676 Silla expanded to the Daedonggang. The T'ang Chinese invaders had to withdraw to Manchuria. At last, in 735 they were forced to recognize Silla's domination over the area south of the Daedonggang.

Among its many accomplishments, Silla could be credited with unifying the three kingdoms by its diplomatic shrewdness in allowing

Gold crown

the T'ang to aid its conquest of Baekje and Goguryeo. Although Silla was unable to control all the former territory of Goguryeo, which extended to much of Manchuria, the peninsula has been governed by a single kingdom since the seventh century.

In the meantime, after the fall of Goguryeo, Dae Joyeong, a former Goguryeo general, founded Balhae (698-926) with most of the remaining Goguryeo people. Its territory extended from the Sungari and Amur Rivers in northern Manchuria to the northern provinces of modern Korea. Balhae gained control of most of the former Goguryeo territory and then confronted Silla. However, later in 926 Balhae was conquered by Khitan.

The Cultural Legacy of the Three Kingdoms Period
Each of the Three Kingdoms had unique and distinctive political, social, and cultural traits and styles, yet all three shared several

common characteristics that have become Korean tradition, having a long-lasting impact on Korea throughout its history.

The cultural legacy of the Three Kingdoms period still lingers in the contemporary Korean way of life. In terms of foreign relations and diplomacy, Silla and Baekje had sought to use Chinese power to beset Goguryeo, which inaugurated a tradition of involving foreign powers in Korean internal disputes (Cumings 1997:34). Such a process was repeated toward the end of the Joseon dynasty in the nineteenth century. After World War II, the peninsula was again divided by world politics, and remains so today.

As for Koreans' attitude toward religion, their hallmark inclusiveness was manifest during the Three Kingdoms period. Their indigenous beliefs consisted of Shamanism, yet foreign-born Buddhism was able to penetrate their belief system. *Hwarang*, Silla's youthful warrior movement, was organized by a monk, yet the warrior oath symbolized the mix of Buddhism and Confucianism that had come to characterize Korean thought by that time. The "*hyangga*" (native song) genre represents a transformation of shamanistic incarnations into Buddhistic supplications. It is perhaps this type of inclusiveness that later made room for Christianity to grow.

There is ample evidence that the Three Kingdoms had a tradition of gender equality. The Goguryeo tomb murals show a group of noblewomen wearing pleated skirts as well as a female armed warrior riding an armed horse. Three Silla rulers, the twenty-seventh, Seondeok Yeowang (632-647), twenty-eighth, Jindeok Yeowang (647-654), and fifty-first, Jinseong Yeowang (887-897) were queens. There was no cultural tradition of patriarchy in the Three Kingdoms period.

Goryeo Dynasty

With unification, Silla reached its peak of power and prosperity. Beginning in the middle of the eighth century, however, Silla was torn to pieces by rebel leaders: Gyeonhwon, who founded the Latter Baekje state in Jeonju; former Silla prince Gungye, who established the Latter

Goguryeo state; and Wang Geon, a former minister of Gungye's from a gentry family in Gaeseong, who overthrew Gungye in 918. Wang Geon's power grew over the next two decades, and he raided the Latter Baekje. Eventually, Silla yielded its power to Wang Geon, who united the peninsula again and founded the new state of Goryeo, whose name was derived from Goguryeo.[28]

Wang Geon adopted a policy of leniency toward the Silla aristocracy and even married a woman of the Silla royal clan. He remained alert to a possible conflict between his state and the northern nomadic states in the former Goguryeo territory. He also advised that Buddhist temples could not be interfered with, and warned against usurpation and internal conflicts among the royal clans. He tried to justify his rule by claming moral superiority.

The fourth king, Gwangjong (949-975), instituted the emancipation of slaves in 956, to restore the commoner status of those unjustly held captive. He also installed a civil service examination system to recruit officials by merit. The fifth king, Gyeongjong (975-981), granted land to officials. As Bruce Cumings (1997:40), a historian and an expert on Korea, has stated, "The Koryŏ [Goryeo] dynasty ruled for just short of half a millennium, but in its heyday the dynasty ranked among the most advanced civilizations in the world," despite the devastating invasion from Mongolia.

Goryeo engaged in trade with Sung China, and its subsistence economy was built on agriculture. Despite efforts to abolish slavery, society was composed of various strata, including farm laborers, miners, producers of silk and paper, pottery makers, and even slaves. While there were all sorts of outcasts, such as butchers, wicker workers, and entertainers, new hereditary aristocratic houses emerged, the elite using marriage as a strategy to expand the power of their families. This established the tradition that a good marriage to a notable aristocratic family could be a shortcut to political power. The residues of such traditions still linger in contemporary Korean society.

Goryeo's political ideology was based on Confucianism. In 992, in order to enhance Confucian ideology, Seongjong (981-997) established a national university, consisting of six colleges, which became a major vehicle for preparation for the civil service examination.[29] Under Injong (1122-1146) schools were set up in rural areas to educate local youth.

Confucianism as well as Buddhism still flourished. There were as many as seventy temples in the capital of Gaeseong alone. The woodblock printing of the first *Tripitaka*, the Buddhist canon in Chinese translation, was completed in 1087.[30] Geomancy based on the ideas of Buddhism and Taoism was also popular among the Goryeo people.[31]

Goryeo celadon ware was the dynasty's most celebrated artistic achievement. Sung porcelain provided the stimulus for the development of this fine celadon ware whose delicate jade-green color and remarkable decorations reflect Taoist simplicity and Buddhist tranquility.

Goryeo science and technology were also highly advanced. The Goryeo woodblock-printing technique allowed for the publication of a wide variety of books, and an advanced cast-metal type printing technology was devised, thus pushing back the date for the first movable metal type to 1234, 200 years before the Germans "invented" it (Steers et al. 1989:129). Gunpowder was also manufactured for the first time in Korean history, and by 1377, it was utilized in the production of weapons. Also, in 1363, clothing was revolutionized by the introduction of the cotton plant from Yüan China, which had been claimed by the Mongols in 1271.

Goryeo's culture was rich, colorful, and sophisticated, but the dynasty suffered a great deal from internal strife between civil and military officials. A military coup challenging favoritism in the royal court of King Uijong (1146-1170) took place in 1170. Military officials rose up against civil officials, many of whom were killed. The second major purge took place three years later, and eventually political power passed from civil officials into the hands of the military. From then on, power shifted from one military strongman to another until 1196. Nevertheless, the military rulers found that they lacked the administrative expertise to run the country and thus invited the participation of civil scholar-officials. In time the civil aristocracy, mainly scholar-bureaucrats, began to fortify its power base.

Internal conflict between civil and military officials had weakened the dynasty, but beginning in the eleventh century Goryeo also suffered invasions from Khitan, Liao, and Jurchen. The most devastating blow came from the Mongols in the thirteenth century. After conquering the Chin of China, the Mongols, equipped with new weapons, chased diehard Liao refugees into the territory of Goryeo, and finally attacked Goryeo itself. During the Mongol invasion, Goryeo moved its capital to Ganghwado. Over the course of the war, the Mongols took more than 200,000 Goryeo captives with them when they returned to Yüan China, leaving behind much death and destruction. They burned property and destroyed numerous cultural treasures and relics, including the original of the *Tripitaka*. The Yüan (Mongols) demanded that Goryeo join with them in subjugating Japan in 1274 and again in 1281. Goryeo was responsible for the construction of warships and the provision of supplies for both invasions. Both campaigns ended in failure.

Because of Yüan's military domination, a succession of Goryeo kings was required to take princesses of the Yüan imperial house as wives, so that their sons would succeed to the Goryeo throne. For Yüan China, Goryeo played the role of a "son-in-law nation." Goryeo would not be free from Yüan influence until the Yüan were driven northward by the rise of the Ming dynasty (1368-1644) of China. Goryeo then had little choice but to adopt a pro-Ming stance.

Besides, Goryeo had to deal with Japanese *waegu*[32] or pirates. In the reign of King Gojong (1213-1259), raids by Japanese *waegu* started to be troublesome, and after 1350 they became rampant. The raiders came by sea, landing randomly along the Goryeo coast and plundering villages.

In 1388, the newly established Ming dynasty proclaimed its intention to claim Goryeo's northern territory. Outraged at this move, Goryeo commander-in-chief Choe Yeong was determined to strike

Ming's forces and mobilized troops, but his deputy commander, Yi Seonggye, opposed the expedition. Leading his army back from Wihwado in the mouth of the Yalu River, Yi Seonggye deposed the king and seized political control for himself in a bloodless coup.

Joseon Dynasty

In 1392, Yi Seonggye overthrew Goryeo's king and usurped the throne to become King Taejo (1392-1398), the founder of his own dynasty, the Joseon. Afterwards, the throne of the Joseon dynasty was either inherited, if there were no apparent heirs, a ruler was chosen from among the royal family members of the Jeonju Yi clan. Because of this monopoly by Yi clan members, the dynasty has also been called the Yi dynasty or Joseon.

The new kingdom maintained a close relationship with Ming because of Yi Seonggye's specific ties to that dynasty. Yi Seonggye also embraced Neo-Confucianist doctrines, which gave the traditional ethico-political cult a metaphysical interpretation. The reformers surrounding Taejo intensified their drive to impose Confucian norms on people's lives, which spelled the decline of Buddhism. By confiscating land and forcing many temples to close, the new dynasty weakened Buddhism to a subservient position.

The changing status of Buddhism in Joseon society brought about many changes. Korean burial rituals that were an amalgam of indigenous customs and Buddhist traditions were replaced by Confucian customs. The Buddhist ritual of cremation, for instance, was thrust aside in favor of Confucian ancestor worship and its related rituals. Before the Joseon dynasty, endogamous marriage,[33] polygamy,[34] and remarriage of widows were permitted. However, Joseon society expanded the number of kin with whom marriages was prohibited, forbade the practice of giving equal status to multiple wives, and discouraged remarriage.[35]

In the end, Taejo became more of a figurehead than a ruler, but the third king, Taejong (1400-1418), who ascended the throne after killing his brother, the heir-apparent, strengthened the monarchy. King Sejong (1418-1450), Taejong's successor, who was known to be intelligent and scholarly, was regarded as one of the greatest kings in the dynastic history of Korea and his rule in the mid-fifteenth century was marked by progressive ideas in administration, economics, science, music, medicine, and humanistic studies. For example, Sejong ordered the development of a rain gauge in 1442 that preceded Castelli's "invention" of the pluviometer in 1639 by almost two hundred years. Sejong's interest in astronomical science was all-encompassing. Sundials, water clocks, orreries of the solar system, celestial globes, astronomical maps, and atlases of the seven planets were the creative results of Sejong's encouragement.

Sejong also established the *Jiphyeonjeon* (Hall of Worthies) to promote research about institutional traditions and political economy. He then directed scholars of the Hall of Worthies to devise an alphabet for the Korean language called *Hangeul*, his most celebrated achievement. *Hangeul* consists of eleven vowels and seventeen consonants and is so simple and scientific that even an uneducated person can learn it in a matter of hours. Despite strong opposition from Confucian scholars, whose mastery of Chinese characters guaranteed their elite positions, the king persisted with his determination to promote *Hangeul* for the benefit of the masses, and distributed the first Korean written language in alphabetic form to the people in 1446.[36] In the meantime, the official written language continued to be Chinese, just as Latin was in Europe at the time, but now ordinary Korean people had a means of writing in their own language.

Sejong also showed great concern for the livelihood of the peasants, providing them with relief in times of drought and flood. He also put into effect a sliding tax scale to ease the peasants' burden. In foreign relations, Sejong took strong measures against the Jurchen tribes, constructing six fortresses in the territory on the northern frontier. In 1443, Sejong created four counties on the northern border and opened three ports to the Japanese to promote trade.

The seventh king, Sejo (1455-1468), defied Confucian orthodoxy by supporting Taoism and Buddhism. Sejo assumed direct control, intimidated his critics with purges and executions, instituted the banishment of officials, and seized property. With the end of his reign, the power of Korean monarchs diminished, and the Joseon dynasty began a long decline. However, the ninth king, Seongjong (1469-1494), reinstated traditional ideas in the form of Neo-Confucianism. State support of Buddhism gradually diminished, and Confucianism once again assumed its place in the royal administration.

The Development of the *Yangban* Legacy in Joseon

In establishing Joseon, the role and strength of the military were essential for the success of Yi Seonggye's coup. However, without strong support from the literati, his coup d'état would not have been successful. Because they provided such crucial support, the literati began to attract the attention of Joseon kings and the literati's potential role in government became quite significant. It was the powerful literati who set about codifying a corpus of administrative law infused with Confucian ideals, principles, and practices that would become the political *modus operandi* of the Joseon dynsaty.

The dominant social class of the Joseon dynasty was the *yangban*. The word "*yang*" means two orders of officials, civil and military. The *yangban* class directed the government, economy, and culture of Joseon. Therefore, Joseon has been aptly characterized as a *yangban* society. The *yangban* was more broadly and widely rooted than the ruling class of Goryeo or earlier kingdoms. The size of the *yangban* class increased via the state examination system used to recruit officials, while "protected appointments" severely limited the dynasty's policies.

The *yangban* devoted themselves to the study of Confucian doctrines, and their profession was the holding of public office. They concerned themselves with fashioning an ideal Confucian polity through the moral cultivation of the people. Yet they did not serve in technical positions, which included medical officers, scientists, engineers, accountants, law clerks, and artists. The *yangban* were not interested in devoting themselves to agriculture, manufacturing, or commerce, so these positions were left to the *jungin* (middle people).[37] The civil order was always more prestigious than the military.[38] Also, since Confucianism places commerce and industry at the bottom of the status hierarchy that consists of, in descending order, *sa* (scholar-official), *nong* (farmer), *gong* (artisan), and *sang* (merchant) (Mason et al. 1980:281), it served as a barrier to the development of science and technology, industry, and commerce in Joseon society (Kim 1992).

The marriage pattern of the *yangban* was exogamous, but the selection of marriage partners was endogamous in order to preserve hereditary status. The *yangban* created a distinct residential pattern. While *samurai* warriors in Tokugawa Japan (1603–1868) were not allowed to live in the countryside, "many *yangban* families resided in the countryside of Joseon, making school, party, lineage, and affinal ties much more important than communal solidarity based on common residence" (Han 2003:12 n.9). Even in the capital of Seoul, the *yangban* resided as a group in certain areas.

In order to protect their status, the *yangban* sent their youths to private tutorial schools, called *seodang*, where they learned basic Chinese characters and practiced writing Chinese and could then proceed further in advanced schools in Seoul and in their local counties. In Seoul, there was the highest National Confucian Academy (*Seonggyungwan*). Certain limitations applied to the descendants of secondary wives of the *yangban*. There was also regional discrimination against the residents of the northern provinces.

As the power base of the *yangban* expanded, particularly as the *sarim* (rural Neo-Confucian literati) emerged into political prominence through the civil service examination process, the majority of *yangban* literati had to compete among themselves, and many power struggles took place. As a result, there were four major purges: in 1498 (*Muo sahwa*), 1504 (*Gapja sahwa*), 1519 (*Gimyo sahwa*), and 1545 (*Eulsa sahwa*). Although the extent of violence differed, these purges were the consequence of factional strife among political cliques vying for political power. The Joseon power holders were bloody and ruthless when attacking other cliques, and much energy was wasted in factional strife. Fear of literati purges and factional strife discouraged many brilliant Neo-Confucian literati from keeping their positions in government and encouraged them to return to their hometowns to devote themselves to scholarship and the education of the younger generation.

Foreign Policy and Japanese Invasions

As anticipated, Yi Seonggye adopted a pro-Ming stance, but he went further by dispatching diplomatic envoys to the Ming each year to offer New Year's felicitations, congratulate the Ming emperor on his birthday, honor the birthday of the imperial crown prince, and mark the passing of the winter solstice. All these missions were political in nature, intended to secure the safety of the new dynasty. Even though it was a strategic maneuver, such a policy was described as *sade*, meaning to serve the great or big. Since then, the word *sade* has had a negative connotation and is used to describe Korea's submissive foreign policy in dealing with countries bigger and stronger than Korea.

During Sejong's reign, the northern frontier was stabilized by the establishment of six garrison forts to fend off the Jurchen people. They were called Yain (or "barbarian") by the Koreans, and by the designation of the Tumen as a permanent boundary. But this did not stop the Yain from pillaging. Joseon also had to protect its seas from Japanese marauders from Tsushima, Japan. In 1419, Sejong sent a strong military force to wipe out the Japanese bases. Through negotiations, Joseon's three ports were opened to Tsushima and limited trade began.

The real Japanese invasions took place under Toyotomi Hideyoshi in the sixteenth century. A military general, Hideyoshi emerged as a strongman after his military victories resulted in a unified Japan. His ambition was to conquer the Ming Empire by way of invading Korea. Even before the Hideyoshi invasions, Korea had been troubled by sporadic attacks on its coasts by the Japanese in the mid-sixteenth century. The *yangban* bureaucrats were content to take temporary measures, fearing that a permanent peace could not be easily attained.

In April 1592, Japanese forces landed at Busan with an overwhelming number of soldiers, and their northward attack was swift. The fourteenth king, Seonjo (1567-1608), and his court fled toward the far northern town of Uiju on the Yalu River. During this invasion, Korean ground forces, inexperienced and inept, were ineffectual against the well-trained Japanese forces. However naval hero Admiral Yi Sunsin (1545-1598) fought effectively against the Japanese navy by devising the "turtle ship (*Geobukseon*)".[39]

The heroic role of Admiral Yi, an increase in the "righteous armies" known as *Uibyeong* (guerrilla forces), and Ming military assistance forced the Japanese to pull back. Through negotiations a settlement was finally reached. However, in January 1597, the Japanese renewed their war efforts, bringing in 100,000 soldiers. This time the Japanese faced stiffer resistance from Koreans and the Chinese garrison, and the invasion was limited to the southern provinces. Nevertheless, Admiral Yi was killed by a Japanese bullet as he was standing in the bow of his flagship in 1598. In the same year, the death of Hideyoshi prompted the Japanese to bring the war to an end.

Hideyoshi's invasion resulted in a massive number of Korean casualties, and Japan benefited from the abduction of skilled Korean workers, artisans such as weavers and porcelain manufacturers, priests, and Confucian scholars, as prisoners of war. These Korean artisans became the instruments of a great advancement in the ceramic arts of Japan.[40] The numerous books seized by the Japanese in Korea contributed to the development of learning in Japan, especially the study of Neo-Confucianism.

After the Japanese invasions, Joseon was once again subject to the depredations of its northern neighbor. In Manchuria, the Jurchen tribes had united under the leadership of Nurhachi (T'ai Tsung) and began sporadic attacks along the northeastern border. Manchu's first major invasion of Korea took place in 1627 (*Jeongmyo horan*). After the invasion, Joseon was granted peace in exchange for its pledge to play the role of "younger brother" to Manchu's "elder brother," as specified in the Confucian norm of hierarchical social relationships.[41] Because of this pledge, the Manchus subsequently withdrew their army from the peninsula. Nevertheless, before long, Manchu (Emperor T'ai Tsung of the Later Chin changed the name of his state to Ch'ing) demanded an annual tribute (suzerainty) from Joseon. In response to Joseon's refusal to comply with this demand, the Ch'ing emperor himself led a second invasion in 1636 (*Byeongja horan*).

During this invasion, the sixteenth king, Injo (1623-1649), sent his court, including his queen, sons, and their wives, to seek refuge on Ganghwado, but his queen and ministers were captured, along with 200 other hostages. Consequently, Manchu was able to exert its power over Joseon to establish a tributary relationship, forcing Joseon to sever ties with the Ming court and securing two Joseon princes as hostages. The Manchu went on to conquer Ming China and rule China as the Ch'ing dynasty (1644-1912). After that, Joseon was unable to escape the influence of Ch'ing until the latter was defeated by the Japanese in the Sino-Japanese war in 1894.

Historians have observed that during the period in which the Joseon dynasty was invaded by Japan and Ch'ing. However, China was ruled by foreign forces for 300 years, France was at war for 100 years, and Germany for thirty years.[42] Nevertheless, although invasions were not rare events during this time, they contributed to the decline of the Joseon dynasty.

Consequently, Joseon in the postwar period witnessed many socio-political and economic upheavals. Also, factional strife among *yangban* literati intensified as competition intensified. The rise of wealthy merchants, who were classed as secondary-status citizens according to the Confucian hierarchy, contributed to the decline of *yangban* society. Upward social mobility, almost nonexistent in the prewar period given the existing stratification system, began to expand. Rich peasants and merchants were able to acquire *yangban* status, and *nobi* (slaves) were able to purchase their freedom.

Neo-Confucian orthodoxy was questioned by a rising spirit of criticism, which in turn engendered distrust of the *yangban*. Attention was drawn to agricultural problems as more *yangban* became involved in land-cultivation issues. As a result, agro-managerial techniques and production methods steadily improved. Privately operated handicraft factories replaced government-operated ones, stimulating the production of goods for sale.

In the seventeenth century, Joseon began to understand the West, mainly through Catholicism, which it called Western Learning (*seohak*). "Practical Learning (*silhak*)"[43] in the seventeenth and the eighteenth centuries led to "Enlightenment Thought" (*Gaehwa sasang*) that aimed to reform various institutions in the Joseon dynasty. Since Enlightenment thought served as a guiding metaphor for future modernization, and the increase in mercantile activities expedited the rise of commercial farming, which in turn began to transform rural life, some critics see the eighteenth century as the earliest burgeoning of indigenous capitalism and the beginning of Korean modernization. However, some Western scholars argue that this was not the case, asserting that Korean modernization started in the nineteenth century (Eckert 1991:5; Deuchler 1977:xii).

CHAPTER 2

Nascent Modernization in the Midst of "Broken Calm"

Moving between East and West for over three decades, I have discovered that some well-informed and widely traveled Western intellectuals tend to respect, envy, and even idealize other cultures, especially those that have modernized. According to these intellectuals, modernization is not synonymous with Westernization per se. Although the impact of the Western world on Eastern modernization has been profound in the past few centuries, influence did not always run in only one direction.

At one time, Asia's influence on Western modernization was the dominant trend. As John Fairbanks and his associates (1965:10) have pointed out, "In 1500 an observer might more logically have looked forward to the 'Asianization' of Europe ⋯ The great series of inventions emanating from China — paper, printing, the wheel barrow, the crossbow, canal lock-gates, the sternpost rudder, the compass, gunpowder, porcelain ⋯ to none of these early influences were there comparable movements in the opposite directions."

Joseph Needham, in collaboration with Whang Ling and later Lu Gwei Djen, has provided a comprehensive list of Chinese scientific and technological inventions and innovations throughout history. As early as 1751 B.C. for instance, the Chinese had worked out a 365 and 1/4 day year, as well as a close calculation of the ratio of a circle's circumference to its diameter; in the latter part of the thirteenth century the Chinese developed an original system of algebra. Also, many other scientific discoveries and inventions were accredited to the ancient Chinese.[1] Koreans also made many advances, as Richard M. Steers and his colleagues (1989:129) have learned: in 1234 they developed the first movable metal type for printing, in 1442 they invented the rain gauge, and in 1592, the world's first iron-clad ships. There are many more inventions that can be attributed to Korea.

Modernization, then, is a phenomenon that has roots in both the West and the East. According to Fairbanks and his associates (1965:9) "The difference is that modernization has been more gradual and evolutionary in the West, going on over a longer period and much of it indeed arising from within Western civilization. In East Asia the shorter duration of modernization and the external origin of many of the stimuli for it have resulted in a more precipitous rate of change and a tendency toward modifications of traditional culture and society that are sudden and revolutionary rather than slow and evolutionary."

Nevertheless, it was only after the middle of the seventeenth century that European thought began to move ahead so rapidly that East Asian modernization came to be overlooked if not forgotten. Perhaps East Asians, Koreans in particular, have been too humble or self-critical of their traditions, manifesting the opposite of ethnocentrism, a perspective I once termed "ethnonihilism" (Kim 1996). Consequently, beginning in the nineteenth century, in order to catch up with the rapid scientific, technological, and economic progress of the West, Koreans began to emulate the West under the name of "modernization." Thereafter, modernization in the East, including Korea, has been understood as synonymous with Westernization or "Europeanization" (Cole 1971:7): the process of adopting Western technology, Western forms of organization, and economic development, though not always essential Western values, such as the importance of the individual, which have at best played a secondary role.

Since the perception of Korean modernization was "Westernization" or "Europeanization," I will discuss Korean modernization within that frame of reference, focusing on "economic modernization." Perhaps belying its title, this chapter delineates Korea's struggles to survive during the most turbulent period in its history.

Because Korea's visibility in the world community has become prominent since its economic development and rapid industrialization, the result of a development plan of the mid-1960s, most foreigners tend to believe that Korean modernization began at that time. Even Koreans acknowledge that Korean modernization began much later than in neighboring countries, most notably Japan. For instance, during a nationwide campaign in the mid-1990s to harness and promote information technology (IT) based on establishing a strong infrastructure throughout the nation, the motto that Koreans adopted was "Although we have been slow to modernize, we must be first in 'informationalization'." Nevertheless, in reality, Korean modernization started at least one and a half centuries earlier than many Koreans and others assume. In fact, Korean "modernization" started even before Koreans acquired the term itself. Pinpointing the start of Korean modernization depends largely on how one defines the concept.

A sensitive issue in discussing modernization in Korea is the role of Japan during colonial rule. Some foreign observers have remarked that the infrastructure for Korean industrialization came from the Japanese (Cumings 1984:20, 1987; Mason et al. 1980:75). Though such a blanket assertion can easily be refuted, it leads to emotional arguments among Koreans, because the legacy of the Japanese colonial period is a topic that invariably wounds Korean pride, stirring up nationalist feelings. David Steinberg (1989:39) most eloquently summarized the situation: "No period of Korean history is fraught with more controversy than that of the Japanese colonial era, and no topic is more likely to excite passion. These sensitivities are easily understandable, even to foreign observers, but the depth and extent of Korean feeling on this subject are more profound than outsiders might imagine, more intense than the reactions of many other peoples to their Western colonizers."

If Korea had never been colonized by the Japanese, would it have modernized to a lesser degree? There is really no way to answer such a question, because we cannot carry out an experiment on two identical Korean societies of the past, one subject to colonial rule, and the other not. However, it is clear that whatever the outcome of such an impossible study might be, colonization can never be justified for the sake of modernization.

Let me begin my description of Korea's journey toward modernization by reviewing the concept and process of modernization itself.

Modernization as a Complex Process

The concept of "modernization" has been defined in many different ways.[2] Some scholars think of "modern" in terms of present-day industrialization and technology, characterized by jet travel, space exploration, and nuclear power (Kim 1992:199). Marion J. Levy Jr. (1966:110) defines modern society as a place where the "members use inanimate sources of energy and/or use tools to multiply the effects of their efforts." Martina Deuchler, a social anthropologist and an expert on Korea, states that "'modernization is generally understood as action that consists of several transformative processes: commercialization, industrialization, secularization, diffusion of education, and expansion of popular involvement in the political process" (Deuchler 1977:233).

According to these definitions, modernization is neither a simple change within tradition, nor a simple self-defensive reflex in response to Western stimuli: instead, modernization must include some significant "transformations" of traditional values as a result of contact with other cultures, especially the West (Kim 1998:11).

If modernization can be understood in this way, then the earliest stirrings of indigenous capitalism and commercialization in Korea in the seventeenth and eighteenth centuries (Deuchler 1977:xii; Eckert 1991:5) can scarcely be interpreted as "modernization." A genuine effort toward modernization in Korea did not start until the nineteenth century with the *Gabo* Reform of 1894 (Deuchler 1977:xii; Lew 1972, 1990), for even the enlightened thought of the seventeenth and eighteenth centuries did not contain the criteria for modernization, but simply added new components to a traditional body of knowledge.

Characteristically, while Japanese modernization emulated that of the West, especially via the Meiji Restoration of the late 1860s, Korean modernization has been modeled after the process in Japan. King Gojong, who was forced by the Japanese to sign the Treaty of Ganghwado, assembled a secret inspection team to study contemporary Japanese civilization in the light of modernization and dispatched the group to Japan at the end of February 1881 (Kim 1998:12).

Modernization in China and Korea followed a different path than in Japan, where it was initiated spontaneously and willingly without foreign domination and had a profound impact. Even though many Koreans from the king to commoners were aware of the need to modernize, they were reluctant and even ashamed to emulate the Japanese model because they were under Japanese domination, not to mention pressure from the West. In this respect, Korean modernization paralleled that of China, including Taiwan.

Proceeding by fits and starts, modernization in Korea escalated during the most turbulent period in its history, which saw the signing of a concessive treaty with Japan, the Russo-Japanese War (1904-1905), Japanese colonization (1910-1945), the fomenting of an independence movement against Japan (1910-1945), the partition of the peninsula (1945), and subsequent horrors of the Korean War (1950-1953).

The partition of Korea by world politics in 1945 was the first time the country had been divided since Silla unified the peninsula in 668 A.D. The subsequent fratricidal war had a devastating impact on all Koreans. Kyung-Koo Han (2000:289-303) assesses that the Korean War was one of the largest, involving the entire nation, and longest-fought wars since the Japanese invasion led by Hideyoshi some 350 years before. Even today, the peninsula remains divided along the DMZ and the relationship between the two Koreas is tenuous at best and openly hostile at times.

North Korea's ambition to acquire nuclear weapons is a violation of the principle of keeping the peninsula free of nuclear weapons and a major challenge to South Korea and its allies. On 10 February 2005, North Korea admitted publicly for the first time that it possessed nuclear weapons and rejected moves to restart disarmament talks. In an effort to resolve the nuclear weapons issue, a six-party talk, composed of the two Koreas, the United States, China, Japan, and Russia, was proposed. Since then, several rounds of six-party talks have taken place, but no significant progress has been made. Suddenly, on 9 October 2006, North Korea conducted a nuclear test. Once again, the Korean peninsula became a security flashpoint.

As punishment for North Korea's nuclear weapons test, on 14 October 2006, less than a week after the test, the U.N. Security Council voted unanimously to slap North Korea with trade, travel, and other non-military sanctions. Eventually, six-nation negotiations reached an agreement to shut down North Korea's nuclear reactor.[3]

Transformation of Joseon Society in the Midst of Japanese Domination

Beginning in the early nineteenth century, when the nascent Korean modernization movement was just emerging, Korea had to deal with yet another threat from the West. Even when Yi Haeung (1821-1898), better known as Heungseon Daewongun, father of the twenty-sixth king, Gojong, adopted a policy of isolationism, he was very aware of the West, and its potential impact on the peninsula. In fact, before and after the Hideyoshi invasions in the sixteenth century, Joseon began to recognize the West through the study of Catholicism, known in Korea as Western Learning. Also, the Practical Learning movement of the seventeenth and the eighteenth centuries led to the adoption of Enlightenment thought and attempts to reform the institutions of the Joseon dynasty.

In the name of modernization, Korea was forced to sign the Treaty of Ganghwado with Japan in 1876. The most important feature of this treaty was the provision for opening Korean ports to the outside world.

Although the treaty was unfair, it brought Korea for the first time onto the international stage. Beginning in the mid-nineteenth century, foreigners competing for Korean trade clashed on Korean soil, leading to the Russo-Japanese War of 1904-1905.

When the Russo-Japanese War came to an end and Russia was ready for a peace agreement, American President Theodore Roosevelt attempted to mediate the terms of the treaty. Despite the recommendation of the U.S. minister of legation in Seoul, Horace N. Allen that his government should intervene in the Korean situation to counteract Japanese aggression, Roosevelt felt that "it was necessary to acquiesce in Japanese domination of Korea as a *quid pro quo* for Japan's recognition of U.S. hegemony over the Philippines" (Lee 1984:309). The deal between the U.S. and Japan was known as the secret "Taft-Katsura Agreement," because it was signed by William H. Taft, U.S. secretary of war, and Katsura, prime minister of Japan, in July 1905. In this agreement, Japan promised not to interfere with American domination of the Philippines in exchange for complete freedom of action in Korea (Choy 1979:64). England took the side of the U.S. and endorsed Japanese wishes.

As a result of its victory in the Russo-Japanese War and with the blessing of the U.S., Japan acquired a firm base in Korea for eventually taking sole control of the peninsula. Japan moved immediately to establish a protectorate over Korea, forcing the Ministry of Foreign Affairs to sign the Protectorate Treaty in 1905, a treaty so humiliating that Koreans call it *Eulsa neungyak*, meaning literally a "humiliating treaty signed in the year of *Eulsa*," a reference to the Korean sexagenarian cycle of time. Five years later, Japan annexed Korea and maintained it as a colony until 1945.

In its nascent efforts to modernize, Korea faced two major challenges: dealing deal with the immediate threat of foreign forces, particularly Japan, and bringing about domestic reform and modernization in order to retain its sovereignty. From the collapse of the Joseon dynasty to the Treaty of Ganghwado to Japanese annexation, various reform movements emerged under the influence of Enlightenment thought.

Efforts were made to find solutions to the pressing problems of nineteenth-century Korea by taking these ideas in new directions. Enlightenment thought stressed national self-strengthening through education and the development of Korean commerce and industry; it exerted a powerful influence on "officialdom," including *yangban* and the royal family.

Nevertheless, the ambitious effort to copy Japan's Meiji Restoration and to make Korea an independent nation failed because of factional strife within the reform movement, the interference of Chinese troops, and the unrealistic goal of winning Japanese support for progressive plans. When the coup d'état of 1884 (*Gapsin jeongbyeon*) led by progressives failed, all these aspirations came to an end.

However, various reforms, revolts, and rebellious movements continued to appear, one after the other, among them the *Gabo* Reform (*Gabo gyeongjang*), the Peasant Rebellion (Donghak) of 1894, and the Righteous Armies (Uibyeong) and Independence Club (Dongnip Hyeophoe) movements of 1895. These actions were all aimed at retaining Korea's sovereignty, resisting foreign threats, and curing the domestic ills that resulted from a class system incompatible with reform, a subsistence-level economy, and an inept government unable to deal with domestic problems.

The reform of 1894 was a sweeping one, affecting virtually every aspect of the administration, economy, and socio-cultural activities. There was an effort to eliminate class distinctions between *yangban* and commoners and to introduce the concept of equality and dignity for all. The reform package was so broad and extensive that it included new standardization of weights and measures, adoption of a new calendar, and an order to cut the Korean male's traditional topknot (*sangtu*).

Deuchler (1977:xii) calls the drastic *Gabo* Reform "the starting point of Korea's modernization because those reforms introduced genuine modern features into Korea." However, the package did not include strengthening the military, which was essential to the security of a state confronting foreign threats. Most of all, since the reforms were planned under Japanese domination, not only were they ineffective, but they also had the unintended consequence of accelerating Korea's penetration by Japan's developing capitalist economy. Also, some of the reform programs, such as ordering the cutting of the topknot, provoked furious opposition from conservative Koreans. However, the reforms as a whole significantly advanced Korea's modernization, although they failed to guarantee Korea's sovereignty.

In a direct response to Japanese domination, in 1895 *yangban* officialdom and Confucian literati mobilized the peasantry and formed guerrilla band of "Righteous Armies" throughout the country. Some bands included hundreds or thousands of fighters, but until they absorbed the government soldiers disbanded by the Japanese in 1907, they possessed neither military training nor military discipline. The bands were for the most part equipped only with the spirit to fight the Japanese. Using guerrilla tactics, some bands were successful in attacking Japanese garrisons.

In 1907, around 10,000 mobilized guerrilla forces from all over the country attacked the Residency-General headquarters and Seoul's East Gate (Dongdaemun). Despite the large number of fighters, they were too weak in manpower and weaponry to defeat the Japanese forces in Korea. The activities of the Righteous Armies reached a peak in 1908 and declined thereafter, and after annexation their soldiers became independence fighters. The Righteous Armies demonstrated the most courageous anti-Japanese fighting in Korean history, yet because they were composed mostly of Confucian literati, they undertook no efforts to institute domestic reform. Instead they represented a movement against Western thought, especially Catholicism, in favor of retaining the status quo, which was Confucian at its core.

Unlike the Righteous Armies, the Peasant Rebellion undertook two major tasks: domestic reform and fighting against Japan to retain sovereignty. After the execution of its founder, Choe Jeu, in 1864, the Peasant Rebellion went underground, but by then it had expanded and was well-enough organized to express the peasantry's deep hostility toward the *yangban* class. The rebels led a resistance movement against the inroads of foreign powers, hoisting banners and calling for a crusade to expel the Japanese and Westerners. The Peasant Rebellion erupted into a revolutionary peasant struggle, employing large-scale military operations.

From its beginnings in Gobu, County of Jeolla-do province, the Peasant Rebellion raged against the county magistrate's abuse of power and corruption. Peasants from all the surrounding areas joined forces with the Righteous Armies, swelling their ranks to over 10,000 men who eventually controlled parts of Jeolla-do and Chungcheong-do provinces after crushing government troops. Eventually, the movement spread to other provinces. When Japan intervened militarily, the Righteous Armies fought the Japanese face to face. However, professional Japanese troops, armed with superior weapons and training, defeated the ill-equipped peasant army. Nevertheless, the aim of the Righteous Armies reflected a recurrent demand in Korean history (Lee 1984).

The founding of the Independence Club in 1896 by Seo Jaepil (Philip Jaison), a self-exile to the United States, and by other new intelligentsia influenced by Western thought, certainly signaled the arrival of the Westernization movement. The Club's activities were focused on three goals: first, to safeguard the nation's independence in the face of external aggression; second, to bring about wider participation in the political process by means of a popular-rights movement; and third, to promote a self-strengthening movement.

Unlike earlier programs and movements, the Club not only dealt with both the nation's independence and domestic reforms, but it also pursued the rights of individuals and civil liberty. The goals of the Club "were to establish schools in each village to provide a new-style of education; to build textile and paper mills and ironworks, thus furthering the country's commercialization and industrialization; and to ensure the nation's security by developing a modern national defense capacity" (Lee 1984:304).

In 1896, to express the views of Independence Club members, Seo founded the *Dongnip sinmun* (Independence), a thrice-weekly newspaper that eventually evolved into a daily. It was the first genuinely modern newspaper written in the Korean *Hangeul* alphabet.

As the activities and goals of the Independence Club gained popularity among the general public, those in power feared that the Club's hidden goal was to abolish the monarchy. They threatened to destroy the Club and drove Seo back to the United States. Eventually, the ailing dynasty arrested the leaders of the Club and then called in troops to clear the street of demonstrators protesting the arrest of their leaders.

Although the Club came abruptly to an end, its purposes and actions had a profound impact on Korean history as a whole and modernization in particular. Even after 1910, when Korea became a Japanese colony (via a provision of the Japanese protectorate in 1905), many Koreans committed themselves to carrying out the programs of the Independence Club with the intent of laying the foundation for an independent Korea.

Japanese Colonization and the Independence Movement

Independence Movement

Japanese colonial policies in Korea can be divided into two phases: the early years of brutality from 1910 to 1919 and the later years of cultural genocide from 1919 to 1945. The Korean fight for independence against Japan had to change in response to changes in colonial policies. By and large, Korean resistance movements against colonial rule were divided into two groups: a radical, confrontational, and revolutionary approach on the one hand; and the moderate, indirect, and gradual strategy of the so-called "cultural nationalists" (Robinson 1988) on the other.

The first phase of Japanese rule began on 22 August 1910 with the appointment of Terauchi Masatake as the first Governor-General (1910-1916), and was known as the "dark period (*amheukgi*)" because of the extensive repression of Korean political and cultural life that took place during this time (Eckert et al. 1990:260). The Japanese banned political organizations and it became illegal to assemble for almost any purpose without police permission. In the cities, the police watched intellectuals, religious leaders, and nationalist politicians, and arrests for political activities mounted. In 1912 alone, there were over 50,000 arrests for all crimes, including arrests for illegal political activity and assembly (Eckert et al. 1990:261).

A plot to assassinate Governor-General Terauchi by An Myeonggeun, brother of An Junggeunwho had assassinated Itō Hirobumi in 1909,[4] resulted in an intensive round-up of nationalists in December 1910. The police arrested over 600 Koreans. The long list of those indicted included many leading Korean nationalists. Japanese officials, by dealing deal with Koreans in this harsh way, hoped to strike a decisive early blow against the nationalist movement.

In order to exploit the colonial economic system, the Japanese mustered their administrative resources and personnel, mobilizing both military and civilian police forces. The colonial government initiated a land survey to lay the foundation for Japan's expropriation of the Korean nation and established the Oriental Development Company as its mechanism. Consequently, the company was able to expand its ownership of land to 154,221 hectares. The number of tenant farmers deprived of their land by the company exceeded 300,000. In the meantime, 98,000 Japanese landowning families settled in Korea prior to 1918. Steinberg (1989:41-42) offers a detailed analysis of the Japanese exploitation of Korean landownership.

Even though Japanese colonial policy was brutal, the Koreans continued to fight for their sovereignty. Between 1907 and 1910, some 150,000 Koreans demonstrated and fought against the Japanese. Although the Japanese claimed that resistance ended by 1912, it may have continued sporadically until 1915 (Steignberg 1989:43). Members of the Korean resistance fled to Manchuria, the Maritime Province, Hawaii, and elsewhere.

Although the Korean nationalist movement was united in the single goal of regaining Korean independence, internal strife hampered its attempts to harness nationalist energies into a unified "drive to unseat the Japanese" (Robinson 1988:15). Instead, Korean nationalists were sharply divided into two factions: radical nationalists who advocated social revolution and overt resistance to Japanese imperialism, and moderate nationalists who advocated gradual solutions to the problem of independence. The latter, who have been labeled cultural nationalists (Kim 1998; Robinson 1988:15; Suh 1967:8–9), advocated for education and enlightenment to nurture new values and skills while shaping mass nationalist sentiment to lay the foundation for Korea's future independence. The cultural nationalists considered their objective not simply the immediate goal of throwing out the Japanese at any cost, but transforming the nation by developing fundamental strengths based on the Western model (Kim 1998).

Whatever its intention, the cultural nationalist movement faced a serious challenge from radical nationalism, which attacked its fundamental premise. Michael Robinson (1988:100), an expert on Korean history, sums up the sentiment of the radical nationalists:

> Heavily influenced by their study of Marx and other Socialist writers, radicals attacked the fundamental precepts of the cultural nationalist program. They questioned the utility of national reform within the colonial system, arguing that without political independence talk of national development was meaningless.
>
> Furthermore, they questioned the basic motives of the cultural nationalist leadership's advocacy of cultural and economic development. Under Japanese colonial rule, did not such movements serve only the interests of the middle and upper class Korean elite? Such criticism diluted the mass appeal of cultural nationalism and, furthermore, split nationalist leaders over issues of class versus national interests as well as tactics for independence.

Because the cultural nationalists had to work within the limits of colonial rule and deal with the Japanese authorities, their tactics required conciliatory gestures toward the Japanese at times, leaving them vulnerable to the charge of collaboration even to this day.

Such factional divisions and disputes were precisely what the Japanese hoped to foment with their strategy of "divide and conquer." Consequently, instead of directing their efforts toward Japanese colonialists, the nationalists were diverted by infighting, and both factions were deeply wounded by their ideological disputes. Even several decades after Korea's independence from Japanese occupation, many Koreans remain scarred by the insidious strategy of the Japanese colonialists to turn them against each other.

March First Movement and Japanese Policy of Cultural Genocide

When Japanese colonial rule intensified, many Koreans participated in a nationwide anti-Japanese demonstration on 1 March 1919. Known as the "March First Movement" (*Samil Undong*), it declared Korean independence from Japan. The doctrine of self-determinism put forward by the American President Woodrow Wilson as an integral part of the post-World War I peace settlement indirectly provided the impetus for this protest. The movement was initially sparked by overseas Korean independence fighters in Shanghai, Japan, Manchuria, and Siberia, but it was coordinated through various religious organizations, including Cheondogyo,[5] Christians, and Buddhists, among others.

A declaration of independence was originally scheduled to be signed on 3 March 1919, the date of funeral rites for King Gojong, but the representatives decided to act on 1 March. Thirty-three representatives met at the Taehwagwan restaurant in Insa-dong, Jongno, and formally promulgated a Declaration of Independence proclaiming that Korea had become an independent nation. The opening line of the declaration read, "We herewith proclaim the independence of Korea and the liberty of the Korean people." Students and citizens gathered in Pagoda Park at Jongno 2-ga in Seoul and marched through the streets. Passions spread quickly throughout the city, and the declaration soon led to a nationwide movement, involving at least two million participants throughout the entire peninsula.

In the brutal military response known as the "*mudan jeongchi*," the Japanese authorities mobilized a 5,402-man police force in 751 stations and several thousand military police. They reinforced these forces by including an additional six infantry battalions and 400 military police troops in the suppression campaign.[6] Defining any Korean taking part in the independence resistance as a criminal, the Japanese decided to cope with subsequent demonstrations by a policy of mass killing. The worst atrocity up to that point took place on 15 April 1919 in the village of Jeam-ri, Suwon, Gyeonggi-do province. Changsoo Lee and George De Vos (1981:29) describe what happened:

> a nearby Japanese garrison had come to the village. Some of the soldiers had roughed up several male inhabitants believed to have joined in the general active protest. The protesters had been part of the Christian community of this village. Two days after this unpleasant episode, some troops returned. They told all the villagers present to assemble in the Church. The villagers did so, thinking they were to hear some word of apology for the brutal behavior of the Japanese soldiers. Once they were all inside, the troops barred the doors, nailed them shut, and poured gasoline about the wooden structure, setting it on fire. Everyone inside was incinerated.

Additional brutal retaliation continued. While the church burned, the Japanese soldiers directed a barrage at the civilians, killing all of them, including women and infants. The Japanese burned thirty-one houses in the village and set fire to 317 houses in fifteen villages in the vicinity of Jeam-ri.[7]

Despite such horrible burnings and mass murder, Korean independence fighting and demonstrations never flagged. Seven years after the March First Movement, on 10 June 1926, the day of the state funeral of King Sunjong (1907-1910), the last king of the Joseon dynasty, students launched a large-scale anti-Japanese demonstration known as the "June Tenth Anti-Japanese Movement" (Yuksip Manse Sageon). There were also several large-scale protests and assassination attempts against Japanese leaders. In 1929, for instance, students in Gwangju, Jeollanam-do province, began demonstrations against the Japanese because they had insulted Korean female students. The protest spread to 194 schools and involved some 54,000 students.

Although the March First Movement and other anti-Japanese independence movements failed to achieve their ultimate goal, they did accomplish several things. Despite the enormous number of casualties, the movements demonstrated the nation's pride, highlighted the inhumane treatment of Koreans by the Japanese occupiers, and demonstrated the potential power of Koreans against their aggressors. The Korean people's political consciousness reached a new stage of awareness. The demonstrations showed that nationalist passions among Koreans at every level could be mobilized for anti-Japanese activities.

The establishment of the Korean Provisional Government (Daehanminguk Imsi Jeongbu) in Shanghai in April 1919 was a by-product of the March First Movement. The independence fighters in Manchuria and the Russian Maritime Territory regrouped under the banner of the General Headquarters of the Restoration Army (Gwangbokgun Chongyeong) in Antung prefecture in Manchuria. The provisional government was able not only to dispatch its envoys to international conferences and to put out its principal publication, *Dongnip sinmun* (Independence News), but also to continue providing information for the independence movement both within Korea and in the outside world.

Obvious changes occurred in Japan's colonial policy, which was now carried out by the so-called the "enlightened administration" (*munhwa jeongchi*). In a conciliatory move, Japan announced that it was abandoning reliance on its gendarmerie police forces to maintain control in Korea in favor of a so-called enlightened administration. Japan even abolished the wearing of uniforms and swords by civilian officials, although all these moves remained gestures at best. Admiral Saitō Makoto was appointed the new Governor-General. Eventually Saitō was proclaimed leader of the so-called enlightened administration.

After experiencing Japanese brutality and coming to terms with the harsh political reality after the March First Movement that Korea's political independence was unobtainable. Knowing the reality, a good many Korean nationalists, particularly cultural nationalists, adopted a secondary goal. They advocated for education and enlightenment to nurture new values and skills while cultivating mass nationalist sentiment to lay the basis for future independence. They established schools and industries (Kim 1998) as well as Korean newspapers in the Korean language, *Hangeul*, including the *Dong-A Ilbo*, the *Chosun Ilbo*, and the *Sidae Ilbo*.

Urbane, well-traveled, and fluent in English, Admiral Saitō Makoto replaced the naked coercion of Japan's earlier colonial policy with softer but more effective policies of coercion known as "harmony between Japan and Korea" (*Naeseon yunghwa*). Ironically, it may have been the March First Movement that allowed Japan to increase its exploitation of the Korean economy, which came to resemble a classic colonial economy. Huge quantities of Korean rice had to be shipped to Japan to overcome a severe shortage there, and Korea became a market for the output of Japanese industry, particularly clothing, yarn, and thread.

In reality, the later period of Japanese colonization was economically and emotionally harsher than the earlier one that had been characterized by overt brutality. Throughout the 1930s, when Japan moved closer to its 1931 occupation of Manchuria and before and after the Sino-Japanese war in 1937, Korea was economically developed and exploited for the Japanese realm. Even the development of Korean hydroelectric facilities, together with various industries that relied on that power, was logistically important to the Japanese to further continental aggression. Korea was also exploited as a rice-exporting region to make up for the deficits that Japan suffered. According to an estimate, about half of the rice produced in Korea was exported to Japan (Steinberg 1989:45). Because of the resulting shortage of rice for Korean consumption, nutritional standards declined and poverty increased.

At the same time, Japan instituted policies of deliberate Korean cultural genocide under the slogan of *Naeseon ilche*, meaning "Japan and Korea are one entity." This movement aimed to eradicate Korean national identity by eliminating traditional Korean culture and transforming the Korean people into Japanese imperial subjects (*Hwangguk siminhwa*). The *Naeseon ilche* policy had several purposes, and the overarching aim was to completely eradicate Korean national identity. Japanese authorities pressed Koreans to adopt Japanese customs and habits, including clothing, food, and housing, in all aspects of daily life. The policy included promoting Shintōism and the imperial cult; strictly enforcing the use of the Japanese language in public and quasi-public places, including all educational facilities after 1938 as well as in homes; and forcing Koreans to adopt Japanese names (*changssi* or identity creation), beginning in 1940.

Parenthetically, because of the *changssi*, I had difficulty answering to a strange name, which was supposed to be my new "Japanese name." Nevertheless, I had to have one in order to enroll in the Japanese-run elementary school. Often, because I was not used to the new name and it was never used at home, I did not respond when my Japanese homeroom teacher called on me. The Japanese authorities pretended that the policy of *changssi* was voluntary, but in reality it was mandatory. Often police were used to enforce the policy. Those who did not conform to the policy were thought to be anti-imperial and were discriminated against in employment. Despite some vehement opposition, less than four months after the announcement of the policy, over 300,000 Korean households (about 87 percent of the total) had changed their names (Kim 1998:202 n.27).

Japanese authorities thought that the major hindrances to their cultural-eradication movement were the Korean national newspapers and other *Hangeul* publications. Another Japanese target was the Korean Language Society. In October 1942, the leaders of the Korean Language Society were arrested; some such as Lee Yunje died in prison. In 1938, Korean-language teaching was banned from secondary school curricula; beginning in 1943 the Korean language was no longer taught in primary schools. Japanese control of writing, speech, books, films, and music was thorough, and anything that obstructed or hindered the implementation of *Naeseon ilche* was a target for eradication. In February 1938, even the map of the Korean peninsula with the rose of Sharon (the Korean national flower) in the background had to be deleted.

Facilitating opportunities for higher education was the top priority of Korean cultural nationalists. Because there were very limited educational opportunities in the colony for Koreans beyond middle school, college-bound Koreans increasingly went to Japan to complete their education. To counteract the undesirable social effects inherent in such a system, nationalists mounted a drive to establish a Korean university (Eckert et al. 1990:290). The cultural nationalists formed the Society for the Establishment of a Korean People's University in November 1922, with the help of 1,170 supporters. The goal was noble, hopes were high, and expectations great, but the movement came to nought because of "Mismanagement of donations, infighting between chapters, and vitriolic criticism from more radical nationalists, including the withdrawal of support from the important All Korean Youth League" (Eckert et al. 1990:291).[8]

In addition, the Japanese pushed the movement toward failure, employing the tactics of "divide and conquer" against cultural nationalists and radical leftists. In 1926, before the Korean nationalists' drive to establish their own people's university, which further diminished public interest in a Korean people's university.[9]

Japanese Mobilization of Koreans

The greatest Korean suffering during the Japanese colonial period, both in scale and intensity, took place when Japan began to mobilize Korean manpower to serve their war machine. This process steadily escalated after 7 July 1937, when Japan launched its full-scale assault on China. When the war began, Japan carried out a total national mobilization policy and put into effect a variety of other extraordinary measures, including the requisition of Korean grain production and various items made of metal. In February 1938, as combat grew more intense, the Japanese announced the Special Volunteer Army Act, and some Koreans were mobilized in June of that year in accordance with the act. In 1939, the Japanese proclaimed the National Manpower Mobilization Act, under which Korean laborers and military draftees were involuntarily brought to Japan to compensate for the manpower shortage created by the expansion of the war to Southeast Asia. These mobilized laborers were forced to work in munitions plants and coal mines, and to perform various other forms of physical labor to support the war. According to South Korean Government statistics, between 1939 and 1945 over 4 million Koreans were drafted into Japanese work programs in Korea, while more than 1.2 million were forced to work in Japan.[10] Many Koreans were sent to coal mines in Japan, Sakhalin, and elsewhere. A good many of them still remain there. In fact, Japanese mobilization became a major contributor to the Korean diaspora throughout the world.

As Japan escalated its war effort, the National Mobilization Law of 1942 entrapped increasing numbers of Koreans. Following the Japanese attack on Pearl Harbor, Koreans were subject to the Japanese military draft. The number of Koreans drafted into the Japanese military totaled 360,000 by the end of World War II. These conscripted soldiers were sent to the South Pacific, Southeast Asia, and China. Almost half of them died or were missing in action. The aggregate number of Koreans mobilized throughout the war by the Japanese government in both Korea and Japan reached almost 6 million (Kim 1988a:24; 1998:114).

The mobilization included females ranging from twelve to forty years of age, who served under the designation of the Women's Volunteer Workers Corps. The mobilized females were forced to engage in harsh manual labor, and a good many of them were sent to the war zone to work in brothels for Japanese soldiers. The Japanese authorities even picked up pregnant women to meet their allocated quotas despite instructions that they draft only single females between the ages of eighteen and twenty-nine.[11]

In February 2007, several U.S. Congressmen led by Michael

Honda, who is of Japanese descent, submitted a resolution that in strong words holds Japan responsible for the sexual enslavement of women during its colonial occupation of Asia, including Korea, in the past century and demands its apology. On 26 June 2007, by an overwhelming thirty-nine votes to two, the House Foreign Affairs Committee passed a resolution calling on Japan to formally acknowledge and apologize for the mass coercion of "Comfort Women." into army brothels. Eventually, on 30 July 2007, the U.S. House of Representatives unanimously passed the resolution, calling for Japan to acknowledge their inhumane deeds fully, not to distort and deny history by blaming the victims.

Korean Modernization in Retrospect: "Development without Development"

According to statistics provided by Edward Mason (1980:75-82) and his colleagues, economic growth in Korea between 1910 and 1940, both in manufacturing, with an annual growth rate of over 10 percent, and in agriculture, with a 2 percent annual growth rate, appeared to be substantial. Korean annual economic growth between 1911 and 1938, for instance, averaged 3.5 percent, compared to 3.4 percent in Japan. Mason (1980:76-77) and his colleagues provide the following explanation for such economic growth:

> In 1940, the Japanese accounted for 94 percent of the authorized capital of manufacturing establishments in Korea, and such key sectors as metals, chemicals, and gas and electrical appliances were almost wholly Japanese. Korean firms, where they existed, were much smaller and financially weaker than those of the Japanese. There were over 1,600 Korean technicians in these industries [in 1944], but this number was only 19 percent of all technicians in Korean manufacturing and construction. The other 81 percent were Japanese, and this percentage rose to 89 percent in such high technology industries as metals and chemicals.

The size of Japanese investment in Korea and Japanese transfer of their technology sound impressive, considering the inventory of the Korean economy at the time.[12]

In an effort to counteract, if not eliminate, this misinterpretation of Japan's role in modernizing Korea during the colonization period, Heo Suyeol (2005) published a comprehensive book with detailed statistics in which he states that economic indicators definitely show that economic growth took place in Korea during the colonial period. Nevertheless, Heo methodically and persuasively asserts that Korean economic growth at this time did not benefit Koreans and had nothing to do with the subsequent expansion of Korean economic growth and industrialization since the mid-1960s. He terms it "Development without Development" (*Gaebal eomneun gaebal*) for Koreans, as he astutely titles his book. For example, despite economic growth during the Japanese occupation, Korean farms suffered great economic privation at the hands of the Japanese.[13]

Even if the Japanese created the infrastructure for economic growth and industrialization in the peninsula, the ultimate question remains, in the words of Steinberg (1989:40), "For whom ⋯ was this infrastructure built and the Koreans trained?" The answer, as Koreans argue, is "that it was for the Japanese, to serve their expansionist and military interests. The welfare of the Korean people was not a primary, not even a secondary concern" (Steinberg 1989:40). As evidence, the Japanese focused on constructing industrial plants in the northern part of Korea, a strategic site suitable for attacking Manchuria and China proper.

Recent Korean Modernization Since the Mid-1960s

It is an indisputable fact that contemporary Korea since the mid-1960s has been a modern, if not ultra-modern, society, however assessed: phenomenal growth of its economy with an unprecedented rate of industrialization, hyper-urbanization, remarkably high literacy rate, and many other factors. Since these aspects will be discussed later on, in this section, I limit my discussion to two characteristics of recent Korean modernization: A legacy common to all previous modernizations in Korean history; and a unique characteristic of the most recent modernization.

First of all, earlier modernization was initiated under the most difficult circumstances socially, economically, and politically — under conditions of the so-called "broken calm." These include the post-war power vacuum (1945-1948), which created a chaotic political condition in Korea and struggles for political hegemony between and among political sectors divided largely by ideological lines; the partition of the peninsula since 1945, which destroyed the economic balance between the industrialized north and agriculture-based south; the subsequent war (1950-1953), which devastated the entire country, including a near total destruction of the existing infrastructure, buildings, homes, and other properties, not to mention the human casualties; political instability with student revolution (1961), followed by innumerable demonstrations, labor disputes; and most of all, the 1961 military coup d'état. It is indeed astonishing that Korea accomplished its economic "miracle" and modernization, overcoming many obstacles; how it did so will be explored in detail in the next chapter.

Second, unlike the earlier modernization that was either forced or induced by foreign countries, the most recent Korean modernization has been initiated and accomplished by the will and determination of Koreans themselves. Recently, because Korea is experiencing slow economic growth, there has been increasing nostalgia for the military regime, and even for President Park Chung-hee and his leadership in Korean economic development. Some sociologists under the sway of the so-called "great man theory" recognize that often a great man or woman influences major socio-economic and political change; Franklin D. Roosevelt (1882-1945) played such a heroic role in pulling America out of the Great Depression in the 1930s (Cole 1975:14-15). Nevertheless, a great man or woman may owe at least a part of his or her greatness to particular social settings and conditions. Indeed, the

Great Depression allowed Roosevelt to adopt the New Deal program. Also, many economists and historians often point out that, despite Roosevelt's New Deal programs, America did not really emerge from its economic depression until America's involvement in World War II, in 1942 to be precise. It was the war that changed basic economic conditions (Cole 1975:15).

In a similar fashion, even though President Park played a heroic role in Korean economic development and rapid industrialization, major credit must be given to the Korean people who carried out the most difficult tasks. Clearly, credit for Korean development must be shared by others besides President Park. Incidentally, the original five-year economic development plan (1962-1966) President Park implemented had been drawn up by the Economic Development Council of the short-lived Jang Myeon regime in 1961 (Mason et al. 1980:253). Chang was elected premier under the newly assembled cabinet government after the student revolution, and fell by military coup. Despite economic development, most Koreans endured difficult times under the military-led government. Some Koreans have already forgotten about the hardships of those years. Perhaps they have a short or selective memory, filtering out the bad elements and remembering only the good.

Role of a Mandatory Draft in Recent Korean Modernization

Because a military-oriented culture has been a major obstacle to Korean democratization for some thirty years, most Koreans, the younger generation in particular, are reluctant to talk about the "military," even though their military experience is a major topic of men's casual conversation. Nevertheless, Korea's mandatory draft system, which excludes physically challenged people, stipulates that virtually every Korean man must serve in the military. If this mandatory draft system did not exist, a great many rural Koreans would have had little or no formal training. Through their military experience, they not only became aware of the outside world beyond their home towns, regions, and provinces, but they also had opportunities to gain skills and knowledge to handle sophisticated equipment and machinery. Also, they acquired leadership skills during their military service, which have been fully demonstrated in a nationwide rural development project, the New Village Movement (*Saemaeul Undong*), which will be described in Chapter 5. After being discharged from active military duty, such men have become effective leaders in various rural modernization projects.

Their military experience has proven particularly useful in the field of construction, improving Korea's ability to bid on jobs in Middle Eastern countries. Older generations of Korean workers and managers understand what it means to hover between life and death, having learned endurance through three wars: World War II, the Korean War, and the Vietnam War. Such experiences help to explain how Korean construction workers have been so successful in undertaking the most difficult tasks in the Arabian Desert under the most inhospitable circumstances. I myself have observed hardworking Korean construction workers in Middle Eastern countries; they work as if they are soldiers in a combat zone (Kim 1992:214–215). Mandatory military service and its experience cannot be underestimated as an important factor in recent Korean modernization.

CHAPTER 3

Political Evolution and Revolution in Contemporary Korea

My generation of Koreans is perhaps one of the most unfortunate, for it has weathered so much socio-economic and political turmoil and endured devastating wars. In writing this chapter I feel as if I am ruminating on my own life history.

I was born one year after the Japanese attacked China at the start of World War II.[1] Until my oldest brother was drafted by the Japanese army, I was too young to understand Japanese colonial rule and the war. Nevertheless, I was old enough to remember the worst part of World War II. I have vivid memories of hurrying into a tunnel-like underground shelter (*bangongho*) when I heard a warning siren. Every public building as well as each individual dwelling had shelters against possible American air raids. Even now, when I ponder my memories of going into these shelters, I am still unable to understand why American warplanes would come to our region of Korea remote, isolated, and mountainous — where there were no military installations, nothing of strategic value, and no Japanese soldiers. However, every once in a while, I was able to spot several tiny silver objects in the sky, which I was told were American warplanes called B-29s.

Although I was unable to comprehend what Japanese emperor Hirohito's unconditional surrender on 15 August 1945 would do to us, I was old enough then to remember a big celebration in the square of our town, even though it was a tiny and remote place. My parents hoped that my brother, who had been drafted by the Japanese Army and sent off to the battlefield somewhere in China, would return home soon. When he did not appear, my parents thought he must have died, because casualties among draftees were so high that not many were expected to make it back. However, my brother did come home several months after the liberation when the Korean Provisional Government (KPG) returned from China. He told us that initially he had been sent to a battlefield somewhere in the Shantung Peninsula in China but later escaped and joined the army of the KPG in Shanghai, Gwangbokgun, attaining the rank of captain by the war's end.

Many people believe that serious fighting in Korea did not begin until the start of the Korean War (1950-1953), but many of the most brutal and gruesome killings actually took place right after the liberation, in remote, rural and mountainous areas. Communist guerrillas attacked right-wing anti-Communists, and police retaliated against the Communists and their sympathizers. Often killings happened in remote regions where police forces could not intervene. Since my hometown is located at the extreme northeastern tip of Gyeongsang-do province, near Taebaeksan, the second tallest and the most rugged mountain in South Korea, it was a natural sanctuary for Communist guerrillas, and killings were common. In fact, we lived in two distinct political systems: by day, we inhabited the capitalistic, democratic, and right-wing-led Republic of Korea; and by night, because the South Korean police force could not protect us, we lived in a *de facto* Communist state.

Very little has been written about these events, but historical research has revealed many details about the horrible tactics the Communists used to gain control. People who never experienced such cruelties firsthand cannot begin to imagine them. Often I was awakened in the middle of the night and had to leave my house when the self-defense militiamen who patrolled the village blew a whistle, warning us that Communist guerrillas had infiltrated the village.

When daylight came, police came by to search for those villagers who had given food and other supplies to the Communist guerrillas under the threat of imminent death. As soon as the police found these villagers, they dragged them to the police station and tortured them. When the police caught Communist guerrillas, they executed them without trial. Accidentally, I once witnessed the execution of guerrillas whose faces had been covered with white towels before they were shot. I closed my eyes so as not to see, but I could not close my ears. Such scenes were not uncommon throughout remote regions of the country. In my village, liberation from Japanese rule (*haebang*) certainly did not bring freedom from fear and pain.

While a guerrilla war was being waged continuously in my home region, a real, all-out war began on 25 June 1950, when I was a sixth grader in elementary school. In less than one month, the North Korean People's Army (*Inmingun*) reached our corner of South Korea. Eventually, the North Korean authorities came to our house, evicted us, and made our house the regional headquarters of the northern forces. We were relocated to a hut with a thatched roof. Meanwhile, our life in this miserable shack continued until Gen. Douglas MacArthur's forces made a spectacular amphibious landing at Incheon on 15 September 1950. Since our village is located in the heart of the Great Baekdu Mountain Range (Baekdudaegan), which runs all the way to the northeastern side of the peninsula, many retreating North Korean troops passed through our village and its vicinity. Eventually, the front line of the war moved north of our region, and finally a ceasefire was declared in 1953.

During my college years in Seoul, as the post-Korean War government, led by Syngman Rhee and his Liberal Party (Jayudang), was tilting increasingly toward autocratic rule, I was an active participant in "the April 19 Student Revolution" in 1960, which brought down the First Republic. Immediately, the Second Republic was born, but it was brought down in turn by a military coup on 16 May 1961. The country was in disarray, and for the next three decades, it was ruled by the military. I escaped this oppressive situation by going to America for advanced study, and stayed there for the next thirty-six years.

As a professional anthropologist living in America, in the early 1980s I conducted fieldwork on dispersed Korean family members in Korea, fieldwork that brought back my childhood memories of the war. While I was engaged in this study, in 1983 the Korean Broadcasting System (KBS) telecast scenes of reunited families via a reunion telethon that attracted the world's attention. Watching these scenes I spent many nights weeping along with the participants as I heard their tragic stories of separation and witnessed the joy and emotion of their reunions. Portions of my fieldnotes were stained with my tears. It has been difficult for me to write about myself and my own people and yet remain objective.

In order to maintain a balance between the compassion I feel as a native anthropologist doing fieldwork with my fellow Koreans and the detachment I need as a scientist, I have decided to downplay my personal feelings in describing the events I have witnessed. In the general survey of modern Korean political history that follows I will only discuss my own experiences and reactions when describing local events I observed and in which I at times participated.

The Post-War Power Vacuum

The dramatic conclusion to World War II on 15 August 1945 after the atomic bombs fell on the Japanese cities of Hiroshima and Nagasaki left Koreans unprepared to organize their own government.[2] Before they could even start debating their future, several key decisions that would affect the destiny of Koreans were made by foreign powers, the most detrimental one being the partition of the peninsula.

Political Chaos after the Liberation

Five days before the Japanese emperor Hirohito officially announced Japan's unconditional surrender on 15 August 1945, a middle-rank Japanese (whose name is unknown) from the Bureau of Political Police, sensing that the Japanese surrender was imminent, visited Song Jinu, a journalist and moderate cultural nationalist, in the early morning of 10 August and proposed that Song lead an interim administration to preserve law and order as the Japanese left Korea. Song refused this invitation and instead demanded freedom of the press, the release of all political prisoners, and distribution of food to starving Koreans. Song also called for a halt to the Japanese surveillance of his residence (Kim 1990; Goha Song Jinu Seonsaeng Jeongi 1990:425-427). The following day, a Korean attorney, Gang Byeongsun, reassured Song that the Japanese surrender would come within the next few days (Go 1976:461).

On 11 August 1945, four Japanese high officials invited Song to an unidentified Japanese home in Bonjeong (current Chungmuro) to induce him to head up an interim administration to preserve the peace (Goha Song Jinu Seonsaeng Jeongi 1990:428).[3] Song refused once again, but the Japanese insistently importuned him until the eve of the day of liberation. As an excuse, Song told the Japanese authorities that he was too ill to accept such a responsibility (Goha Song Jinu Seonsaeng Jeongi 1990:427). Bruce Cumings (1981:70) reports that Song "refused the Japanese efforts because (1) he realized that any Korean administration would have to await the sanction of the incoming Allied forces; and (2) he believed that the Korean Provisional Government (KPG) in Chungking [Chongqing] was the legitimate government of Korea. ··· Song did not want to give the Japanese the benefit of cooperation in their time of need." At the final meeting with the governor of Gyeonggi-do province at his office on 14 August, Song again refused the Japanese request.

The Japanese were becoming desperate to create an interim administration run by an influential Korean, so they turned to Yeo Unhyeong, whose views were a mixture of socialism, Christianity, and Wilsonian democracy. Yeo had always been willing to work with Communists, and he embraced Marxism as a "good idea" (Cumings 1981:474-475 n.114). Eventually Yeo met with Endō Ryūsaku, the Governor-General's secretary for political affairs, in the early morning hours on 15 August and accepted the Japanese offer. Yeo in turn demanded the following of Japan: "(1) Release all political and economic prisoners immediately throughout the nation; (2) Guarantee food provisions for the next three months; (3) Absolutely no interference with the maintenance of peace or with Korean activities for the sake of independence of peace or with Korean activities for the sake of independence; (4) Absolutely no interference with the training of students and youths; (5) Absolutely no interference with the training of workers and peasants" (Cumings 1981:71).

Yeo did not waste any time. He gathered his followers at his home and began to create an organization that would serve as an administrative body for a political movement above and beyond the interim peace-keeping administration. Mobilizing for this purpose his existing underground political organization, the Korean Independence League (Joseon Geonguk Dongmaeng or Geonmaeng), Yeo and his followers formed the Committee for the Preparation of Korean Independence (Joseon Geonguk Junbi Wiwonhoe or CPKI). The launch of the CPKI did not go smoothly, because the Japanese authorities thought it went above and beyond its original mission of peacekeeping. On or about 18 August, the Japanese demanded that Yeo scale back the CPKI's functions to the original mission.

Partition of the Peninsula and Ideological Divisions

Although the official announcement of the division of the Korean peninsula along the thirty-eighth parallel was made on 2 September 1945, the United States had actually planned this division four days before the end of the war. The initial decision to draw a line and divide Korea was made on 10-11 August, 1945 in an all-night session of the U.S. State-War-Navy Coordinating Committee (SWNCC). As previously mentioned, according to Bruce Cumings (1981:120; 1997:186-187) John J. McCloy of the SWNCC directed Col. Charles H. Bonesteel and Maj. Dean Rusk, both of whom knew very little about Korea (Collins 1969:25 n.26), to come up with a plan to define the zones to be occupied by American and Russian forces. Preoccupied with dividing the peninsula evenly, they were unaware that Korea would suffer economically if the industrialized north and agricultural south were separated, not to mention oblivious to the potential for war between the two Koreas. The U.S. officials who made this hasty decision were satisfied because the Soviet Union had no objections and would agree to the placement of the capital city of Seoul in the American-controlled zone.

On 20 August, while Yeo was mobilizing his CPKI, an American B-29 dropped leaflets signed by Gen. Albert Wedemeyer announcing that the U.S. military would soon arrive and that until then, the Japanese authorities should maintain law and order (Go 1976:470; Goha Song Jinu Seonsaeng Jeongi 1990:442). The Japanese promptly ordered the dismantling of all Korean law-and-order and political organizations. The leaflets clearly announced that the troops entering Seoul would be American.

American forces arrived a full month later than Soviet forces. However, U.S. Maj. Gen. Archibald V. Arnold replaced Abe Nobuyuki as Governor-General. Two days later, Endō Ryūsaku and all Japanese bureau chiefs were removed from office, and the administration changed to the United States Army Military Government in Korea (USAMGIK, hereafter the U.S. Military Government). Having lost its vital mission, Yeo's CPKI gradually shifted toward organizing Communists. In the meantime, right-wingers, encouraged by the fact that Seoul and the south would be ruled by Americans, began to mobilize.

Koreans were sharply divided along ideological lines into Right and Left. The Commanding General of the United States Armed Forces in Korea (USAFIK), John Reed Hodge, handled Korean affairs poorly; he and his officials were clearly ill-prepared to rule over fifteen million Koreans because they had no experience in dealing with Korea and its culture. Hodge was also ill-informed about the purpose of the partition of the peninsula (Cumings 1981:126; Henderson 1968:21). Native Korean Baek Nakjun (George Paik) who served as an adviser to Hodge's military government observed that "The American military forces drifted away from the mission due to a lack of a clear policy and goal" (Baek 1982:216-217).

Meanwhile, as a result of sharp ideological divisions among Koreans, South Korea was bustling with many small political parties and organizations.[4] The most visible activity was organized by Yeo Unhyeong, who used the CPKI as a basis for forming the Korean People's Republic (Joseon Inmin Gonghwaguk or KPR). In early September (Lee 1946:260), Yeo published a list of its officers and cabinet members and their departments.[5] He had made an effort to include both left- and right-wing adherents, and cabinet members were chosen according to their various specialties.[6] While Yeo's KPR became active, the rightists led by Song Jinu, using the organizational backbone of the Preparatory Committee for National Congress (Gungmin Daehoe Junbihoe) together with the other four right-wing factions, formed a political party, the Korean Democratic Party (Hanguk Minjudang, KDP), that was anti-Communist, conservative, and politically right-wing. Some critics point out that "unlike the KPR, the KDP never tried to reach across Korea's political divisions and include Koreans on the Left" (Cumings 1981:96).

Relations between Yeo's KPR and the U.S. Military Government were becoming strained, and the KDP began to receive full support from the U.S. Military Government, a manifestation of the "American-KDP camaraderie" (Cumings 1981:150).

Trusteeship vs. Anti-Trusteeship

Because of this rapport between the U.S. Military Government and the KDP, the U.S. Military Government supported the latter's request for the return of Syngman Rhee and the Korean Provisional Government (KPG) leaders. Subsequently, Rhee returned on 16 October, and Kim Gu and twenty other KPG leaders returned on 23 November. Their return, however, exacerbated the existing factional strife in Korean politics.

Although the KDP was instrumental in the return of the KPG leaders, those leaders were critical of the KDP,[7] and the KDP and KPG quickly became estranged. If KPG leaders were to exercise political hegemony, they knew they would have to eliminate the KDP leaders;

in response, the KDP supported Syngman Rhee instead of the KPG leaders. In the meantime, Hodge and his advisors were clearly less trusting of Kim Gu, former president of the KPG in Shanghai, than of Syngman Rhee (Go 1976:485–486).

While all of this political manuevering was going on, at a conference in Moscow in December 1945, the foreign ministers of the United States, Great Britain, and the Soviet Union adopted a trusteeship plan for five years under the assumption that Koreans were not yet prepared to govern themselves. The announcement of the trusteeship triggered public outrage and violent opposition from Koreans. Although at first the Communists and leftists joined in the anti-trusteeship movement, on 2 January 1946, the Communist groups in Korea, doubtless on Russian instruction, suddenly changed their attitude and came out in favor of trusteeship. Well-rehearsed demonstrations in favor of trusteeship were held in North Korea and by leftist groups in the South.

On 28 December, Song Jinu attended a strategy session against the trusteeship at Kim Gu's residence. While Song urged the avoidance of direct confrontation with the U.S. Military Government, Kim Gu and his KPG leaders not only insisted on using radical and violent means if necessary, but also on clashing head-on with the U.S. Military Government. The argument between Song and the KPG continued until 4 o'clock in the morning on 29 December. At 6:15 A.M. on 30 December, Song Jinu, aged fifty-six years, was assassinated at his home.[8]

At this point, Kim Seongsu took over leadership of the KDP. With his involvement in party politics, the anti-trusteeship movement became an anti-Communist movement: when the Communists shifted their position from anti-trusteeship to pro-trusteeship on 3 January 1946, the anti-trusteeship movement became the anti-Communist movement. As the leader of the KDP, Kim Seongsu made it clear that the KDP absolutely opposed the trusteeship. At the same time, Kim made it clear that he and the KDP supported the KPG leaders, and persisted in trying to bring about cooperation between

Syngman Rhee and Kim Gu (Lee 1991:370).

In the meantime, Syngman Rhee organized the National Headquarters for Unification (Minjok Tongil Chongbonbu) to establish an autonomous Korean government. Kim Gu and others from the Korean Independent Party (Hanguk Dongnipdang or Handokdang) also formed a National Assembly (Gungmin Hoeui) to succeed the Extraordinary People's Assembly in launching an anti-trusteeship movement and in bringing about national unification between the leftists and rightists. The left-wing political parties formed the Democratic National Front (Minjujuui Minjokjeonseon) and carried on a unified pro-trusteeship campaign. The left-wing hoped that by giving their positive support to the work of the Joint Commission they might in turn create support for the trusteeship concept. Nevertheless, "when the police found evidence of large-scale currency counterfeiting at a press used by the Korean Communist Party (May 1946), the U.S. authorities put out an order for the arrest of its leaders, whereupon the Communists went underground" in willy-nilly fashion (Lee 1984:377).

The General Election and the Birth of the Republic of Korea

When the U.S.-Soviet Joint Commission reconvened in May 1947, the United States proposed deferring the Korean issue for further discussion at a conference of the foreign ministers of the four powers. When the Soviet Union rejected this proposal, the United States submitted the question of Korea's independence to United Nations supervision. As a result, a U.N. Temporary Commission on Korea was created to oversee and facilitate the implementation of Korean independence. However, the U.N. Commission was unable to enter North Korea because of Soviet opposition. On the basis of the Commission's report in February of 1948, the Interim Committee of the United Nations General Assembly authorized elections to be held in those areas of Korea open to the supervision of the Commission, which meant only the southern half of the country, which effectively nullified the trusteeship issue.

While Syngman Rhee welcomed the United Nations' decision, Kim Gu wanted to leave room for North Korea to participate in the election after the Soviet Union's interference had been removed (Go 1976:530-531). At this juncture, it appeared that a coalition among the nationalists, especially Syngman Rhee and Kim Gu, could be accomplished. However, the effort to unite Korean leaders on the issue of elections ultimately failed. While Syngman Rhee and Kim Seongsu insisted that elections be held exclusively in the south, Kim Gu and his followers urged dialogue between the north and south (Lee 1991:384).

The first general election in the history of Korea was carried out only in the south on 10 May 1948. 100 seats were allocated to the North Korean provinces, and 200 representatives were chosen by South Korean voters.[9] The general election results indicated that Syngman Rhee's National Society for the Rapid Realization of Korean Independence (Daehan Dongnip Chokseong Gungminhoe or NSRRKI) had fifty-five seats, while Kim Seongsu's KDP had only twenty-nine seats.[10]

Rhee's shrewd initial political maneuver after the election was to adopt the first Korean Constitution. In January 1948, Yu Jino had been asked by the U.S. Military Government and Kim Seongsu to draft a constitution (Lee 1977:214-215). Yu's original draft included a parliamentary system, but Syngman Rhee manipulated it into a presidential system. The revised version of the constitution was passed by the General Assembly on 12 July, and formally promulgated on 17 July 17 1948. The National Assembly held presidential elections on 20 July and elected Syngman Rhee the first president of the Republic. Rhee took the helm of the government and promulgated the birth of the Republic of Korea (ROK) on 15 August 1948.

In the meantime, the Provisional People's Committee for North Korea, led by Kim Ilseong, was formed in February 1946, serving as a virtual government in the North. The Democratic People's Republic of Korea (DPRK) was formally established on 9 September 1948.

Syngman Rhee's inauguration address as the first president of ROK

The Fratricidal Korean War

Outbreak of the Korean War

Syngman Rhee continued to be plagued by ideological confrontation between left and right, and there were many clashes and confrontations between the two factions. There had also been several major pro-Communist military rebellions in Yeosu and Suncheon, in October 1948. Because of such turmoil, Rhee's government hardened its anti-Communist policies.

While the Rhee government was busy strengthening its anti-Communist stance, at dawn on Sunday, 25 June 1950, North Korea attacked South Korea along the thirty-eighth parallel. The South Korean army was caught completely off guard. Some scholars speculate that the South provoked the war (Stone 1953:44), but documents relating to the origins of the Korean War that have come to light from

Russian sources confirm that the North that attacked the South, putting earlier speculation to rest. Park Myung Lim (1996, 2 vols.), a Korean political scientist, addresses this issue well in his comprehensive and voluminous book on the Korean War, supporting the conventional view that the North was the aggressor.

On the second day of the war, the South Korean army had to give up Uijeongbu, the gateway to Seoul, the capital city of South Korea. North Korean tanks reached Seoul on 28 June, the third day of the war, and while President Syngman Rhee assured frightened citizens over the radio that he would make every effort to secure the capital city, the South Korean army blew up the Hangang Bridge, cutting off the major route leading south.[11] Over one and a half million Seoulites were isolated and trapped, panic-stricken and unable to flee. This thwarted retreat separated many family members.

On 25 June, at the request of the United States, the U.N. Security Council passed a resolution calling for the immediate cessation of hostilities and the withdrawal of North Korean armed forces to the thirty-eighth parallel.[12] The Security Council also called upon all United Nations member countries to render assistance in the execution of this resolution. Concurring were sixteen countries, including the United States, Britain, France, Canada, Australia, New Zealand, the Netherlands, the Philippines, Turkey, and seven other countries. These sixteen nations constituted the U.N. forces.

On 29 June, 300 planes under United Nations command entered the Korean peninsula, followed by the arrival of United Nations forces in Busan on 1 July. The Council authorized the United States to designate a commander of the unified forces, and President Harry S. Truman named Gen. Douglas MacArthur commander-in-chief of the United Nations forces. Nevertheless, the tide of the war was not easily reversed. U.N. forces continued to retreat. By the end of July, North Korean troops occupied most of the southern peninsula. North Korean forces ferreted out reactionary elements, including members of the South Korean armed forces, police, anti-Communist rightists, and many others who became subject to arrest, imprisonment, abduction, and persecution. There were innumerable massacres by the Communist occupation authorities.[13] The North Korean authorities forced the residents of the occupied area to collaborate with the People's Army of the north. Many South Korean political leaders, scholars, intellectuals, and prominent writers who were unable to escape Seoul were kidnapped and forcibly taken to the north.

While most of South Korea had fallen under northern control, on 15 September 1950, Gen. MacArthur's forces made an amphibious landing at Incheon, and the tide of the war turned abruptly in favor of the United Nations. Seoul was recaptured, and the U.N. forces broke out of the Busan perimeter. As the North Korean army retreated northward, the United Nations forces crossed the thirty-eighth parallel and marched north, securing the area to the Yalu River.

However, the war then moved into a new, more complicated stage as Chinese People's Volunteers (CPV) appeared at the front in October and again in November. China had mobilized a massive number of "volunteer soldiers" who swept over the area in continuous waves without concern for high casualty rates in a military maneuver that came to be known as "human-wave tactics" (Whiting 1960:118).[14]

The CPV and reorganized North Korean troops were able to halt the advance of U.N. and South Korean troops, forcing them to withdraw from the area they had occupied in North Korea, and causing them to relinquish Pyeongyang on 4 December 1950.[15] The military decision to abandon Pyeongyang and the subsequent flight of Pyeongyang citizens over the Daedonggang resulted in bedlam. The damaged iron bridge over the river had not yet been fully repaired, and many desperate refugees appeared to be performing acrobatic contortions on the severed and crooked railings of the bridge as they tried to cross the river. Some fell to their deaths in the waters below; others were severely injured. The retreat was equally dramatic from the area of the Dumangang in the northeastern part of North Korea.

When Chinese troops crossed the thirty-eighth parallel and entered Seoul on 4 January 1951, the South Korean government and the United Nations troops pulled out of the city and abandoned the port of Incheon. Once again, they had to deal with the evacuation of refugees. The war during the winter months of 1951 consisted of attacks and counterattacks to the south of Seoul, and in early March, U.N. troops began to make substantial gains and move steadily forward. Then, on the nights of 14 and 15 March, U. N. troops moved once more into Seoul, which by now had changed hands four times. The U. N. forces fought their way to the thirty-eighth parallel, and on 4 April they broke through that line, opening the door once again for a northward march. However, on 11 April, President Truman relieved Gen. MacArthur of his command and replaced him with Gen. Matthew Ridgway.[16]

When the tide of the war turned in favor of the United Nations under Ridgway's command, after U. N. troops and South Korean forces had successfully pushed the invading forces north of the thirty-eighth parallel, the Soviet Union proposed cease-fire discussions among the participants in the war. The Truman administration was eager to end the fighting, now that it was possible to establish a division of Korea near the thirty-eighth parallel.[17] When the rulers of China indicated their interest in a truce, Truman authorized Gen. Ridgway to begin negotiating with enemy generals. The talks opened on 10 July 1951 at Gaeseong, and on 27 July 1953 at Panmunjeom an agreement was reached on terms for an armistice. Each side would pull its forces behind a newly drawn DMZ established between the battle lines in effect at the time of the armistice. Prisoners of war would be exchanged, and a Neutral Nations Supervision Commission set up to ensure that both sides adhered to the agreement. At the end of the war, Korea lay in ruins.[18]

Family Dispersal

Although the literature on the Korean War is relatively rich, accounts of the suffering of the civilians, particularly those who were separated from their family members, has been scarce, except for a few narratives (Kim C.S. 1988a, *passim; idem* 2002:158-174).

Korean family dispersal stemming from the partition of the

peninsula along the thirty-eighth parallel has been the most devastating effect of the Korean War. Although a cease-fire went into effect more than a half century ago, the splintering of families persists to this day. Once it was estimated that 10 million Koreans (5 million from each side) were separated from their family members (Kim C.S. 1988a, *passim; idem* 2002: 158-174).[19] While 10 million may be an exaggeration, no one can be certain. Today, the South Korean authorities estimate that the figure is between 750,000 and 1.23 million first-generation displaced family members (Kim C.S. 2002:158).

The physical displacement of such a large number of people was painful for the nation, but adding to that pain was the fact that family members who were dispersed to the north and the south found it virtually impossible to communicate for more than a half a century. Despite the fact that millions of Koreans have suffered from this extended diaspora, the misery created by family dispersal was poorly publicized until the summer of 1983, when the Korean Broadcasting System (KBS) aired its reunion telethon.

The KBS reunion telethon came about almost by accident. On 30 June 1983, while I was conducting fieldwork on the subject, KBS

KBS Telethon

broadcast a television special on families separated during the war. Originally it had been scheduled to air for only ninety-five minutes, but the program was so successful that KBS found it difficult to end it at the scheduled time. Thousands of people rushed to the studio to register for an appearance on camera. In the end, the program lasted four and a half months, from 30 June to 14 November 1983, claiming 450 hours of airtime and reuniting more than 10,000 thousand persons with lost family members. With the permission of the Korean Red Cross, which was monitoring the reunion for KBS, I was able to gain access to Yeouido Square (later named Reunion Plaza), where the KBS building is located.

Following the telethon, the thirty-ninth North-South dialogue produced the first North-South exchange of home-town visitors and art troupes.[20] On 20 September 1985, 151 visitors, headed by their respective Red Cross presidents, arrived in Seoul and Pyeongyang by way of Panmunjeom to begin a four-day visit. Excluding the art troupes, fifty members from each Korea were chosen for reunions with family members, close relatives, and friends.

When Kim Dae-jung became president of South Korea in February 1998, he implemented a policy of détente, and later, in his visit to North Korea in June 2000, he facilitated an exchange of visits between the dispersed families of North and South Korea. One hundred people from each Korea would make visits to Seoul and Pyeongyang for reunions with family members separated for more than half a century. Since then, there have been numerous exchanges, involving a total of 9,977 persons from both sides, and such exchanges are continuing today.

Unfortunately, since the number of exchange visitors is limited to 100 per side for each reunion, it will take a very long time for all separated families to be reunited. For people who had long anticipated such reunions, the process is moving very slowly. The eighty-one-year-old president of the Association of Pyeongannam-do province noted that if reunion meetings continue at their current pace, it would take twelve and a half years to accommodate the next 150,000 registrants. If he were placed in the last group, he would be ninety-three years old. Since time is growing short for elderly first-generation dispersed Koreans (Kim C.S. 2002:173), in order to pick up the snail's pace of the reunion process, the South Korean National Red Cross plans to establish a permanent meeting place where dispersed Korean family members can meet their loved ones anytime they wish. The South Korean National Red Cross also facilitates family reunions via on-line video meetings, utilizing fifteen stations throughout South Korea, including the Red Cross headquarters in Seoul.[21] As of July 2006, there had been fourteen meetings and four on-line video meetings among Korean family members dispersed between the North and the South.

Construction of a permanent center to accommodate family reunions was originally scheduled to be completed by 30 August 2005. However, on 19 July 2006, North Korea made a shocking announcement: it was calling off all family reunions in retaliation for South Korea's refusal to provide rice and fertilizer to North Korea in response to North Korea's drastic and unannounced missile test. On 11 March 2007, however, the two Koreans agreed to restart the construction of the reunion center, and visits between dispersed families have resumed.

Evolution and Revolution of Korean Politics

The Syngman Rhee Government and Student Revolution

After Syngman Rhee became president, he exerted complete control over Korean politics (Eckert et al. 1990:348). Because his presidency was a long one, Rhee's autocratic ideas had time to take root and grow stronger. His skilled political manipulation, enhanced by fierce anti-Communist slogans and aided by sycophantic subordinates, allowed him to wield enormous power during and after the Korean War (Kim C.S. 1998:149). Favoritism and corruption in the temporary wartime capital of Busan were widespread in the government and in the upper ranks of the military.[22] Rhee's arbitrariness and self-righteousness threatened to dissolve the National Assembly. He built up his power base by devising a new and more subtle tool for controlling that body. In late 1951, Rhee formed Jayudang (the Liberal Party), which was composed of a motley assortment of opportunists, who employed police surveillance, armed thugs, and gangs to preclude any public criticism of Rhee's regime. In 1952, when Rhee was up for reelection, he proposed the same constitutional amendments that the National Assembly had refused to approve in 1951, which were election of the president, vice president, and a bicameral legislation by popular vote. Rhee then declared martial law and arrested several dozen assemblymen.

By 1954, employing various immoral, unethical, and illegal tactics, Rhee's Liberal Party had achieved a clear majority in the Assembly. In order to amend the constitution to make himself president for life, Rhee and his party employed every available means to bribe, banish, or threaten independents in the Assembly. The vote for the constitutional amendments on 27 November 1954 resulted in 135 in favor, sixty against, one invalid, and six abstentions. The vote fell one short of the 136 required for passage. The next day, Rhee's Liberal Party came up with a mathematical principle that said that two-thirds of 203 was 135.33, but 0.33 should be rounded down, so that the required votes should be 135, not 136. The idea came from Jang Gyeonggeun at a strategy session at Lee Gibung's residence after the vote (Go 1976:672). On the basis of this mathematical principle of rounding down, the amendment was considered passed. Consequently, Rhee returned to office for a third term.

The 1960 election was marred by fraud so blatant that it could not be ignored. In March and April 1960, massive student demonstrations broke out in Seoul and other cities throughout South Korea. On 19 April 1960, some 300,000 university and high school students marched toward the presidential mansion, where they were fired upon directly by police. About 130 students were killed, and 1,000 wounded. This occurrence is now known as the April 19 Student Revolution. Rhee finally resigned on 26 April, and the First Republic

19 April 1960

came to an end.

The collapse of Rhee's government was followed by a brief interim administration, and the constitution was changed to a parliamentary cabinet with a bicameral system, consisting of a lower and upper house. Yun Po-sun assumed the figurehead position of president, and Jang Myeon (John M. Chang) took on the role of prime minister to lead the new government. However, the tasks proved too daunting for a weak government to handle largely because of incessant political wrangling within the ruling Democratic Party (Minjudang) and the social instability brought about by the never-ending street demonstrations. The short-lived (15 August 1960 to 16 May 1961) Second Republic fell when a military junta led by Maj. Gen. Park Chung-hee seized power.

The Coup d'État of 1961

Using social and political unrest as a pretext, Maj. Gen. Park Chung-hee took power in a coup d'état on 16 May 1961.[23] Park suspended the constitution, formed a military junta to impose an absolute

Maj. Gen. Park Chung-hee

military dictatorship, and created the Supreme Council for National Reconstruction (Gukga jaegeon choego hoeui). Park emerged as its chairman, and ruled the country until 1963. With presidential elections scheduled for mid-October of that year, Park retired from the army, ran as the presidential candidate of the Democratic Republican Party (DRP), defeated Yun Po-sun, former president of the Second Republic, and became president of the Third Republic.

In 1967, Park won reelection, and two years later secured a constitutional amendment to open the way for a third term. He was elected again in 1971. In an attempt to ensure his unchallenged command of Korean affairs, Park declared martial law on 17 October 1972, and called for a program of "revitalizing reforms" (*yusin*)," modeled after the Japanese Meiji Restoration.[24] The *Yusin* Constitution was approved by an intimidated populace through public referendum in November 1972, and this effectively transformed the presidency into a legal dictatorship. Under the terms of the new constitution, the president was to be chosen indirectly by members of the National Council for Unification (Tongil juche gungmin hoeui), which was headed by the president himself. Moreover, the president was empowered to appoint one-third of the National Assembly members.

Park's eighteen-year rule saw the devolution of the movement for Korean democracy, but his government revolutionized Korean economic growth and industrialization, employing effective economic development plans with the help of a new and studious apolitical group of technocrats and a well educated, disciplined, and dedicated work force.

In contrast with Syngman Rhee, who maintained strong anti-Japanese sentiments, Park normalized diplomatic relations with Japan by signing a bilateral pact in 1965. Facing vehement opposition, especially from student groups, against such a normalization agreement, Park tried to persuade the public that any compensation resulting from the normalization agreement with Japan could be used as seed-money for Korean economic development and industrialization.

Whatever his ambitions, goals, and accomplishments, Park's rule was brought to an abrupt end on 26 October 1979, when he was assassinated by his close aid and confidant, Kim Jaegyu, director of Park's own Korean Central Intelligence Agency (KCIA).

Parenthetically, Park's regime presents us with an irony. During his authoritarian rule, when he exerted tight control over Korean politics in what amounted to a dictatorship, many Koreans demanded a liberal democracy, rejecting his system and exerting strong resistance against it. However, recent polls by the Committee for Evaluating Korean Presidents have rated Park favorably, as most desirable CEO (59.2 percent);[25] most likable president (51.4 percent);[26] most respectable person throughout all of Korean history (20.1 percent), above and beyond King Sejong (16 percent), Adm. Yi Sunsin (15.3 percent), and Kim Gu (7.9 percent);[27] and best president (63.56 percent) in five separate categories.[28]

The period of transition immediately after Park's assassination was characterized by uncertainty, confusion, and contention. Under the 1972 constitution, the prime minister, Choi Kyu-hah, became acting

President and was supposed to serve out the remainder of Park's term. However, a new military (Singunbu) force emerged and staged yet another coup on 12 December 1979 to fill the power vacuum in the aftermath of Park's death. The new military group was led by Maj. Gen. Chun Doo-hwan, head of the Defense Security Command, the agency responsible for investigating Park's murder. He was promoted to three-star and, soon after, four-star general within a year, and retired from the military in 1980 to devote himself to politics. In late August, Chun was named president by indirect elections in accordance with the *Yusin* Constitution, and was inaugurated on 1 September 1980.

With Park's death, Kim Dae-jung, whom Park had sentenced to death, and Kim Young-sam, another opposition leader, regained prominence. At the same time, demonstrations against the new military leader spread. The most furious and brutally repressed demonstration took place in May of 1980 in Gwangju-si, the most populous city in the provincial capital of Jeollanam-do province. Many civilians and students were killed.[29] The Gwangju Rebellion may have started in response to specific government abuses and to a general sense that the Jeolla region had suffered repeated discrimination under all the governments of the previous twenty-five years. Many Koreans blamed the United States for not interfering when such brutal mass killings took place during the Kwangju uprisings. David Steinberg articulates Korean sentiment against the role of the United States and America's dilemma in dealing with the situation:

> The Kwangju [Gwangju] Rebellion seriously impaired any sense of legitimacy that the Chun region might have hoped to have. The United States was severely damaged by it as well, for the popular impression was that all Korean forces were under the control of the U.N. Command and, thus, under U.S. leadership. Although this was (and is) largely incorrect, as the special forces and certain other troops were excluded, it has become increasingly apparent that there are dangers inherent in any system under which a foreign power,

lacking real authority, may be held popularly responsible for actions or tension. Some say the populace had fully expected the United States to intervene and force negotiations and were astonished when it did not do so, further attributing U.S. inaction to support for the Chun government (Steinberg 1989:60).

Despite the demonstrations, commotions, and social unrest, Chun adopted a new constitution that established indirect election of the president, who would serve a single seven-year term. By doing so, Chun was able to assume the presidency in early 1981. After Chun's inauguration in January of that year as president of the Fifth Republic, U.S. President Ronald Reagan invited Chun to be his first official foreign guest. Reagan hoped to improve relations with Korea that had cooled during Jimmy (James Earl) Carter's administration because of Carter's pressure on human rights issues and his advocacy. As part of his campaign platform in 1976, Carter also promised to withdraw U.S. troops from Korea. According to Steinberg (1989:60-61), President Reagan's invitation of President Chun actually saved the life of Kim Dae-jung, who was under a death sentence for allegedly instigating the riots that led to the Gwangju incident. Nevertheless, I speculate that for many Koreans, Reagan's invitation to Chun might have been interpreted as the United States' endorsement of the legitimacy of the Chun government. From that time, anti-U.S. sentiment began to rise among Korean youth (Steinberg 1989:60-61). Demonstrations by students and labor unions became frequent. In 1985, for instance, there were 3,877 on-campus demonstrations. As massive protests against the Chun government escalated in June 1987, the government was forced to accept the people's demands for a set of democracy measures on 29 June. The constitution was revised again, reintroducing direct popular election for the president, with a single five-year term.

At the ruling Democratic Justice Party (Minjujeonguidang or DJP) convention on 10 June 1987, Chun designated Rho Tae-woo, a former major general who had played a central role in the success of

Chun's coup, as the party's candidate for president. As the DJP candidate for president, Rho announced a sweeping liberalization program, maintaining a cautious distance between himself and the increasingly unpopular Chun. Rho won the presidential election, and his government was able to institute some positive foreign policies toward the Communist block, including establishing diplomatic ties with Eastern European countries, the Soviet Union, and China. Also, Rho was credited with diplomatic initiatives that enabled both North and South Korea to join the United Nations simultaneously. Rho's administration allowed for rapid liberalization on the labor front, but furious labor strife and student demonstrations were still prevalent. Rho limited his term to five years as specified in the constitution.

Democratic Development

As Rho's government came to an end, so did military rule. Finally, a civilian government was restored when one of the opposition leaders, Kim Young-sam, became president in 1993. Kim's government had the distinction of eradicating corruption in the bureaucracy by legislating a property registration system for public officials and the practice of using real names in financial transactions. He also restored autonomous local governance (*Jibang Jachi*), which had been suspended since the 16 May 1961 military coup. Despite all these moves, Kim's government suffered severely, and the country faced financial exigencies when the foreign currency crisis swept across Asia during 1997-1998. Kim's government failed to defend the national financial system, and eventually invited the aid and intervention of the International Monetary Fund (IMF) for a bailout.

When Kim Young-sam's five-year term as president ended in February 1998, another opposition party leader, Kim Dae-jung, was inaugurated as the new president. Kim's biggest single accomplishment was the first-ever inter-Korean summit with North Korean leader Kim Jeongil. Kim's détente policy even resulted in the North and South Korean teams forming a single group when they entered the Olympic stadium together in the opening ceremony of the Sydney Olympics in 2000. This accomplishment in North-South relations led Kim to become the first Korean to receive the Nobel Peace Prize in 2000.

In the December 2002 presidential elections, Roh Moo-hyun, a straight-talking and self-educated former human-rights lawyer from the ruling Millennium Democratic Party (Saecheonnyeon-minjudang), the same party to which Roh's predecessor Kim Dae- jung belonged, won by a narrow margin over the opposition party leader. After he became president, Roh left the Millennium Democratic Party on 11 November 2003 to create his own party, Yeollin-uridang (the Uri Party), with forty-seven members of the National Assembly, proclaiming that his goal was "to realize clean politics, create a nation where the middle and working classes flourish, promote a warm-hearted society with people helping each other, and achieve peace and mutual prosperity in the Korean peninsula." In the seventeenth general election on 15 April 2004 the Uri Party won a landslide victory, gaining 152 (out of 227 from single-member electoral districts) members of the newly elected National Assembly.[30] Roh could easily initiate any program he wished with such a large number of National Assembly members.

Indeed, Roh's government initiated reforms leading to the pursuit of a full realization of democracy in government operations as well as in social practices and emphasizing the fair distribution of wealth. His policy of fair distribution of wealth has been hindered by a slow-growing economy, rising unemployment rate, escalating housing prices, and inadequate policies to address these problems. His naive manner and straight talk have often been interpreted as imprudent by his critics. His "sunshine policy" and generosity in aiding North Korea have been criticized, especially after North Korea's push for its nuclear programs. In Roh's administration, the general and ideological division between Koreans became clearly manifest. While younger and more liberal forces were supportive of the Roh government, older people and conservatives tended to be resentful. The major task of the Roh government was to negotiate this division while still pushing Korea's economy forward. Time may be growing short to implement Roh's policies. In the meantime, Roh's Uri Party has begun to lose its popularity as evidenced by a miserable defeat in various local, regional, and national elections as late as 6 February 2007. More than twenty members of the National Assembly who belonged to the Uri Party have left the party and formed their own cliques. As the presidential election draws closer, it seems that a growing number of the National Assembly members wish to disassociate themselves from an unpopular president. Seeking a peaceful solution that will lead to a nuclear-free peninsula has remained another challenge.

Regionalism vs. "Generationalism" in Contemporary Korean Politics

Regionalism

In politics, regionalism plays a role in virtually every society, but in Korea it plays a greater role than in most. Even if there are still strong regional emotions between North and South in the United States since the Civil War (1861-1865), the polarization has been tempered. For example, Bill Bredesen, a Harvard-educated Yankee from New York, came down to the South, became mayor of Nashville, and was twice elected governor of Tennessee. However, it is unrealistic to expect that in Korea any man or woman from Gyeongsangbuk-do province will be elected governor (*dojisa*) of Jeollanam-do province, and *vice versa*.

No one knows exactly when such strong regionalism emerged in Korea. Perhaps its genesis can be traced back to the peninsula's division in the Three Kingdoms period. Edward Mason and his associates (1980:74) have recognized that "Koreans long ago knew that they were one people, however faction-ridden the court or however much the people of Kyongsang province might not like those of Chŏlla province." Even though we are unable to document the exact emergence of regionalism and subsequent prejudice against certain regions, regionalism and its clichés, if not outright prejudice against certain regions, were evidenced in Yi Hwang's writing. About 500 years ago, Yi Hwang traveled and wrote about the specific characteristics of the people living in the various provinces.[31] As Paul Crane (1978:85), the son of a missionary who dedicated himself to medical mission work in Korea, has pointed out, Yi Hwang's characterizations "have remained as the abiding prejudices that many people hold today about people from other areas. Each characteristic is subject to various interpretations, both complementary and otherwise, which many people still apply to the eight provinces. There are also popular vulgar labels that are used to describe various provinces and the people who come from them."[32]

Regionalism in Korean politics has manifested itself prominently since the 1961 military coup d'état and military leaders who led the coup displayed provincial favoritism. Three consecutive Korean presidents, Park Chung-hee, Chun Doo-hwan, and Rho Tae-woo, were not only ex-generals but also from Gyeongsangbuk-do province. Most Koreans from non- Gyeongsang-do provinces, particularly from Jeolla-do province, have long been convinced that strong provincial favoritism has been at work. Koreans often used the terms "TK" and "Non-TK," which come from abbreviations for Daegu [Taegu] and Gyeongsangbuk-do [north Kyŏngsang] province, to differentiate and label people in the business world and in the arena of politics.

Nevertheless, about Gyeongsang-do province's favoritism, Leroy Jones and Il Sakong (1980:302) had a different view:

> It is widely believed that the government discriminates in favor of entrepreneurs from Park Chung Hee's Kyŏngsang province. However, our results show that while Kyŏngsang province dominates in absolute numbers, its citizens are actually underrepresented relative to the population as a whole. If there is any discrimination, it operates in favor of those born in the north, Seoul, or Kyŏnggi province. Even this, however, is probably due to differences in education and parental occupation rather than discrimination.

However, people's perceptions tend to be at odds with the outcome of Jones and Sakong's study. For instance, in a national survey conducted in January 1989 by a Korean daily newspaper, more than 85.3 percent of respondents acknowledged that regional competition and conflict, especially between Gyeongsang-do and Jeolla-do provinces, were severe.[33]

Korean anthropologist Kwang-Ok Kim [Kim Kwang-Ok] has concurred with public perception, and broadened the range of discussion to the entire region of Yeongnam that includes both north and south Gyeongsang-do [Gyeongsangbuk-do and Gyeongsangnam-do] provinces, and of Honam, that combines both south and north Jeolla-do [Jeollanam-do and Jeollabuk-do] provinces. Kim (1989:18) states that "Evidence of this regionalism was seen in the recruitment of high government officials, where most key posts were filled by people from the Yŏngnam region. Officials who graduated from certain regional high schools were positioned in elite posts. As a result, the Honam region became the stronghold of the opposition party. In this way, regionalism was promoted, and even exploited, both by the government and the opposition party as political capital." According to Kim (1989:19), such regionalism was strengthened by the military regime of Chun Doo-hwan: "This resulted in a more widely-spread regionalism marked by the Kwangju massacre and greater privileges accorded to people from the Yŏngnam region."

If we use the boundaries of Yeongnam and Honam to determine regional favoritism or "dis-favoritism," and if the president was able to influence this regionalism, then Kim Young-sam, who became President in 1993 at the end of the military-led government and hailed from Gyeongsangnam-do province, could not have been free from the controversies of regionalism. In fact, regionalism was a hot political issue until Kim Dae-jung, who was from Jeollanam-do province, was inaugurated as president in 1998. In a sense, Kim Dae-jung may have been a beneficiary of regionalism. Without the wholehearted support and backing of Honam voters, Kim might not have been elected president, even though he won over the opposition leader by a narrow margin. Indeed, in Korean politics, regionalism has played a pivotal role.

Generationalism

In the December 2002 presidential election, in addition to the regional factor, two other dimensions, the age of voters, and the Internet and e-mail, were crucial in electing Roh Moo-hyun as President. During the campaign, even Roh's party "leaders were so convinced that this had all been a mistake that they hardly bothered to campaign for him" (Breen 2004:254). Nevertheless, Roh was elected primarily with the support of Honam voters, even though he was originally from Gyeongsangnam-do province, which is in Yeongnam. In fact, although Roh received only 27.1 percent of the vote from his home state of Gyeongsangnam-do province, while his opponent received over 67 percent, Roh received over 90 percent of the vote from Honam. Surprisingly, Roh received over 95 percent of the vote from Gwangju-si, a stronghold for Kim Dae-jung's political power base.

Roh Moo-hyun was a major beneficiary of the young voters who used the Internet extensively, especially e-mail, for the first time in a Korean election. During the 2002 presidential election, even around noon on election day, exit polls indicated that Roh was losing. In response to that news, led by the "Rohsamo [Nosamo] Fan Club" (a group of people who loves Roh Moo-hyun),[34] Roh's supporters, mostly young people who could use the Internet better than the older generation, went to chat rooms and sent out hundreds of thousands of e-mails and text messages to encourage voters to get out and vote. Consequently, after lunch, exit polls showed that Roh had pulled ahead, becoming the sole beneficiary of the young voters' support. The age of voters — generational differences — had become as decisive a factor in politics as regionalism had been in the past.

Also, during the course of campaign, whether it was genuine or not, Roh's ambivalent stance toward the United States was interpreted as indicating that he was anti-US. Because of this assumption, Roh benefited from the anti-American sentiment that had long prevailed among young voters. During the 2002 presidential election campaign, I witnessed a candlelight vigil in central Seoul on a weekend in early December that turned into an anti-American rally. Triggered by a June accident in which two Korean teenagers were killed by a U.S. military vehicle, and the subsequent acquittal of the two soldiers involved, large and frequent demonstrations took place in Seoul and other cities. The tone of these demonstrations was becoming increasingly anti-American. Nevertheless, my American friend who has been in Korea as long as I have been in America commented that "it might have been anti-American sentiment, but certainly it was not 'anti-Americanism.'"

So beginning with the 2002 presidential election, age emerged as an important factor in Korean politics. When Roh became president, an age group that came to be known as the "386 generation" began to enter politics as key aides for the president, cabinet members, National Assembly members, and also as key decision makers. Kyung-Koo Han (2000:355 n.1) defines the "386 generation" as "those now in their thirties (3) who attended college in the 1980s (8), and who were born on [in] the 1960s (6). The '386 generation' are characterized by their collective experience or participation in the popular democratization movement of the 1980s against government that oppressed individual rights and freedom."

Han (2000:355-356) points out that the "386 generation was not only great in number, but was composed of the very people who could free themselves from the influence of the old values and resist the old practices in the work place. Many of their parents and supervisors who were educated in the postliberation period could not get away from the old values and practices; instead, they tended to have a part in continuing these values and practices, until the so-called 386 generation, who had a very different character, came on the scene."

Indeed, generational differences between Korean voters that emerged in the 2002 election were evident in the 2004 general election. In the 2000 general election, only thirteen members in their thirties were elected, but in the 2002 election almost twice (twenty-four members) as many in that age group were elected. In the 2000 election there were seventy-eight members under forty, but that number increased to 129 in 2002. In the meantime, the number of members sixty and older decreased from eighty-nine in the 2000 election to forty-nine in the 2002 election. The Korean National Assembly members who were elected in the 2004 general election were much younger than their predecessors who were elected in the 2000 general election.[35] Age and generational differences now play a pivotal role and are a decisive factor in the Korean political process.

Structure and Organization of the Current Korean Government

Since the Republic of Korea was born in 1948, the Korean Constitution has been amended nine times. Nevertheless, except for the months between August 1960 and July 1961, Korea's constitution has called for a presidential system in which the president is the head of the state and chief executive. Under the current constitution, the government has three branches: the legislative, judicial, and executive. In addition, there are two other constitutionally based institutions, the Constitutional Court and the National Election Commission.

The legislative branch consists of a single house, the National Assembly, whose 273 members serve a four-year term. As a lawmaking body, in addition to deliberating bills for legislation, examining government budgets, and ratifying international treaties, the National Assembly is in charge of inspecting and auditing the administration, and approving the appointments of the prime minister and the director of the Board of Auditing and Inspection. The National Assembly can impeach public officials, and may recommend to the president the removal of executive officials, including the prime minister.

The judiciary consists of three tiers of courts: the Supreme Court, which consists of 13 justices and a chief justice; Appellate Courts, which are established in five large cities; and District Courts, which are located in Seoul and twelve other provincial cities. The judiciary also operates a family court, an administrative court, and a patent court.

The executive branch, headed by the President, consists of the prime minister, the State Council, eighteen executive ministers, seventeen independent agencies, the Board of Auditing and Inspection, and the National Intelligence Service. The President is elected by popular vote for a single five-year term, and the prime minister is appointed by the President, subject to the approval of the National Assembly.

Also, the self-governing powers are given to sixteen higher-level (provincial) governments and 234 lower-level (municipal) governments, including seventy-five cities (*si*), eighty-six counties (*gun*), and sixty-nine districts (*gu*) within metropolitan cities. The local chief executives are elected by direct popular vote.

Current Inter-Korean Relations

From the partition of the peninsula until the 1960s, South Korea viewed North Korea as an illegitimate government, and treated it as such.[36] By the 1970s, South Korea began to accept the reality of the partition, and acknowledged the *de facto* existence of the northern regime. In his Liberation Day message on 15 August 1970, President Park Chung-hee announced the idea of peaceful unification, acknowledging North Korea as an independent political entity. In 1971, the two Koreas began a formal inter-Korean dialogue for the first time.

If the major concern of the two Koreas in 1971 was peaceful coexistence, during the 1980s the emphasis lay on co-prosperity in addition to coexistence through economic cooperation. The 1980s saw a series of declarations, particularly one made on 7 July 1988, that South Korea would not regard North Korea as a subject of competition or confrontation but as a good partner with whom South Korea needed to pursue co-prosperity.

Throughout the 1990s, the South Korean government's understanding of the political reality of the division became manifest. Consequently, the two Koreas were able to sign the Agreement on Reconciliation, Nonaggression, Exchange and Cooperation on 19 February 1992. South Korea's desire to achieve unification based on an inter-Korean consensus was reaffirmed during this period. Nevertheless, despite the rhetoric on the road toward Korea's unification in the nineties, all the talks, dialogue, joint communiqués, and declarations produced no tangible outcome until lifelong opposition party leader Kim Dae-jung became president of South Korea in February 1998. Up to that point, the only exception had been the North-South exchange of home-town visitors and art troupes on 20 September 1985.

In an effort to achieve peaceful coexistence between the two Koreas, Kim Dae-jung implemented his "sunshine policy" of détente toward the North. This policy was spelled out in Kim's Berlin Declaration, a speech delivered at the Free University in Berlin, Germany, on 9 March 2000, during a nine-day European tour. His declaration encompassed four points: (1) support for North Korea's economic recovery; (2) an end to the Cold War on the Korean peninsula and peaceful coexistence between South Korea and North Korea; (3) resolution of the issue of separated families; and (4) talks between South and North Korean authorities.

Kim Dae-jung's Berlin Declaration eventually led to a historic summit between Kim Dae-jung of South Korea and Kim Jeongil of North Korea on 13-15 June 2000. Both leaders signed the Joint Declaration in Pyeongyang on 15 June.[37]

Since the declaration provided for an exchange of visits between the dispersed families of North and South Korea, a reunion of family members took place on 15 August 2000. Because President Roh Moo-hyun continued to follow the same policy as Kim Dae-jung regarding inter-Korean relations, reunions continued under Roh's government and take place on an irregular basis whenever the two Koreas agree to have them.

Also, a cabinet-level inter-Korean meeting was held to discuss follow-up measures aimed at implementing the agreement signed by the two Kims. This cabinet-level meeting eventually produced many promising results. Plans were made to reconnect the inter-Korean railroad for transport of goods from the Korean peninsula to Europe via the Trans-Siberian Railway (TSR). Since the first cabinet-level meeting on 29-31 July 2000, there have been more than a dozen meetings in Seoul and Pyeongyang alternatively. Thus far cabinet talks have been focused on economic aid for southern rice and fertilizer production, and on promoting tourism.

Given this progress in relations, the rather dramatic announcement by North Korea on 10 February 2005 that it possessed nuclear weapons shocked not only South Korea but also many concerned parties around the world. In an effort to make the peninsula nuclear-free, six parties — the two Koreas as well as China, Japan, the United States, and Russia, nations with a vested interest in Korea — have been working toward a peaceful resolution of the issue.

On 5 July 2006, however, North Korea launched seven missiles, including one long-range Daepodong-2 missile, into the East Sea. Once again, the test shocked the entire world, including South Korea, and especially Japan and the United States. When North Korea went on to conduct a nuclear weapons test on 9 October 2006, the U.N. Security Council has adopted a resolution to apply sanctions in response.

On 13 February 2007, after more than three years of effort, the six-nation negotiations finally reached an agreement to shut down North Korea's nuclear reactor and eventually dismantle its atomic weapons program, just four months after North Korea had shocked the world by testing a nuclear bomb. The agreement was reached by the six-party nations — the two Koreas, China, Japan, the United States, and Russia — in a conference room at a Chinese state guesthouse in Beijing, China. According to this agreement, the North will receive initial aid equal to 50,000 tons of heavy fuel oil within 60 days for shutting down and sealing its main nuclear reactor and release facilities at Yeongbyeon, to be confirmed by international inspectors.

The North will also get, in increments, future aid amounting to

950,000 tons of heavy fuel oil. The details of the agreement were delegated to five working groups that would deal individually with denuclearization, US–North Korea relations, Japan–North Korea relations, economic cooperation, and peace and security mechanisms in northeast Asia. If North Korea follows through with its promises, these will be the first moves it has made to scale back its atomic development after more than three years of six-party negotiations that were marked by delays, deadlock, and the North's first nuclear test explosion in October 2006.

One day before the North Korean agreement to disable all of its unclear facilities, announced in Beijing on 3 October 2007, on 2 October, South Korean President Roh Moo-hyun visited Pyeongyang for a three-day of summit meeting with North Korean leader Kim Jeongil. President Roh's journey to Pyeongyang by car took three and a half hours from Seoul. About thirty miles north of Seoul, President Roh stepped out of his vehicle to make the symbolic gesture of walking across the border that separates the two Koreas. On 4 October 2007, the two leaders signed a declaration that contained a number of specific projects that could build closer economic and security ties between two Koreas.[38] Most South Koreans are cautiously optimistic about the actual implementation of the projects.

CHAPTER 4

Kinship, Marriage, and Family

When I was teaching a course on comparative family systems at an American university, my students expressed curiosity about the system of "arranged marriage." Some of them asked how one could marry someone without first experiencing "love" or "affection." I entertained my class with the following verse to illustrate the logic behind the system and its justification: "I never knew what love was, I don't know what love is, I don't care what love is, I don't to intend to be told what love is. Get married? Love does not lead to marriage but marriage leads to love, if such a thing as 'love' exists."

Nevertheless, my "pseudo-verse" was not sufficient to convince American students of the logic of arranged marriage, because most Americans have been so deeply enculturated within the system of "free choice" or "love marriage," in which love is supposed to lead to marriage and not vice versa. Indeed, as Francis L.K. Hsu (1970:40) has pointed out, "When two American lovers appear in public with their arms around one another, the rest of the world is excluded." In the minds of most Americans, there is scarcely any room for the concept of arranged marriage.

This does not mean that "romantic love" is a concept totally foreign to East Asians — Koreans, Chinese, and Japanese. In fact, the main theme of one of the most popular and beloved Korean novels, *Chunhyangjeon*, depicts a romantic love story between the son of a local magistrate and the only daughter of a retired *gisaeng*, a female entertainer who serves as an escort at men's drinking parties. Although the man was of noble origin (*yangban*) and the women was a *cheonmin* (commoner), the man was able to marry her after all by overcoming many obstacles simply because he loved her so dearly. This story has generated many movies, TV soap operas, and musicals over a long period, and is still popular among Koreans. As Stuart A. Queen and Robert W. Habenstein (1974:105) have reported, "In ancient feudal China, falling in love was not an unusual antecedent to marriage, although parental consent was necessary before the various ceremonies preparatory to marriage could go forward."

Even in the West, romantic-love marriage has a relatively short history. Such marriage was not common before the end of the Middle Ages in Europe. In fact, "marital selection in medieval England was a matter of clear bargaining and formal routines, in contrast to the romantic adventure it has become in modern England and America" (Queen and Habenstein 1974:255). In America, even in colonial times marriage required parental permission (Queen and Habenstein 1974:336).

One may surmise that since Korea has experienced rapid industrialization, hyper-urbanization, and increasing globalization, the traditional system of arranged marriage is gradually diminishing. Indeed, as Laurel Kendall (1996:109), an anthropologist and a Korea expert, has observed, "Today, as the workplace and the coeducational university provide unprecedented opportunities for romance, increasing numbers of women and men have love marriage without a matchmaker's introduction."

It appears that a great majority of Koreans of marriageable age now favor love marriage over arranged marriage. Statistics regarding the number of people who practice arranged marriage as opposed to love marriage vary considerably, mainly because of the varying definitions of "arranged marriage."[1] For instance, if two people are introduced by a fellow worker or college classmate and later get married, this could perhaps be counted as an "arranged marriage." Certainly it would be difficult to discern in such an example the system of free choice reflected in the Shakespearean love tryst. And we would perhaps be too hasty to conclude, on the basis of unusual news stories such a seventy-nine-year-old woman seeking a divorce,[2] the increasing number of single person families, and other socio-economic and demographic changes, that the system of arranged marriage has actually diminished.

One should not assume, observing the daily activities of middle-class Seoulites who wear Western-style clothes, drive their own automobiles, and live in Western-style apartment complexes, that they are just like Westerners. One has to see what they do after they come home from work. Then they take off their Western clothes, sit on the floor even though their apartments are furnished with complete sets of Western furniture, and deal with their family members in accordance with traditional Korean family and kinship rules. Contemporary Koreans are complicated beings.

Many Korean lineages have launched campaigns to update their genealogies as symbolic reflections of a revitalized interest in kinship. Gatherings of lineages occur more often than before, despite the increasing participation of Koreans in various formal organizations not based on the family. Walking along the streets of Seoul, one can easily find more signs for lineage offices than signs for Rotary, Kiwanis, and Lions clubs. Recently, I received a copy of my own lineage genealogy even though I have lived overseas for more than thirty years.

As an analogy, while looking around at the scenery of contemporary Seoul, I am amazed by the contrasts between different types of buildings. If one focuses on a certain section of downtown Seoul, it looks like any Western city, with high-rise office buildings. But if one walks along the northern district of Jongno-gu and the foothills of Bugaksan, one sees many tiled roofs of traditional homes. If one concludes that Seoul is no longer a Korean capital just because one has only seen the high-rises, plainly one has failed to see the other side of Seoul.

Likewise, without understanding the inner workings of the traditional Korean family system, the contemporary Korean family system can only be superficially understood.

Kinship is the Key

Traditionally, anthropologists have been interested in studying kinship mainly because in traditional, non-Western, and noncommercial societies the kinship system is the most dominant form of social organization and structures many areas of social life.[3] Anthropologists note that in some societies "kinship connections have an important bearing on matters of life and death" (Ember and Ember 1996:393). Hsu (1983:211) considers that kinship "holds the key to social and cultural development in the same sense that the germ cell holds the key to the biological organism and provides us with some idea of what the unfolding animal is going to be like." Marital and consanguineal (blood) relations are the two major structural components of kinship, the very pillars of the kinship system.

Since the early modern period, with the introduction of various legislations and court orders, the structure and function of the Korean kinship system has undergone a rapid transformation.[4] Despite these changes and modifications, faithful remnants of Korean kinship still profoundly influence the Korean way of life.

Marriage

The Korean kinship system dictates certain rules, regulations, and principles as well as taboos regarding marriage.

Marriage between Relatives

Historically, Goguryeo and Baekje practiced free-choice marriage, although marriage within the same lineage (or clan) was prohibited. Silla allowed free choice of marriage partners, and also encouraged close kin marriages beyond the third degree of relationship (beyond uncle and aunt),[5] and with members of the same clan, especially among royal and upper-class families (Lee 1983:71).

In its early dynastic period, Goryeo followed the Silla system, allowing close kin marriage even within a two-degree relationship (even brother and sister, if the mothers were different) in royal families as an effort to maintain the "same blood" so to speak (Lee 1983:71). In fact, King Taejo of the Goryeo dynasty encouraged such close kin marriages.

Rules regulating marriage customs, specifically those prohibiting marriage between close relatives, were first initiated by the tenth king of the Goryeo dynasty, Jeongjong (1034-1046). During his reign, the children of close kin marriages could not be appointed to government positions. Nevertheless, such a prohibition mainly had an impact on upper-class nobility, and not commoners. Some believe that such a rule reflected the influence of China, but others disagree. If Goryeo was either forced to imitate or willingly adopted the Chinese system, the incest taboo rule (meaning that a sexual and/or marital relationship between individuals who are in a real, assumed, or artificial bond of kinship is prohibited) might have extended to entire surname groups as in China. Instead, Goryeo merely imposed a prohibition of marriage between close relatives (Lee 1983:64-65).

Prohibition of marriage between members of the same clan (the same surname group) came into being in the Joseon dynasty after the Ta Ming Lü (Law of the Great Ming), the comprehensive body of administrative and criminal law of the Ming dynasty (1368-1644) of China, was adopted. Martina Deuchler (1977b:4) offers an explanation for the adoption of this law: the Joseon literati-officials (*sadaebu*) became aware that indigenous Joseon customs often stood in the way of implementing reform policies, which could not be carried out successfully without legal sanctions. The adoption of the Ta Ming Lü was therefore an introduction of the "rule of law" to supplement the "rule of goodness." However, Joseon interpreted the entire Ta Ming Lü so literally that lineage and clan exogamy, the rule of marriage that requires a person to marry outside his or her own group, was institutionalized in Korea (Lee 1983:66). Nevertheless, *yangban* continued to marry matrilineal cousins (siblings of mother's sisters and father's sisters) (Deuchler 1977b:8–9).

However, Korean clan exogamy differs from that of the Chinese. The Chinese exogamy rule extended to the entire surname group of a clan such as Kim, Lee, or Park, whereas the Korean rule was limited to members of groups that have a common origin, called *bongwan* or *bonhyang*, meaning the name of the place from which a clan's common ancestor came. Deuchler (1977b:9) translates *bongwan* as "clan seat." For instance, my wife and I have the same surname of Kim, but while my clan seat (*bongwan*) is Uiseong, my wife's clan seat is Cheongpung, so our marriage does not violate the rule of clan exogamy. In Korea, unlike in China, several different clans may share one surname, and clans with different surnames may share a clan seat, in which case the rule of "clan seat exogamy" is applied. Under this rule, even some prolific clans that have millions of members have been prohibited from marrying among themselves. There have been many heartbreaking stories of people who fell in love without knowing they were members of the same clan, and could not marry because of the taboo rule.

In July 1997, however, the Constitutional Court of Korea handed down a landmark decision ruling that prohibition of marriage between clan members beyond eight-degree relationships (third cousins) was unconstitutional. Since then, clan members whose kinship was beyond eight degrees could marry legitimately, and family registries could issue marriage licenses for same-clan couples.

Furthermore, on 3 February 2005, the Constitutional Court ruled that the "*hojeok* system," a male-oriented family registry, was unconstitutional and violated the spirit of gender equality in the Korean Constitution. Until this decision, in Korean families only male members could be the "head" (or "*hoju*"), and children had to take their father's surname. Concurring with this court decision, and after strong lobbying from women's organizations, on 2 March 2005 the Korean National Assembly passed a statute abolishing the *hoju* (male headship) system, effective beginning 1 January 2008. After this date, children will be able to choose their mother's surname if they wish, or combine their father's and mother's surnames. Some women already use their mother's surname in their names.

Before the Constitutional Court decision, the incest taboo was justified by the assumption that all kin-group members shared the same blood.[6] There is a theory that inbreeding, or marrying within the family, can increase the possibility of genetically damaged offspring, since members of the same family might carry the same harmful recessive genes (Stern 1973). However, it is incorrect to apply this theory to all same-clan-member marriages, since many millions of people who belong to the same clan are not blood relations. These court decisions and subsequent new statute governing the Korean incest-taboo rule still appear to follow the principle of kinship that goes back to the time of the Three Kingdoms, and even the early period of the Goryeo dynasty.

Parenthetically, it has to be stressed that in most human societies, the incest taboo exists as the prohibition of marriage between mother and son, father and daughter, and brother and sister. However, a few societies in the past did permit incest, mostly within royal and aristocratic families, including the Incan, Hawaiian, and Egyptian; in the latter there is the famous case of Cleopatra, who was married to two of her younger brothers at different times (Middleton 1962:606).

Arranged Marriage

The system of arranged marriage in Korea was firmly established during the late period of the Goryeo dynasty when it was in close contact with the Yüan dynasty (1279-1368).[7] In the later period of Goryeo, while aristocrats practiced arranged marriage, commoners followed free-choice marriage. The Goryeo aristocrats used marriage as strategy to expand the power of their families and as a direct shortcut to personal political power. "The more influential the family with which one formed marriage ties, the more quickly one might enhance the standing of one's own house and bring it into greater political prominence. There was a strong aspiration among ambitious young to marry with an aristocratic family member — particularly with the royal family clan" (Eckert et al. 1990:69). The system of arranged marriage appears to have coincided with or paralleled the emergence of a social stratification system. Historically in Korea certain privileged classes have used arranged marriage as a major mechanism for maintaining or improving their own class status.

This was further evidenced during the Joseon dynasty, when arranged marriage came to be considered an ideal form, and was firmly institutionalized after the *yangban* class emerged, as a means of maintaining its status quo. Consequently, during the Joseon dynasty, the system of arranged marriages contributed to class endogamy, in which most Koreans married within their own class. Nevertheless, for non-*yangban* commoners, free-choice marriage was the norm.

The Korean arranged-marriage system began to decline when Korean society started to transform itself from premodern to modern society. Certain socio-economic and demographic changes led to a transitional form of marriage. An individual might select several candidates and then ask his or her parents to choose from among them, or parents and kin members would recommend several marriage candidates and the individual would select from among them. One can surmise that today, while arranged marriages are still the means by which less educated, rural people acquire their spouses, highly educated and urban Koreans tend to choose their spouses themselves. Nevertheless, even today, well-to-do Koreans often choose to make an arranged marriage in order to maintain their status or improve their socioeconomic standing.[8]

In traditional arranged marriages, matchmaking was done by relatives, most often female members who would search for a spouse among their natal kinsmen and the relatives of their husbands, since they were familiar with both kin groups. Their chosen man and woman would marry with the approval of the elders of both families. Most of the time, such approval was no more than a formality, because the male elders trusted that the female marriage-arrangers would know the betrothed well since they belonged to both clans (Kim 1974:577). The matchmakers would serve as collateral for both families since they would be relatives of both. Also, because of such a selection process, the bride and groom tended to be of the same rank socially and economically. Jo Gangui (1984:79-121), a Korean anthropologist, has documented an elaborate network of marriages among *yangban* groups in Gyeongsang-do province from the later period of the Joseon dynasty to the present. He claims that the boundaries of marriage were limited to some thirty clans in geographic proximity within the province via the mechanism of *yeonjulhon* or "chain-string" forms of marriage arrangement which operate by mobilizing networks of relatives, mainly females.

Because increasing urbanization altered and diminished the tradition of arranged marriages, during the 1970s and 1980s a legion of unlicensed semiprofessional matchmakers (called Madam *Ttu* or Madam Procure) emerged in urban areas. These matchmakers mostly arrange marriages between children of the newly rich and privileged. Madam *Ttu* matchmakers did not charge any fee for their activities until their arrangement was finalized successfully. Commissions would run about 10 million *won* (about $106,600).[9] However, at times, they became so expensive that it was considered a real social problem (Kim 1988a:38).[10] Nowadays, this kind of matchmaking has diminished but it has not disappeared altogether. It has been reported that some former Madam *Ttu* matchmakers have become consultants for commercial marriage consulting centers.[11]

Matchmaking as a New Business Enterprise

As the credibility and reputation of the Madam *Ttus* have declined, licensed and commercial marriage consulting centers (*gyeolhon jeongbo hoesa*), which use computerized matchmaking and multimedia technologies, have become increasingly popular.

The marriage consulting center originated in Japan during the early 1980s, where it became popular and prosperous, with many branches opening throughout the country. The first marriage consulting center in Korea was founded in 1986, and a few others followed soon after. But in 1999 when the Family Ritual Code (*Gajeong uirye junchik*) that regulated marriage rituals was suspended, government licenses were no longer required to engage in the commercial matchmaking business. Since then, consulting centers have sprung up throughout the country, and their numbers have increased dramatically. Currently there are over 1,000 centers, ranging from small local ones with few members (applicants), to those that have over 40,000 members and operate globally, including the United States (L.A. and New York) and New Zealand. Some centers also support homepages and videotaped narratives in English. In 1994, when I visited such a place in Seoul with my students during my tenure as a visiting professorship at Yonsei University, it looked like a small private counseling center. Now it has become a genuine business enterprise.

Anyone who wishes to register and seek a spouse has to be a member. Annual membership fees vary from center to center and by category of membership. An average membership fee runs from 880,000 *won* (about $9,381) for a general membership to as high as 5.5 million *won* (about $58,635) for a special membership for unusual cases, such as those with outstanding educational credentials or those with disabilities. One center that specializes in second marriage or remarriage offers three different categories of membership for women (not for men for some strange reason) and charges different membership fees: a general membership is 880,000 *won* (about $9,381); a special membership costs 1.95 million *won* (about $20,788); and a *"noblesse"* membership (for the well-Known or rich) charges 3 million *won* (about $3,198). The center's services depend on membership category.[12] The total annual earnings of all Korean marriage consulting centers in 2006 were over 70 billion *won* (about $74.6 million). This is a newly emerging business enterprise in Korea that plays the role of matchmaker.[13]

Korean Marriage Tends to be Endogamous
Investigating arranged marriage, Kim Yonghak (2005), a Korean sociologist, analyzed almost 800 megabytes of data compiled at a marriage consulting center between 2004 and 2005. According to his analysis, men and women seeking a compatible marriage partner cared

less about a person's appearance or wealth than about their educational background which has become an important measure of social status; degrees from reputable universities were seen as highly desirable. The study also indicates that prettier women tend to have richer husbands.[14]

Arranged marriages in Korea, whether brought about by relatives, Madam *Ttu*, campus dates, or even via marriage consulting centers, tend to be endogamous. That means they follow a rule of marriage that requires a person to take a spouse from within their own social group as defined by class, kin, wealth, education, or some other form of social organization. In traditional Korea, class, particularly *yangban* status, was such a category, but in recent times education has come to serve as the most important group boundary as demonstrated by the marriage center study.

Parenthetically, in America, since mate selection is a "free choice" based on romantic love, an American youth is free in principle to choose a spouse from any socio-economic or educational background. In fact, marriages often happen across ethnic, racial, and religious lines as well as across class lines, which are hazier. Nevertheless, eligible mates do not exist randomly in society but are located in culturally defined groups or cliques such as college and the work place. One tends to marry someone known through long association as a member of such in-groups. Consequently, this situation results in a sort of "social endogamy."

Form of Marriage and Rule of Residence

Monogamy, a single spouse system, has always been the ideal form of Korean marriage. Historically, according to Deuchler (1977b:8), "Marriage during Koryŏ seems to have been a rather loose institution which was not restricted by a multitude of rules and regulations. It was easily entered into and easily gotten out of. The relationship between men and women was open and unceremonious." In fact, during the Goryeo dynasty, a wealthy man might marry three or four wives. These wives were not ranked and seem to have enjoyed roughly the same status. Deuchler (1977b:8) tells us that "Their social origins were apparently not indicated by different hair and dress styles." However, during the Chosŏn dynasty, in the spring of 1413, "a law was enacted according to which a man who had a legal wife was prohibited from taking a second wife (*yuch'ŏ ch'wichŏ*); a man who broke this law was forced to separate himself from his illegally acquired second wife (*ii*)" (Deuchler 1977b:31).

Despite this explicit law, although cases were limited, conditional, and exceptional, the system of polygyny (the marriage of one man to two or more women at the same time) was tolerated in the past if there were no male heirs to reinforce the patrilineal system that traces kin relationship through the male line only (Lee 1982:113-114). Unlike concubines and their children, which had been tolerated since the beginning of the Three Han period around the first century B.C. through the end of the Joseon dynasty, co-wives and their children were treated in the same way as first wives and their children.

Although the Korean Civil Code does not recognize the plural spouse system (Kim 1983:111-112), in the mid-1970s, Lee Kwang-kyu [Kwang-gyu Lee], a Korean anthropologist, recognized that nearly two percent of Koreans were unlawfully practicing polygyny (Lee 1982:117). Nowadays, however, it would be difficult to find anyone who practices polygyny.

Traditionally, upon marriage, following the patrilocal rule of residence, a newlywed couple lived with or near the parents of the groom. Currently, largely because of urbanization and industrialization, many young Korean couples practice neolocal residence, which is the establishment of an independent household.

Under the traditional system, the bride's adjustment to the groom's family was often difficult (Janelli and Yim 1982:40) because the mother-in-law could exercise absolute authority over her daughter-in-law. The bride had to endure all kinds of hardships, called *sijipsari* (Kendall 1996a:221-2; Kim 1988a:38). In any conflict between his mother and his bride, the husband had to remain neutral or take his mother's side. This was more prevalent in *yangban* families, because they were more inclined to conform to socio-ethical ideals. Nowadays, most Korean parents would like to maintain their own independent households without living with their sons and daughters-in-law. According to a social survey conducted in 2004 by the Survey Research Center at Sungkyunkwan University, only 2.8 percent of married Korean couples live with their fathers and 6.7 percent with their mothers.[15]

Age of Marriage

In traditional Korean society, people tended to marry at an early age, especially among elite or aristocratic families. Any person beyond marriageable age was labeled an old bachelor (nochonggak) or old maid (nocheonyeo), and stigmatized. Unmarried persons, whatever their age at death, were not granted the full ritual for a dead person, and never became subjects for ancestor worship. Kendall (1996:92, 94 n.15) has noted that in the day when an early marriage was the norm, a bride and groom might still technically be children. In 1925, for instance, most Korean women were married before the age of sixteen. The median age at marriage for women rose by about one and a half years between 1925 and 1940. In 1925, the median age at marriage for men was twenty-one; by 1940, it had risen by a little more than half a year. Ever since the Korea National Statistical Office (Census Bureau) started keeping the official census in 1970, the average age at marriage among Koreans has increased steadily. In 1972, for instance, the average age at marriage for men was 26.7 and 22.6 for women. By 2004, it had increased to 30.6 for men and 27.5 for women.

Another prominent social change is that a good many women are choosing to remain single for life. According to a survey conducted by the school newspaper of an elite university in Seoul, nearly one-third of the respondents did not plan to marry.[16] The reason they cited was that they did not want to be tied down by a family, and for Korean women it is difficult to manage a family and pursue a career at the same time because of inadequate childcare.[17] Many young Korean women now consider a career more important than marriage. In fact, by July 2005, the Korean female workforce had reached 10 million for

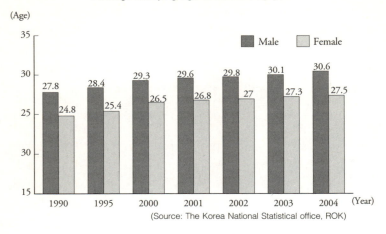

Average marrying age of Koreans by year
(Source: The Korea National Statistical office, ROK)

the first time in the history of Korea.[18]

Another interesting development is the increase in international marriages, resulting from close contact between Koreans and other foreign nationals, because of increasing globalization. From 1990 to 2004, over 66,000 Korean men married foreign women, mostly from East and Southeast Asian countries, including China, Japan, and other nations, and the number is increasing yearly.[19] A shortage of marriageable women now exists because many Korean women have opted for the single life following a mass exodus to the cities and industrial zones for job opportunities, especially in factories. This shortage is particularly acute in rural areas and consequently an increasing number of rural men are marrying foreign women.

Incidentally, while preparing this book, I was quite startled by the number of foreign women who are marrying Korean men, a phenomenon that is rapidly increasing. The language barrier between these women and Korean family members is a serious cultural problem, because almost all foreigners who marry Korean men do not have even rudimentary Korean language skills. Family squabbles develop at times, abuse may take place, and the divorce rate is rising.[20]

The most serious problem is adjustment difficulties experienced by children born to foreign mothers who lack the Korean language. Such children tend to learn their mother's language, and thus do not have sufficient command of Korean to succeed in school. The number of these struggling children is predicted to be over 100,000 by the year 2010.[21] If this problem is not addressed, it may become a potential burden for schools and Korean society.[22] A preliminary study of this social problem has concluded that an educational program addressing cultural diversity and targeted at Korean husbands who have married foreign women is an important and necessary project.

Since these foreign women are widely distributed throughout the country, it would be difficult to educate them in a given place at a specified time. To overcome this problem, beginning in February 2006, Korea Digital University, under the auspices of Pohang Iron and Steel Company (POSCO) and with administrative support from provincial governments and various local governments, launched a nationwide campaign entitled "e-Learning for Multicultural Families in Korea." The project offers a comprehensive educational program for

Southeastern Asian women

international marriage families, emphasizing the Korean language and culture. Beginning in February 2007, this project was put into effect in Gyeongsangbuk-do and Jeollanam-do provinces.

International marriage among rural Korean men has brought about a new configuration in Korean marriage patterns and family life. Such a change means that it will be difficult for Koreans to claim that they are racially, ethnically, and culturally homogeneous. One might say that a multicultural way of life has started to affect rural areas as well as urban areas in Korea.

How Does One Marry? : Ceremonial Aspects of Korean Marriage

Under the strict arranged marriage system that prevailed among *yangban* families until the second half of the twentieth century, there was virtually no courtship. Trusting the word of the "go-between," since she was usually a relative, the bride and groom allowed their wedding day to be set and the marriage to take place without their being consulted. The bride and groom were not even allowed to meet or see each other from a distance before the marriage. In some cases, bride and groom might glimpse each other without the knowledge of other people. But typically the couple saw each other for the first time on their wedding day. Among the underprivileged and lower classes, the matrimonial ceremony was simple and humble, and some ceremonies took place collectively in a later period of the Joseon. Sometimes families adopted girls before they reached the age of ten as future daughters-in-law, a custom called "*minmyeoneuri*" (Harvey 1983:45-61); the adoption of boys as future sons-in-law was called "*daerilsawi*."[23]

As the arranged-marriage system has been evolving into a system of "free choice," a transitional form of marriage arrangement has emerged in which meetings between the would-be-bride and would-be-groom, called "*matseon*" (or "mutual first") (Kendall 1996a:109), can take place in various places, such as tearooms, restaurants, and any other decent establishment with or without the presence of the arrangers or parents of both families. *Matseon* might still be classified as an arranged marriage in a broad sense, or at least a "modified system of arranged marriage."

Despite all the recent changes in marriage customs, the long-standing Korean tradition of "*gunghap*," which figuratively means destiny and involves the year, month, day, and hour of a person's birth, plays an important role, especially in arranged marriage. Usually marital harmony is predicted by a fortune-teller who determines whether the potential couple's *gunghap* are compatible. Even if all other conditions are satisfactory, some marriages cannot be finalized because of the fortune-teller's prediction of unlucky *gunghap*. Even today, a good many people tend to believe that if a married couple has marital troubles, they are due to bad *gunghap*.

Traditionally, fortunetellers played a significant role in setting wedding dates. Wedding dates for most Koreans were set by the parents of both families in close consultation with fortune-tellers, who would select an auspicious time for the wedding. In certain years like 2007, considered the luckiest year for many years to come, a particularly auspicious date would be recommended by so many fortune-tellers that one could scarcely get an appointment in the most desirable commercial wedding halls. Some Christians marry in their churches, and since the Christian population is increasing yearly, church weddings have become common among Christians in Korea. Interestingly, very few Buddhist temples in Seoul provide wedding services to their members. I have heard that there are some weddings in Buddhist temples, but I have never had the opportunity to attend a Buddhist wedding ceremony.

This overview of Korean marriage and the setting of wedding dates reminds me of my own wedding. My fiancée and I had to marry before my departure for the United States for advanced study before the school year began in September 1965. However, my intended bride and I were unable to obtain a wedding hall in which to be married (a church wedding then was rare in Korea). Every wedding hall in

Seoul was booked for the next several months. We eventually found an open date on 25 June 1965 in the wedding hall of the Chosun Hotel. We asked why this day was available. They told us that no one wanted to marry on such an "unlucky day," for it was anniversary of the start of the Korean War (25 June 1950). We requested the day anyway, and permission was granted. At that time in Korea, setting one's own wedding date was almost unheard of and practically revolutionary. I had already stunned my parents by telling them that I had selected my own spouse. Many people attended our wedding because it was a holiday and we were allowed to keep the wedding hall as long as we wanted, because no other weddings were scheduled on that "unlucky day."

Gift Box Delivery

Sending a formal letter to announce a wedding was an official practice among yangban during the Joseon dynasty that has almost disappeared. However, presentation of the formal wedding contract (*honseo*) and a variety of gifts still takes place to a certain extent. The groom's parents prepare the marriage contract and betrothal gifts with colored silks or thread and place some special items — most of them fertility symbols — in the lacquered wedding gift box (*ham*),[24] and deliver them to the groom's house.

Who delivers the gift box varies depending upon the time and place. Eugene Knez (1959:70) has observed in Gyeongsangnam-do province that the gift box "is carried by a servant, or possibly a hired pack board (A-frame) carrier, who is accompanied by one, usually more, representatives of the family of the bridegroom." A photograph displayed in the National Anthropological Archives of the Smithsonian Institution (NAA MS-7355) depicts a scene of gift box deliverers accompanied by two men carrying lanterns and wearing formal attire and horse-hair hats (*gat*) in nineteenth-century Korea.

In recent years, the gift box is usually carried by the groom's friends, normally no more than five, and they extract a very large delivery fee from the bride's family when they deliver the box. In order to raise this delivery fee (*hamgap*), "the bearers delay their final surrender of the gift box for as long as possible, haggling with the bride's family every inch of the way as they shout their demands through the neighborhood alleyways" (Kendall 1996:191). The box deliverers cry loudly, "Gift box for sale!" repeatedly. The fee for the gift box delivery varies, depending on the wealth of the bride's family. The bearers are doing it for fun, and the fee they receive usually pays for an evening's expensive celebration, much like a bachelor's party in America.

During the mid-1960s before I left Korea, gift box deliveries were common scenes in the streets of Seoul in the early evening. However, since I have returned to Korea in 2001, I have not witnessed a single one. Perhaps high-rise apartment complexes are not ideal places for this practice. I have also been told that young people today do not want to be bothered with this custom. Some say they do not like to waste time and money in this way. Even in the mid-1960s, I delivered the gift box myself. My son who married in Korea in 1998 did not want to ask his friends to deliver the box, his friends did not want to do it, and my would-be-daughter-in law did not care much about it. Finally, my son delivered the gift box himself. I surmise that a good many contemporary young Koreans are not very anxious to carry on this old custom.

The groom's friends used to practice the custom of groom hazing (*sillang darugi*). Traditionally, right after the wedding, they would hang the groom on a beam and literally beat him until he agreed to ransom himself with food, drink, and even cash. At times, beatings and jousts not only caused real discomfort for the groom, but also put him in harm's way. Nowadays, an innovative modification of this custom has appeared: the groom's friends take the groom "by force" to a restaurant, and make him or his in-laws pay for an expensive drinking and eating party. This custom too is fading away, because most grooms tend to treat their friends well anyway.

Wedding

Some people prefer to have a traditional Korean wedding ceremony, wearing traditional wedding outfits, while others choose a modern-style wedding with a Western-style wedding gown for the bride and a tuxedo for the groom. Interestingly, while rural Koreans have opted for modern-style weddings in commercial wedding halls, some urban, well-educated elite Koreans are choosing a traditional wedding, a manifestation of a nostalgic feeling for the past and tradition.

Deuchler (1977b:17-18) describes, as part of the traditional Confucian wedding, "the groom's presentation of the wild goose to the bride (*ch'inyŏng*), and it was performed just before the groom led the bride away to his house where the actual nuptial rite took place. In Korea, this act was made the centerpiece of the wedding ceremony. The goose, often a wooden replica, replaced other wild animals that had customarily been sent to the bridal home in advance ···. According to Korean tradition, bridegroom and bride exchanged ceremonial bows and the nuptial cup in the house of the bride (*sŏbu kyobae*) thus

Modern wedding

preserving Korean matrilocal marriage custom."

In weddings at commercial wedding halls, a master of ceremonies, the *jurye*, conducts the wedding rites from behind a podium as does the minister or preacher in a church wedding. The *jurye*, who is selected by the groom or his family, has to have a reputation for virtue and a flourishing family. Up until the present, the *jurye* has usually been a man. Recently, it has been reported that some females are also serving as the *jurye*, although I have never attended such a wedding. Instead of throwing a bridal shower or giving actual items as in the West, the invited guests from the bride's and groom's families, relatives, and friends give money as wedding gifts in the form of white envelopes containing cash. The amounts ranging from 10,000 *won* at the minimum (about $10.6), to 100,000 *won* (about $106.6) in most cases, and to unlimited amounts in the upper range. Hardly anyone will hand in less than 10,000 *won*. If one cannot afford at least 10,000 *won*, he or she will not attend the wedding.

The amount of the cash contribution has risen compared to the 1980s as described by Kendall (1996a:29). "Today, most of the envelopes will contain 3,000 to 5,000 *wŏn* ($3.75 to $6.25 U.S.)," she reports. "Five years later, 10,000 *wŏn* ($14.50 U.S.) will be standard, and by the early 1990s, the figure will double to 20,000 *wŏn* ($25.00 U.S.). Inflation, coupled with a rising standard of living, is a common place of contemporary Korean life; the overall cost of getting married will nearly double between 1985 and 1990."[25]

Wedding Costs

Marriage exchanges in Korea altered significantly as Korea's economic growth and industrialization rapidly made great strides. The price hike in wedding costs is most noticeable. Kendall (1996a:168) notes that "in 1990, weddings, with all their attendant exchanges, cost the average couple and their families 18.32 million *wŏn* (roughly $26,000 then)." According to a survey by Sunoo (one of the major marriage consulting centers) of 294 couples from five major Korean cities, in 2000 the average marriage cost per couple was estimated to be 78.45 million *won* (about $78,450), but it has increased to 134.9 million *won* (about $134,980), including housing expenses. The groom pays 60 percent of the total cost, because he is in charge of providing the housing which is the most expensive item, while bride supplies all the furnishings.[26]

The dowry differs according to the status and wealth of the family. A familiar tale concerning the dowry for upper and upper middle classes is well summarized in the so-called "three keys" story. Kendall (1996a:168) describes a story she once heard:

> I soon learned the urban folklore of the "three keys," that if one wishes to marry one of the three sa (the three professions of doctor *ŭisa*, lawyer *pyŭnhosa*, or professor *paksa*), then one must provide the house key, the car key, and the office key (purchase a professional practice) ⋯. The ubiquitousness of this folklore is indicative, rather, of the cynical and hyperbolic humor regarding matchmaking. I learned recently, when I made reference to the three keys in a public lecture, that at least in the popular imagination, the ante has now been upped to five keys, including the golf club key and the vacation condominium key.

Even working women have to prepare the basic dowry, which includes a large wardrobe cabinet, a dressing table, a dish cabinet, quilts and sleeping pallets, dishes and cooking utensils, television set, electronic rice cooker, *kimchi* refrigerator, a list that potentially has no end.

Often the dowry list serves as a yardstick to measure the "market value" of the bride. If the list doesn't measure up to the expectations of the bride's mother-in-law, this could lead to a squabble between the two families and ultimately to divorce. According to a director of a marriage consulting center, the exorbitant cost of marrying has become yet another reason why Koreans are delaying or deferring marriage.[27]

Family

Decline of the Extended Family

The traditional Korean family structure is extended, meaning that it is composed of two or more nuclear families, each consisting of a man, his wife, and their unmarried child or children.[28] When Korea was an agrarian society, each of those nuclear units in the family engaged in a single economic activity such as farming. As Korean society evolved economically and socially, the pattern of the extended family has shifted to that of the nuclear family, which today is the most common form of family in Korea (82.8 percent). The proportion of Korean nuclear families has increased from 71.5 percent in 1970 to 82.8 percent in 2005, whereas the proportion of extended families declined from 18.8 percent to 6.9 percent during the same period.[29] In 1960, 1.6 percent of Korean households were composed of four generations, but in 2000 only 0.2 percent of Korean families consist of four generations living together.[30]

In the meantime, the "stem family" developed, once an ideal form in Japan, although it is disappearing rapidly (Befu 1971:38). The stem family is a transitional form of family from extended family to nuclear family. It is defined that after retirement or death of its head, the family is continued through succession and inheritance, usually by one of the offspring, who stays with the parents after marriage and maintains the family line. In rural Korea, before rapid economic growth and industrialization took place starting in the mid-1960s, many firstborn sons and their brides tended to live with the groom's parents, while other sons moved elsewhere to establish their own nuclear families.

When we discuss the Korean nuclear family, some Americans may assume that it is exactly the same as the nuclear family in America. Structurally, the two systems are identical, but there are some differences in their functional relationship. The American nuclear family is more autonomous, and its relationship with the rest of the family tends to be very limited, mainly because most married couples are located far from their parents since they are mobile and dispersed throughout the continent of North America. Most Americans cannot interact frequently with their parents and in-laws except on special occasions such as Thanksgiving and Christmas Holidays. However, since Korea is such a small country, even if families create their own nuclear units, they are still in close geographic proximity to each other. If they want to meet or interact with one another, they can do it within a few hours.

Recently, a good many young couples are deciding to live near their parents or parents-in-laws, mainly because couples with small children can take advantage of the free babysitting services offered by mothers and mothers-in-law. Some young couples even prefer to live in the same apartment complex with their parents or parents-in-law. My next-door neighbors, for instance, now have their parents living on the next floor of our apartment building. I often wonder whether or not young American couples would do the same thing. If I can characterize the Korean nuclear family, it tends to be closer to the stem family in its functional relationship to parents or parents-in-law than the American nuclear family.

Changing Authority Pattern

The traditional authority pattern of the Korean family is patriarchal, which means authority is allocated to the males. Such an authority pattern is reinforced in the relationship of parents and their children; in particular, the relationship of father and son is considered to be of the utmost importance. Such absolute control can be seen in Hsu's. (1983:338) observations that "no parents are wrong vis-à-vis their children (*tien-hsia wu pu-shih chih fu-mu*)." Roger Janelli and Dawnhee Yim (1982:50) report that "the proper relationship between father and son soon became the paradigm for all hierarchical relationships in a moral society." The relationship between father and son was governed by the virtue of filial piety (*hyoseong* in Korean and *hsiao* in Chinese), which was greatly emphasized after the seventh and eighth centuries under the influence of the Confucianism from China.[31]

Korean patriarchal rules are closely related to the position of women in Korean society in general, and they set the tone for gender discrimination in Korean society in particular. Patriarchy was the basis and justification for discrimination against daughters, which in turn created a preference for male children. However, women's rights movements challenged traditional patriarchal rule and have been successful in achieving an equal-rights system, called an egalitarian system (*pyeongdeung juui*).

Emerging Women's Rights

Because of the functional consequences of patriarchal rule and the preference for males, traditional Korean families discriminated against their daughters. Roger Janelli and Dawnhee Yim (1982:36) learned of female infanticide resulting from extreme poverty during their fieldwork in a rural Korean village: "One lineage woman, in the presence of her seven-or-eight-year-old maternal granddaughter, told us how she had placed the girl on a cold floor immediately after birth, hoping she would die." The woman unhesitatingly said, "But look how well she grew up." Unwanted female babies were sometimes abandoned at the gate of a stranger's house (Harvey 1979:63, 260-269). Even in ancestral worship, "women were excluded from officiating at the rites, and ritual responsibility could not be assumed by a wife or a daughter's son in the absence of an agnatically related male heir" (Janelli and Yim 1982:13; Deuchler 1977:29; Lee 1977:13). Clark W. Sorensen (1983:64), an anthropologist and an expert on Korea, has observed that "At meals ⋯ women serve the men first, in sequence by status and seniority within the family."

Recently, however, such discrimination against women has diminished dramatically in accordance with the improvement of female status in Korea. According to a nationwide survey conducted by the *Chosun Ilbo*, a Korean daily newspaper, via Gallup Korea in 2005, of 1,027 married women with at least one child, 48.7 percent of those in their twenties favored girls rather than boys (28.4 percent); 43.7 percent of those in their thirties selected girls over boys (27.5 percent); and 34.8 percent of those in their forties chose girls over boys

(34.1 percent). Only those in their fifties (38.3 percent) favored boys over girls (24.1 percent). While older Korean women still prefer to have boys, younger Korean women clearly indicate a preference for girls, observing that in general girls tend to understand parents better than boys do (33.5 percent) and girls can be good "friends" with the mother (20.1 percent).[32]

Another challenge to patriarchal rule has been a sequence of court rulings and new statutes upholding equal rights. On 21 July 2005, there was another Supreme Court ruling to abolish a centuries-old system that denied women, especially married women, the right to an equal share of the clan property, which is a major step in ending gender discrimination in the Korean kinship system. This ruling will require a revision of kin group organization.

In the past, the marital bond in Korea used to be so strong that seeking divorce was unthinkable, especially among *yangban* families, and thought to be dishonorable. Drawing upon the Ta Ming Lü, Koreans developed the "three rules of obedience," which state that a woman must follow her parents in youth, her husband in marriage, and her sons in old age. Equally, the "seven evil causes of divorce" allowed a man to divorce his wife when she was disobedient to his parents, failed to bear a child or children, committed adultery, succumbed to jealousy, contacted a repulsive disease, offended with her loquacity, or stole from the family, usually for her mother.

After the fall of the Joseon dynasty and under Japanese rule, male-centered norms regulating divorce persisted. After liberation from Japan and under the influence of the Western concept of egalitarianism, the South Korean Civil Code was revised to denote specific conditions for divorce that were equally applicable to men and women.

For instance, in an extensive study of divorce cases presented to the Seoul District Court during the ten years after the liberation of Korea from Japan in 1945, Lee Taeyeong (1957), the first Korean woman lawyer, found a total of 144 divorces. Except for a few cases, the defendants were all women. This study focused on the heart of urban

South Korea but still revealed a male monopoly in initiating divorce suits. If the study had been done in rural districts, male domination in divorce would have been even greater. Also, in February 1962, Choi Jae-seuk (1966:405–407), a Korean sociologist, surveyed residents of two apartment complexes in Seoul and three rural villages in different South Korean provinces to discern the attitudes of Korean people toward divorce. In Seoul, on the issue of wife abuse, 35.2 percent of the women responding indicated that they would accept abuse within marriage while 21.4 percent said they would seek separation to avoid it. In the rural villages, 67.9 percent of women surveyed indicated that there would be no choice but to endure abuse while hoping for better relations in the future; only 5.4 percent indicated that they would seek separation.

Even in the 1950s and early 1960s, divorce in Korea was uncommon, and cases were mostly male-centered and male-initiated. Times haves changed. The divorce rate in Korea is fairly high now — the highest in Asia and the third highest among members of the Organization for Economic Cooperation and Development (OECD), after the United States and Great Britain.[33] Recent Korean divorces deviate from the traditional pattern in that more women now initiate divorce than men, and the figures are on the rise. In 1990, among all divorces, 43.0 percent were initiated by women. This has increased to 64.2 percent in 2000,[34] and to 66.7 percent in 2005.[35]

Achievement of Korean Women

Much credit should be given to Korean women in achieving an egalitarian authority pattern in society. Overcoming all obstacles, Korean women have recently achieved many distinctions in society and continuously excel in various fields. In 2000, 25.1 percent of women passed the higher civil service examination (*haengjeong gosi*), which leads to appointments to key government positions, and that number increased to 44.0 percent in 2005. In 1994, only 31 (10.7 percent) women passed the bar examination (*sabeop gosi*), which leads to professions such as lawyer, public prosecutor, and judge, but in 2005 the figure rose to a surprising 323 (32.3 percent). In the higher civil service examination for diplomats (*oemu gosi*), 40 percent of those who passed were women.[36] In 2007, 55.6 percent of all newly appointed Korean judges were women.[37]

In 2006, 40 percent of public prosecutors and 55.6 percent of judge-trainees (who will be appointed as judges after two years of training in courts) were women, an astonishing accomplishment for Korean women.[38] In all three of these examinations given in 2005, women earned the highest scores in each category. In various other junior civil service examinations given that same year, women comprised the great majority (71 percent).

Another interesting aspect of increasing gender equality in Korea is that women dominate teaching positions in elementary and middle schools. The success rate of women who took the qualifying examination for elementary and middle school teachers in the Seoul School District was overwhelmingly high (89.8 percent). Currently, 60 percent of all Korean elementary and middle school teachers are women.[39] Korean women have become quite prominent in other professions as well. Among all Korean physicians, 18.4 percent are women, while 21.9 percent of dentists and 62.1 percent of pharmacologists are women.[40] In politics, women constituted only 1 percent of all National Assembly members in 1992. The proportion of women representatives, however, increased dramatically to 13.0 percent (39 members out of 299 total members) in 2004.[41] Most dramatic of all, on 20 April 2006, a sixty-two-year-old woman, Han Myeongsuk, became the first woman prime minister of Korea.

Despite such progress, according to a survey a great majority of Korean women (72.4 percent) feel that gender discrimination still exists in contemporary Korea. For instance, in the twenty top Korean business firms, including Samsung, Hyundai, LG, SK, and Kia Motors, women constitute 18.6 percent of the total workforce but occupy less than 1 percent of managerial positions.[42]

Kin Group Organization and Kinship System

Patrilineal Descent

The major pillar for every kinship system is the rule of descent that connects individuals with particular sets of kin on the basis of known or presumed common ancestry. Within the kin group, each member addresses the others using kinship terms instead of personal names.[43] The rule of descent also determines the scale and complexity of kin groups, including lineage (a set of kin whose members trace their descent from a common ancestor through known links) and clan or sib (which is made up of related lineages). Under the bilateral rule of descent, as seen in most Western societies, the size of a kin group can be limited because it links a person with a group of close relatives through both sexes.

The Korean rule of descent has been a patrilineal system: within a given kin group, a member affiliates with other kinsmen who are related to him through males. The origin of the patrilineal system in Korea may have been prehistoric, although the bilateral descent system was practiced in Goguryeo and Silla. The patrilineal system was strengthened under Chinese influence at the beginning of the Three Kingdoms period around the first half of the first century B.C. The system was further developed during the early seventeenth century (Janelli and Yim 1982:10; Osgood 1951:242). Since the patrilineal system by definition requires tracing one's kin relationships through males, up until most recently, it has fostered a preference for males.

In the past, when families were heirless, polygynous arrangements were sometimes made, although such instances were extremely rare. Traditionally, an heirless family would adopt a male as heir, which had been a widespread custom since the middle of the Joseon dynasty, but the range of males available for adoption was very limited, mostly agnates (persons related by patrilineal descent).[44] However, this practice of adoption began to change with the revision of the South Korean Civil Code in 1977 to permit adoption of someone with a different surname and the entry of the husband's name into his wife's family registry.[45]

More recently, the Constitution Court abolished male headship in the household and the male-oriented family registry, and the National Assembly passed a statute abolishing the limitation of the range of adoption. However, Koreans still adhere to the agnatic principle in adoption.

Perhaps the greatest influence of patrilineal rule on the Korean kinship system is that it gave rise to a number of elaborate kin groups, such as lineage (*munjung*) and clan or sib (*ssijok* or *chinjok*). In Korea, there are about 1,100 clans, each of which includes scores of lineages (Kim 1988a:158 n.27), although how many Koreans are actually affiliated with active lineages or clans is difficult to ascertain (Kim 1974:576-577). The most important mechanism for promoting a sense of belonging to a kin group is the extensive use of kinship terms to encompass the entire membership of the kin group, the basic medium being the genealogical record (*jokbo*).[46] Lineage and clan members address one another by using kinship terms, regardless of how remote the relationship may be. Most Koreans tend to believe that the same lineage or even the same clan members are all kin, even though they may be many generations removed from the common ancestor.

Solidarity of kin-group members is further fostered by participation in worship of the common ancestor and in communal ownership of property. Regarding the communal property of a kin group, each member feels that he is the owner of that kin-group property, even if he is too poor to own property as an individual. In the rural Korean village where I conducted my fieldwork in the early 1960s, a lineage owned three different communal properties: ritual land for the lineage, land for the support of formal education of capable young members, and land for the common welfare of all the members (Kim 1968:73-78). If young members are brilliant and capable of pursuing further education but cannot afford it, the lineage gives such individuals scholarships provided by profits from land designated for this purpose. The idea of supporting the education of the young members of a lineage is based on the belief that if they obtain high positions in government or gain prominence as scholars, prestige and fame are automatically bestowed on the entire membership of the lineage.

Currently, properties owned by some lineages and clans are quite sizable, and assets can reach several billion *won* due to the appreciation of real estate. Some lineage and clan members of certain kin groups have become rich as a consequence. Since the Korean kinship system has been patrilineal, with the rule of inheritance favoring male members, female members of their natal lineages and clans have felt discriminated against.[47] In order to uphold gender equality, quite a few women of several kin groups have challenged the inequity of sharing property within the patrilineal kin groups. Finally, on 21 July 2005, the Korean Supreme Court abolished such discrimination against women members of kin groups. Consequently, from that point on even a married woman has the same rights as an adult male to claim equal shares in property owned by her natal (father's) kin group.

Not only does this court ruling affect the property ownership of Korean kin groups, but it is also going to be a major driving force in altering Korean kin-group organization and solidarity. The court ruling will probably spark a transformation in the Korean rule of descent from a patrilineal to a bilateral system. A spokesman from the Korean Confucian Society at the Seonggyungwan called the court decision "outrageous," claiming that it would bring "chaos" to South Korea's male-dominated social order.[48]

The Faithful Remnants of Korean Kinship

Despite all the changes in the Korean kinship system, the old system has been with Koreans for so long that its remnants still profoundly affect their way of life. Some of the social characteristics that influence present-day Korean traditions and thought patterns can be traced to their origins in the Korean kinship system.[49]

Korean kinship attributes of continuity, authority, inclusiveness, and asexuality have influenced every Korean institution, including business, politics, and even religion. With respect to continuity, "which is the condition of being, or the attitude of desiring to be, an unbroken sequence, or concerned with others" (Hsu 1965:638-661, 1971,

1983:217-247), I have witnessed it in both tragic separations and rapturous reunions of Korean families dispersed by the partition of the peninsula. Under the circumstances of war, North Koreans have made every effort to save the male heirs of their families by sending them to the south in order to secure the continuity of their family lines (Kim 1988a).

With respect to political institutions, for instance, during the Joseon dynasty, the Yi clan made every effort to rule the dynasty continuously, even if there were no apparent heirs for kingship. Under the current system, which limits the president, who is elected directly by popular vote, to a single five-year term, continuity cannot be maintained. However, North Korean ruler Kim Ilseong transferred his power to his son, Kim Jeongil, for the sake of continuity. Likewise, many chairmen of big Korean business conglomerates inherit the chairmanship from their fathers.

In terms of authority, which refers to "personal power that commands and enforces obedience, or the condition of being under such power" (Hsu 1965:638-661, 1971, 1983:217-247), Korean presidents enjoy more power than American presidents even though both nations have the same presidential system. A Korean chairman of the board of any business corporation also has more authority than his American counterpart.

Inclusiveness, which means the "act of incorporating or the attitude of wishing to be incorporated" (Hsu 1965:638-661, 1971, 1983:217-247), can be seen in regional ties and school ties, which create a fictional kinship (a socially defined equivalent of marital [affinal] or blood [consanguineal] ties) similar to the Japanese *oyabun-kobun*, or patron-client relationship (Cole 1971:196-199). In Korea, the relationships between *seonbae* (senior) and *hubae* (junior) students of the same school are analogous to fictional kin relationships between older and younger brothers (sisters for female schools), and these students even address each other using the real kinship terms of older and younger brothers (sisters). This is similar to the *senpai-kohai* (senior-junior) relationships of the Japanese, and both are described by the same Chinese characters

(Kim 1992:50).

During my fieldwork on a Korean industry in the late 1980s and early 1990s (Kim 1992), I found that the chairman of the corporation took advantage of the inclusive fictional kin category that he shared with two Korean presidents, Chun Doo-hwan and Rho Tae-woo. All three men came from the same province and had school ties as alumni to the same high school (Kim 1992:50). Hak Chong Lee (1989:156-157) observed that in the Korean business world, school connections, regional ties, and kinship networks were essential not only in power-group formation at the top levels but also in the formation of informal relations and cliques at all levels throughout Korean society. These relationships work as important factors affecting the behavior of employees. Similarly, regional connections give those from the same region a feeling of common background and compatibility, and this too affects the social interactions and personal decisions of employees. Such inclusiveness is well reflected in the Korean view of religion. Koreans see all religions as equally good; religions are not regarded as exclusive as in Japan and China (Befu 1971:96; Hsu 1981:255).

With respect to asexuality, which denotes "the condition of having no connection with sex" (Hsu 1971:11), although much has changed recently, traditionally in Korea sex could not be discussed openly, particularly in public or quasi-public places. Any intimate relationship between men and women could not be displayed publicly. For example, none of the reunited husbands and wives during the reunion telethon in 1983 by KBS kissed each other. Similarly, not wanting to display affection in front of millions of viewers, most did not even hug each other when they were reunited (Kim 1988a, 1989:318).

A stark contrast was the scene in February 1973 when American P.O.W.s from Vietnam were reunited with their wives. For instance, when Air Force Maj. Arthur Burer arrived at Andrews Air Force Base, his wife shrieked, streaked across the tarmac, and leapt into her husband's waiting arms. Burer lifted her up in a bear-hug embrace. Their exuberant hugging was so vivid that televisions and magazines reported every aspect of their greeting in detail. If they had not displayed such an intimate exuberance in public, most Americans would have wondered what was going on between the reuniting couple (Kim 1989:318).

It appears that every human being is related to other human beings and behaves on the basis of many different principles, but for Koreans the foremost principle organizing their lives is kinship.

CHAPTER 5

Traditional Rural Life and the Current Exodus

As in most agrarian societies, in Korea, before its urbanization in the early 1970s, the rural village or hamlet (*maeul*)[1] was the center of all socio-economic and political activities. However, Korean villages, unlike those in other rural societies, were not populated only by peasants. In fact, a good many members of yangban families and lineages resided in the rural countryside, establishing private academies (*seowon*), and educating many renowned Neo-Confucian scholars, such as Yi Hwang and Yi I, and innumerable scholar-bureaucrats. Indeed, traditional Korean culture has its roots in rural villages.

Even in the modern era, all Korean presidents except for one have been from rural villages and the founders of the top three Korean business conglomerates, Samsung, Hyundai, and LG, all have rural roots. Vast numbers of Koreans who have achieved distinction in Korean society come from rural backgrounds. Therefore, an in-depth look at rural Korea is essential for understanding the modern Korean elite and the most recent changes in Korean society.

Before Korea took a major step toward successful industrialization, the vast majority of Koreans lived in rural villages. In the 1960s, the ratio of rural to urban dwellers was seven to three (Lee 2003:177), but according to the most recent census of 2005, this ratio had become two to eight. The rate of urbanization increased from 79.7 percent in

2000 to 81.5 percent in 2005.²

The most obvious decrease in population has taken place and is still taking place among Korean farmers. In 1965, one year before the first five-year economic development plan (1962-1966) had been completed, the farming population was slightly more than 55.1 percent of the total Korean population. However, toward the end of the second economic development (1972-1976), the farming population had fallen from over 14 million (44.7 percent) in 1970 to less than 4 million in 2001, a 75 percent decrease over the previous thirty-five years.³ Indeed, Korean rural villages are experiencing a drastic decline in population.

Maeul as the Center of Social Life in Rural Korea

The Origins and Development of Rural Korean Villages

The origin of the Korean village goes far back to prehistoric times. Archaeologists believe that settled villages in the Korean peninsula appeared as early as 12,000 years ago (Nelson 1993:10). Therefore settled village life in Korea started long before the domestication of plants and animals, which happened about 4,000 years ago, during an era analogous to the Jōmon in Japan. During the Early Village period (6000-2000 B.C.), villages were closely related to specific habitats and situated on riverbanks, along coasts, and on coastal islands (Nelson 1993:59).

Characteristically, most Korean villages have been small in size, not only because they were sparsely populated in prehistoric times but also because of the physical environment: over 70 percent of the Korean peninsula is occupied by mountains, hills, rivers, and small streams, and Korean villages have had to adapt to a rugged terrain. As geographer and Korean specialist Shannon McCune has pointed out, "the Korean mountain system is over six thousand feet in altitude in some sections. ···There are no plains deserving of the name and much of the land is in slope" (McCune 1980:15). Even in the late Goryeo dynastic period, a good many villages consisted of fifty and sixty households, and villages with fewer than ten households were not uncommon (Lee 1996:18). Village size gradually increased during the Joseon dynasty.[4]

Until recent times, due largely to the natural barriers of rugged mountains and mighty rivers, transportation and communication were difficult. As a result of this relative isolation, each village developed unique characteristics. Perhaps sociologist Lee Man-gab (1960:23) is correct when he says, "it may appear that each village is the same, but each village is distinctively different in its human relations." Some Korean villages are located on flat land, but most are located at the base of a mountain facing south and overlooking a plain. According to Kwang-kyu Lee (2003:147-148), this is not "based on geomancy,[5] but rather on a long experience of living in Korea. Having the mountain on the north side of the village protects the village from cold winter winds, and the plain on the south gives the village lots of sunshine." Since Korea is located in the northern hemisphere, the sun rises higher in the sky in summertime: roofs and long overhangs block the direct sunlight, creating shade for the house. In winter, the direct sunlight from the south works like natural solar heating. Therefore, a "mountain behind and water or a plain in front" has become the traditional ideal site for a village or house.

There are no accurate statistics on the number of villages in Korea. Kwang-kyu Lee (2003:143) estimates that there are about 50,000 villages in South Korea alone, while In-Joung Whang (1981:27) accounts for 34,871 villages as of 1979. However, since then, many new villages have been established, while others have disappeared largely because of rezoning and the construction of dams, highways, and other development projects. Still others have merged to form combined villages, known as "*i*" or "*dong*."

Types of Rural Villages
In addition to the typical rural farming village, where peasants engage mainly in wet-rice cultivation, there are other distinct types of villages

defined by their locality and occupations of their residents. There are suburban villages, mountain villages, slash-and-burn cultivation villages, and fishing villages. In the past, according to Kwang-kyu Lee (2003:144), "suburban communities were settled primarily by outcasts. They were villages composed of special workers, such as leather workers, basket weavers, shamans, etc. At a distance of about four kilometers from the cities were located villages for manufacturing and villages which processed and provided wood for fuel. Especially around Seoul, there were lots of satellite villages which had facilities for lodging and food for the benefit of travelers going between the city and outlaying areas." Nowadays, however, because of the development of modern transportation and the expansion of city limits, such suburban villages have mostly been incorporated into larger cities. For example, most small cities in Gyeonggi-do province near Seoul have become a part of the Greater City of Seoul.

Mountain villages are located at higher altitudes and are sparsely populated, the houses scattered widely at the foot of a mountain or in a valley. Unlike the occupants of farming villagers in the plains, who cultivate mainly wet rice, mountain-village farmers grow mainly barley, wheat, Indian millet, millet, potatoes, and corn. They also collect and gather bee honey and mushrooms. Recently, mountain villages have experienced a sharp decline in population because of people moving to cities and industrial zones. Today, only a small population remains in these villages, planting cash crops for herbal medicines and cabbages, which can grow in the highlands. In the past, the roofs (made of tree bark, called *neowa*) and buildings of mountain villages were distinctive, made from natural elements found in the mountain environment. Nowadays, however, bark roofs have been replaced with the same tin, plaster, and tile roofs found on most farmhouses in the plains. From 1976 to 1977, Clark W. Sorensen conducted anthropological fieldwork in a mountain village in Gangwon-do province. Because these villages are disappearing so rapidly, his work (1988) remains a valuable documentation of the mountain culture and ecology of Korea.

Up until 1968, slash-and-burn cultivation villages, whose farmers grew mainly millet, Indian millet, and potatoes, were scattered in deep and high mountain regions. The slash-and-burn method of cultivation is generally understood this way: farmers cultivate a field for a while, then move on to a new field, letting the bush reclaim the old one; later they return to cultivate the first field again, slashing and burning it so minerals can be re-deposited without the use of fertilizers. However, Korean slash-and-burn cultivators did not change their place of residence when they burned their fields because their sphere of activities was limited geographically.

During the Japanese occupation, farmers who lost their lowland farms often went to mountainous regions to become slash-and-burn cultivators. In 1933, while Korea was still under Japanese occupation, the number of slash-and-burn cultivators amounted to about 82,000 households. Beginning in 1968, however, the Korean government prohibited such farming methods, and in 1974 the government introduced a new bill calling for slash-and-burn cultivators to be relocated. Slash-and-burn cultivation villages no longer exist in Korea.[6]

The spatial arrangement of fishing villages, both on the seacoast and on islands, is one of clusters, and most houses are smaller than those in villages of the mountains, valleys, and plains. Even if a village is classified as a fishing village, very few of its inhabitants engage solely in fishing. Most families have some rice fields or a dry paddy that they cultivate in addition. Generally, fishing exists as an alternative means of livelihood for those with insufficient land. Consequently, the income of fishing families is determined by the amount of land they own. Traditionally, fishermen have been regarded as poorer, less educated, and of lower social status than farmers (Lee 2003:146-147).

In the mid-1960s, Vincent S.R. Brandt (1971), an American anthropologist, conducted fieldwork in a small farming and fishing village in south Chungcheong-do province. Brandt's study delineates the contrast between the strictly traditional agrarian way of life and the increasingly money-oriented fishing economy in a rural village. His writing reflects the prejudice held by the local inhabitants against the fishermen: "There is considerable difference between farmers and fishermen in their personal conduct ⋯ Idleness (often enforced), drunkenness, its behavioral corollary quarreling, and adultery all are more prevalent in the neighborhoods where fishermen are preponderant" (Brandt 1971:65)

Today, however, the Korean fishing industry is flourishing, thanks to technological and economic development, especially the great success of aquaculture (sea weed, shrimp, and oyster), and changes in dietary patterns, notably the increased consumption of fish. In fact, in 2005, fishermen's annual income per household in Wando County, Jeollanam-do province, which consists of more than 200 islands, was estimated at about 50 million *won* (about $53,304), almost twice that of the national average for rural farm household's of 26 million *won* (about $26,000).[7] Fishing villages have persisted and prospered.

The Social Structure of Korean Villages

Yangban-Dominant Lineage Villages

Lee Man-gab (1960:23) identified three distinct social structures that defined three types of Korean villages: (1) villages where a formally aristocratic (*yangban*) lineage is predominant,[8] (2) those where a commoner lineage is predominant, and (3) those where power and wealth are shared by more than one lineage. However, "lineage-dominant" villages are not necessarily controlled by a single lineage, but sometimes more than one as Brandt (1971) has documented in his field study.

Nevertheless, Korean villages can largely be classified into two types: lineage-dominant villages dominated by one or more *yangban* lineages,[9] and commoners' villages that lack any dominant *yangban* lineage. Kwang-kyu Lee (2003:151-152) calls the latter category "mixed villages." These two types of villages are distinctively different in their history, culture, and structure.

An overview of the village of Hahoe

Comprehensive ethnographic research has yielded much information on lineage-dominant Korean villages. Fieldwork conducted by Korean anthropologist Kim Taek-kyoo (1964, 1979) resulted in an ethnography on the Yu lineage-dominated village of Hahoe, a compact village cloaked in a mysterious aura of ancient folk culture that was founded near the end of the Goryeo dynasty, 1355. The village included residents of two lineages in addition to the Yu lineage, but the Yu clan came to dominate sometime between 1635 and 1642, after one Yu member, Yu Seongryong(1542-1607), had served as prime minister in the Joseon dynasty during the Japanese invasion in the mid-sixteenth century. Designated a Korean folk village by the government in 1972, Hahoe has aroused keen public interest throughout the country and received intensive international media exposure when Her Majesty Queen Elizabeth II of Great Britain visited on 21 April 1999. Since then, the village has had a record number of visitors (Kim 1992:32-38, 2002:177-178).

Parenthetically, the style and scale of traditional Korean houses in the *yangban*-dominant villages reveal something more than the class distinction between the yangban and the commoners. The rooflines of the tiled roofs of Korean houses reflect the nation's character and style of arts, particularly its architecture. Although the eaves of buildings in the three principal East Asian countries, China, Japan, and Korea, all curve upward, subtle differences exist in the manner of these upturns. While China's traditional architecture is vertical and Japan's tends to be diagonal, Korean rooflines form soft curves that float ever so gently heavenward, flowing with nature's rhythms. This architectural style is prominently featured in many Buddhist temples. A detailed description of the artistic traits of Korean roof eaves can be found in Seock Jae Yim's *Roofs and Lines* (2005).

Roger L. Janelli with Dawnhee Yim (1982) conducted fieldwork in a farming village they call Twisŏngdwi (a fictitious name), located only fifty kilometers from downtown Seoul, in order to document ancestor worship rites and rituals among many other things. The village is dominated by the Andong Gwon [kwon] lineage. The Gwon lineage settled in the village during the latter half of the sixteenth century, and the village has grown ever since. In the 1930s, as the village continued to grow and their farm holdings increased, the Gwon lineage started hiring non-lineage members to work with them, and the number of non-Gwon residents increased during the 1940s and 1950s. Non-Gwon members of the village have generally been poorer than the Gwons for whom they work, and have second-class status socially, economically, and even politically. Janellis' ethnography demonstrates that even what one calls a lineage-dominated village can have non-lineage members. Brandt's (1971) ethnography of a village motivated between land and sea depicts not only the relationship between farmers and fishermen, but also relationships among the two dominating gentry lineages and non-lineage members or commoners.

It is not necessarily true that in a lineage-dominated village the greatest number of villagers belong to the dominant lineage or lineages. In Hahoe, for instance, the proportion of Yu lineage members in the population was 57 percent between 1589 and 1618, and diminished to 39 percent from 1615 to 1635 (Lee 1996:60 n.64). It appears that as the lineage-dominated village became more prosperous and politically powerful, the number of non-lineage members needed as farmhands and general laborers increased.

Lineage villages emerged after the formation of lineages as kin groups. Political factionalism and competition for government positions among various lineage groups might have encouraged politically prominent lineages to form such kin-group organizations in rural communities. Each lineage began to record their respective genealogies after 1600 during the Joseon dynasty (Janelli and Yim 1982:10), a practice that intensified after the Japanese invasion in the sixteenth century. Once a lineage-centered village had been formed, a second or subordinate lineage might then be established through the son-in-law or grandson of a daughter of the lineage. In some cases new lineages and their villages were dominant over the original lineages (Lee 2003:153).

There are no accurate statistics on the number of lineage villages in existence since the 1600s. However, in 1930, a Japanese colonial official, Zenshō Eiske, made a survey of Korean lineage villages and estimated that there were some 15,000 of them, about one-third of the total number of Korean villages. According to Zenshō's analysis of 1,685 prominent villages, 207 were known to be older than 500 years; 646 were between 300 and 500 years old; 351 were between 100 and 300 years; and 23 were less than 100 years; while the age of 458 villages remained unknown (Lee 1996:291).

The Major Characteristics of Lineage Villages

In lineage-dominated villages, behaviors and interactions among the inhabitants are largely governed by kinship rules and follow a clearly structured hierarchical system of rank and authority closely linked with Korean aristocratic traditions. Ranking by age is important, yet generational order from the common ancestor in the clan and lineage takes precedence over age. Lineage members address each other using kinship terms rather than personal names. For instance, sibling terms extend to every lineage member who belongs to the same generation from the common ancestor. Most prosperous and well-to-do lineages possess communal properties that become the material basis for providing ancestor-worship rituals, scholarships, and other welfare for their members.

In lineage-dominated villages, the overall sense of "community" is known to be rather weak. According to Brandt's (1971:26-27) report, "In much of traditional rural Korea the *yangban* probably felt a greater affinity for kin and other members of their own class in neighboring villages or towns than they did for the commoners next door." However, this does not mean that even in lineage-dominated villages, lineage members interact exclusively with themselves. In fact, they cooperate with non-lineage members through several channels such as "*dure*," a system for mutual assistance and cooperation among all the members of a village.[10] Under the spirit of the *dure*, everyone in the village takes very seriously their moral, ethical, and social obligations to help others on certain occasions. Such cooperative labor includes house-building, transplanting rice, threshing grain, moving, weddings, funerals, death anniversaries, etc. If for any reason a villager cannot participate in a cooperative project, another member of the household will do his or her share.

It is generally true that members of lineage-dominated villages, which tend to be more static and rigid than non-lineage villages (Lee 1996:60 n.62), are less harmonious in their relations and less willing to cooperate with one another. "Without a strong sense of community," Brandt (1971:25) reports, "conflict between kinship groups and after World War II, tensions between the *yangban* and commoner classes and among political factions were all readily expressed in strife within such villages." However, those conflicts and tensions have been reduced, if not eliminated, since the Land Reform Act introduced in 1949.

Lineage-dominant villages in Korea have forced a revision of the stereotypical image of "peasants" long held by anthropologists such as Robert Redfield (1960), Lloyd A. Fallers (1961), and others who have defined a "peasant" as someone who is "poor," "ignorant," "uncouth," and often harbors "partial hostility" toward the elite (Fallers 1961:109). Such a view has largely been shaped by "a European mental category" (Brandt 1971:11 n.).[11] Many Korean rural inhabitants who have lived in lineage-dominated villages and engaged in farming do not match this stereotypical image. In fact, a good many Korean *yangban* who lived in such villages wielded enormous influence in the Joseon court.

Yi Hwang, whose hometown of Dosan was a typical rural lineage-based village of Yi clan members, is a classic example of a village dweller who by no means fits the Western-based category of "peasant." Upon retirement from his government position in the Joseon court, Yi Hwang taught his students at Dosan Seowon, a Confucian academy he had founded. One of Yi's students, Yu Seongryong, became prime minister of the Joseon dynasty during the Japanese invasion in the mid-sixteenth century, and others became scholars who carried on Yi's school of thought.[12] Following Yi's example, several of his students returned to their home villages and became teachers themselves. Yu Seongryong, for instance, returned to his hometown of Hahoe upon his retirement as prime minister and taught his students at Byeongsan Seowon, near the village. Such a trend was prevalent throughout the country and resulted in trained scholar-bureaucrats who were able to pass the national civil service examination (*gwageo*) and exercise enormous power. As these examples show, students and teachers were not peasants but the local *yangban*-elite who happened to be based in rural villages.

Commoners' Villages or Mixed Villages

As Zenshō Eisuke's survey shows, two-thirds of Korean villages were commoners' or "mixed villages,"[13] composed of members of several lineages, none of them dominant in number or influence over other villagers. These groups were — and still are — equal in social class as well property holdings. Traditionally, such mixed villages have been composed largely of commoners without the presence of elite or *yangban*. They also tend to be smaller than lineage-led *yangban* villages, with much smaller houses. Until very recently, these houses

Tile-roofed houses of the yangban-led lineage village

Well-preserved thatched-roof houses in the mixed village

had thatched roofs covered with straw, not the tiled roofs that are a common sight in *yangban*-led lineage villages. In sum, mixed villages are poorer than *yangban*-led lineage villages, closely resembling the common image of a "peasant village."

Several studies (Brandt 1971; Kim 1964; Lee 1996) reveal that everyday activities in mixed villages were more harmonious and cooperative than in *yangban*-led lineage villages. Even village heads (*ijang*) in a lineage village did not have to share their authority and administrative power with senior members of the village. While *yangban*-led lineage villages were dominated by the norms and regulations of kinship and controlled by kin-group organizations, communal cooperatives such as *dure*, *pumasi* (exchange of labor), and various *gye* (mutual financial associations) played a more vital role in mixed villages. Since the values and norms of mixed villages tend to be more egalitarian, their leaders were also more democratic in their decision-making than their counterparts in lineage-dominant villages. Consequently, mixed villages tended to be more mobile, dynamic, and open to the outside world (Lee 1996:60).

Distinctive characteristics of lineage-dominant and mixed villages were most pronounced prior to the 1949 Land Reform Act, which abolished institutionalized class differentiations. Nowadays the differences between the two types of rural Korean villages have been significantly reduced, if not extinguished completely.

Transformation of Rural Korean Villages

Rural Villages as Objects of Exploitation

Before the formation of kin-group organizations (lineage in particular) and the emergence of lineage villages in the sixteenth century, Korean farmers and fishermen were indeed peasants in every sense of the word.

From the Three Kingdoms period, villages as administrative districts were regularly reorganized and subdivided, a process by which new villages were established and old villages redistricted and consolidated. No detailed information on these villages is available, but the "Castle lords exercised economic jurisdiction in the villages over which their power extended. They both levied taxes on the peasant population and exacted corvee labor service from them" (Lee 1984:97).

Rural village farmers were of course the objects of this exploitation, which continued during the Joseon dynasty and intensified as *yangban*-led lineage villages emerged. When the Joseon dynasty redistricted provincial counties, villages were labeled as *dong, ri, po, pyeong,* or *chonhyang*, all Chinese loan-words, but no efforts were made to improve rural farming villages. Instead, peasants and all rural farmers other than *yangban*-led lineage members were denied freedom of movement. "Peasants were fixed on the land and were unable to move as they wished," Ki-baik Lee (1984:184) reports that :

> In order to prevent them from abandoning the land they worked, 'identification tag' (*hop'ae*) law was enacted ⋯ by the provisions of a law (*oga chakt'ongpŏb*) that organized households into units of five, neighbors were made mutually responsible for ensuring that members of the unit did not abscond from their locality of residence. In consequence, the peasant household of Yi [Chosŏn] Korea in general was a self-sufficient unit living generation after generation in one place, providing its own needs for food, clothing, and shelter.

Peasant Rebellion

The first peasant rebellion recorded in Korean history took place during the late Silla dynasty. In an effort to overcome a fiscal crisis in 889, the government enforced the collection of heavy taxes from local peasants. Protesting the tax burden imposed on them, the peasants abandoned their land and roamed the countryside, seething with rebellion. The rebellion began in the area of Sangju and spread throughout the country, becoming a large-scale movement. Eventually, the government had to battle these powerful peasant insurgents. Through this insurgency, angry peasants expressed their rage and frustration, but their revolt did not accomplish anything to improve their lives.[14]

Numerous intermittent peasant uprisings occurred throughout subsequent dynasties. At times, some *yangban*-turned-farmers convinced peasant farmers to take part in these uprisings as happened in the Hong Gyeongrae Rebellion of 1811 and Jinju Uprising of 1862 (Lee 1984:254-255). However, most of the rebellions and uprisings followed the same pattern: several thousand discontented farmers would attack local government offices; the central government would send troops to put down the rebels; the rebel leaders would be arrested and some executed, and the rebellious peasants would have accomplished very little beyond demonstrating their frustration and anger.

However, one of the largest rebellions, which took place during the Joseon dynasty in 1894, grew out of a syncretic religious belief called Donghak (Eastern Learning) and erupted into a revolutionary peasant struggle that employed military operations on a large scale. Under the leadership of Jeon Bongjun, the head of Gobu County's Donghak parish, the peasants occupied the county office, seized weapons, and distributed the illegally collected tax rice to the poor. When they took up arms, the peasant armies demanded that the *yangban* be prevented from draining the life-blood of the peasants through their illegal extortions. Later, the activities of the peasant armies evolved into a patriotic movement for national independence from foreign domination.[15]

The Reform of 1894 (*Gabo gyeongjang*) (Lew 1972, 1990, 1998) is considered the starting point of Korea's modernization (Deuchler 1977:xii). This reform was a sweeping one, affecting virtually every aspect of the Joseon administration, the economy, and socio-cultural activities. Local government was restructured in an effort to adapt local administration to local conditions. The prefectures were subdivided into uniform county (*gun*) units, thus simplifying an earlier structure. Also, an effort to eliminate class distinction between *yangban* and commoners was made. Nevertheless, the county and village units of local government were left intact, and no systematic effort to improve rural conditions was made then or after the reform. The *yangban* took this opportunity to strengthen their influence by establishing lineage villages, and wresting control of economic and political resources from non-lineage villagers, thereby ensuring their position as the dominant class. Some small natural villages were consolidated into the larger unit of villages, called *ri*, under the domination of *yangban* lineage members (Lee 1996:30-32, 42).

Ever after the 1949 Land Reform Act, which marks the beginning of the new republic, peasant-farmer protests took place. Nancy Abelmann (1996), a cultural anthropologist and an expert on Korea, depicts a farmers' protest in the late 1980s in a southwestern village and in Seoul against corporate ownership of tenant plots that were exempted from the 1949 Land Reform Act. Her descriptions are not limited to rural farmers but also include student activists and organizers who joined the protest, in an effort to examine the broad issues of class, nation, capitalism, and democracy in the context of modern Korean history. Sociologist Gi-wook Shin (1997) has written a comprehensive book tracing the roots of peasant activism from 1910 to post-1945 Korean rural society.

Recently, Korean rice farmers and supportive farmers' organizations felt so threatened by the 2004 World Trade Organization (WTO) and FTA for market liberalization that they staged demonstrations and protests that now extended overseas. During the six days of WTO ministerial meetings that began on 14 December 2005 in Hong Kong, some 1,000 Korean protesters clashed with Hong Kong's riot police. Over 800 Korean protesters were detained at police stations, although they were subsequently released.[16] When Korea and the United States began formal negotiations on a bilateral FTA in June 2006, a 146-member delegation of Korean activists, workers, farmers, and students went to the United States to protest.[17] Despite opposition by farmers, on 2 April 2007, Korea and the United States announced an FTA between the two nations, which awaits congressional approval in both countries.

The Japanese Land Grab and Exploitation of Peasants

Japanese interest in Korean real estate, especially farmland, had begun before Japan officially annexed Korea in 1910. In order to acquire Korean farmland, in 1908 the Japanese government established the Oriental Development Company. Within the first eighteen months of its operation, the company acquired 73,500 acres of Korean farmland, and an increasing number of Japanese immigrant-farmers relocated to Korea as landlords (Lee 1984:318). In order to expand their possession of Korean farmland, the Japanese established the Land Survey Bureau in 1910, the year of the Japanese annexation of Korea. Japan then promulgated the Land Survey Law in 1912.

The Land Survey Law allowed the Japanese to grab even more Korean farmland, which they did swiftly by expropriating it from Korean peasant farmers. This skillful Japanese tactic has been described by Ki-baik Lee (1984:318-319):

> The land survey law ⋯ required that a landholder, in order to have his ownership rights recognized, report his name, address, and the name under which his land was registered — as well as the type of land use, the dimensions, and other pertinent data. This report was to be made to the director of the Land Survey Bureau within a comparatively short stipulated time period. Koreans, however, felt very uneasy about reporting their landholdings to the Japanese Government-General. Moreover, the registration procedures were not adequately made known to the general farming population and many peasants were negligent about making their reports. Nevertheless, all those who failed to register their land had it confiscated by the Government-General.

Consequently, the Japanese Government-General became Korea's largest landowner, owing 40 percent of the total land area in Korea (Lee 1984:319), and by 1941 Japanese ownership had swollen to 54 percent (Heo 2005:32). A good many Korean peasants ended up working their own land for the new landlords, the Japanese.

With the development of dams and waterways on farmland, along with the introduction of new varieties of rice seeds with higher yields and new farming methods, Korean rice production increased 24.9 percent from 1910 to 1944 (Heo 2005:67).[18] Nevertheless, the beneficiaries of this increase were mostly the Japanese, along with a few Korean landlords. Heo Suyeol (2005), a Korean economist, methodically and persuasively delineates both Korean farm production and the circumstances of Korean peasant life in the period of Japanese exploitation.

Despite the increase in farm production and economic growth, this period is recorded as the most difficult that Korean peasants had to endure. David Steinberg (1989:46) describes these conditions: "By 1930, 75 percent of farmers were in debt, and three-quarters of that debt was to Japanese financial institutions. Tenancy and partial tenancy became the norm; some 12 million people (2.3 million families) were tenants, paying exorbitant rents. There was migration out of such rural areas: in 1925, 2.8 percent of such migrants went to Manchuria and Siberia, 16.9 percent to Japan, and 46.4 percent to Korean urban areas, where living standards were so low."[19] Korean peasants were not only exploited by the Japanese but uprooted from their own farms, which marked the beginning of the Korean diaspora as more farmers left rural communities. Korea was basically forced to become a rice-supplying colony for Japan, which had a rice shortage.

The Japanese history of colonialism described in this and a previous chapter explains why Koreans became so frustrated, if not downright angry, about the recent attempt by Japanese revisionists to misrepresent this history in revising a history textbook. The Japanese Educational Ministry's approval of these middle school history texts, published by Fuso Publishing, Inc. is an attempt to whitewash Japan's brutal imperialist behavior in the first half of the twentieth century. The textbooks omit or are evasive about critical aspects of Japan's inhumane behavior in its war of aggression, denying the 1937 Nanjing Massacre, omitting any reference to "comfort women," and deceptively describing the policy of *changssi* (identity creation) for Koreans that began in 1940. The textbook claims that *changssi* was carried out in accordance with the wishes of Koreans. This is incorrect, because I was there at the time, and I was forced to adopt a Japanese name. Otherwise, I would not have been able to enroll in public school.

Also, several Japanese prime ministers have visited or threatened to visit Yasukuni Shrine in Tokyo, where Japanese soldiers, including Class A criminals, are buried. This has renewed anti-Japanese sentiment throughout Korea and China. There have been territorial disputes over the tiny uninhabitable island of Dokdo, a rich fishing area, and over the name of a body of water between the Korean peninsula and the Japanese island of Hokkaido: Koreans claim it is the East Sea (Donghae), while the Japanese argue that it is the Sea of Japan. The recent moves of Japanese revisionists and the resurgence of a strongly right-wing ultra-conservatism is causing friction between Korea and Japan, and prompting emotional public rallies and protests across Korea and China.

I cannot speculate about the final outcome of these disputes, but I do know that most contemporary Japanese college students, judging from those who took my classes when I was teaching at the University of Tennessee, were not well informed about the Japanese role in Korea and China before and during World War II. In that sense they are analogous to North Korean youngsters who do not know much about the outside world. The question remains whether the Japanese can emulate what the Germans have done: admit their guilt for the past and move on.

Land Reform of 1949 and Egalitarianism

The Japanese colonialists not only robbed Korean peasant farmers by charging 50 percent or more of their crop in rent while leaving them no security of tenure on the their land (Brandt 1971:55), but they also made no effort to ameliorate social injustice by eliminating *yangban* privileges institutionalized during the Joseon dynasty. During the entire period of Japanese domination, the *yangban* class was left intact.

A major transformation in rural Korean communities took place through land reform that occurred after Korea's liberation from Japan. The Land Reform Act was introduced in 1949, one year after the formation of the Republic of Korea and following the U.S. Military Government policy to distribute Japanese-owned land to Koreans. Initiated by the leading right-wing KDP (Cumings 1981:98), the reform initially restricted the maximum amount of land a family could own to 29,752 square meters (9,000 *pyeong*). The tenant who received ownership of the land from the existing landlord would pay, over five years, a price equivalent to 1.5 times the average annual product of the land.

Unlike the North Korean Land Reform Act of 1946, which confiscated land from landlords without compensation, the Land Reform Act of 1949 allowed landlords in South Korea to receive bonds from the government, which took on the task of collecting the payments from the former tenants (Kim 1992:460–474). Edward S. Mason and his associates (1980:237) have calculated that "In actual practice, landlord bonds with a face value of 30 *sŏk* (equals 5.12 U.S. bushels), of rice sold on the market for the equivalent of only 3.5 *sŏk*, in effect virtually wiping out landlord assets.[20] An average former tenant, on the other hand, might be paying 6 *sŏk* a year to the government, 30 percent of his harvest."

Many believed that the Korean Land Reform Act of 1949 was very successful, because "confiscation and redistribution of the land and income of a relatively small number of landlords thus can be seen to have had a large impact on a great many people" (Mason et al. 1980:237–239). Steinberg (1989:189) sums up the meaning of the Land Reform Act rather convincingly:

> Land reform was important to Korea in equity terms in both South and North. It may have only marginally improved production and did not in any major sense redistribute income in the society as a whole, but more important in the short term it produced a state of shared rural poverty that, with other factors, defused political activism in the countryside; in the longer

perspective, land reform prevented some of the inequalities of maldistribution of income in the early years of independence. Whether the reform was accompanied most effectively is a separate issue, but all the Confucian states have implemented major land reforms (China, Japan, Korea, Taiwan, and Vietnam) or, like Singapore and Hong Kong, have no rural base.

Most of all, the Land Reform Act officially eliminated some residual aspects of former *yangban* class status and brought about egalitarianism in the minds of peasant farmers. Even though some elements of yangban governance still linger to a certain extent, other criteria such as educational attainment and individual wealth for all are now considered more important. In this sense, the Land Reform Act brought revolutionary change to the long-rooted *yangban* tradition and its legacy.

New Village Movement

As the military-led Korean government was bringing about unprecedented economic growth and rapid industrialization via the successful implementation of the first and second five-year economic development plans (1962-1971), it was able to give some attention to Korea's rural-sector development. In 1970, because of his own personal zeal to bring about modernization in rural Korea, President Park Chung-hee introduced the New Village Movement, "*Saemaeul Undong*."[21] Perhaps it was no accident that President Park initiated the movement because he was born and grew up in a remote mountainous village, and later taught there for a few years as an elementary school teacher. The experience of rural poverty was in his bones, and he believed it necessary to improve the condition of rural villages and their infrastructure (Kim 2002:53).

The New Village Movement was a nationwide movement that mobilized over 30,000 Korean villages. Centered primarily on rural-area development, it was devoted to improving the welfare of rural people. It was a deliberate process in which different kinds of agents and personnel (often young and vigorous, with military experience, but not members of the traditional village elite)[22] were mobilized to bring about fundamental changes in various aspects of rural villages. The central training headquarters was established at Suwon in 1972, and eventually there were eighty-five training institutions throughout the country.[23]

The New Village Movement's projects ranged from plans for improvement in the physical environment, such as building farm roads, village entrance roads, sanitary water systems, rural electrification, village halls, small bridges and small-scale irrigation systems, to income-generating projects such as special crops, livestock, and marketing arrangements. Whang (1981:25-27) provides a full list of these various ventures.

Beginning in 1974, as it spread across the nation, the New Village Movement expanded to urban and suburban areas, including industrial plants and schools, and even to military bases. The objectives of the movement were broadened in scope to include spiritual enlightenment and urban factory projects. The movement extended to social leaders such as university professors, journalists, and lawyers. At its height, government officials wore uniforms to symbolize the movement. Even taxi and bus drivers wore distinctive caps. Eventually, the movement no longer focused on rural-development projects became a national mobilization project for political purpose.

Although the Korean government allocated a huge budget for the movement, a large share of the investment in the project was made by rural people themselves in the form of donations of labor, land, and even cash.[24] For instance, the government provided each of over 30,000 villages with over 300 free bags of cement for the improvement of village dikes, roads, and community wells. An unfortunate byproduct of this development was the so-called "concrete mania," which destroyed the ecological and aesthetic beauty of the rural villages.

Even after the assassination of President Park in 1979, the fifth republic under President Chun Doo-hwan inherited the New Village

Movement. President Chun's emphasis was on various welfare projects, including the extension of medical-care centers to rural areas and special education programs for rural young women. However, in the Sixth Republic, under President Rho Tae-woo, the movement ground to a halt largely due to the scandal resulting from the overcharges, abuse of funds, corruption, and tax evasion committed by President Chun's younger brother, who had been head of the organization from 1981 to 1987. He was finally sentenced to seven years in prison for the illegal appropriation of $5.8 million (Lee 2003:180; Steinberg 1989:149).

There is no question that the New Village Movement brought about many improvements in rural villages. Most obvious were physical changes: straw or thatched roofs were replaced with roofs made of cement tiles, tin, plaster, or galvanized sheets of iron in various colors; easy-access roads for vehicles and roto-tillers, culverts, and bridges were built with cement; latrines were dug; village wells were remodeled; the introduction of a new variety of rice, which guaranteed a higher yield than traditional ones, was readily accepted. A more significant change affected the spirit of the villages. The villagers' tendency to depend on government initiation for every project was replaced by a reliance on their own initiative and cooperation. Furthermore, the New Village Movement, "by providing status to young, non-traditional leadership, has been one of the most effective means of destroying the traditional-oriented social system, one of the goals of the movement" (Steinberg 1989:149-150).

On a personal note, when I visited my home village in the late 1980s after having been away since the early 1960s, I was shocked by changes to the village's landscape brought about by the New Village Movement. As a classic countryside village, it is located in a remote and isolated mountainous region in the northeastern region of South Korea. Because of the movement, however, access roads to the village had been widened and paved with cement. The houses now had both hot and cold running water in indoor kitchens, refrigerators and TVs (because electricity was available), and direct-dial telephones that could reach anywhere in the world.

Perhaps it might be naive sentimentality, but I was yearning for the old thatched roofs. I was disappointed to find odd-looking styles of housing of dubious aesthetic quality at best. Villagers assumed that those houses were Western style, but to me the style was neither Western nor Korean. The villagers complained that the new roofs that replaced the old thatched ones were inefficient for heating and cooling. The thick straw roofs used to provide insulation that prevented heat loss in winter and served as a barrier against the blazing sunlight in summer. Now, the roofs of the houses are so thin that people can hardly endure the summer heat. Clearly, some changes introduced by the New Village Movement were incompatible with the traditional way of life in rural Korea, which has evolved for thousands of years in harmony with the weather and other ecological conditions.

Despite the obvious improvements brought about by the New Village Movement, it has also attracted criticism. Kwang-Ok Kim (1998:18) sums up these concerns:

> ⋯ the Saemaŭl Movement was far from being a civil movement as its communal ideology was produced and controlled by the state. Furthermore, the state evaluated and justified the legitimacy of the communities. In short, individuals became the object of state management through the medium of competitive performance. During this period, traditions gradually disappeared as state power strengthened in the course of industrialization and urbanization. These changes led to the migration of people from villages to cities. Thus, traditional sociocultural elements that constituted traditional life-style were lost.

Steinberg (1989:150) points out that in such a movement, "the potential for mobilizing is obvious. Few societies in ostensibly democratic states are so mobilized and controlled."

Ironically, while Koreans themselves became increasingly critical of the New Village Movement, many delegations from 133 countries, including a nineteen-member delegation of Iraqis from northern Iraq (where Korean troops, called "Zaytun,"[25] were stationed in Arbil) came to Korea to learn something about the New Village Movement in order to adopt it as a role model for their own rural development.[26] China likewise looked to the movement as a model to revitalize rural Chinese villages.[27]

Massive Exodus of Rural Peasants to Urban and Industrial Zones

Despite the deliberate effort of the Korean government to revitalize Korean rural villages via the New Village Movement since 1970, these villages have nonetheless faced a most difficult time largely because of the massive exodus of rural peasant farmers to urban and industrial zones, a side effect of the inequity of Korean income distribution between urban and rural areas. By the late 1960s, before the initiation of the New Village Movement, the income of rural peasant farmers had fallen to about half that of urban salaried wage workers (Steinberg 1989:153).[28]

However, improvements in the rural sector brought about by the New Village Movement along with increases in rice prices reduced the income gap between rural and urban areas. The average annual household income in rural areas in 1970 when the New Village Movement was initiated was 75.6 percent of what it was in urban areas. From 1974 to 1988, except for three years (1979, 1980, and 1987), the average annual household income in rural Korea even exceeded the urban average. Nevertheless, rural household income started to lag behind urban areas once more, beginning in 1989. In 2000, rural household income had returned to its level in 1970, and this disparity continues.[29]

On the one hand, rapid economic growth gave the Korean government energy and resources to spare for the improvement of the rural economy and way of life. On the other hand, unprecedented economic growth and industrialization through a series of successful five-year economic development plans also had detrimental consequences for rural development. The lower income and poor living conditions in rural areas — despite improvements brought about by the New Village Movement — motivated rural farmers to leave their villages for urban areas, where higher wages and modern living conditions, especially a better prospect for the education of their children, were major attractions. Urban and industrial zones have become a "black hole" into which massive numbers of rural migrants are absorbed. Some farmers abandoned their rural farmhouses when they left their villages. There are no reliable statistics on how many rural houses have been abandoned, but one can easily see them in rural villages.

Consequently, the largest proportion of the rural population is now those fifty and older (52.4 percent).[30] Korea's Rural Development Administration estimates that by 2010, the proportion of the rural population aged sixty and older will swell to 46.9 percent. Since the average life expectancy of Koreans has increased to 78.2 years, an increase of 8.4 years over the past 20 years (one of the fastest growing rates in the world), the population of the elderly in rural Korea will continue to increase.[31]

Most farmers who remain in rural villages tend to be older, while young productive workers leave, creating a critical shortage of farm labor. This shortage in turn reduces the amount of land under cultivation because the farming capacity of the elderly is so limited. Farmland is also shrinking each year. It went from 2,298,000 hectares in 1970 to 1,876,000 hectares in 2001, an average annual reduction of 21 percent from 1970 to 2001.[32]

An uneven distribution of age and sex in the rural population has created several problems. Next page Figure, which shows the age and sex distribution of Koreans in 1955, resembles a fine pyramidal triangle, while the other Figure, which reflects the results of the 2005 census, looks like a flattened pot. Since there are fewer children of elementary school age, between six and twelve (only 8.4 percent of the total population), many rural elementary schools have already closed,

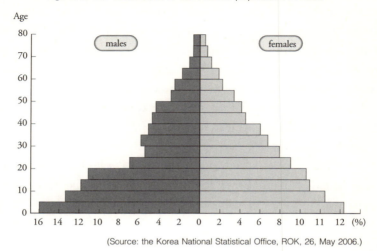
Age and sex distribution of the Korean population in 1955
(Source: the Korea National Statistical Office, ROK, 26, May 2006.)

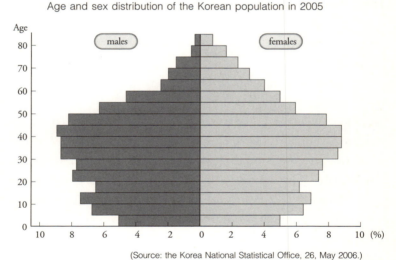
Age and sex distribution of the Korean population in 2005
(Source: the Korea National Statistical Office, 26, May 2006.)

and the number of such closures is on the rise.[33]

In Gangwon-do province, to the east of Seoul, has a rugged terrain of mountains and rivers that attract tourism and sports enthusiasts,

However, 310 elementary schools in the province were closed between 1990 to 2000, and many others are scheduled to close in the near future or be forced to merge with other schools for lack of students. This problem is not limited to Gangwon-do province but is a nationwide phenomenon. In fact, the Ministry of Education and Human Resources Development has to decide either to close or merge 1,976 elementary schools throughout the country.[34] The crisis extends to middle and high schools as well.[35]

Furthermore, there are a limited number of women of child-bearing age in rural areas (16.6 percent of the total female population in rural villages), and that number is decreasing each year.[36] Newborn babies are deemed precious, literally, because they are scarce, so much so that some municipal governments, such as Donghae, Inje, Yangpyeong, Yeoncheon, Mokpo and eight other cities give mothers of newborns gold bracelets, silver necklaces, and other precious gifts to congratulate them for bearing children. Still, many people are skeptical about whether such gifts will induce a high fertility rate.[37] The low fertility rate in rural areas is clearly exacerbated by the low birth rate nationwide.

In addition, in rural Korea there are fewer marriageable women than men between twenty and thirty years of age; consequently, there is a shortage of women these men can marry. Furthermore, rural women tend to avoid marrying rural men because they know that if they do, they will have the same difficult life as their parents, with hard work on the farm, few rewards, and limited educational opportunities for their children. This exacerbates the scarcity of marriage partners for rural men. Because of this imbalance between supply and demand, an increasing number of men from rural areas are marrying foreign women as discussed above.

The Changing Paradigm of Korea's Rural Villages

Rice: A Sentimental Crop for Korean Farmers

Traditionally, Koreans have considered rice to be more than just a staple food. Rice has been "an essential element in the moral order of the farmer's universe" (Brandt 1971:82; Hahm 2005:89-106). As Brandt (1971:80) recognized during his 1969 fieldwork in a rural village, "Most wealth is still calculated in terms of rice — a commodity that is, of course, readily transferable into other forms of property." Anthropologist Hanhee Hahm (2005:89-106) reports that since rice has been so deeply embedded in Korean culture for so long, Korean people's morality, values, and even worldview are attached to the culture of rice farming.

Koreans' preoccupation with rice has been so profound that Korea's yearly rice production has steadily increased from 1970 (4,090,000 tons) to 2002 (5,515,000 tons), due largely to an adequate supply of fertilizer and insecticide, mechanized farming methods, and the introduction of new varieties of hybrid seeds that give better yield than the old varieties. From 1970 to today, Korea has supplied over 90 percent of its own rice, except for a couple of bad years, 1994 and 1996. In addition, the surplus of rice that is stockpiled is also increasing, amounting to over 1 million tons in 2004.[38]

Despite these accomplishments, wet-rice farmers have been discouraged by the external pressure imposed by the Uruguay Round Agreement (UR), which requires the implementation of a Minimum Market Access of from 1 to 4 percent of the total consumption of rice. Since the 2004 WTO and the FTA push for market liberalization, Korean rice farmers have felt threatened by such agreements. Most Korean farmers worry about the imminent opening of the domestic rice market to foreign imports. In December 2004, Korea reached an agreement with nine rice-exporting countries, including the U.S., China, and Australia, to keep its tariff-waiver status on rice imports in exchange for expanding market access.

Beginning in the middle of October 2005, a series of farmers' protests were aimed at stopping the ratification of the rice-pact agreement by the National Assembly. Korean farmers worry about the opening of the domestic rice market to relatively inexpensive foreign rice. For instance, the Korean rice price is more than six times the U.S. market price. Korean farmers predict a gloomy future in which Korea might be forced to open its market to other agricultural products as well. On 1 April 2004, Korea and Chile signed a FTA, but rice was excluded from that agreement because Chile is not a rice-producing country by any means.[39] In the FTA between Korea and the United States, which was agreed upon on 2 April 2007, rice was excluded from the package of the agreement.

Because of these bleak prospects for the domestic farming of rice, the size of Korean rice farmland shrank from 1.2 million hectares in 1974 to 980,000 hectares in 2005. Jeollanam-do province, the highest rice-yielding province, has been hit most severely: in Jeollanam-do, for instance, about 204,602 hectares of wet-rice farmland in 2001 has shrunk to 190,090 hectares in 2005.[40] Korean rice consumption has also diminished from 5.4 million tons in 1980 to 4.7 million tons in 2004, the lowest amount since 1975.[41] One possible explanation for this reduction in rice consumption despite a population increase is the change in diet patterns from rice-centered Eastern food to Western food, including bread, pizza, and other fusion food, especially American-style fast food.

It is noteworthy that McDonald's, the American fast-food giant, opened its first store in Seoul in 1988. One year later, in 1989, its annual sales volume reached 100 billion *won* (about $106 million), and a decade later, in 2000, its sales doubled to 200 billion *won* (about $213 million), with 300 restaurants in Korea. The Korean fast-food brand Lotteria and Domino Pizza's annual sales volumes are identical to that of McDonald's. Pizza Hut has sold the most: in 2004 Pizza Hut sold nearly 400 billion *won* (about $426 million) worth of pizza to Koreans, especially to young Koreans. The market share of non-rice fast food may be the biggest challenge to Korean rice consumption.

Commercialization

As the rice-centered rural farming paradigm is changing, Korean farmers have begun to cultivate various cash crops. They have recognized that, for market-oriented cash crops, un-irrigated paddy farmland (*bat*) is more valuable than irrigated wet farmland (*non*). Using paddy lands, farmers have started to raise cucumbers, tomatoes, watermelons, strawberries, mushrooms, Chinese cabbage, bell peppers, turnips, herbal plants for herbal medicines, and other vegetables. In 2006, for instance, Korean farmers exported bell peppers, eggplants, cucumbers, and pears to Japan, which accounted for almost the entire Japanese import market share of those products. Together with those crops, by exporting lilies (92.6 percent of Japanese import share), paprika (63.9 percent), and watermelons (58.1 percent), in 2007 Korean farmers earned $1,723,200 from Japan.[42] Such market-oriented cash crops can be grown year-round using greenhouses. Even in cold winter weather,[43] farmers can supply fresh fruits and green vegetables to customers. Such market-oriented farmers tend to be more aggressive in increasing produce per unit of land by utilizing a variety of means. They also tend to specialize in specific products and to become commercialized.

Several auspicious conditions have encouraged the commercialization of farming.[44] First, demand for non-staple and non-grain items, such as fresh fruits, vegetables, and fish has increased due to a growing urban population resulting from industrialization and the influx of rural migrants into cities. Second, because of the development of transportation and the expansion and paving of highways, farmers can now easily access urban consumers in a matter of a few hours, thus preserving the freshness of the produce. Such a speedy delivery system has revolutionized cash-crop farming (Keidel 1980:148). Third, urban demands for a variety of food are further met by technological advances, especially the introduction of vinyl greenhouses, coupled with the zeal, motivation, and commercial outlook of today's farmer.

Most fishermen have taken advantage of the advanced technology of aquaculture instead of depending on traditional fishing methods that employ small vessels. Seaweed, shrimp, and other shellfish, especially high priced ear shells (*jeonbok*), have been grown domestically in aqua-farms. The income of fishermen has risen steadily since the introduction of aquaculture on a large scale. There are many aqua-farms in inland ponds that raise all sorts of freshwater fish through the application of new fish-farming technologies.

Technological Innovation

Not that long ago in Korea, human muscle and oxen were the major sources of energy for tilling farmland and harvesting crops. Now, roto-tillers have replaced oxen for tilling fields, and combines, like moving factories, are used to harvest crops. Currently, many farmers have taken advantage of information technology. A growing number of Korean farming villages now have the skills and technology that can connect them to the commercial opportunities in cyberspace.

Beginning on 27 December 2001, the provincial government of Gangwon-do province and the city of Wonju designated the mountainous village of Hwangdun-ri, near Wonju of Gangwon-do province, a "Cyber Village" to demonstrate how modern information technology could be applied to farming. Computers with broadband connection were installed in the village's 160 households. Internet TV and telephones with visual screens were installed in sixty-six households. The village headquarters office provided training facilities to teach Internet skills and other information technology. The results have been astonishing. The villagers can now find all the necessary information about farming, including the prices of farm products, daily. Also, each household has an e-mail address with which to communicate with the outside world, thus freely and easily overcoming physical isolation. Government documents can be readily requested or acquired online without villagers having to make actual trips to various offices. Village students can submit their homework to school via the school homepage. Parent-teacher conferences can also be conducted online. The village health office monitors the community's patients, diagnosing and consulting with physicians who work in large hospitals in Wonju, the largest city in the region, via the Internet without the necessity of visiting those hospitals.[45]

It has been reported that farmers in Doheung-ri in Gyeongsangbuk-do province are now in the habit of checking the daily weather and the price of farm products on their home PC via the Internet every morning at about 6 o'clock.[46] Recognizing farmers' growing interest in information technology and its practical application to farming, the Ministry of Government Administration and Home Affairs and the provincial and municipal governments have selected additional villages to receive information technology. As of 13 March 2003, over seventy such villages have been designated. The numbers are growing, and eventually this will become a nation-wide campaign.[47]

Farmers have also begun to see the impact of information technology on produce sales, as demonstrated by the increase in mushroom farmers' income in Tosim-ri, a village located 1,000 meters above sea level in Bonghwa County, my home county, in the northeastern corner of Gyeongsangbuk-do province. The county is known to be one of the most isolated, remote, and resource-poor counties in Korea. Nevertheless, it is well known for its pine-tree mushroom (*songi* or *Tricholoma matsutake*), which holds the special aroma of pine trees. This species grows only under pine trees and cannot really be domesticated. Because of its remoteness and isolation, the village was designated a model cyber village by the government in August 2003. One-hundred-and-twenty villagers received PCs from the government, and the villagers have been trained to use them.

Since the villagers learned how to use computers, they have begun to sell their mushrooms via the Internet directly to urban consumers. Before the introduction of information technology, the village's mushroom sales were only 4 million *won* (about $4,264) in 2002, but after using the Internet in 2004, sales-volume went up to 245 million *won* (about $261,000), almost sixty-times more than the sales of the pre-information technology year. The villagers expected that in 2005 sales would go up to 300 million *won* (about $319,800).[48] Because of the practical application of information technology in mushroom gathering and sales, cash-hungry villagers in a rugged and remote mountainous village have become richer than ever.

Now information technology is poised to bring about another revolution in rural villages. In October 2005, SK Telecom (SKT) together with Green-net introduced a ubiquitous system that can control the temperature inside vinyl greenhouses and poultry farms from anywhere and at any time through a cellular phone connection (mobile hand phones). If this system is widely adopted by rural farmers, there is no telling what the future will hold for farming methods.[49]

An Emerging New Elite in Korean Farming Villages

The massive exodus of Korea's rural population, particularly younger people, toward urban and industrial zones has created an "empty-nest" situation in rural villages. Nevertheless, despite these changes, the outlook is positive for the future of Korea's rural villages because there is now a trend of highly educated young professionals moving into the rural sector.

During the financial crisis of 1997 and 1998, Korea received a loan from the IMF to address the critical shortage of foreign currency in the country. At that time, some highly educated people decided to seek employment in the rural sector where there was less competition for jobs. Some chose to go to rural areas in order to take advantage of government aid of some 60 million *won* (about $63,965) that would be provided for their relocation and adjustment to a new life. Although their numbers may be relatively small, some urban elite now choose to live in rural areas and raise their families there simply because the quality of life is better than in urban areas.

According to a report,[50] in 2005, although the overall number of farmers had declined by 1.5 percent since 2004, the number of highly educated people, those with an education level of two years of college and above, had increased in rural areas by 7.7 percent. The proportion who graduated from four-year colleges and universities was 15 percent (87,000), the highest ever. Some educated Koreans have relocated to rural areas to improve their quality of life by avoiding crowded conditions, traffic jams, pollution, congestion, and other ills that pervade large cities. Despite the challenges of rural life, they prefer this environment to an urban one. In order to enable a smooth transition for these relocated people, the National Headquarters for Back to Rural Farming (Jeonguk Gwinong Undong Bonbu), a non-profit organization founded on 19 September 1996, provides various adjustment programs and offers vocational training in various schools.

If these new farmers can draw upon their education and talent, as well as the professional experience they acquired during their previous urban jobs, Korean villages will have a new breed of cultivators. Mechanized farming methods, coupled with information technology, may enable a highly motivated, energetic, and skillful few to accomplish the same tasks that required more workers in the past.

Even if the demand for rice, its production, and the farmland devoted to its cultivation have all decreased in recent years, shifting to a value-added variety of rice and replacing the heavy use of chemical fertilizer with organic farming methods may attract Korean consumers conscientious about eating healthy food. Then rice, which has been such a vital part of Korean life for so long, may regain its status as a major staple.

CHAPTER 6

Religion and Belief

Foreign observers often ask, "What accounts for the phenomenal growth of the Christian population in Korea?" and "How have Koreans acquired an international reputation for their ardent devotion to Christianity?" To answer such questions, we need to examine the historical context of Korean religious belief. As Michael Breen (2004:44) has observed, "Many women go to 5 A.M. worship services before starting their children off to school." Breen was also curious about the phenomenon of people within the same family following different faiths: "It is common to find a husband who could loosely be called Confucian, a Buddhist wife and Christian children. What is striking is how similar Koreans are, whatever their formal religious affiliation" (Breen 2004:42).

Perhaps it is no exaggeration to say that the Korean peninsula is something of a "repository" for world religions. As a multireligious society, Korea is presently host to all sorts of religious beliefs, some animistic[1] and polytheistic,[2] and others monotheistic.[3] Some beliefs are homegrown and others have been introduced from abroad. Not only are a variety of religions present in Korea, but also a large percentage of the population follows one or more systems of belief. The number of Christians in Korea, both Protestants and Roman Catholics, is the greatest in Asia, with the exception of the Philippines, both in proportion as well as absolute numbers: in 2005 nearly 14 million Koreans, about 29.2 percent of the total Korean population, were Christians.[4] In the capital city of Seoul alone, there are over 1,000 Buddhist organizations and temples and over 7,000 Christian organizations and churches, as well as the Confucian headquarters of *Seonggyungwan*, the headquarters of Cheondogyo, and several Muslim mosques. All these religions coexist symbiotically, yet none of them is an exclusive representative of Korean culture.

Inclusiveness and Syncretism

Inclusiveness

Korean religious inclusiveness is one reason why Korea is a multireligious society. There is a general assumption that all gods, whether one knows something about them or not, must be honored equally or at the very least not made objects of contempt. Koreans trust that all religions benefit humanity in some way, so they are all equally good. To a certain extent, Koreans respect the religious beliefs of all other people, so there is no particular reason to foist one's own particular religion onto others. Such a view is in stark contrast to the Western, and especially American, notion that "religion is to be more and more exclusive" (Hsu 1981:254).

Korean religious inclusiveness is such that different members of a family can believe in different religions. Anthropologist Jo Heung-yun and his colleagues (Yun et al. 1994:ii) offer this example: on a given weekend within a family, the mother-in-law goes to a shaman to attend a *gut* (a shaman ritual), one daughter-in-law attends a Christian church, another has joined a new religious group, and yet another visits a Buddhist temple. Meanwhile, the father and head of the household participates in a discussion among Confucians while mountain climbing. Such religious independence among family members seldom disturbs the harmony of family relations. Usually no one in the family coerces or antagonizes other members because they have different

Several Buddhist monks decorate a Christmas tree in Jogyesa in Seoul to celebrate Christmas

religious preferences.

On 9 October 1993, at a memorial service for a former professor of mine and several other dignitaries who died in a terrorist bombing in Rangoon, Myanmar (formerly Burma) while accompanying the President of South Korea on a state visit ten years earlier, I witnessed another example of religious inclusiveness. A Catholic priest, Protestant minister, Buddhist monk, and three other religious clergymen officiated, and no one who attended the service complained about how it was conducted.

The celebration of national holidays provides further evidence of Korean religious inclusiveness. Religious holidays include Buddha's birthday on 8 April of the lunar calendar, Chuseok (the Harvest Festival), Gaecheonjeol (National Foundation Day based on the Dangun mythology), and Christmas. Korea is probably the only country in the world to have such diverse religious holidays.

It is interesting that China and Japan practice a similar religious inclusiveness. Francis L.K. Hsu (1981:254), a well-known anthropologist who studied China reports that "The Chinese may go to a Buddhist monastery to pray for a male heir, but he may proceed from there to a Taoist shrine where he beseeches a god to cure him of malaria." Japanese anthropologist Harumi Befu (1971:96) has observed that in Japan "the same person may worship deities of different religions without any feeling of conflict. For example, a Japanese might pray at the Buddhist altar at home in the morning and go to a neighborhood Shinto shrine in the afternoon ··· Moreover, there are religious edifices which enshrine deities of different religions. For instance, there may be a Buddhist temple on the premises of a Shinto shine, or vice versa" (Befu 1971:96).[5]

Syncretism

Korean religious syncretism is another factor contributing to Korea's multireligious society. In a sense, all religions are syncretic, yet syncretism is more prominent in the religious attitude of Koreans than that of any other people. A Korean religious concept of a deity may combine elements derived from different religions.

The distinction between indigenous Korean beliefs and Shamanism, for instance, is so blurred that sometimes it exists only in the mind of the scholar analyzing Korean folk beliefs. An anthropologist Kim Seong-Nae (2002:359-394), for example, has provided detailed information about whether Shamanism is part of Korea's indigenous beliefs or imported. Most ordinary Koreans, however, are unconcerned with the historical derivation of a religious concept.

In addition to Shamanism, most new religions, such as Donghak (later Cheondogyo), Wonbulgyo (Won Buddhism), Daejonggyo, and many minor religions, which were founded in the late nineteenth century and the early twentieth century, are syncretic, arising from the combination of two or more other religions. The number of new religions formed in this way is estimated to be over 300. The socio-economic and political environment of nineteenth-century Korea, which was facing challenges from the West and Japan, made Koreans more receptive to new religious hope and promises in the same way that the mass of the T'ang Chinese were inclined by the tenor of the times to accept Buddhism.

Korean religious inclusiveness and syncretism make it difficult to determine the precise numbers of believers in Korea. If Koreans were asked about their religious preferences, a great many would say that they do not have any particular religion. In fact, according to the 2005 Korean census, 46.9 percent of the total population responded in just this way.[6] For this reason, trying to assess the size of Korea's religious population is an art, if not a dubious venture.

Korean Native Beliefs

Anthropologists have demonstrated that although culture, including beliefs and religions, varies from society to society, the human personification of supernatural power in the form of gods or deities is a cultural universal, and Korea is no exception. Archaeologists have found signs of religious beliefs in cave paintings in which the predominant images are animals of the hunt. Many scholars think that this reflects a belief that the image was thought to have some power over events. Bangudae, a Korean archaeological site located in Ulju in Gyeongsangnam-do province, which is dated earlier than the Megalithic (2000 to 500 B.C.) by Sarah M. Nelson (1993:98) or from the late Bitsalmunui (comb and pit marked pottery) pottery period (Choe and Bale 2002:98), is home to an incised rock drawing that probably represents sun worship. The Dangun mythology symbolizes a sun god for the nation at its origin. Nevertheless, since the details of religions practiced in the distant past cannot be reconstructed by archaeologists simply from the remains of material culture, this chapter will cover only a few select religious beliefs.

Ancestor Worship and House Gods

Ancestor worship is one of the oldest Korean indigenous beliefs. Although Confucianism has also emphasized and promoted ancestor worship, Koreans practiced ancestor worship long before Confucianism was introduced to the peninsula. The "practice of lavish burials in Goguryeo is indicative of belief in ancestor worship, which in turn was based on the conviction that the living soul of an ancestor exerts a continuous influence on the well-being of descendants of a later generation" (Lee 1984:34). Ancestor worship became an elaborate ritual in the Goryeo period and was further enhanced during the Joseon dynasty as Confucianism was emphasized as a guiding metaphor for the destiny of the dynasty. Most wealthy *yangban* families built their own family shrines to store the tablets that symbolized their ancestors.

As part of ancestor worship, in an ordinary Korean's household there is also a house god in a jar called *josangdanji* (or jar of ancestors), which symbolizes the spirits of the ancestors of the house (Lee 2003:216-219).[7] Rice is stored inside this jar, which is covered with white paper and placed in one corner of the inner room on a high shelf. Food is served once a year in October by the housewife, who prays for good luck for her family.

There are also numerous deities for the house. The House Master God (*Seongju*), which is supposed to protect the family head, is symbolized by another jar filled with rice and barley and placed on the wooden floor (*maru*). Gyeongsang-do province uses a white paper instead of a jar. The housewife pays homage to this god with food. The Fire God (*Jowang*), which is supposed to protect the housewife, is placed in the kitchen and the housewife serves it clean water in a white cup every morning. The House Site God (*Teoju*) and the God of Wealth (*Eop*) are placed side by side in the backyard, near the platform that holds the jar. Both of these gods are also honored and recognized by the housewife once a year in a special ceremony. There is also the Young Lady of the Toilet God, who is still considered to be a young lady with a perverse nature. Ritual services for all house gods are performed by housewives, except in the Confucian style of ancestor worship.

Village Gods

In the past, almost all Korean natural villages had village gods whose role was to protect the village. These gods were called mountain gods or *Seonghwangdang*, also the name of a ritual performed in their honor on the fifteenth of January in the lunar calendar, and overseen by a master selected by the villagers. Nowadays, however, the observance of rituals concerning house gods and village gods is fading away, especially after the advent of the New Village Movement. For many Koreans, particularly young and educated villagers, worshipping both house gods and village gods is considered superstitious rather than genuinely religious. Recently, however, there has been a revival of these activities in what is called the "village-coming" gathering (*hyangto moim*), influenced by the Korean popular culture movement.

Dangun Myth and a Belief for the Nation

In Dangun mythology, the sun god symbolizes the origin of the nation. The god Dangun was the son of Hwanung, who came down from Heaven, and a bear-turned-woman, who lived on earth. The myth represents not only the beginning of the first Korean kingdom that was supposedly established in 2333 B.C., but is also the source for the national shrine to Korea's ancient religion at Pyeongyang. This mythology appears to be an attempt to enhance symbolically the divinity and authority of Dangun as a political leader in the first kingdom. According to Charles Allen Clark (1961:139), an American missionary, "In 2265 B.C., according to tradition, Tangoon [Dangun] first offered sacrifice to 'Hananim,' the God of the Heavens, at Hyulgu on the island of Kanghwa in the mouth of the Han River, twenty-five miles below the modern Seoul. Later he erected on that island on the Marisan Mountain a great altar of stone and earth seventeen feet high and six feet six inches square at the top, and that alter is still standing today."

Throughout Korean history, there have been numerous "founder's altars" erected by founders and/or kings who visited these altars to worship, an act that in turn promoted the unity and harmony of their subjects. Most of these altars developed into shrines, some of which were dedicated to the king's forebears and others to *sajik* or the gods of land and harvest. As late as the Joseon dynasty, emulating an old Chinese practice, the founder-king Taejo (Yi Seonggye) built an altar, *sajikdan*, in 1394 to worship the gods of land and harvest, offering prayers four times a year. This site and the shrine-like altar of *sajikdan* were erected to the west of the Capital building in Jongno-gu, Seoul, and the city block where the altar is located has been called Sajik-dong, after the altar, which has been preserved to this day.

Shamanism

Shamanism is one of the oldest religious beliefs in Korea and can be traced back to 4000 B.C. in the Neolithic period (Lee 1984:7-8). Although Shamanism is widely dispersed on the Eurasian continent, Korea has preserved it well, and it is still active (Lee 2003:222). Kim Seong-Nae (1999:139-207) has summarized the scholarly work on Korean Shamanism undertaken by scholars at home and abroad over the past 100 years.

Shamanism has a dualistic religious worldview in which the body and soul are seen as separate. Therefore, a particular soul or spirit can enter another body to create a phenomenon known as "possession." One particular characteristic of Shamanism is that the medium, known as "*mudang*" (female shaman), perceives this possession physically. The major functions of a shamanistic ritual service are performed for the purpose of securing good luck, for effecting a cure of physical or mental illness, or for pacifying the spirits of deceased family members.

Shaman rituals are performed by shamans or *mudang* who make contact with gods (benign spirits) or evil spirits through special ritual techniques: *gut*, a major shaman ritual, and *chiseong*, a minor offering. *Gut* includes paraphernalia that echo the distant past and use ancient percussion instruments. The whirling *mudang's* ritual performance is very noisy because of the sounds of the large drum (*janggo*), fiddles, gongs, pipes, and dangling ornaments attached to clothing that glitter and make rhythmic sounds during the whirling dance. The ritual service usually lasts for two days, and since one shaman alone cannot dance for two days straight, usually four or five shamans, along with musicians, perform together as a group.

A scene of a shaman ritual

Since ancestor worship, Dangun mythology, and other native Korean belief systems all include some shamanistic elements, it is difficult to deny a close relationship among them (Kim 1982:3-8). Nevertheless, many scholars (Akiba 1957; Brandt 1971:23; Dix 1980:47; Kendall 1979:159-191) indicate that ancestor worship and Shamanism are different ritual systems. Roger Janelli and Dawnhee Yim (1982:166-167) point out an additional difference. They assert that while ancestor worship idealizes ancestors who are benevolent and never harm their descendants, in Shamanism ancestors are sometimes threatening, and their dependency on their closest relatives channels their acts of affiliation toward them.

To become a shaman, one has to experience the "shaman illness." During her lifetime, mostly in her adolescence or late in life, a woman might suffer from an unknown illness, either bodily pain or mental exhaustion, dreaming of demons or gods and experiencing hallucinations and illusions. Knowing that there is no cure for these symptoms, the woman visits a shaman to ascertain whether or not she has a shaman illness. If so, she becomes a novice shaman, and the older shaman she consulted becomes her godmother. The novice takes the god who appeared in her dream as her guardian deity (Lee 2003:222).

In the Joseon dynasty, shamans and shaman devotees were classed with other outcast groups and subject to discrimination. During the Japanese occupation, the Japanese attempted to eliminate Shamanism in their effort to eradicate Korea's native religious beliefs. The Japanese imposed their Shintōism on Koreans under the pretext of creating a single Japanese entity (*naeseon ilche* in Korean and *naisen ittai* in Japanese).[8] Arresting Korean shamans was a common occurrence (Yun et al. 1994:57). The liberation of Korea from Japan after World War II did not liberate Shamanism. The Western thought and ideology that came along with Christianity relegated Shamanism to a primitive belief or superstition, a view propagated widely by the Japanese during their occupation.[9] In the 1970s, shamans had to face yet another challenge, this time from the New Village Movement (*Saemaeul Undong*). Believing that Shamanism and its rituals were in the same category as excessive drinking and gambling, the movement declared war on the practice. Leaders of the movement together with some civil servants destroyed numerous shaman shrines and prohibited the performance of *gut* rituals.[10] Because of this repression, in Jeju-do, for instance, only twenty or thirty out of 100 or so shaman shrines have survived (Cho 1998:99). The ordeals of Jeju-do shamans seem to epitomize the history of shamans in Korea as a whole.

After enduring all these hardships imposed on them for so long, Korean shamans finally have allies and sympathizers. International scholars and tourists from Japan and the United States were the first groups in recent times to be sympathetic to Shamanism (Kendall 1996:517). Laurel Kendall immersed herself in Shamanism, and on the basis of her fieldwork in a village published the book *Shamans, Housewives and Other Restless Spirits* (1985), which has had a broad audience in the English-speaking world.

Another group sympathetic to Shamanism, mostly young, anti-government protesters and intellectuals who initiated the Korean popular-culture movement, emerged in the 1970s. These proponents often romanticized Shamanism as the most victimized segment of Korean culture. During their anti-government demonstrations and rallies, they utilized *gut* rituals, including shaman dance and music. College students often invited shamans to their festivities, believing that Shamanism represents traditional Korean culture.

Shamanism has also been rejuvenated by the Cultural Heritage Administration (Munhwaje Gwallicheong) of the Ministry of Culture and Tourism, which in 1980 designated the shaman *gut* as one of the "intangible cultural properties (assets)" or *muhyeong munhwaje*. This designation means that Shamanism and its rituals are protected by the government, and that shamans receive some financial assistance from the government for their ritual performance, which has given Korean Shamanism a great boost.

Shamanism is being transformed as shamans adjust to Korea's increasing urbanization, industrialization, and commercialization. Nowadays, rural-based shamans move to cities and perform *gut* for urban clients engaged in high-risk petty-capitalist enterprises. Kendall (1996b:512-527) has traced the movement of shamans from rural villages to cities. Some shamans now work in women's beauty parlors, telling the fortunes of foreign clients from Japan and Taiwan while these tourists receive massages. Some shamans have their own websites to advertise their services, and others teach short courses in becoming a shaman at private tutorial schools.

There are some indications that although Shamanism is seeing a revival in cities, this is not the case in rural villages. However, no one knows for sure how many shamans and shaman devotees there are in Korea, because the National Statistical Office does not keep statistics on Korea's religious population. This is the responsibility of the Ministry of Culture and Tourism, which does not have a separate category for shamans and shaman devotees. The Korean Overseas Information Service (2003:441) estimates that there are well over 50,000 dues-paying shaman members of different shaman organizations in Korea. One of the largest shaman organizations, Daehan seunggong gyeongsin nyeonhapoe, has 183 branches and 40,000 members throughout Korea.

Foreign-born Religions in Korea

Confucianism

Originating in China, Confucianism was founded by Confucius. The name by which he is commonly known is actually a Latinized form of his real name, K'ung-fu-tzu (551-479 B.C.), which means Great Master K'ung. Nevertheless, Wei-ming Tu (1984:4), one of the foremost authorities in the studies of Confucianism, points out that "Confucius was not the founder of Confucianism in the sense that Buddha was the founder of Buddhism and Christ was the founder of Christianity." Rather, the story of Confucianism does not begin with Confucius alone but with the "family of scholars" or disciples who followed or advocated Confucian doctrines. Confucianism is not an organized religion, does not have clergymen, and does not teach the worship of a god or gods. Nor does it promise life after death (Tu 1998:3). Nevertheless, millions of Confucian devotees in China, Korea, Japan, and other Asian countries honor Confucius in much the same way that other peoples honor founders of religions.

The Basic Principle

The basic tenet of Confucianism teaches that humans are compelled by their nature to live with other humans in society. The universal human quality that leads them to do so is called *Jen*, which can be rendered in English as "benevolence," "human-heartedness," "person to personness," and "perfect virtue."[11] "Right action" is defined by Confucians in terms of the duties and obligations implicit in five basic relationships: ruler and subject, father and son, elder person (elder brother) and younger person (younger brother), husband and wife, and friend and friend. Except for the category of friend-and-friend, all these relationships involve the authority of one person over another.

Confucianism insists that the terms "father," "son," "ruler," "subject," "elder brother," "younger brother," "husband," "wife," and "friend" dictate a certain type of conduct. When a son is lovingly obedient to his father and the father dutifully responsible for his son,

Confucians say that the names of father and son have been rectified. The Chinese government made Confucius's teachings the official state philosophy, and in 124 B.C. the government established the Imperial University to educate future government officials in Confucian ideals.[12]

Nevertheless, from about A.D. 200 to 600, interest in Confucianism declined in China, and many Chinese turned instead to Buddhism and Taoism. Sometime in the 600s, however, a revival of interest in Confucian philosophy began. Starting with Han Yu (768-824) and ending with Chu Hsi (1130-1200), a new school of thought within the Confucian doctrine was developed to rediscover the meanings that had been lost over the centuries. Known as Neo-Confucianism, it emphasized the study and investigation of Li, which can be translated as "etiquette," "ritual," "ceremony," and "sacrifice" (Welty 1984:170). Beginning in the thirteenth century and continuing to the present, the thoughts and teachings of Chu Hsi became the orthodox interpretation of Confucianism. Many distinguished Neo-Confucians, such as Yi Hwang and Yi I, emerged during the Joseon dynasty, and the impact of Neo-Confucianism on Korea has been profound.

Introduction of Confucianism to Korea

Confucianism was introduced to Korea during the Three Kingdoms period (37 B.C.-A.D. 935). Goguryeo established a Confucian academy in 372 . In 682, a Confucian academy was also built in the Silla capital of Gyeongju (Deuchler 1992:14). During the late Goryeo and early Joseon periods, numerous exchanges between Korean and Chinese scholars stimulated the growth of Neo-Confucianism studies in Korea.

By the fourteenth century, Confucianism had become an integrated part of Korean culture, and since the sixteenth century, it has almost completely dominated Korean thought and philosophy (Yang and Henderson 1958). In a sense, Koreans were more Confucian than the Chinese, particularly in their devotion to Neo-Confucianism (Janelli and Yim 1982:177; Osgood 1951:332; Peterson 1974:28; Reischauer and Fairbank 1960:426). "Confucianism, for example, featured prominently in Korea, especially in the Yi dynasty [Joseon dynasty]," writes Weiming Tu (1984:10). "Indeed, from roughly the end of the 14th century to as recently as the 20th century, Korean culture has been greatly shaped by Confucian thought."

Neo-Confucian scholar officials were allies of the founder of the Joseon dynasty. The best-known Confucians of the time were appointed teachers at the highest National Confucian Academy, *Seonggyungwan*. Both teachers and students of the academy gathered to debate outstanding problems of Neo-Confucian thought. The kings of Joseon were pressured by the Confucians to replace traditional aspects of the people's religious life with Confucian principles (Deuchler 1992:106). Throughout the Joseon dynasty, the two most prominent Neo-Confucian scholars were Yi Hwang and Yi I. Yi Hwang was the foremost Korean Confucian philosopher of his age and interpreted Neo-Confucianism in Korea. He has often been quoted as the Chu Hsi of Korea, and he maintained a position that emphasized personal experience and moral self-cultivation as the essence of learning. His views had a great influence on Confucian scholarship in Japan,

Dosan Seowon where Yi taught his students

eventually evolving into one of the main schools of Japanese Confucian thought (Yoshio 1965, 1972:3–27). Yi I, the other prominent Korean Neo-Confucian scholar, was not only a philosopher but also a practitioner who put forward many reform proposals concerning the government, economy, and national defense.[13]

Religious Aspects of Confucianism
Debate about whether Confucianism is actually a religion in the Western sense may have no resolution. Tu (1998:3) states that although Confucianism is often grouped together with Buddhism, Christianity, Hinduism, and Taoism[14] as a major historical religion and has also exerted a profound influence on East Asian spiritual life, "it is not an organized religion." If Confucianism is a "religion," it is a religion without a god, and without any organized missionary tradition.

David L. Hall and Roger T. Ames (1987:245) aptly characterize Confucianism as a religion in these terms:

> We can illustrate the difference between the Judaeo-Christian emphasis upon worship and the classical Confucian focus upon achieving authoritative humanity (*jen*) by characterizing Confucius' religiousness as it is presented in the *Analects*.[15] If we were to understand Confucius' religiousness by interpreting it through Western categories and demanding an equal concern for worship, we would have to conclude that Confucius is religious in a limited sense.

For Confucius, religiousness is not characterized simply by worship. A more important component is how a person chooses to live his life (Hall and Ames 1987:246).

Despite scholarly arguments on the religiousness of Confucianism, Confucius himself was very concerned with religion as such, mentioning it only in passing. Although he appeared to believe in heaven (*cheon*)[16] and ancestors, Confucius spoke little about these beliefs. As Paul Thomas Welty (1984:171) has indicated, when

Confucianism became the orthodox doctrine of the empire, religious functions were incorporated into it.

Since its introduction to Korea, Confucianism has worked smoothly in tandem with native Korean religious beliefs and has provided a supernatural framework, cosmology, and moral guidelines for other religions. Some Confucian elements were incorporated with Shamanism, Cheondogyo, and even Shintōism in Japan in a syncretic way.

Aside from the religious aspects of Confucianism, in Korea Confucianism emphasizes traditional social relations, teaches the importance of a hierarchical order, and contains five basic principles of human social relations, of which the parental authority of father over son is the most valued. The highest virtue is filial piety (Choi 1979; Hsu 1970:78; Kim 1988b:127-128). Specifically, Confucianism emphasizes and highly values (1) education and training; (2) emphasis on the group, such as the family, organization, and state, over the individual, as distinguished from individual-centered Western values; (3) the family as the most important unit for economic activities; (4) five basic principles of human social relations for a harmonious social relationship; and (5) a positive rather than a pessimistic worldview (Kim 1992:13).

Confucianism and Its Role in Korea's Recent Economic Growth
Scholarship on the influence of Confucianism on economic development has not yet been fully evaluated. Some scholars, following Max Weber (1951), view Confucianism as a hindrance to economic development. Young-iob Chung (1989:152) is specifically critical of the role of Confucianism in Korean economic development: "Confucian teachings rejected training in economics for the pursuit of wealth and held business people in low esteem. The ruling elite, *yang-ban* [*yangban*], did not allow themselves to participate in profit-making enterprises."

Kyung-Koo Han (2003:9) reports that while the *yangban* "took great pride in the high degree of the Confucianization of Koreans" during the Joseon dynasty, many Koreans subsequently changed their evaluation of Confucianism. Specifically, "when Korea became colonized in 1910, Confucianism and all that was associated with it were identified as the main reasons for Korea's misfortune, and came under heavy attack." Kwang-Ok Kim (1998:20) also points out that the people who led the popular cultural movement challenged Confucianism because it "represented a hierarchical view of the world order, a tool to indoctrinate the people with the idea of absolute obedience to state authority. They claim also that these ideas were used by the political elite as ranking ideological base." Korean sociologist Kyuhan Bae (1987:79) has observed during his research on Hyundai automobile workers how "the government took advantage of traditional Korean values in order to build a loyal labor force." Without any doubt, Confucianism has been included as a part of traditional Korean values.

Nevertheless, even its critics agree that Confucianism had some indirect positive influence on Korean economic development, especially through its effect upon education (Kim and Kim 1989:208; Steers et al. 1989:130). "The Confucian emphasis on learning and competitive examination as a means of social achievement has long motivated the Koreans to pursue scholarly and educational endeavors, which are crucial to the acquisition and diffusion of knowledge — skills indispensable to development" (Chung 1989:130). Dwight H. Perkins' (1986:7) observation that leaders of economic development in Japan, Korea, Hong Kong, Taiwan, and Singapore "were influenced by Confucian values, used Chinese characters, and ate with chopsticks" may not be a frivolous one.

In explaining the role of Confucianism in East Asian economic growth, Tu (1984:90) distinguishes between politicized Confucianism and the Confucian ethic:

> Politicized Confucianism is the power of the state over society; politics over economics; and bureaucratization over individual initiative. This type of Confucianism, as a political ideology, needs

to be thoroughly critiqued before a country can be made dynamic. The other is the Confucian personal ethic which values self-discipline, going beyond egoism to become actively involved in the collective good, education, personal involvement, the work ethic and communal effort.

Tu believes the ethical aspects of Confucianism promote economic success. In fact, unexpectedly, the Confucian ethic has contributed to the rise of modern capitalism in East Asia. "This is analogous to the influence of what Max Weber has described as the Puritan ethic in the rise of traditional Western capitalism" (Tu 1984:142). Carter J. Eckert (1990:410), a historian and an expert on Korea, has expressed a similar view that the effect of Confucianism on East Asian economic growth, including Korea, was a case of "unintended consequences, similar to that of Calvinism on early Western capitalists."

Regardless of their positive impact on Korean industrialization and economic growth, Confucian values have been, and still are, thoroughly pervasive in Korean industrial relations. Clear evidence of Confucian influence has been demonstrated in anthropological fieldwork conducted in a Korean manufacturing plant. Examples include a system of male dominance, a paternalistic reward structure with extra fringe benefits, Confucian academy training, the New Factory Movement, the Labor Management Council, and formal authoritarian relations, which have grown out of the Confucian family concept (Kim 1992, esp. chapters 2-6).

Number of Confucian Devotees in Korea
Any assessment of the number of Confucians and Confucian devotees is dubious at best, for unlike Christians, Confucians do not have any notion of so-called "hard membership." Nor do they have churches, temples, or shrines where they gather together on a regular basis.

There are numerous Confucian organizations, including *Yurim*, which has 234 regional branches (*Hyanggyo*), and about 12,000 officials work within them. Judging from the number of people who practice

Confucian-style ancestor worship, *Yurim* estimates that the number of Confucians and Confucian devotees is over 10 million.[17] Others estimate that at least 91.7 percent of Koreans practice and believe in Confucianism (Yun et al. 1994:26). Geum Jangtae (Yun et al. 1994:140) reports that there were nearly 7 million Confucians in 1982. Nevertheless, according to the 2005 Korean Census, only 105,000 (0.2 percent) Koreans were classified as Confucians.[18]

Buddhism

Buddhism, an offshoot of Hinduism, was founded in the sixth century B.C. by Siddhartha Gautama (Gautama Buddha, 563-483 B.C.), son of a chieftain of the Sakya tribe, who was dissatisfied with Hinduism and founded the new religion by practicing asceticism. Buddhism in its original form was a highly esoteric, philosophical formula for personal salvation through the renunciation of worldly desires, thus avoiding rebirth in the endless cycle of reincarnation of the soul and resulting in the enlightened state of "Nirvana" or "desirelessness." Buddhism was originally a religion without a god, as was Confucianism, and consisted of a set of premises on how to avoid earthly suffering by following the proper procedures of spiritual mechanics or discipline specified in the Four *Noble Causes of Truth* and the *Eight-fold Path*.[19]

As Buddhism spread from India to the outside world, all kinds of local superstitions and theological systems were absorbed into it, producing an elaborate array of deities, saviors, saints, heaven, and hell that Gautama Buddha had never envisioned. Such an altered image of Buddhism is clearly evidenced in the settings of Korean Buddhist temples: "For example, almost every Korean Buddhist temple complex has a side chapel near the main worship containing a shrine to the mountain spirit, or tutelary deity of the spot, usually depicted as an old man with a pet tiger. This symbol is derived both from Chinese Taoist and its union with local animistic beliefs. The shrine receives due veneration along with the ceremonies in honor of Buddha that are performed at the temple, lest the local mountain spirits on whose land the temple stands should become angry" (*Handbook of Korea* 1983:196-

197). Such syncretic elements are visible in the *Mahayana* (or Greater Vehicle) school of Buddhism, which has been more prevalent in northern Asia, including China, Japan, and Korea than in the *Hinayana* school of Buddhism, which has been dominant in Southeast Asia.

Buddhism in Korea has been largely practical in nature. Its aim at the individual level has been to attain Buddhahood and at the social level to save living things. Individuals, the objects of salvation, are in the category of living beings; thus, regardless of their religious preference, people are regarded as objects of Buddhist salvation. In the spirit of inclusiveness, Koreans have incorporated Buddhism into the ancestor worship services for dead spirits. Descendants may have ritual services performed for their dead ancestors at any time. Although Buddha himself never mentioned it in his original writings, a characteristic of Korean Buddhism has been the addition of geomancy and superstition; thus, the most popular prayers are for childbearing (for a male offspring), for the development of the family, and for

Parents pray for their children to score well on the college entrance examination at a temple in Seoul

expelling bad spirits and illness (Lee 2003:233, 236), the same prayers that have been popular in Shamanism.[20] Nowadays, many Koreans go to Buddhist temples to pray that their children score well on the college entrance examination required for admission to Korea's prestigious colleges and universities.

Introduction of Buddhism to the Korean Peninsula

Buddhism arrived on the Korean peninsula in the fourth century, during the middle of the Three Kingdoms period. The northern kingdom of Goguryeo, which bordered on China, made the first contact with Buddhism when the Chinese monk Tudo visited the kingdom in 372, bringing with him a Buddha statute and Buddhist scriptures. Eventually, Buddhism was accepted by the royal houses of Goguryeo. In 384, a dozen years after Goguryeo had first encountered Buddhism, an Indian missionary, Marananta, came to Baekje via China. Buddhism was eventually accepted in Baekje without any significant discord. A century later, Buddhism was brought to the Silla royal house, with the arrival of the monk-envoy Wonpyo from Liang (502-557). King Beopheung (514-540) made every effort to secure the acceptance of Buddhism, but he was thwarted by the opposition of the Silla aristocracy, which led to the storied martyrdom of the high court noble Ichadon in 527 (Lee 1984:59). After that event, Silla officially recognized Buddhism in 535.

Buddhism flourished in the Three Kingdoms period under royal patronage.[21] Many temples and monasteries were constructed and hordes of believers converted. Buddhism became rapidly and deeply rooted in Korean society, eventually spreading to Japan. By the sixth century, Korea was exporting priests, scriptures, and religious artisans to Japan, forming the basis of early Buddhist culture in that country. Eventually, Buddhism became the state religion in all the Three Kingdoms, although government systems were still run along Confucian lines. United Silla produced magnificent Buddhist arts and temple architecture.

Bulguksa, the most famous of the Korean Buddhist temples, was built between 751 and 774, during the United Kingdom of Silla. The temple sprawls on the western slope of Toamsan and is the terrestrial paradise of the land of Buddha. From cornerstone to eave bracket, the design achieves the perfection of the golden mean and is a perfect combination of religion and art. The temple also boasts many priceless treasures and was registered on the UNESCO World Cultural Heritage List in December 1995.

Seokguram, the stone Buddha statue, sits in a grotto with a domed ceiling. This sculpture is the epitome of Korean Buddhism of the mid-eighth century, when Buddhist art flowered into its full glory following the unification of the Three Kingdoms by Silla. This sculptural work sums up the religious enthusiasm, architectural technology, and aesthetics of the Silla people and, like the Bulguksa, was also registered on the UNESCO World Cultural Heritage List in December 1995.

One non-material cultural impact of Buddhism in Silla was the development of the *hwarang* (*flower of youth*) warrior, a youth movement established by the Buddhist monk Wongwang in the early 600s. *Hwarang* consisted of young elites, often in their mid-teens, who

Bulguksa

primarily served a military function. The *hwarang* also had religious elements, however, and made pilgrimages to sacred mountains and river sites in Silla to pray for national peace and prosperity by performing ceremonial singing and dancing (Lee 1984:55). The ideal of *hwarang* combined the traditional age-rank system with the Buddhist concept of charity and the Confucian concept of order.[22]

The Goryeo dynasty that replaced United Silla supported Buddhism so enthusiastically that it created a Buddhist state. Priests became politicians and courtiers. In the thirteenth century, when the Mongols invaded Goryeo, the reaction of the Buddhist-oriented court was to seek divine assistance by carving the Buddhist scriptures onto wooden blocks for printing. The resulting *Tripitaka Koreana*, which consists of 81,258 panels and took sixteen years to complete, is considered to be one of the most outstanding contributions to the Buddhist canon. It is still on display at the Haeinsa, and was also registered on the UNESCO World Cultural Heritage List in December 1995.

Nevertheless, Buddhism in Buddhist-dominated Goryeo experienced a setback when King Gongmin (1351-1374) in the mid-fourteenth century appointed a corrupt priest, Sindon, to a high official post, sparking protests among the Confucian literati of the court. Anti-Buddhism was further perpetuated by the Neo-Confucian scholar Jeong Dojeon, who was a major figure in assisting Yi Seonggye to found the Joseon dynasty. Jeong rejected Buddhism as disruptive of mores and ruinous to the state. From this time on, Buddhist-style funerals and memorial rites were discontinued, replaced by the establishment of household shrines for ancestral tablets in the Confucian manner.

During the five-hundred-year history of the Joseon dynasty, Buddhism was suppressed, and the vast wealth and land holdings of the temples were seized. Buddhist monks were now treated the way shamans had been earlier, and denied entrance to the capital city by the Joseon court. To become a monk, one now had to receive permission from the government (Yun et al. 1994:34). In the late sixteenth century, during the Japanese invasion led by Toyotomi Hideyoshi, Buddhism was revived. Armies of monks rose up to protect the nation against the Japanese, but the invasion itself took a terrible toll, and temples and sacred objects were destroyed or plundered. Also, because of sporadic persecutions by the kings of the Joseon dynasty, most temples were built in or moved to remote mountainous locations. Nowadays, however, some small Buddhist temples or shrines are returning to the big cities, and one can easily spot them in the streets of Seoul.

When the Japanese took over as colonial rulers in 1910, there was some attempt by Japanese Buddhist sects to infiltrate Korean Buddhism. Nevertheless, to a certain extent Korean Buddhism has been acculturated to that of Japanese Buddhism. For instance, Japanese monks were allowed to marry, while Korean Buddhist monks were celibate. Under Japanese influence, some Korean monks adopted the custom of marriage (*daecheo*). After liberation in 1945, there were legal battles for years between married and celibate sects over the legitimate ownership of certain temple properties.

Revival of Buddhism
After the Korean War, Buddhism experienced a considerable revival among the young. There has been a deliberate effort to turn "mountain Buddhism" into "community Buddhism" and "temple-centered Buddhism" into "socially relevant Buddhism." As evidence of this effort, there are forty-six Buddhist organizations for young members; thirty organizations for college students; and sixty-six organizations for middle and high school students. Buddhist organizations sponsor various schools, including universities, high schools, middle schools, primary schools, and kindergartens. They also manage three major hospitals, two daily newspapers, and one radio and television station (Yun et al. 1994:112-113).

Socially relevant Buddhism has made many positive contributions to society and has had a powerful impact on it, as recent trends have brought secluded, temple-centered congregations down from the mountains and right into the heart of urban centers. However, a person like myself, from the old school of thought, with a stereotypical notion of traditional Buddhism and Buddhist monks, experiences culture shock when seeing a monk driving a luxurious sedan or sitting in a first class hotel sipping coffee instead of mountain-grown herbal tea. At a restaurant once I even saw two monks and their followers ordering meat, which embarrassed me because of my "outdated" image of Buddhist monks. I even moved to another seat where I could not see them. But most Koreans who have experienced such changes do not seem to be bothered by them. I may be the only one who finds them disturbing because of my prolonged absence from Korea during the time when all this change was taking place.

Traditionally, since Buddhism and its temples have been associated with the aesthetics of the natural environment, some foreigners might surmise that Buddhists are natural environmentalists. There are some Buddhist environmental conservationists, especially Jiyul who has been one of the most active (and whom I will discuss in more detail later). However, whenever I visit well-known Buddhist temples, it looks as if Buddhists, including monks and lay adherents, are as development-oriented as other Koreans. Since most visitors to the temples as well as the monks themselves drive automobiles nowadays, roads leading to the temples are now wide and paved, and there are huge, splendid parking lots. What I find most astonishing is how Buddhist rituals and praying have come to resemble Christian church services, within the singing of Buddhist hymns sounding like a Christian church choir. Perhaps the services of various Korean religious groups tend to become similar to one another.

Buddhist Membership
Unlike Christian communities, which are "hard communities," meaning that membership is clearly defined, the Buddhist community is a "soft community." Hence, as in the case of Confucians, it is difficult to determine the definite number of Buddhist adherents (Yun et al. 1994:25). Even if a good many people commit to Buddhism as their religion, a large number of them seldom attend the temples to pray.

Currently, there are eighteen different Buddhist sects in Korea. According to Kwang-kyu Lee (2003:235), in 1980 there were 1,912 Buddhist temples, of which 1,093 belong to the Chogye sect within the *Seon* (or "*Chan*" in China and "*Zen*" in Japan) Buddhism school,[23] and 18,629 monks. The 2005 Korean Census reveals that there were over 10 million Buddhists in 2005, or 22.8 percent of the total Korean population.[24]

In sum, the cultural contribution of Buddhism as a major religion for millions of Koreans for over 1,600 years has been profound. As one scholar has noted, over 90 percent of Korean material cultural relics and national treasures are related to Buddha and Buddhism (Yun et al. 1994:101). Nearly 2,000 Buddhist temples are aesthetically situated in the most beautiful sites located deep in mountainous regions. In an atmosphere of beauty and tranquility, over the centuries Koreans have created world treasures of art, including temples, pagodas, paintings, sculptures, carvings, and much more.

Christianity

Catholicism

In Korea, Catholicism was first understood as "Western learning." Korean Confucian scholars such as Yi Ik and An Jeongbok, who were oriented toward the practical-learning school of thought, were exposed to Catholicism in the eighteenth century through European Jesuit missionaries in Beijing of Ming China, before foreign missionaries carried out their work in Korea. However, their initial interest in Catholicism was more intellectual in nature than spiritual.

Catholicism as a religion was not introduced to Korea until 1784, when Yi Seunghun (1756-1801) was baptized by a Western Catholic priest while on a court visit to Beijing. Following Yi, several other Koreans converted to Catholicism. Most early converts were not *yangban* but of the *chungin* class (middle-class commoners), mostly technical specialists who had had little access to political power for a long time (Lee 1984:239).

Nevertheless, no priests or foreign missionaries came to Korea until 1785, when the Jesuit Father Peter Grammont crossed the border and began baptizing believers and ordaining clergy. During the late eighteenth century and the early nineteenth century, the promulgation of foreign religion in Korea was still technically against the law. Many ruling Confucians in the Joseon court viewed Catholicism with suspicion, believing that the religion would undermine existing societal norms, particularly ancestor worship, and eventually lead to the destruction of the dynasty. Nevertheless, a lax administration allowed for a relatively tolerant view of the Catholic movement, although there was sporadic government persecution.

Despite the efforts of the government to suppress Catholicism, it continued to spread, appealing to many from the lower classes. By 1795, following the martyrdom of a Chinese priest, Peter Ju Munmo, there were 4,000 believers in Korea, and by 1863 membership had increased to 23,000.

As the number of Catholic believers grew, government persecution intensified, especially after Hwang Sayeong's persecution in 1801. Hwang (1775-1801), who was born into a *yangban* family and had the potential to become a successful scholar-official, converted to Catholicism and attempted to send his "silk letter" (so called because it was written on silk) to a Catholic bishop in Beijing, asking Western nations to dispatch naval and land forces to compel the Joseon court to grant religious freedom. However, his letter was intercepted, and he was eventually executed for his actions. Another notable persecution, after Hwang's, was the 1836 persecution of three French priests and 300 Korean believers (Lee 2003:245).

Beginning in 1880, after years of persecution and martyrdom, Korean Catholics gained some degree of freedom to participate in religious activities, a freedom further enhanced after the signing of a treaty between Korea and France in 1886. In 1898, a Cathedral was built in Seoul, and Catholicism in Korea gradually became popular until the Japanese interference started in 1910. Beginning in 1940, as part of Japan's assimilation policy under the slogan of *naeseon ilche*,

Shintōism was imposed upon the Korean people, and Catholic believers were forced to attend and observe Shintō religious services and practices. Many Catholics joined the forces fighting for Korean independence.[25]

The visit of Pope John Paul II in May 1984 during the bicentennial commemoration of Korean Catholicism is the biggest event in the history of Catholicism in Korea to date. During his visit, the Pope canonized 103 of Korea's martyrs, making Korea the fourth country in the world in total number of saints. On 24 March 2006, the Korean Catholic Church received additional recognition when Pope Benedict XVI appointed Archbishop Nicholas Jeong Jinseok cardinal. With Cardinal Jeong and Cardinal Kim Suhwan, who was appointed in 1969, the Korean Catholic Church now has two cardinals. Since the Korean Catholic Church had long wished for a second cardinal, the appointment of Cardinal Jeong has done much for its morale. According to the 2005 Korean census, the Korean Catholic Church now has two cardinals, three parishes, about 4,000 priests, and over 5 million followers.[26]

In addition to its religious function, the Catholic Church in Korea has provided various socio-cultural, educational, and social-welfare projects. The Church sponsors twenty-seven hospitals, fifteen nursing homes, 220 kindergartens, 652 Sunday schools, seven primary schools, 65 middle and high schools, ten special and vocational schools, and nine universities (Yun et al. 1994:172). Most of all, the Catholic Church has served as a source of strength during the turbulent political upheavals of the 1980s by providing sanctuary to many dissidents.

In particular, Myeongdong Cathedral (Myeongdong Seongdang) has provided such sanctuary from the mid-1970s through much of the 1980s, up until the mid-1990s, when the military-led government was replaced by a civilian government. Notably, in 1975 when President Park Chung-hee's *yusin* policy was at its height, the Catholic Priests' Association for Justice in Korea (Cheonjugyo jeonguiguhyeon jeonguk sajedan) used the church to declare their demand for restoration of civil rights and to call for boycotting a proposal for referendum by direct vote to amend the Korean Constitution. In 1972, the *Yusin* Constitution was passed with the overwhelming support (91.9 percent) of Korean voters. In response, the Catholic Priests' Association for Justice in Korea was organized in 1974 upon Archbishop Ji Haksun's arrest for his declaration that President Park Chung-hee's *Yusin* Constitution was null and void.

The Catholic Priests' Association for Justice in Korea was so loosely organized that it is difficult to know the exact number of members, but it is assumed to be around 500 priests. In 1976, at the same church Kim Dae-jung attended as a dissident, several Catholic priests made a statement calling for the revitalization of democracy in Korea. Because of its record, Myeongdong Seongdang has become a symbol of sanctuary for many political dissidents, student protesters, and labor union leaders who have called for the revitalization of Korean democracy and the restoration of civil rights.

The initial martyrdoms of Catholic believers in Korea were due largely to their refusal to observe ancestor worship rites. But in 1995, the Catholic Church in Korea officially allowed its members to observe ancestor worship as they pleased. This effort to embrace local customs and traditions has contributed to an increase in Catholic believers.

Protestantism

Unlike Catholicism, Protestantism was introduced to Korea by American missionaries: Horace N. Allen in 1884 and Horace G. Underwood and Henry G. Appenzeller the following year. Protestantism was introduced a century later than Catholicism, and given the relatively tolerant late-nineteenth-century political environment, Protestant missionaries did not have to endure the persecution that Catholics experienced a century earlier. Since Allen and Appenzeller were physicians, it was efficient for them to combine their missionary work with medical practice (Clark 1986:6), and with permission from the king they founded a medical clinic. Early Catholicism was popular socially, politically, and economically with the underprivileged class. However, "Protestantism was most warmly received by the new intellectual class and by the business community" (Lee 1984:335) in the midst of modernization efforts. By then, Koreans viewed the late-arriving Protestants as bearers of modern knowledge, which was desperately needed in Korea's efforts to modernize and protect its independence.

The role of early missionaries was not limited to evangelicalism. Early missionary organizations established the first Western medical clinic, Gwanghyewon,[27] and founded several schools: Baeje School for men in 1886 and, a year later, Kyeongsin School and Ewha School for Women, which was Korea's first educational institution for women. Between 1885 and 1909, Protestant missionary organizations established thirty-nine schools. Currently, Protestant missionary schools include ten primary schools, 123 middle schools, 165 high schools, seven two-year junior colleges, and thirty-four four-year colleges and universities.[28] Many national leaders attended and graduated from these missionary-founded schools, including the former independence-fighter and first president of the Republic Syngman Rhee, who was a graduate of Baeje.

Indeed, Koreans are well aware of the positive contributions made by Christianity to Korean modernization. Kim Jedeuk and his associates (2004) asked 200 prominent scholars in religion and related disciplines what religious group had made the greatest contribution to Korean modernization in the past century. The respondents answered that Protestant churches (60.8 percent) had made the most contribution, with Catholic churches second (33.3 percent), and a combined group of Buddhists and other indigenous religions third (1.6 percent) (Kim et al. 2004:4).

After the annexation of Korea by Japan in 1910, many missionaries offered assistance to the Korean independence movement. Many Christians played a vital role in the March First Independence Movement. Of the thirty-three signers of the March First Declaration of Independence fifteen were Christians (Clark 1986:10). The missionaries' support for Korean independence continued until 1938, when Japanese authorities began to enforce Shintō shrine worship. The Japanese expulsion of the missionaries took place in 1940, on the eve of World War II. There had been many persecutions of Korean Christians, because Japan assumed that the Korean church was opposed to Japanese dominance over the Korean peninsula. Incidentally, in Japanese retaliation for the March First Independence Movement, forty-seven churches and two missionary schools were burned, one such incident being the Cheam-ni massacre.

After World War II, Protestantism in Korea was revitalized after Korea's liberation reopened opportunities for missionary work, and many missionaries returned after 1946 with permission from the U.S. military authorities. Protestantism received another boost during and after the Korean War, which brought Korea to the attention of many foreign missionaries, and new denominations began to flow in after 1953. Donald N. Clark (1986:18) states that "Protestant Syngman Rhee, a member of the First Methodist Church in Seoul, supported the church and wished it well. Many of his closest associates were Christians and much was said about the Christanization of South Korea while he was President."

During the endless series of upheavals, student demonstrations, and labor disputes that erupted in the process of modernization and rapid industrialization that began in the mid-1960s, Protestant churches supported the "underdogs" — workers, students, and protestors. Notably, the Urban Industrial Mission (Dosi saneop seongyohoe), which originated in the United States in 1956 and was introduced into Korea in 1957, was created to carry out missionary work among workers in industrial settings. In earlier years, the mission focused mainly on providing religious services at factories instead of churches, and offering social services and consultations. However, since their mission activities were directed toward industrial workers, they were inevitably involved in organizing labor movements, strikes, labor disputes between employers and employees. In 1979, when women members of the mission occupied the main office of Korea's ruling party, the mission atttracted much national attention. Some industries, including YH trading company and several others factories, went out of business because of prolonged labor disputes.

Since then, government and industry have been well aware that the mission played a major role in instigating labor disputes. Consequently, the mission had to face government repression in the 1970s and 1980s, years during which many college students, dissidents, labor leaders, and activists were involved in the Dosi saneop seongyohoe. At one point, the mission had fourteen branches throughout the nation with around 3,000 members. Nowadays, however, with a civilian government, the mission's activities are not as vital as they used to be.

Regardless of their own religious preferences, Koreans perceived that "the only organization that could realistically claim to ensure both Korea's survival as a people (as emphasized by nationalists) and adaptation to the times (as emphasized by reformers) was the Protestant church" (*Handbook of Korea* 2003:439).

With nearly 9 million members, or 5.49 percent of the total Korean population, the Protestant church is currently the most active religious organization in Korea.[29] A church in Yeouido, downtown Seoul, has nearly 800,000 members. Korea may be the only country in the world where daily prayer services begin at 4:00 A.M. in many churches, an apt demonstration of the ardent enthusiasm of Korean Protestant churchgoers.

Many Westerners wonder how Protestantism has seen such phenomenal growth in Korea. There are many plausible theories, yet no definitive answer. David Chung and Kang-Nam Oh (2001) believe that the syncretic worldview of Koreans may have been the main reason for the remarkable growth of Christianity in Korea. Donald N. Clark (1986:36–37) explains that it can be attributed to:

> a spiritual hunger among Koreans arising from suffering through colonialism and civil war, the attractions of Christian ideas of salvation, the echoes in Christianity of other faiths such as Buddhism (heaven and hell) and shamanism (miracles, sacrifices and priesthood), and the fact that the use of *Han'gŭl* made scriptural study possible for large numbers of people.[30] The church's stress on personal evangelism on a one-to-one basis has been especially

effective in urban areas, where migration from the countryside has created large communities of strangers who miss their village neighbors and are desperately lonely in the cities.

Perhaps Protestant churches were able to play this role to meet the needs of the Korean people.

Korean Churches in the United States

One of the best illustrations of the role of Protestant churches in meeting the needs of the Korean people can be seen in the United States. The history of Korean immigrants to the U.S. is shorter than that of their East Asian neighbors from China and Japan. Korean immigration began in 1903 with the migration of sugar plantation workers to Hawaii, and their first church was established in the same year.[31] Since then, and especially after the passage of the Immigrant Act of 1965 that made it easier for minority groups to immigrate to the United States, the population of Korean immigrants has experienced phenomenal growth. According to the 2000 U.S. Census, in the United States there are 1.3 million Koreans and people of Korean ancestry and an additional 150 thousand Americans of part-Korean ancestry. The establishment of Korean churches has kept pace with this number. There are approximately 3,400 Korean American churches in the United States, and 350 in the Washington D.C. area alone. About 75 percent of the Korean American population is estimated to be Christian (Choi 2003:3).

In earlier years, when Korea was under Japanese rule, the Korean American churches supported the liberation movement to free Korea from the Japanese by providing monetary and spiritual aid to independence fighters. During the years of military rule, the church supported activists who fought for Korea's democratization. With the phenomenal growth of the Korean American population, as well as the Christian population, the churches have provided the immigrants with religious as well as social services. The pastors of these churches help church members get their driver's licenses, find jobs, enroll in schools, and carry out many other chores (Choi 2003:3). Sociologists Won Moo Hurh and Kwang Chung Kim (1984:135) described the functions of Korean churches in the following way: "the immigrants are drawn together in the ethnic church not only to meet intimate friends but also to see 'new faces' other than their family members, relatives, and close friends. In short, they miss both the informal and formal aspects of the Korean society back home, and the ethnic church seems to provide a microcosm of both."

These descriptions were made nearly a quarter of a century ago, but the functions of Korean churches remain the same. Indeed, "Such a large church performs associational functions similar to those performed by the Korean society at large in Korea" (Hurh and Kim 1984:135). For early Chinese immigrants, the family association or clan was the primary associational focus (Kitano and Daniel 1995:27). However, for Korean immigrants, it was the church that helped them adjust to an alien society by functioning like a large "fictional kin group."

Islam

Muslim merchants were Korea's first contact with Islam, which occurred around 1024 during the Goryeo dynasty. About 100 Koreans who were agricultural immigrants in Manchuria were exposed to Islam through contact with Arabic people there and showed some interest in Islamic religion (Yun et al. 1994:193-203). However, there was no mission work to introduce Islam to Korea until the early 1950s during the Korean War, when Islam was introduced to the peninsula by an imam attached to the Turkish army, one of the sixteen nations that comprised the U.N. forces participating in the war. Through the imam's efforts, some Koreans worshipped with the Turkish soldiers and converted to Islam. In 1966, a Korean Islamic organization was formed, and a mosque was established in Seoul. Since then, seven more mosques have been erected throughout Korea. The *Handbook of Korea* (2003:442) estimates that there are more than 20,000 Muslims in Korea.

New Religions

There are about 300 new religions in Korea whose membership ranges from less than ten in some religious sects to more than 600,000 in others. The total number of believers in new religions has been estimated to be between about 1 and 1.5 million.[32] Despite their variations, these new religions have two common characteristics: they appear to be nationalistic, if not ethnocentric, because most were founded in response to or in reaction against foreign-born ideology, religion, and political dominance; and they are syncretic in their theology, combining several elements of existing religions. Since there are too many to review, this chapter will be ruthlessly selective, describing sects that have the most adherents according to the Korea National Statistical Office.

Donghak

Donghak (Cheondogyo) was founded in the 1860s by Choe Jeu (1824-1864) as a movement of Eastern learning in reaction to Western learning, as exemplified by Catholicism, and the dominance of Western power. Choe's main belief was "in the unity of man with God, that mankind and the Supreme Being are one and the same" (Lee 1984:258). It was a nationalistic proclamation that only Eastern learning could stop the negative influence of Western learning in the minds of Koreans. Donghak is a syncretic religion that includes elements of Confucianism, Buddhism, and Taoism as opposed to Western learning or Catholicism. The government was so alarmed by the popularity of Donghak that in 1863 Choe was arrested on the charge of misleading the people and sowing discord in society, and executed the following year (Lee 1984:258-259).

After the execution of Choe Jeu, under the leadership of Choe Si-hyeong (1829-1898), second parish, an Donghak movement became a well-organized force, and made an effort to restore its good name (or correct the distorted image of its founder), which has been deliberately created by the government. At the same time, the Donghak followers organized, made demands, and threatened the government to prevent the *yangban* from draining the lifeblood of the peasants through illegal extortions, and to expel the Japanese and Westerners. In the meantime, the membership of the Donghak increased to several thousand, and in 1894 the movement erupted into a revolutionary peasant rebellion, employing military operations on a large scale. As the Donghak movement gained momentum, Jeon Bongjun, the head of Gobu County parish, and his peasant army occupied the county's office, seizing weapons, and distributing to the poor the rice illegally collected as a tax by the magistrate of Gobu County. At times, the peasant army was able to crush the government's troops.

As the peasant army gained strength, its influence extended to other provinces. When the panicky government sought military support from China and Japan, Japan intervened militarily, and the Donghak peasants ended up fighting well-trained Japanese soldiers equipped with modern weapons, and they were no match for them. The Donghak rebellion was a revolutionary movement of peasantry against Joseon's oppressive *yangban* society that had demonstrated the power of the peasants.

The Donghak later changed its name to Cheondogyo in 1905 under the leadership of Son byeonghui, who took a religious-nationalist approach and played a leading role in the March First Independence Movement, serving as head of the thirty-three signers of the Declaration of Independence. At one time, membership swelled to 2 million but later declined to 600,000 because Japanese suppression was lifted. Membership became stagnant after liberation (Yun et al. 1994:214). Cheondogyo followers were estimated to number 28,184 according to the 1995 Korea National Statistical Office's figures. Figures for membership do not appear in the 2005 census, however.

Wonbulgyo
Wonbulgyo (Won Buddhism) is an offshoot of Buddhism, and was founded by Park Jungbin in 1916 at Iri, Jeollabuk-do province. As a syncretic religion combining elements of Confucianism, Buddhism,

and Taoism, Wonbulgyo emphasizes modernization, secularization, and revitalization of Buddhist doctrine. In addition to religious activities, Wonbulgyo runs a university, hospital, high school, and middle school and also sponsors various welfare programs, including a nursing home and orphanage. Kwang-kyu Lee (2003:249) reports that "there are 681,000 believers in Wŏnbulgyo. The 2005 Korean census recognizes 130,000 members."[33]

Daejonggyo

This new religion was founded in 1904 by Paek Bong, and in 1909 Na Cheol and Jeong Hunmo promulgated a version of it in Seoul that was centered around the mythology of Dangun, founder of Gojoseon. "The main doctrine was to return to three truths, the three truths being the basic elements of a human being: one's disposition, life, and energy" (Lee 2003:250). To avoid Japanese suppression, believers changed the name of their religion to Daejonggyo and moved the center of its mission to Manchuria, where they engaged in anti-Japanese independence fighting. *Daejonggyo* once had 145,000 believers (Lee 2003:250), but the Korea National Statistical Office lists 7,603 believers as of 1995. The 2005 census, however, does not list Daejonggyo as a separate category.

Daesunjillihoe

The Jeungsan religion was founded in 1902 by Gang Ilsun, who was once a believer in Donghak but recognized its limitations and proposed a new religion that preached belief in a paradise in the afterlife. Jeungsan is a combination of Confucianism, Buddhism, Taoism, and the realm of diviners, geomancers, and medicine men. It teaches that the universe is a heaven that can be realized in the mind of a person through homage and prayer (Lee 2003:248-249). A branch of Jeungsan headquartered in Seoul, Daesunjillihoe, has grown steadily since it was established in 1969 and includes 650,000 members (Yun et al. 1994:217-218). The Daesunjillihoe sponsors regular seminars and lectures.

Unification Church

As a new religious movement, the Unification Church (Tongilgyo) was started by Moon Seonmyeong in 1940. It was formally and legally established in Seoul as the Holy Spirit Association for the Unification of World Christianity, reflecting Moon's original vision of an ecumenical movement.

The beliefs of the church are explained in the book *Divine Principle*, which draws from the Bible as well as Asian tradition, and includes belief in a universal God. According to Breen (2004:44), "Moon's view of God is quintessentially Korean, combining shamanist passion and Confucian family patterns in Christian form." In the 1990s, Moon began to establish various peace organizations, including the Family Federation for World Peace and Unification. Members of the Unification Church are found in fifty countries. In Korea, its members are estimated to number from 250,000 to 3 million.

In sum, with its more than 300 religions, Korea is indeed a multireligious society. Unlike some other multireligious nations where the threat of disintegration exists, in Korea multireligious groups live symbiotically and even respect other religions. Koreans practice inclusiveness in religion and trust that all religions benefit humans in one way or another. Therefore, from the Korean perspective, all religions are equally good.

However, whenever a new religion was introduced, it was not always welcome. Although Koreans have experienced direct and indirect suppressions, overt persecutions, and even martyrdoms in the name of religion, such actions were undertaken by the ruling elite of the dynastic courts, and not by ordinary people. There have been quarrels within given religious groups over hegemony, but rarely has there been any major inter-religious strife. Also, despite the existence of so many diverse religions, no religious people in Korea want to divide the Korean nation on religious grounds, which shows that "Koreanness" may be more important than any religious value.

Not only has religion granted Koreans spiritual enrichment, but it has also brought tremendous cultural enrichment to the country as well. Koreans have incorporated the foreign cultural elements that came along with these religions into their native culture, adopting them and making them their own. When the country faced an imminent threat from foreign powers, various religious groups joined together and fought for Korean independence. Religions have indeed made a profound contribution to Korean history.

CHAPTER 7

Class, Mobility, and Education

I may be a member of the last generation of Koreans to have witnessed the remnants of the *yangban* class, although it was officially abolished after the *Gabo* reform in 1894. Before Korea's liberation from Japan, when I was a young boy, in my home village, which was a single-lineage-dominant village with *yangban* origins, I observed an elderly farmhand (*meoseum*), a commoner, using an honorific expression in addressing the little son of the landlord. The boy answered the farmhand without using an honorific.[1] In the past, the *yangban* had privileges of higher social status even in casual conversations between yangban and non-*yangban*.

I can also attest to the efficacy of the open-class system, which allows individuals to achieve their maximum potential on the basis of talent, training, and education, and a bit of luck. A son of the farmhand above managed to go all the way to college by taking night-school classes (*yagan hakgyo*) while working in a small business firm as an errand boy (*sahwan*) in Seoul. Eventually, because of his hard work and drive, he passed the higher civil service examination (*haengjeong gosi*) and became a civil servant. Now retired, he lives in a lavish apartment in Seoul. Because of his high aspirations, hard work, and determination, he was able to make use of the competitive examination system, which was open to everyone, to attain his personal goal in less than fifty years. One can easily understand why Koreans strive so hard for a good education, because they consider it a shortcut to improving their class affiliation.

Historical Survey of Korean Social Classes

The social stratification system in Korea has a long history. Classes began to emerge during the Bronze Age. Early social-class distinctions were ascribed and hereditary in nature, and social mobility to upgrade class affiliation was limited. When class categorization became achievement-oriented, education became the single most important key to status in Korea.

By examining various kinds of burial markers, dolmens, and cairns, Sarah Nelson (1993:11) has observed that social class began to appear in the Korean peninsula in the second millennium B.C. Later, the Three Kingdoms created centralized aristocratic states in which power and prestige were exercised by a limited number of aristocratic families and lineages of kings and queens. However, very little is known about the Goguryeo social-class order other than the upper aristocracy. Baekje aristocracies were limited to eight renowned families, and power was vested only in these family members (Lee 1984:48-49).

Silla developed a unique, rigid, and hereditary class system, manifested in what was called the "bone-rank" (*golpum*) system. There were two levels of bone-rank: "sacred-bone" (*seonggol*)[2] and "true-bone" (*jingol*). The royal family came exclusively from the latter. According to Ki-baik Lee (1984:50-51), "Not only this, but bone-rank also determined the scale of the residence in which a Silla citizen might live. For example, a true-bone house could not exceed 24 'feet' in length or width, a head-rank six house 21 feet, a head-rank five house 18 feet, a head-rank four or commoner's house 15 feet. Moreover, sumptuary regulations based on bone-rank governed the color of official attire, vehicles and horse trappings, and various utensils." Below bone-rank, there were several grades and classes, which were rigid and clearly demarcated.[3]

During the Goryeo dynasty, aristocrats expanded their power base to many prominent lineages.[4] In addition to enabling aristocratic lineage connections through marriage, the Goryeo system allowed a large number of men to become government officials, which required a new method of selecting personnel, the civil service examination. This examination provided a means of advancement for members of all the hereditary aristocratic families. Artisans, however, had their occupations determined by heredity and could not change them. The peasant population, called *Baekjeong*,[5] was not eligible to hold government office, and below the *Baekjeong* were the *cheonmin* (lowborn), who were slaves.

Joseon Social Classes with Yangban

Joseon's social class system was dominated by *yangban*, which consisted of two orders, the literati and military positions. The Joseon dynasty broadened the base of recruiting officials to serve the government by instituting a state examination system. There were four major classes: *yangban* (upper class), *jungin* (middle people), *sangmin* (commoners), and *cheonmin* (the lower class or outcasts).

Yangban (Upper Class): the First Class

In the Joseon dynasty, *yangban* directed the government, economy, and culture. In principle, a person could serve the government as an official if he (always he, not she) could pass the state examination,[6] but this opportunity was in reality limited to those of *yangban* rank. Since *yangban* were exempted from the usual service obligations to the state, including corvée labor and military duty, they could devote themselves exclusively to study and preparation for the examinations. *Yangban* discriminated against the other classes in all aspects of social life, maintaining their own areas of residence in the southern and northern sections of the capital and creating their own villages in the countryside.

Jungin (Class of Middle People): the Second Class

Second in status to the *yangban*, the *jungin* were engaged in science and technology. People in the *jungin* class were eligible to take the civil service examination but in the miscellaneous category. If they passed, they could become low-ranking government officials or take jobs as interpreters, medical officers, astronomers, geographers, mathematicians, lawyers, musicians, and painters.

Sangmin (Commoner Class): the Third Class

This class included people who were engaged in production, such as farmers and workers in manufacturing. Among the commoners, there was also a rank order: farmers were considered the highest, followed by workers in manufacturing, then merchants at the bottom. All commoners were obliged to pay taxes, were subject to compulsory labor, and had to serve in the military.

Cheonmin (Lowest Class): the Fourth Class

This class included slaves, butchers, shamans, singing girls, and performers. Slaves, who occupied the lowest layer, were sold, given as gifts, and inherited. People who belonged to this class were discriminated against by the people above them.

The tradition of the four-class system of the Joseon dynasty led to the development of a distinct classification of occupational prestige in Korea: *sa* (scholars and literati-bureaucrats) was considered the highest occupation; *nong* (farmers) was regarded as the second highest; *gong* (artisans) ranked third; and *sang* (merchants) was placed at the bottom of the social ladder (Jones and Sakong 1980:252-253; Kim 1992:103).

Emergence of the Open-Class System and Change in Occupational Ranking

The *yangban*-led Joseon class system was reevaluated by scholars of the Practical Learning School (*Silhak*) during the eighteenth century in an effort to reform Joseon dynastic social institutions. These scholars recognized that the nation could no longer ignore people who were engaged in farming, science and technology, commerce, and industry by treating them as second-class citizens.

Silhak thinkers focused their attention not on the landlord class but on farmers who actually cultivated the soil. They proposed to abolish all distinctions of social status, in other words, all social classes. Ki-baik Lee (1984:236) sums up *Silhak* thought as follows: "··· they took the position that the well-being of the people was to be achieved through abolishing the social status system and determining the division of labor in Yi society on the basis of ability alone." Eventually, under the influence of *Silhak* thought, as well as a government policy of permitting slaves to perform military duty in exchange for their freedom, government slaves (*gong-nobi*) were set free.[7] Private slaves (*sa-nobi*) as well as government slaves, if any still remained, were eventually freed as part of the *Gabo* reform in 1894. The reform program also included the elimination of class distinctions between *yangban* and commoners, and made it possible to open the ranks of officialdom to men of talent regardless of social background (Lee 1984:293; Lew 1990:214-216).

The fall of the Joseon dynasty in 1910 brought with the abolishment of the Joseon class system, but the Japanese did little to acknowledge its disappearance. Nevertheless, some lower-class Koreans such as butchers did try to escape from the stigma of their class status. Despite many instances of being barred from schools, by the mid-1920s some 40 percent of butchers' children were in school (Breen 2004:107-108). After the liberation of Korea, the Western concept of equality was introduced, especially through Christianity. As a new republic was born in 1948, equality was guaranteed in the Korean Constitution, and Article 11 is specific about not recognizing any privileged class. Before the 1949 Land Reform Act, landlords were mostly of *yangban* origin and still exercised certain power and privileges. It was the Land Reform that finally "undermined the economic base of the former aristocracy [*yangban*]" (Brandt 1971:38).

Ranking of Occupational Prestige

The previous social ranking order of the Joseon dynastic period — *sa, nong, gong*, and *sang* — became obsolete as Korea experienced rapid economic growth and industrialization beginning in the mid-1960s. As a reflection of changing trends, according to survey data from 1964 to 1971, the occupation most students at Ewha Womans University[8] ranked highest for a prospective spouse was "businessman," a category at the bottom of the ranking system during the Joseon dynasty (Jones and Sakong 1980:252-253).

According to a 2001 study of how Koreans rate occupations that was carried out by Choe Taeryong (2002:29-86) (based on a sample of 656 citizens from the city of Chinju), among the thirty-three occupations listed, "physician" was rated the highest and "general laborer" the lowest. The top ten occupations in the 2001 list had also been included in the top ten rankings in previous studies that had been carried out in 1967 (Lee and Kim 1970), 1978 (Kim 1979) and in 1983 (Choe 1983), although there were slight changes in order.

Among these occupations, that of university professor was consistently rated highly in all surveys.[9] Whatever the precise ranking of professor over the years, contemporary Koreans tend to rate professional specialists, including physicians, lawyers, university professors, big businessmen, and higher officials in government as having the most prestigious jobs. Among the top five most prestigious occupations, in addition to university professor and member of the National Assembly, are three occupations that used to belong to the second class of *jungin* (class of middle people) and the third class of *sangmin* (class of commoner) in the Joseon dynasty. An entertainer was considered a member of *cheonmin* (lowest class) in the Joseon class system, but currently that occupation's prestige is fairly high (below radio or television producer, but above newspaper reporter): twelfth out of thirty-three listed occupations.

Recent Social Classes

Unlike the bone-rank system of the Silla dynasty and the *yangban*-led four-class system of the Joseon dynasty, under the current open-class system, an individual's class affiliation is determined by several informal criteria such as income, occupational prestige, educational attainment, residential area, and family background, among others. There has been no anthropological study of social status in contemporary Korea comparable to the classic case study conducted by American anthropologists in the 1940s.[10]

After dividing the class system into upper class, middle class, and lower class groups mainly on the basis of income, a Korean daily newspaper determined in 2004 that 22.5 percent of the Korean population belonged to the upper class, 63.9 percent to the middle class, and 13.6 percent to the lower class. Comparison of these results with a 1997 study shows that the Korean middle class decreased by 5 percent points between 1997 and 2004.[11]

In terms of self-perception regarding class affiliation, by 2005 only 1 percent of Koreans believed that they were upper class, while 56 percent saw themselves as middle class, and 43.0 percent thought they were lower class.[12] These figures indicate that fewer Koreans than in the 2004 study saw themselves as upper or middle class, while many more thought of themselves as lower class.

Given this rapid transformation, some Koreans have expressed concern about the eroding middle class.[13] Recently, in March 2007, the Institute for Health and Social Affairs reported that the Korean middle class tumbled to 43.7 percent of the population from 55.54 percent a decade ago, indicating that about a quarter of middle class households had become financially weakened over the years.[14] Several explanations for this trend are plausible, including the high unemployment rate for highly educated white-collar workers and the massive layoffs resulting from the restructuring of business and industry after the IMF bailout in 1997. Most troubling is a widening disparity in income between a limited number of highly paid income earners and a growing number of poor people. The top 20 percent of

Korean households earned 7.64 times more than the bottom 20 percent, far above the earning gap in major European economies and Japan.[15] According to a recent report, for instance, a lawyer in a reputable international law firm in Seoul is paid over 4.7 billion *won* (about $5.7 million) per month, which is the average monthly income for 5,654 households,[16] while there are over 7 million Koreans whose income is less than 1.2 million *won* (about $1,270) per month, a figure that was 120 percent below the absolute poverty line in 2006.[17]

Education for Korean Upward Mobility

In accordance with the modern class system, education determines entry into preferred occupations in Korea; consequently, education has become almost an obsession in the minds of Koreans. Emphasis on education has a long tradition in Korea and there have been several contributing factors.

The Cultural, Historical, and Social Tradition of Education

Confucianism and Its Emphasis on Education

The recognition of the importance of education in Korea can be traced to the impact of Confucianism. During the Three Kingdoms period, education was not available to the general public, but each kingdom did establish a Confucian academy for the education of the elite.

During the Goryeo dynasty, the school system was institutionalized in Taejo's reign (918-943), and the nation's highest academy, *Gukjagam* (National University), designed principally for the study of Chinese tradition and Confucian classics, was established in 992, under King Seongjong (981-997).[18] The state's civil service examination motivated youth to obtain a university education.

During the Joseon period, in 1398 the National Confucian Academy of *Seonggyungwan* was established. In order to prepare for the civil service examination, "from an early age *yangban* youth attended private elementary schools (*seodang*) where they learned the basic Chinese characters and practiced writing them. Then, from age seven, they advanced to one of the Four Schools (*sahak*) in Seoul or to the County School (*hyanggyo*) established in each county. The Confucian students of these schools, after several years of study, were thereby qualified to sit for the licentiate examinations. If they passed the first stage of the examination held at the provincial level, they proceeded to Seoul for the second stage, which determined those who would receive degrees (Lee 1984:180). These licentiates might then enter the nation's highest academy, *Seonggyungwan*, in Seoul, where they could excel even further.

Also, many Neo-Confucian literati played an important part in teaching scholarly tradition to members of their own clans or lineages in order to retain social power. In the vicinities of their homes in the countryside, these literati established *seowon* (private academies)[19] where they educated their youth and carried on the teachings of Neo-Confucian literati, thus perpetuating the scholarly tradition in which they played an essential role. During King Sukjong's reign (1674-1720), there were about three hundred *seowon* throughout the nation that taught Confucian scholarship.

The importance of education was recognized early, as well as the means to deliver it: establishing many *seowon* and high academies such as *Gukjagam* and *Seonggyungwan*. Teaching was centered on the Confucian classics, not the practical fields of science and technology, medicine, law, and commerce. Education was limited to aristocrats and *yangban* and served as the major route to government office. Even in *Gukjagam*, while sons of officials of the third rank and higher could enroll in University College, sons of eighth- and ninth-ranking officials could only enroll in Law College, the College of Calligraphy, or the College of Accounting. At *Seonggyungwan*, only Licentiates (*saengwon*) in classics were allowed to enter. In all likelihood, giving priority and preferential treatment to the study of Confucian classics probably hindered the development of science, technology, and other fields considered essential for modernization.

Hunger for Education

Modern education was introduced to Korea by American Protestant missionaries: the first Western medical clinic opened in 1885; the Baejae School for men in 1886; and the Gyeongsin School for men and Ewha School for women in 1886. At the same time, Koreans themselves recognized the importance of education as the vehicle for modernization and national independence and strength. In 1895, King Gojong (1864-1907) proclaimed in an edict that education was essential to the nation's future. During the period of Japanese domination in the early 1900s, Koreans further emphasized education, trusting that it would eventually provide the foundation for future Korean independence. Many Korean nationalist intellectuals who were once active in political movements decided to devote themselves to education. In the scant few years before Korea fell completely under Japanese colonial domination, the number of private schools reached 3,000, and they were particularly numerous in the northern half of the country (Kim 1998:39).[20]

In addition to disseminating new learning, many private schools in the years of Japanese domination served as hotbeds for the nationalist movement. Naturally, Japan frowned on these schools and felt it necessary to control Korean education, particularly private educational institutions, during the Residency-General period. As a consequence of this control, the number of schools diminished. In 1907 missionaries alone operated 508 primary schools, twenty-two high schools, and two theological schools. By 1917, this number had been halved, and by 1937 only thirty-four missionary schools remained (Eckert et al. 1990:262). Also, after annexation, Japan's educational policy changed; Japan started to direct its efforts toward elementary and vocational level education, which would teach Koreans to perform menial tasks in the Japanese language for Japan.[21]

In order to "Japanize" the Koreans effectively, Japan made primary education in Korea a minimum requirement for everyone, and the Government-General built hundreds of public schools in the first decade of its rule. By 1910, some 110,800 students attended these schools, and this number increased to nearly 2 million by 1941 (Eckert et al. 1990:263).²² By contrast, the Japanese strictly limited higher-education opportunities for Koreans. It was estimated that "Only five percent of Korean students passed beyond the primary level, and although there was a tremendous expansion of student numbers over time, in 1945 only about twenty percent of the population had received some schooling, while the general rate of literacy was still below fifty percent" (Eckert et al. 1990:263).

Higher Education as "Han"

In response to the discriminatory policy of the Japanese that banned higher education for Koreans, Koreans started a movement in November 1922 to establish a Korean People's University (Minnip Daehak).²³ The rationale for this attempt was that "although mass education was necessary for overall development, a society is judged, in the end, by the quality of its upper level educational system, which, in turn produced national leaders" (Robinson 1988:86).²⁴ However, the movement was unable to raise the necessary funds (Kim 1998:85), and its momentum was slowed by the mismanagement of donations, infighting between chapters, and vitriolic criticism from more radical nationalists (Eckert et al. 1990:291). The Japanese helped to bring about the failure of this movement, employing the tactics of "divide and conquer" to set moderate and radical nationalists at odds.

Although the Korean drive to establish a people's university was widespread, in 1926 Japanese authorities announced a plan to establish Keijō Imperial University (currently Seoul National University) in Seoul, which further diminished public interest in the Korean People's University, and soon the movement withered away (Kim 1998:86). Because the door of the imperial university was not open to most Koreans, some Koreans who wished to receive an elite education and could afford to do so went to Japan or overseas with the help of American missionaries. Because of these limiting circumstances, in 1945, for example, less than 1 percent of Koreans had received higher education.

However, there were several Korean institutions of higher education, such as Joseon Christian College (later changed to Yeonhui and then to Yonsei University), Boseong Junior College (currently Korea University), Ewha Womans Junior College, and Sungsil Junior College, but Japan did not allow them to become integrated universities.[25] For many Koreans yearning for further education to acquire upward mobility, higher education remained a *han*, meaning an unfulfilled wish or desire.

The Korean word *han* is one of the most widely used Korean euphemisms, yet it is the most difficult to translate into English with the right nuance. Some scholars who are quite competent in both Korean and English have attempted to translate the word *han* into English, but the translations do not come to close to the original nuance of native Korean usage. Laurel Kendall (1983:101, 1988:8) translates it as "unfulfilled desires," Haesung Chun Koh (1983:170) suggests it is "a haunting sense of regret," and Carter Eckert (1990:400) offers yet another translation as "catalytic bitterness and anger." Michael Breen (2004:38) elaborates on the meaning of *han* as "a kind of rage and helplessness that is sublimated, and lingers like an inactive resentment."

Between 1945, when Korea was liberated, and 1965, before Korea made great economic strides, educational institutions grew exponentially. By 1947, there were 15,400 public schools, compared with 3,000 at the time when Korea fell under Japanese domination (Mason et al. 1980:345). Student enrollment in institutions of higher education increased from 7,819 in 1945 to 141,626 in 1965 (Mason, et al. 1980:348, table 89).[26] After liberation, many Koreans were able to fulfill their long-enduring *han* for higher-education opportunities.

Higher Education as a Means for Upward Mobility
Although some Koreans have become celebrities, including presidents, without the benefit of higher education,[27] higher education has played a pivotal role in providing upward mobility and success for many individuals. For instance, according to a survey by Leroy P. Jones and

Il Sakong (1980:232) in the early 1980s, 69.1 percent of entrepreneurs, 51.1 percent of *jaebeol* (big business conglomerates) leaders, 62.7 percent of high civil servants, and 84.2 percent of public managers had completed college or above.

People recognize the importance of education not only because of their cultural heritage and their need to fulfill the *han* resulting from historical adversity, but also for the economic reward of higher education: more highly educated people are paid more than those who have less education; they have greater marketability, and they gain mobility for advancement. A recent study based on figures from 2004 indicates that the average monthly income of people who graduated from four-year colleges or universities is over 1 million *won* (about $1,066) more than the average monthly earnings of those who only graduated from high school.[28]

Higher Education Enhances the Opportunity to Meet a Desirable Marriage Partner

In selecting a marriage partner via marriage consulting centers (*gyeolhon sangdamso*), educational background is considered to be of the utmost importance. Young Koreans consider the appearance or wealth of a prospective marriage candidate secondary to the person's educational attainments, trusting that a highly educated candidate has a better chance of acquiring a reputable white-collar job, a secure income, and future success. It is assumed that any individual who holds a degree from a reputable and sought-after university must be intelligent and capable, and therefore have a higher potential for future success.

Edward Mason and his associates (1980:350) share this view: "Because of the belief that graduates from several of the universities (Seoul National, Yonsei, Korea) have a better chance of obtaining employment in government or leading businesses upon graduation, places in those universities are in high demand, while provincial universities may have assigned to them students who have low scores on the examination." The most desirable marriage partner, therefore, has to graduate from a first-class university; this pressure, in turn, increases the competition to enter first-class universities. "Examination hell," the metaphor often used to depict this reality, is not an exaggeration.

Education in Contemporary Korea

Educational System and First-Tier Schools

During the Japanese occupation, the Korean school system was structured the same as that of Japan: six years of primary school, five years of secondary, and several junior colleges such as Ewha, Boseong, and Yeonhui, until the four-year Japanese-run Imperial University (Keijō Imperial University) was established in 1926. After the liberation, under the initiative led by the U.S. Military Government in close consultation with Korean members of the Advisory Council for Education, the Korean education system was restructured into 6-3-3-4: six years of primary school, three years of middle school, three years of high school, and four years of higher education.[29] Currently, the four-year colleges of medicine, pharmacology, and law are on the verge of creating three-year professional schools, like similar programs in the United States.

By the way, the Korean Ministry of Education and Human Resources Development is responsible for issues and concerns pertaining to both formal and informal education in Korea. However, the Korean Ministry of Education is more centralized and powerful than its U.S. counterpart, which delegates much of its functions to the states and other relevant organizations such as regional accreditation organizations, etc., while dealing mostly with the public school system, focusing on grades K–12. The power, authority, and jurisdiction of the Korean education ministry are extensive and regulate all Korean educational institutions, including higher educational institutions and privately endowed schools. The ministry also regulates the admissions policy of private colleges, and even the board of trustees of private colleges. The ministry can regulate virtually everything related to education, including the so-called "Three

'Nots' Policy," which will be described later.

By 2005, there were nearly 20,000 schools, ranging from kindergarten to university, and almost 9 million students enrolled in those schools.[30] In 1945, when Korea was liberated from Japan, out of all the students enrolled in the school system, 93 percent were in the primary grades (Mason et al. 1980:344). By 2005, students enrolled in primary grades accounted for only 44.9 percent of all students.[31]

In Korean education, private schools play a major role. Over 2 million students, 30.2 percent of a total of nearly 9 million, are enrolled in private schools, which number nearly 6,000, or 30.2 percent of a total of 20,000 schools. Of 349 institutions of higher education, 301 schools (86.2 percent) are private colleges and universities, and of over 600,000 students who enroll in those institutions of higher education, over 500,000 (85.5 percent) are studying in private colleges and universities.[32]

The nation's annual budget reflects the Korean concern for education. In 2001, for instance, the Korean central government allocated 8.2 percent of the total Korean GDP for education, the third largest proportion in the world.[33] In 2002, the Korean central government education budget was 22.3 trillion *won* (about $0.23 billion), which was 19.6 percent of the nation's total budget of 113.9 trillion *won* (about $121 billion),[34] a figure that has increased steadily around 7 percent per year through 2007.[35] For instance, in 2003, the budget for education was 4.6 percent of Korea's GDP, which made Korea seventeenth among OECD counties (5.4 in the United States, 5.1 percent England, 5.8 percent France, 6.0 percent Finland). However, Korea spends the highest percentage of private funds (2.9 percent) on education to its GDP than all other OECD member countries.[36]

Reflecting the Korean devotion to education, in 2003, for instance, 99.9 percent of students who graduated from primary school enrolled in middle school and 99.7 percent of students who graduated from middle school were going to attend high school.[37] The proportion of Korean students who graduated from high school and went on to colleges and universities increased from 79.7 percent in 2003 to 82.1

percent in 2005.[38] Parenthetically, in the United States, the percentage of high school graduates going to college was 56.6 percent in 2002, and fell slightly to 55.7 percent in 2004.[39] This indicates that the percentage of Korean high school graduates going to college is about 25 percent higher than in the United States. Also, in 2005, some 68,439 Koreans received masters' degrees, and 8,602 received doctoral degrees at home and abroad. Korean educational institutions have made great progress quantitatively and qualitatively. Right after the liberation in 1945 and before, during, and after the Korean War, there were not enough qualified teachers. Also, because of the war's widespread destruction, existing school buildings were used for double and triple teaching shifts due to the great number of students that had come from North Korea. In 1952, in the midst of the war, the student/teacher ratio was 66.5 in primary school, 37.4 in middle school, 27.3 in high school, and 26.7 in universities (Mason et al. 1980:352, *table* 93 in particular). At that time, there used to be nearly 70 or 80 students per classroom, but by 2002, class size had been reduced to 34.9 students in primary schools (*Handbook of Korea*, 2003:341). It is noteworthy that in 1985 the Korean government began to extend government-paid compulsory education from primary through middle school (nine years), starting with agricultural and fishery communities and gradually expanding to include all areas of the country by 2002.

Before the mid-1960s, when I left Korea, compulsory education until middle school would have been unthinkable and English lessons beginning in primary school unimaginable. However, Korea's Ministry of Education and Human Resources Development has plans to require, as of 2008, a two-hour weekly lesson in English starting with the first year of primary school.[40] Before English teaching became an integral part of the primary school curriculum, it had already been instated in private kindergartens and many *hagwon* (private tutoring centers) in most major cities throughout Korea.

During my stay at Yonsei University (1993–1994) as a senior Fulbright scholar, I had been asked by friends and relatives, "Is teaching preschool children English harmful or not?" Since I am not a professional linguist, I was unable to offer any professional opinion. I did tell them that I had seen European children learning several languages simultaneously, so presumably there would be no harm in doing so. My children are also bilingual, having been exposed to both Korean and English ever since they were born, and they experienced no delay in learning and conceptualizing.

Whatever its impact, the teaching of English in Korea is now an unstoppable phenomenon. English teaching has become a thriving business for private tutors and *hagwon*. Why are Koreans so enthusiastic about learning English? There are probably several reasons. First of all, we cannot deny the importance of American influence, resulting from intensive contact between the two countries ever since the end of World War II. Also, an unusual zeal for learning English was greatly reinforced when the wave of "internationalization" and "globalization" started sweeping the world, Korea in particular, in 1993 and 1994, before and after the signing of the Uruguay Round (UR) agreement.[41] Korea was facing the unavoidable challenge of internationalization and globalization. In 1993 and 1994, while I was still at Yonsei University, I observed the upheaval firsthand, when I was invited by several branches of the government and private organizations to talk about my views on globalization.

In order to meet the challenge of globalization, in November 1994 President Kim Young-sam introduced the neologism "*Segyehwa*," which combines several meanings: globalization, internationalization, and an open-door policy toward the outside world. There was a consensus at the time among informed Koreans that *Segyehwa* was to become a major world trend and an unavoidable destiny.

Recognizing that English competency would be essential for survival in the global arena, Korea has emphasized English instruction at all levels of schools, business communities, and government. In an effort to prepare for *Segyehwa*, many first-tier universities promote international student exchange programs. Some reputable Korean universities not only encourage their students to study abroad but also invite foreign students to come to Korean universities.[42]

Korean Enthusiasm for Overseas Education

Worth noting is the number of Koreans who have received terminal degrees from American educational institutions. According to information compiled by the Korea Research Foundation in 2004, from 1948 to 2004 a total number of 15,756 Koreans received their doctoral degrees from U.S. educational institutions.[43]

Currently, a large number of Koreans enroll in institutions of higher education in the United States. During the academic year 2003-2004, there were over 50,000 Korean students in institutions of higher education in the United States, the third largest number among all foreign students, after those from India (79,736) and China (61,765). In 2006, Korean students comprised nearly 15 percent of the total number of foreign students in the United States, followed by those from India (76,708), China (60,850), and Japan (45,820).[44] Considering the population sizes of the countries involved, the proportion of Korean students who study in the United States is truly astonishing.

The enthusiasm of Korean students for overseas education is not limited to higher education but is found at every level. Currently, among students who study overseas, primary school students outnumber middle and high school students. In 1998, only about 200 primary school students went overseas, but this number swelled to over 6,000 in 2004, about a thirty-fold increase over the past six years.[45]

Why have these numbers increased so dramatically? I have several interpretations of my own. First of all, a more lenient policy concerning overseas education has removed certain obstacles. Overseas educational opportunities used to be limited to those who had graduated from colleges and universities. Beginning in January 2000, a new law permitted those who had graduated from middle school in Korea to study overseas. When policy restrictions were eased, a large number of primary school students seized the opportunity for overseas study.[46] In August 2001, for instance, nearly 150,000 Korean students from all levels traveled to seventy-two foreign countries to study. As of September 2005, the total number of Korean students studying in the United States at all levels was over 86,000, 13.5 percent of the total number of foreign students. There were more students from Korea in the U.S. than from any other country.[47] In 2006, the number of Korean students of all ages studying in the United States neared 100,000, 15 percent of the total number of foreign students.[48]

Secondly, both students and their parents take the route of overseas education to avoid "examination hell." In Korea, the college entrance examination to top tier schools, particularly top tier colleges, is complicated and highly competitive, and preparation is furious. Before the Roh Moo-hyun government declared the so-called "Three 'Nots' Policy" (*sambul jeongchaek*), to be described later on, competition to get into the best schools began in the fifth and sixth grades in primary school, and sometimes even in kindergarten. From an early age, students work long hours after school with tutors or attend private tutoring centers (*hakwon*), additional study needed to memorize subjects likely to be on the examinations. Some children carry two meals with them, lunch for school and supper for tutorial school, leaving home at dawn and returning near midnight. Some young children's spinal cords are deformed because of their heavy school bags. For many children and parents, preparation for entrance examinations has become physically exhausting, emotionally draining, and financially burdensome. Failure to pass can mean a serious slide down the social ladder. Some students take the college entrance examination twice or even three times until they get acceptable scores.

Occasionally, children who did not do well enough to enter reputable schools or those who are afraid of get poor scores even commit suicide. On 24 November 2005, for instance, on the eve of the taking the College Scholastic Ability Test (CSAT),[49] a nineteen-year-old boy who graduated from high school and was scheduled to take the test for the second time committed suicide in Seoul.[50] According to a report prepared by the Korean Education Committee for the National Assembly, 462 students committed suicide from 2001 to 2004 because of examination pressure. It is alarming to note that, of 3,117 middle and high school students who were included in a nationwide survey conducted in 2005, nearly one half (48.6 percent) thought of committing suicide because of their low performance on the test.[51]

Since a good score on the CSAT opens many doors in addition to enrollment in a prestigious university, students and their parents take the test very seriously. Enrolling in a selective university not only means that a student will receive a quality education; perhaps even more important is the social network that connects the student to an alumni chain of tens of thousands of graduates who have fanned out into influential positions in society.

Because the test had not yet been introduced when I was applying to college, I was unfamiliar with it until after my return to Korea in 2001. At first, I thought it would be about the same as the Scholastic Aptitude Test (SAT) or American College Test (ACT) for American high school students who are going on to college. However, Korean parents, teachers, students, and the even government take the CSAT very seriously. In America, since standardized tests are offered several times during the academic year, and American students take the test, including the pre-SAT, during their junior year in high school, not many parents know their children's testing dates. However, in Korea, not only do students and parents know the test date, but the entire nation is aware of it. In fact, the entire nation tries to accommodate the test. On the test day, for instance, subways and buses extend their rush-hour schedules while all airplanes are grounded at Incheon and Gimpo airports for 15 minutes at 8:40 A.M. and for 20 minutes at 1:20 P.M., so students are not disturbed during a listening component of the test.

For college entrance, the CSAT score is not the only criterion. High school records and other factors, such as extracurricular activities, personal essays, and an in-depth interview, determine a student's chances of going to a good university. Nevertheless, the CSAT score carries the most weight. Therefore, students prepare intensively for the

CSAT test. Years of investment and hard work come down to one eight-hour test. Parents make every effort to prepare their children for this examination.

Among those students who have gone overseas for their early education, some high school graduates have received poor scores on the CSAT. Instead of enrolling at poorly rated colleges in Korea, they went abroad for their education, particularly in the 1980s and 1990s when competition was severe. However, competition to enter colleges and universities then began to ease because of demographic changes. In the academic year 2006-2007, there were 640,000 openings for freshmen in Korean colleges and universities but only approximately 557,134 students graduated from high schools in 2006. So, there are over 80,000 more positions than high school graduates to fill them, even if all high school graduates enroll in college, which is not the case. This trend will continue in the future because of Korea's slow population growth.[52] Korean women on average gave birth to 1.08 children in 2005.

Given this situation, there should not be any competition at all to enroll in college. It should be a "buyer's market." However, the burning desire of Koreans to be educated at top-tier colleges still fuels intense competition. Prestigious colleges are flooded with applications, while not-so-well-known colleges, especially in provincial areas, are having a difficult time recruiting students.

Thirdly, the dramatic increase in Korean students studying abroad has been fostered by Korea's national mood that stresses the importance of learning English. Students and their parents surmise that pursuing an education overseas means learning English effectively in the process. Many parents trust that if their children start learning English at an early age, they will become as fluent as native speakers.

Where Korean students choose to study overseas supports this observation. For primary, middle, and high school students seeking to study abroad, the United States was the most popular destination (28.7 percent of the total), followed by Canada, New Zealand, Australia, and Great Britain.[53] In selecting their destination, Korean students clearly prefer to study in English-speaking countries, a choice that reflects the Korean government's interest in offering English lessons in first grade and using native English-speaking teachers. Globalization has been another stimulus for Korean children going abroad for education from an early age.

In relation to early overseas study, a neologism has recently been introduced: *gireogi appa*, or "wild geese fathers." *Gireogi appa* refers to the father of a family whose young children and mother leave so the child can study overseas at an early age, while the father remains in Korea to support them. *Gireogi* (geese) are migratory birds, flying north to Siberia in the summer and south to Korea in the winter. Like geese, some fathers visit their families seasonally or occasionally. However, some fathers cannot afford to do so, and for them there is another neologism: *penguin appa* (penguin fathers), because penguins cannot fly, nor can they cross into warm ocean water from the cold Antarctic. There is still another group of fathers called *doksuri appa* (eagle fathers), who visit their wives and children overseas whenever they wish because they can afford frequent trips. This terms was probably coined because the eagle is a large and powerful bird, and symbolizes freedom.

To support the expense of early overseas study, parents not only have to make financial sacrifices but also disrupt normal family life. Eventually, this situation creates a family separated by an ocean, a phenomenon so common, widely diffused, and at times tragic that the *Washington Post* ran a detailed story entitled "A Wrenching Choice."[54] Some fathers who remain in Korea become so lonely that they commit suicide.[55] In 2005, educational expenses to support students studying abroad at an early age were estimated to be $3.5 billion. If spending by an accompanying family member were included, total expenses that year would have reached $10 billion.[56]

The Korean Obsession with Education and the "Three 'Nots' Policy"

Emphasis on education in Korea has brought about a highly

competitive entrance examination system that certainly lives up to its billing as "examination hell." It is apparent that Korean parents are determined to sacrifice everything so their children can obtain good scores on the CSAT test. Most Koreans seem to think that receiving degrees from top tier universities is almost the same as passing the high civil service examination (*gwageo*) of dynastic times. Graduates of the nation's top leading universities have a better chance of obtaining employment in government and leading businesses, and even of acquiring desirable marriage partners.

Perhaps educational policymakers in the Roh Moo-hyun government might even have envisioned some similarities between the college entrance examination and the civil service examination (*gwageo*), especially the *jinsa* (Literary Licentiates) section, of the Joseon dynasty. Those who passed the *jinsa* examination could enter the National Confucian Academy (*Seonggyungwan*) in Seoul, the nation's highest educational institution, for further study, and could then sit for the Erudite Examination (*mungwa*). Having passed the latter, they would then be able to take the Palace examination in the presence of the king. The man who attained the highest score in the Palace examination was accorded the title of *jangwon*, and could be appointed to a mid-level post in the government. If a man did not pass the first examination, he could not proceed to the next level of the *gwageo*, and would have no chance for a career as a civil servant. In a similar way, any modern-day student who is not accepted to a top-tier college is thought to have no chance for a promising career.

The civil service examination system was introduced from T'ang China to Silla in 788, and to Goryeo in 960. The system was further elaborated during the Joseon dynasty as a means of recruiting officials. However, since the examination system required extensive knowledge of the Confucian classics, it ended up promoting Confucian learning, even if unintentionally. Also, during the Joseon dynasty, although in theory any commoner or man of free status could sit for the examination, in reality, the *yangban* monopolized the examinations leading to appointment to civil offices.[57] This was because the opportunities for the kind of education needed to pass the examination were available almost exclusively to the *yangban*. In response to the negative impact of the traditional examination system, Korean education policymakers, particularly members of the "386 generation," who stood up against the privileged and the establishment during the military regime, have made a deliberate effort to deny any privilege to any group or institution, including first-tier universities. Such an ideology has brought about the so-called "Three 'Nots' Policy" as the principal directive of contemporary Korean education.

The Three 'Nots' Policy

Because the entrance examination for middle school was unfair and had many adverse effects on young children, it was abolished in 1969.[58] Only the high school entrance examination remained until it too was abolished in 1974 in an effort to eliminate rank order differences among high schools. Instead of the entrance examination, the Ministry of Education and Human Resources Development initiated a lottery system for admission to high school, beginning with Seoul and Pusan and eventually extending to the entire nation. However, the college entrance system remains the same, and competition for the top-tier universities has not changed, and may even have intensified.

In an effort to eliminate the differences among high schools and to implement an educational policy that offers equal opportunities for all, the Roh Moo-hyun government adopted the "Three 'Nots' Policy," which prohibits schools from managing their own college entrance examinations, accepting financial donations for admitting students and making students' high schools a factor in admissions. President Roh stresses that the "Three Nots Policy has only protected equal education opportunities for the nation, but also it is the fundamental element of education policy to maintain a cooperative society."[59]

Several leading members of the ruling Uri Party concur with the president: "Considering how bad the polarization of our society has become — especially with education, job and economic opportunities

— the Three Nots Policy should remain." Also, in order to mitigate the overwhelming importance of CSAT scores for entering college, Education Minister Kim Shin-il said in a letter to the nation, "Until now, many universities have accepted students who get high scores on national college entrance exams but have bad high school grades. But there will be very limited paths for students with bad high school grades from now."[60]

However, "the Three Nots Policy" has been challenged, particularly by administrative officials at various universities, including Seoul National University and numerous private universities. They demand that the government guarantee universities freedom in administrating and selecting students, and call for an educational policy that allows for fair competition. Most university administrators consider the Roh government's policy an obstacle to fair competition among universities in the globalizing world. It appears that this debate will be an ongoing one.

The Heavy Financial Burden for Parents

The emphasis on education has in turn increased the financial burden on parents. In 2002, for instance, about 83 percent of Korea's educational budget, 23.3 trillion *won* (about $24 billion) or about 20 percent of the annual budget, came from the central government. The remaining 17 percent, or 23.42 billion *won* (about $26 billion), came from the revenue of local governments. This budget, of course, does not include the funds from private foundations that support private schools. Most of the budget covers management costs at primary and secondary schools, the operating budget of national universities, and partial support for private universities and for educational administration and research organizations.

Korean parents seem to think the national budget for education is inadequate and that they need to supplement their children's education. Private contributions cover the costs of reference books, school supplies, transportation, and extracurricular activities. The largest sums are frequently spent on after-school tutoring. Some parents hire private tutors to prepare their children for the national examinations, and others pay for room and board for their children to stay in the best school district.

Korean parents spent $3.5 billion in 2005, excluding the living expenses of the accompanying family for their children's overseas study. In addition to this, a researcher at the Korean Educational Development Institute (KEDI) estimates that Korean parents spent 13.6 trillion *won* (about $144.9 billion), a figure which almost doubled between 1995 and 2005. An average parent spends 238,000 *won* (about $253) per child per month. The largest share of this sum — 7 trillion *won* (about $7.4 billion) — goes to primary school students.[61] The total annual educational cost paid by Korean households, including both overseas education and living expenses for the accompanying family member and domestic private spending on education, is over $17 billion, or over one-fifth of the total Korean annual budget. By 2003, Korea was spending the most private funds for education in relation to its GDP (2.9 percent) of all OECD member countries.[62]

Exodus of Rural Migrants and Soaring Real Estate Prices in Certain School Districts

Parents want to enroll their children in the best schools, and many leave the country for the city in order to do so. According to a study conducted in March 2005 by the Korean Center for the Study of Rural Economy (Hanguk Nongchon Gyeongje Yeonguwon), among 441 Koreans who left rural farming villages for cities, 123 (27.9 percent) indicated that they did so to provide better educational opportunities for their children.[63]

School attendance is determined by residency within school districts, and preference for school districts dictates migration within a city as well. Seoulites tend to relocate from poor school districts to better ones. A lavish school district located south of the Hangang called Gangnam (literally meaning south of the river) is known to be the best. Gangnam's many private tutoring institutes, called *hagwon*, are crowded with students. In order to take advantage of these resources, parents who can afford it purchase houses or apartments in the district, while others rent a room or apartment in order to meet the residency requirement. Because of this demand, real estate prices in that district are outrageously high.

Surplus Highly Educated Workforce
Korean higher education has expanded much more rapidly than the economy can incorporate college graduates. For the past several years, annual economic growth has slowed, and the number of college graduates has exceeded the manpower requirements of the economy.[64] The number of jobless Koreans hit a four-year high in 2005 with an annual unemployment rate of 3.7 percent as more people failed to land jobs amid a faltering economy.[65] The rate of unemployment among college graduates was 3.4 percent in 2005 and 3.5 percent in 2004, according to figures released by the Korea National Statistical Office.

Interestingly, for the past seven years, from 1999 to 2005, on average the employment rate of two-year junior college graduates (78.5 percent) has been higher than that of graduates of four-year universities (57.9 percent).[66] Consequently, in desperation, some four-year university graduates are seeking work that only requires a high school degree. For example, when five positions for expressway tollgate clerk became available, three of the 163 applicants had masters' degrees and forty-four had graduated from four-year universities.[67] Worried about the lack of employment opportunities, some students defer graduation, hoping to see an improvement in the job market.

Because of this "inflation" in educational qualifications, there is growing social pressure to reduce the number of four-year university graduates. The Ministry of Education and Human Resources Development has proposed the closing of fifteen national universities and has encouraged the remaining twenty-five to reduce their numbers by consolidating.[68]

Challenges for Korean Education

The Korean *han* to acquire better and higher education seems to have been satisfied to a great extent. From 1973 to 2004, in fact, over 8 million (8,396,170) Koreans received degrees from institutions of higher education, including two-year junior colleges, a national open university, and several "100 percent online universities." Now, with nearly 10 million graduates from institutions of higher education, it is time for the Korean educational system to upgrade the quality of education to match that of world-class universities. There are several challenges that must be met to bring this about.

First, an effort has to be made to reduce the gap in quality of education among various schools in Korea. Of the 349 colleges, some are world-class, yet others are poor in both facilities and the quality of the education that they offer. As long as there are great differences among universities, the extreme competition to enroll in the top-tier universities will continue. Because of Korea's low population growth, many provincial colleges are facing difficulties in recruiting students, and will suffer a severe shortage of applicants.

Demographers predict that by 2050 the total number of high school graduates will be 250,000, while available positions in colleges and universities will be 640,000. Even if all high school graduates go on to higher education each year, 380,000 positions will remain vacant. Consolidation among national universities alone will not solve the problem. Of 349 institutions of higher education, 39.1 percent are in Seoul and its vicinity, a situation which has contributed to a concentration of the Korean population in Seoul.

A second major challenge is restructuring the content of the curriculum as well as improving teaching methods. Korean textbooks are loaded with factual information, and instructors tend emphasize memorization rather than creative thinking, because it is easier and quicker to check, correct, and assign grades; "excellent students" are those who can retain large amounts of information. Perhaps this system has its origins in Confucian teaching, where the main aim was to memorize the Confucian classics and reproduce them well. In the words of foreign observers (Mason et al. 1980:372), "Especially at the higher levels of [Korean] education, curriculum and examination content would seem to discourage creativity and innovation." A German and former consultant of Booz Allen Hamilton Korea, Tariq Hussain (2006:185-218) is critical about the shortcomings of Korean education, which does not create globally competitive resources. In Hussain's view, the Korean educational system does not reinforce critical thinking and problem-solving skills, communication skills, diversity, and leadership.

A third challenge that Korean education has to confront is multicultural education, as the number of students with diverse cultural backgrounds and different languages is increasing. Unlike multiethnic societies such as the United States, Korea has been a homogeneous society with a common culture and language until recently. Hence, Korea does not have the experience needed to educate ethnically diverse students. The recent trend in marriages between rural men and foreign women has created a situation in which an increasing number of rural Korean students have diverse ethnic and cultural backgrounds.

Perhaps the greatest challenge Korean education has yet to face will be competition from foreign educational institutions in Korea. In order to meet the demands of the new century, Korea has not only lifted restrictions on overseas study but has allowed for the establishment of foreign schools. In May 2005, the National Assembly passed a bill allowing foreign schools to open in Korea's free economic zones, which include the entire provinces of Jeju, Songdo, Gwangyang, Busan, and Jinhae. On 19 January 2006, Korean President Roh Moo-hyun announced in his New Year's address that he would eventually allow foreign universities to establish themselves in Korea,[69] although no specific date has yet been set.

If Korean institutions of higher education meet these aforementioned challenges properly and wisely, this may be the best opportunity for Koreans to attain world-class status in higher education.

CHAPTER 8

Ethos

My attempt to describe the Korean ethos reminds me of Emmett Grogan's remark that "anything anybody can say about America is true,"[1] for it may also be the case that "anything anybody can say about Korea is true." It is difficult to depict the ethos of a nation like America because its racial, ethnic, and cultural diversity is so great that the end result may be superficial generalization. Individual variations within a nation or society can be greater than the variations between nations or societies. Some scholars such as Erich Fromm assert that national character is not only an obsolete concept, but the process of determining what it might be is analogous to constructing a "market personality": in figuring out national character, scholars "give the customers what they want," selecting some characteristics and omitting others.[2]

Korea is not as diversified as America, and it is by no means a small country in terms of its population. As of 2006, Korea was the twenty-fifth most populous country in the world out of 193 nations.[3] It is not completely isolated, nor is it as homogeneous as many Koreans claim, particularly in beliefs, values, and ideologies. We cannot assume that "all Koreans are alike and that they are different from other people" (Han 2003:26). After a prolonged absence from Korea, when I returned in 2001, I found that I was perhaps closer to the older generation of

American southerners (since I lived in the American South all along) in my way of thinking — though not in appearance, of course — than to the younger generation of Koreans. This is not an exaggeration. In fact, some conservative southerners resemble Asians. As my good Southern friend John Shelton Reed (1972:85) says, "Somebody once called Charlestonians [meaning aristocratic southerners] 'America's Japanese [indicating East Asians inclusively],' referring to their habits of eating rice and worshipping their ancestors, and the Southern concern with kin in general is indeed well known."

There is another pitfall in conceptualizing ethos: treating all characteristics as if they were synchronic without considering their historical origins, changes, and alterations resulting from national crises as well as socio-cultural transformations. It would be equally fallacious for anyone to assume that any characteristic quality of Koreans is a permanent one. The Korean ethos has changed in accordance with changes in Korean society — a new Korean ethos comes into being, or an old ethos is altered and reshaped as Korea changes. Because of such changes, it is difficult to categorize and generalize a single Korean ethos.

Another difficulty in dealing with ethos is choosing the most appropriate term from existing terms — "national character," "patterns," etc. Since the term "national character" has other connotations, some scholars prefer to use "ethos" (Befu 1971:151-179) instead. Yet, if ethos is defined as a "characteristic quality" (Biesanz and Biesanz 1973:98) of a society that "expresses a people's qualitative feeling, their emotional and moral sensing of the way things are and ought to be — their ethical system" (Hoebel 1958:543), then it is difficult to discern any difference between national character and ethos. In order to avoid both of these terms, other writers have coined the term "patterns" (Crane 1978). Still others have opted to use the term "Koreanness" instead of ethos or national character in delineating the characteristic qualities of Koreans (Han 2003:5-31). Regardless of the term I use, I intend to delineate what Koreans believe in as an ideal culture or value, and how they really behave as a practical or real culture. Most of all, I am interested in what makes Koreans "tick."

However I proceed and whatever my justification in attempting to delineate the Korean ethos, It will probably not be popular among today's anthropologists. National character was once a popular subject in anthropology, during the 1930s, 1940s and even the early 1950s, pursued by psychologically oriented anthropologists through the study of culture and personality. For instance, during World War II, in order to study Japan, a group of anthropologists developed a method to "study culture at a distance" since they were unable to conduct fieldwork in Japan because of the war (Benedict 1946; Gorer 1943; Mead 1951, 1953, 1962; Mead and Metraux 1953). However, the popularity of national-character studies faded after the war, and recent anthropology textbooks do not even have terms related to such studies in their indices (Hsu 1979:528).

Nevertheless, Francis L.K. Hsu (1979:528) perceives "a new urgency for studies of national character" as business and industries become increasingly global. A growing number of multinational business and industrial corporations have shown a keen interest in contrasting values cross-culturally (Ferraro 1998:88-114; Reeves-Ellington 1999:5-13; Serrie 1999:35-41; Young 2000:13-17). In the late 1980s in Korea, a new type of *hanguginnon* [Koreanness] developed as a form of cultural nationalism (Han 2003:25), which can be defined as the effort to revitalize the national community through creating, maintaining, and strengthening the nation-state's cultural identity (Han 2003, Kim 1998, Yoshino 1992). Interest in national character studies by anthropologists resembles slash-and-burn agriculture, an analogy anthropologist Anthony Wallace (1966:1254) once used to describe theory-building in cultural anthropology: "After cultivating a field for a while, the natives move on to a new one and left the bush take over; then they return, slash and burn and raise crops in the field again" (Wallace 1966:1254). If this analogy is correct, anthropologists may return to the "field" of national character and cultivate it again.

In categorizing traits associated with national character, the researcher's own identity as insider or outsider can result in bias, which is important to minimize. In complex, modern, industrialized and urban societies like Korea, it is difficult for anyone to characterize researchers in terms of "insider" versus "outsider," or "native" versus "foreigner." Nevertheless, when one studies one's own society, there is a tremendous advantage if one is already familiar with the culture and can easily arrive at generalizations from an insider's point of view. As anthropologist Magorah Maruyama (1969: 229-280) puts it, "Inculture persons are full of hypotheses of their own. These inculture-relevant hypotheses are often of the sort that cannot be dreamed up by outsiders." Nevertheless, one of the major concerns of the insider is maintaining objectivity (Kim 1977, 1987:943-946, 1990:196-201, 2002). Outsiders may have many handicaps, but can be less biased toward the society they are studying than insiders. If objectivity is essential for scientific work, being free from bias is important. While insiders may take things for granted, outsiders see things with fresh eyes (Kim 2002:88).

My dual identity as an anthropologist has been an advantage: I am in a sense an insider who was born, raised, and partly educated in Korea for twenty-seven years, and I am also an outsider who has been absent from Korea for thirty-five years during which I was living, working, and conducting fieldwork in the West (Kim 1977). In each of these settings, as an Asian fieldworker my identification has shifted from "insider" to "outsider," from "native" to "foreign" anthropologist, and from "marginal" to "perpetual marginal" to "reflexive" anthropologist (Kim 2002:xii). Because I have spent so much time outside of Korea, the bias inherent in the approach of an insider (or "native" anthropologist) is reduced.

Historical Circumstance and the Korean Ethos

The Korean Ethos during the Japanese Colonial Era

A particular historical circumstance can be very influential in the formation of an ethos. This was clearly the case for Korea during the

Japanese colonial period. The Japanese colonizers made efforts to describe the Korean ethos in papers such as "The Characteristic Features of the Korean People," issued by the Japanese Governor-General's office in 1927, and "The Real Nature of the Korean People" and "The Causes of Ills," both written by Choe Namseon (1890-1957) in the 1930s. These works listed a wide array of supposed characteristics of the Korean people, too numerous to mention here, ranging from "emotional volatility to lack of public-mindedness" (Han 2003:16), all of which are very negative.[4] Collectively they are no better than George Kennan's derogatory description of Korea and Koreans mentioned earlier in this book.

Yi Gwangsu (1892-1950), a cultural nationalist and well-known writer,[5] summarized the Korean ethos (*minjokseong*) in *Gaebyeok* (Creation), a monthly magazine, under the title of "Treatise on the Reconstruction of the Nation (*Minjok gaejoron*)" (Yi 1922:18-72). In that article, Yi "lashed out at the Korean tradition as an obstacle to progress, became a champion of individualism and free will, criticized early nationalist reformers for failing to maintain Korean independence, and encouraged capitalistic economic development as the basis for the rise of a middle class leadership" (Robinson 1988:67). Yi thought that it was his responsibility as a leading intellectual during that troubling time to find and condemn the shortcomings of the Korean national character so it could be dealt with in order to gain national independence.

Nevertheless, Yi's latent purpose of regaining national independence by getting rid of many harmful traditional traits was not fully acknowledged and appreciated by all Koreans, especially the radical nationalists.[6] Condemning Yi's pro-Japanese stance, they criticized his depiction of the Korean ethos because it had been made under the extraordinary circumstances of Japanese oppression and exploitation of Koreans as colonial subjects.

Major National Crises and Their Impact on the Korean Ethos

Historically, Koreans have experienced many major crises that have threatened their existence — Chinese domination, Mongol invasion, Japanese colonial rule, war mobilization on behalf of Japan during World War II, and the fratricidal Korean War. Koreans had to manage to survive during these harrowing times, and this in turn influenced the formation of the Korean ethos.

Han Kyung-Koo (2000b:289-303) argues that because of their history, Koreans have developed a particular kind of personality adept at surviving, adapting, and overcoming crises. The resulting modes of behavior include (1) an emphasis on "effectiveness over efficiency": employing any available means to accomplish the goal even if they are improper and ineffective to survive by any available means, even if it is improper; (2) an attitude of "now or never," a belief that if something cannot be attained now, there will be no second chance; (3) a "sojourners' mentality," meaning instead of having long-range plans and pursuing a goal methodically, carrying out a task hastily within a short period of time, even if it proves less profitable; (4) a belief that it is acceptable to violate existing rules because employing the correct and legitimate procedure to accomplish a task will cause one to lose out to those who use illegitimate means; and (5) the development of "factionalism" to attract and assemble sympathizers and defeat opponents, which fosters further factionalism. Many traits of the Korean ethos may have resulted from this "crisis-ridden" personality.

The liberation of Korea from Japan did not change the negative characteristics of the Korean ethos right away. In the early 1960s, one of the most popular writers of the time, Lee Eoryeong, described mostly negative Korean characteristics such as feudalism, irrationalism, cowardice, cruelty, etc. However, in the revised fortieth year anniversary edition of his book, published in 2002, "Yi [Lee] (2002) changed many aspects of his position and reinterpreted the same cultural patterns and artifacts in a more positive way, justifying his former statements as well-intended criticisms to help Korean society achieve the goal of modernization and economic growth" (Han 2003:18). Lee Gyutae (1981) listed mostly negative traits of the Korean ethos, including an inferiority complex, a disposition to conceal, introversion, fatalism, a tendency toward self-deprecation, dependency, etc. Lee's intention in revealing such negative traits seems to have been the same as Yi Gwangsu's.

Generational Character and Ethos

Changing aspects of Korean patterns and new interpretations of the traditional Korean ethos began to emerge in the 1980s with Korea's remarkable economic ascent. A new generation of Koreans appeared that had not been influenced by the negative traits linked to a "crisis-ridden personality." These new Koreans are probably best represented by the 386 generation, which is not only great in number, but also composed of the very people who were able to free themselves from the influence of the old values and resist the old practices in the workplace. As Kyung-Koo Han (2000a:355) has said, "We could perhaps discuss generational character, instead of national character."

While previous generations of Koreans could not escape the old values and practices, and tended to perpetuate them, the 386 generation has a very different character. As Korea achieved economic affluence, although there was some self-criticism, for example denouncing young people for their carefree attitude and lifestyle of conspicuous consumption[7] because of their newly acquired wealth and privilege, entirely new and positive characteristics also began to emerge: self-confidence, self-assurance, and pride under the slogan, "We can do it." This transformation is described in a book written by Lee Jangu and Lee Minha (2000),which uses the metaphor "*sinbaram* (wind of God)" to describe this new attitude of doing things willingly and cheerfully, going at tasks "like crazy." Koreans and Japanese use the same Chinese characters to write this word, but it has different sounds and meanings for each: in Korea, the word is "*sinbaram*," meaning the state of ecstasy a shaman falls into when possessed by a spirit; in Japan it is "*kamikaze*" (divine wind), a divine wind which saved Japan from attack by Mongols.[8]

Other aspects of this transformation in attitude have been pointed out by Kyung-Koo Han (2000a:354): "To be unruly, hasty, disobedient, uncooperative, overly competitive, etc. is no longer considered bad; such qualities are now expected to make Koreans into creative, resourceful, and independent-minded workers suitable for venture industry in the rapidly changing future."When Korea was colonized by Japan in 1910, Confucianism was identified as a major cause of Korea's misfortune, and came under heavy attack. Now, however, some native Korean scholars as well as foreign scholars are reevaluating the role of Confucianism in the Korean ethos. Koreans' view of Confucianism is indeed confusing, contradictory, and inconsistent at times. Michael Breen (2004:192), for instance, in categorizing the Korean character during the Joseon dynasty, found that "Koreans are governed by an ethos that is predominantly Confucian." Nowadays, Koreans no longer adhere to Confucianism as much as they used to.

Emergence of a New Ethos

I have personally witnessed the drastic shift in the Korean ethos from the 1960s to the 1980s. When I left Korea in the mid-1960s, it was a poor agrarian nation with a GNI of about $100. Because of the poor state of the Korean economy and resulting low standard of living, before I went to America, I had never used a Western-style toilet with toilet paper. It was also the first time I saw both hot and cold running water in a restroom. I had never had a full-course Western-style dinner. I did not know what to do with the many forks and knives when I was invited to a lavish Thanksgiving dinner at a grand hotel in Atlanta, Georgia, as a student at Emory University. Because of these experiences, during my early years in America I always felt uneasy and even ashamed at times, and became unnecessarily defensive.

However, within less than two decades, most Korean students who came to the university where I was teaching looked confident, self-assured, and even complained about the poor facilities in a rural Tennessee college town. Upon their arrival, most were able to buy expensive automobiles which they paid for in full with cash. Unlike my generation of Korean students who had come to America for advanced studies, most Korean students who arrived after the mid-

1980s were supported by their parents, and were well acquainted with Western manners. As a result they looked confident, apparently lacking even a trace of the defensiveness I once felt.

Display of the New Korean Ethos during the 2002 World Cup

Koreans' pride, their upbeat mood, and self-confidence as manifestations of this new Korean ethos were fully on display during the 2002 Fédération Internationale de Football Association (FIFA) World Cup hosted jointly by Japan and Korea. As the Korean team kept defeating several strong European teams, millions of cheering supporters, called "*Bulgeun angma*" (Red Devil), followed the team on and off the soccer field chanting, "*Daehan minguk*" (the Great Han People's State or Republic of Korea)," "*O, Pilseung Koria*" (Oh, victory Korea), and "*Urineun hana*" (We are one). At the semi-final-four game, some 200,000 red-shirted cheering young people roared, shouting these slogans, and at least 7 million Koreans poured out into the streets all over the country to cheer for the soccer team. Amazingly, there were practically no mishaps even though thousands and thousands of people, if not millions, gathered together spontaneously in the city plaza. After the cheering was over, the participants even picked up the litter, cleaning the streets themselves.

Ki-Wook Shin (2006:1–2) reports that such rallies were held overseas by Koreans in the Staples Center in Los Angeles (home of the Los Angeles Lakers), the city center of Paris, the Korean Embassy in Germany, and the Netherlands. Over 5.6 million overseas Koreans were roused to pride in being ethnic Korean based on a common bloodline and shared ancestry Shin (2006:2). According to Shin (2006:1), the fervor over the World Cup was not simply about soccer, but was an expression of Koreans' pride, identity, and confidence. It might have been a manifestation of a new "ethnic nationalism."

Previously, Korean nationalism (*minjok*) has been demonstrated throughout Korean history, for example in the March First Movement. However, the nationalistic slogan "We are one," alluding to national unity, pride, and confidence with a winning spirit, differs from previous slogans and displays of nationalism in scale and intensity. The use of this phrase did not signal a revolt against any oppression. Also, it did not exclude "non-ethnic elements," as evidenced by the honoring of Guus Hiddink, the Korean soccer team head coach, a native of Varsseveld in the Netherlands. After the Cup, he was granted honorary Korean citizenship. During the summer months while the FIFA World Cup was taking place, there had been the "Hiddink syndrome" and "Hiddink mania," because of the coach's managerial skills that helped the team to become one of the four semi-finalists in the FIFA World Cup, a ranking the Korean team had never before attained in the history of Korean soccer.

Hiddink's strategy was to select the best possible player for each position regardless of his previous reputation and without considering his background, such as family origin, regional ties, and school connections. Hiddink asked his players to become adept at the basic skills of soccer, to believe in themselves, to apply all the rules to everyone fairly, and to become innovative. No one aspect of his approach was unique or extraordinary, but because of Hiddink's personal popularity and the great success of Korean soccer, many labels appeared, such as the Hiddink style of management (*Hiddink-sik gyeongyeong*), the Hiddink style of personnel policy (*Hiddink-sik yonginsul*), and the Hiddink philosophy (*Hiddink cheolhak*). Many Korean business firms, including the Samsung Economic Research Institute (SERI), were interested in analyzing and learning from Hiddink's success so they could apply his strategy to managing their businesses. During the games, there were even a few placards that said, "Hiddink for President."[9]

It seems that the character Koreans displayed throughout the World Cup differed significantly from descriptions of the Korean character in the past — such as "hard to move emotionally," according to the Japanese Governor-General's office in 1927; having "weak will power," "lack of confidence," and "lack of pride," according to Choe Namseon in 1930; showing feelings of "inferiority" and "fatalism," according to Lee Gyutae in the 1970s and 1980s; and displaying "defeatism" and "cowardice," according to Lee Eoryeong in the 1960s. When I look at

Koreans today, I wonder whether we are talking about the same Koreans who were depicted by scholars and intellectuals during the Japanese colonization.

Parenthetically, millions of cheering supporters, that "Red Devil" who followed the Korean team on and off the soccer field, impressed soccer fans all over the world. Fans cheering for their teams via huge screens on the streets and in city squares throughout Korea created a new culture of positive team support in stark contrast to the commotions of "hooligans" that have marred European soccer. During the 2006 FIFA World Cup in Germany, soccer supporters copied the Korean behavior seen at the 2002 FIFA World Cup, watching large screens in the streets and on open squares. After watching the 2006 FIFA World Cup, on 10 July 2006 the *Financial Times* reported, "Anybody who stood with 750,000 people on Berlin's Fan Man Mile for any game — but particularly a Germany one — will never forget the experience."

Clearly, new traits have emerged in the nature of Koreans, replacing the old ones or merging with them, though some older characteristics still persist. Each period in history contributed to certain ideals and events that make up the sum total of the heritage of modern Koreans. In addition to the emergence of the new ethos, some traits have been reinterpreted in different time.

Aspects of the Korean ethos can be grouped into three categories: contradictory patterns, diminishing traditional patterns, and faithfully persisting patterns.

Contradictory Patterns

Vincent S.R. Brandt (1971:28) has stated that "contradictory forms of behavior are found in all cultures, but they seem to have been more dramatically expressed in Korea than in some other parts of the world." He has further noticed that Korean patterns of behavior are not only contradictory but that such contradictory formal values are often quite acceptable and may even be regarded as praiseworthy

(Brandt 1971:23). Brandt does not differentiate between ideal and real culture, but he uses a dualistic model of ideal cultures.

Breen (2004:17) has noted that "the Koreans have a way of upsetting you and getting into your heart at the same time." He has also observed that most Koreans' view *chaebŭl* (big business conglomerates) with great ambivalence, which could be interpreted as a contradiction: "On one hand, they [*chaebŭl*] are credited with having built the country and directly provided employment opportunities for millions. On the other hand, they are resented. The corrupt collusion with politicians, speculation in real estate, and domination of their local markets create an impression of capitalist greed and murky hands controlling the country" (Breen 2004:147).

According to Kwang-kyu Lee (2003:287), Koreans are preoccupied by the notion of "first class" famous brand names. Even a wrist watch has to be first class. Nevertheless, Koreans also strongly criticize the "conspicuous consumption" of others. The current level of the foreign currency reserve in Korea is so much higher than anticipated that the government has made an effort to encourage Koreans to invest in real estate overseas, yet Koreans who live Gangnam (south of the Hangang) have been penalized with an excessive real estate tax.

These are some of the contradictions found in Korea today. In the next section, I review some basic patterns of contradictory behavior that seem to characterize the Korean ethos.

Values Unhurried Calmness, Yet Craves Fast Results

Paul Crane (1978:13) reports that he had difficulty understanding "what the Koreans really think," adding that "the Oriental has had a distorted reputation for being inscrutable and impossible for the Westerner to understand." I have lived in the American South for as long as Crane has been in Korea, and just as Crane had difficulty understanding Koreans, I have had difficulty understanding southerners, and have come to the conclusion that they are inscrutable.[10] Contradictory patterns probably make a people's behavior even more confusing to outsiders.

If anyone from Mars had visited Korea during the Joseon dynasty and observed a Confucian gentleman and his mannerisms, the Martian would have concluded that Korean behavior was not hasty and never seemed hurried. Instead, the Martian would have seen Koreans as slowly and gracefully moving through life, a polite and gentle people. Crane (1978:16) depicts the unhurried, calm, and quiet behavior of a typical Confucian *yangban* gentleman:

> The fast-vanishing dignified Korean gentleman with his long white robe and horse-hair hat is the embodiment of Confucian culture. He walks as though his feet were heavy and his eyes were viewing the distant hills. He has a ready, earthy wit and is a born actor and comic, as well as a philosopher and autocrat. He demands respect (and he usually receives it) from those whom he meets. He is used to periods of tremendous work and long periods of unhurried quiet. He has, above all else, learned to endure. Of all the people on this globe, he is second to none in ability to suffer and survive in the face of impossible odds. He somehow eases through, and has been doing this under oppression, corrupt governments, and foreign invasions for thousands of years. He is like the tides, slow of motion but impossible to stop.

In early childhood, Koreans of my generation (those 60 years and older) were instructed repeatedly not to run, dash, or hurry, but to walk as cautiously and slowly as possible. A hurried culture was interpreted as rash, imprudent, and, most damning of all, "un-Confucian."

A hurried culture was not only denigrated by Confucians, but by traditional scholars and farmers. Crane (1978:54) elaborates:

> This rushing to meet the clock is not appreciated by traditional scholars and farmers, for it seems to them undignified and immodest to be rushing about like a flapping duck or a scared rat just to satisfy someone's obsession about the clock. Many people still do not think in time-space relationships, and are yet to be adjusted

to the concept of exactness in time or anything else. A new generation of men with military experience may eventually bring time-consciousness to the Korean scene. To appear to be in a rush is still considered impolite and unbecoming to a gentleman.

Crane (1978:54) further discusses the unhurried nature of Korean interactions with this anecdote: "There was a time when the driver of a Model T Ford wishing to pass a missionary in another Model T stopped his car after passing and apologized and explained how he had to catch a train, and asked forgiveness for the impoliteness of passing an honorable teacher."

Times have changed, however, and so have Korean patterns of behavior. As Crane (1978:54) has noticed, "Modern drivers in Seoul seem to practice the same tactics as the famous *kamikaze* taxi drivers of Tokyo, and have lost all pretense of courtesy on the road." Here Crane is actually describing life on Korean roads in the kindest and mildest way. As anyone who has ever driven a car in any Korean city knows, it is dangerous to even slow down to read a road sign. Countless cars behind will honk to show their impatience as if ready to run right over you. Many cut in front of you dangerously without any warning, refusing to wait or follow behind a slow-moving vehicle. Because of its "hurried" culture, Korea is now reported to have the highest rate of traffic accidents in the world.[11]

Dick Advocaat, a Dutchman who was appointed head coach of the Korean National Soccer team in September 2005 to prepare them for the 2006 FIFA World Cup in Germany, knew only two Korean words, "*ppalli ppalli*" (hurry up) and "*gamsa-hamnida*" (thank you). He has said that he loves the word *ppalli ppalli* the best because of its application to soccer games.[12] Any foreigner who had known any Korean Confucian gentleman of the past would certainly be shocked by these fast, aggressive, and hustling contemporary Koreans. Indeed, he would probably wonder whether they are the same people. Which one is the real Korean? Was the stereotypical Korean *yangban* in his dignified Confucian robes, who was seemingly never in a hurry, simply the product of Confucian influence?

There is evidence that the hurried Korean culture we see today is not a new phenomenon. Witness the twenty-second king of the Joseon dynasty, Jeongjo (1776–1800), who constructed the stone wall, Hwaseong, in Suwon, Gyeonggi province. This 5.74-kilometer stone wall with forty-eight gates was originally supposed to be completed in ten years, but the construction took only two years and nine months (Kim 2007:19). And this happened in a period dominated by Confucianism.

So no one really knows whether the Koreans' hurried culture was a dominant pattern before the introduction of Confucian-oriented *yangban* culture, but Korean journalist Guk Heungju (1986:117–119) believes just that. He proposes several reasons why the Korean national character is so hurried: first, since they were descendants of horse-riding, nomadic northern people (Goguryeo people), Koreans became accustomed to making quick decisions on horseback while moving swiftly; second, Koreans had been attacked so often and so many times by foreign enemies that they had become used to finishing everything quickly in order to either run or hide (Guk 1986:117–119).[13]

Because of such hustling and bustling, Koreans have a well-earned international reputation for being hard workers. Breen (2004:175) reports, "On construction sites in the Middle East and South-east Asia, they have impressed governments with their round-the-clock operations and their ability to beat deadlines." Breen (2004:176) offers a story about his own experience with Korean hustle:

> Car breaks down? No problem. Once I was on the motorway with my family when the accelerator cable snapped. We were spotted by a pickup vehicle that patrolled the roads looking for victims. In no time the driver and his mate had hoisted the car off its front wheels and were tugging us along the road. We were still in the car of course. Going along a road at about fifty m.p.h. on your back wheels with no view except the back end of a truck may be exciting for children but is unnerving for adults. We were pulled

to a small village where they had a workshop. A lad was dispatched to the nearby town to get the part and we were shown the village restaurant. After some noodles and kimchi, the car was done and we were back on the road.

Korea remains one of very few countries in the world where one can get many things done immediately. Because of Koreans' reputation for demanding fast results, Alan Cassels, a newly appointed CEO of German-based DHL (Dalsey, Hillblom, & Lynn)-Korea, an international express-mail service firm, has declared that it is his ambition to satisfy fast-paced Korean customers.[14] Of course, there are bound to be a few downsides to such speedy work in terms of quality. In the 1990s, this rushed approach to building bridges and department stores brought about major disasters.

Nevertheless, despite the downside of such a fast-paced work ethic, in Korea it is widely accepted as ideal. Most Koreans believe that without this characteristic Korea would never have been able to catch up with its neighbors, particularly Japan. Thanks to this culture of hurry, Korea was able to achieve formidable economic progress and industrialization in a very short period of time. By the mid-1980s, for instance, the small fishing town of Pohang had become the world's single biggest steel production plant, POSCO, second only to Japan's Nipon Steel. While Japan took nearly 100 years to become one of the world's top automobile manufacturers, Korea became internationally competitive with Japan in automobile sales in only fifty years. Recently, the chairman of one of the top Korean conglomerates whose annual sales total 21 trillion *won* (about $22.3 billion) told his employees, "We have to be faster to keep a competitive edge over other countries. Nowadays, a big firm is not taking over the small one, but the faster one will take over the slower one. Let's move faster and swifter!"[15]

It appears that in order to survive in Korea, one always has to move fast, rush, and hurry. If not, one will not merely stand still, but actually be pushed back. Certainly this norm contradicts the norm of the ideal Confucian gentleman who was required to move as gracefully as possible with all the dignity in the world.

An Inclusive Worldview with Exclusive "One-ness"

There is ample evidence of Korean inclusiveness when it comes to religious beliefs. If inclusiveness means "the act of incorporating or attitude of wishing to be incorporated" (Hsu 1965:638–661), this quality is also prominent in Korean family and kin groups, either through lineage or clan, and in other socially defined groups determined by locality and school networks. Koreans extend the family-group concept not only to their immediate family but to the entire kin group to which they belong. As long as they can identify that they were descended from a common ancestor, real or presumed, regardless of how remote they might be from this ancestor, they address their fellow "descendants" with basic kinship terms, interact with them like family members, and demonstrate loyalty to them accordingly. Loyalty goes first and foremost to the immediate family, then to known blood relatives, and then to lineage and the clan (Crane 1978:32).

If there is no kinship relationship, Koreans extend the boundaries of inclusiveness to school ties, following the pattern of kinship ties.[16] The bonds among school classmates and alumni are very intimate and strong. Jaeyeol Yee (2000:330) reports that "average Koreans invest more time and energy to maintain their personal network than average Americans. ⋯ Koreans tend to choose more homogeneous people as their network partners." Classmates and schoolmates are obliged to look after each other when in need. For example, the 1961 *coup d'état* led by Maj. Gen. Park Chung-hee was initially carried out largely by members of the Eighth Class of the Korean Military Academy. "Every Eighth Class member, whether or not he actually took part in the *coup*, became a powerful person" (Crane 1978:46). In addition to classmates, the relationship among alumni, especially between seniors (*seonbae*) who graduated earlier and juniors (*hubae*) who graduated later from the same school are analogous to kin relationships between older and younger brothers (or sisters), and they actually address each other using the real kinship terms of "older" and "younger" brother (or sister).

When school and regional ties overlap, this combined bond becomes even stronger than kinship ties, and inter-personal relationships are indeed inclusive. Hak Chong Lee (1989:156-157), a Korean business professor, has observed that in the Korean business world, school connections, regional ties, and kinship networks work not only in the formation of power groups at the top, but also in the formation of informal relations and cliques at all levels throughout Korean organizations.

While Koreans are extremely open to religious beliefs and interpersonal relationships within the boundaries of the group with which they have identified themselves, they tend to shun those who do not belong to their group. As Kwang-kyu Lee (2003:275) observes, "To someone they do not know, members of an intimate circle tend to show attitudes and behaviors that are cold, unkind, unpleasant, and rude." Some foreign observers who have been in Korea for a prolonged period of time share this view. British Catholic priest Clifford E.J. Smart (1978:117-123) who has lived in Korea since 1956, says, "Koreans are kind in treating strangers when they visit their homes [within their fence], but outside the fence of their boundary or on the street, their attitude toward the strangers is different. They pretend not to know them, and even ignore the strangers." Breen (2004:52) points out that "there is no guilt about behaving unfairly or rudely towards someone who is outside. ⋯ Koreans can be extremely rude towards non-persons. There is a remarkable lack of civic mindedness. ⋯ The Koreans can also be extremely cruel to non-persons."

According to Crane (1978:30), a foreigner is categorized as a "un-person." Some foreigners such as Breen (2004:20) have felt that "Korean intellectuals become more xenophobic, nationalistic, and perpetuate the idea that all of Korea's problems are the result of willfulness by foreigners. This is the mark of a scoundrel." According to a survey conducted by the Corea [Korea] Image Communication Institute (CICI) of 213 foreign "opinion leaders," including foreign companies' CEOs, diplomats, foreign professors, correspondents, branch managers of the foreign banks, and business expatriates[17] who live in Korea, Koreans are not open-minded, and are xenophobic toward foreigners. Whether such a criticism is valid or not, Breen (2004:68) notes that "Koreans see virtue in unity; one mind, one people, one system, one race, one path." Clearly foreigners are not seen as belonging to this category of "one." Perhaps Hiddink, the winning head coach for the Korean national soccer team, was an exception to the rule of "oneness."

Evidence of this attitude toward foreigners can be seen in Korean society's institutionalized discrimination against children of mixed marriages, who were often born into poor families and stigmatized. There was even a ban on mixed-race men in military service. It was imposed on the assumption that they would not fit into barracks life. However, despite this discrimination, Korea's mixed race population has increased and diversified, as farmers and blue-collar workers have turned to Southeast Asian countries in search of spouses. Although it is a slow process, the traditional Korean fear and distrust of foreigners has begun to change.

Korean xenophobia is the result of countless foreign invasions and domination by hostile neighbors, including numerous nomadic northern tribes, Mongols, successive Chinese dynasties, Russians, and Japanese. Korean uneasiness in dealing with outsiders and overt displays of hostility toward strangers and foreigners are by-products of the long historical ordeal Koreans have experienced over many centuries.

Until recently, most Koreans had very limited interaction with outsiders beginning in early childhood. In the Korean child-rearing process, Koreans are seldom exposed to strangers, spending all their time with members of their extended family. Since most American parents as a matter of course often leave their children with baby sitters who are complete strangers to the children, American children are used to adapting to people they do not know well. Until very recently, as is the case in Japan as Harumi Befu (1971:155) pointed out, few Korean children had babysitters. They rarely had a chance to deal with non-family members in the child-rearing process. Korean children would receive all of their comfort exclusively from family members — mothers, grandmother, aunts, nieces, and siblings — and they did not have the chance to learn to live with outsiders and strangers.

Remarkable Endurance, Explosive Impatience (A Thin-pan or "Naembi" Culture)

As Crane (1978:96) has indicated, "One of the great virtues of many Koreans is their ability to endure hardship. Korea is the land of those who have learned to endure in order to survive." The geopolitics of the Korean peninsula has ensured that the country has been vulnerable to attacks from hostile neighbors. In addition to invasion and domination by Chinese dynasties over the centuries, including the CPV during the Korean War, there have been continual intrusions from nomadic northern tribes such as the Yen, Khitan, Jurchen, and Mongols. Two full-scale Japanese invasions of Korea led by Toyotomi Hideyoshi in the late sixteenth century devastated the peninsula and eventually led to Korea's annexation by Japan in 1910.

When Korea lived under Japanese rule from 1910 to 1945, Japan tried to eliminate Korean culture in order to assimilate it into Japanese culture. Although Koreans adopted some external traits from the Japanese that fit into traditional Korean patterns, they rejected most mannerisms and customs that were distinctly Japanese. Despite the invasions by Chinese, Mongols, and others, "Koreans have remained true to their own culture and patterns of thought as developed through the centuries" (Crane 1978:125).

Not only has Korea as a nation demonstrated its endurance, but Koreans as individuals have exhibited remarkable endurance under the tragic circumstances of family dispersal before, during, and after the Korean War. Although some separated couples have remarried, a great many have not done so over some sixty years, choosing to remain single, hoping someday to be reunited with their loved ones.

Until most recently, Koreans have accepted such misfortune and suffering as fate. Fate is understood to be a destiny beyond one's own power and control. Some writers view fatalism as a Korean characteristic. Yun Taerim (1971:390-391) indicates that such fatalism is a core Korean value and traces its origin to the socio-economic and political structure of the Joseon dynasty. Kim Inhoe (1980:iii–v) recognizes fatalism as an important Korean pattern but traces its genesis from Shamanism. Kim Taegil (1977:16-20), a Korean ethicist, acknowledges that fatalism in Korea novels is an important pattern. As early as 1836, French missionary Clause-Charles Dallet (1829-1878) noticed that Koreans believed that everything would be decided by predetermined fate (Hong 1975:196-197). Edward Poitras (1978:29-35), John Gibson (1978:269-274), and Uting Ti (1978:241-247), a Chinese, all of whom have been in Korea for a prolonged period of time, share the same view of Korean fatalism.

In Korea, endurance (if not fatalism or predeterminism) has been considered a virtue; impatience, by contrast, is thought to be "a major sin" (Crane 1978:97). Nevertheless, in a contradictory pattern, Koreans display explosive impatience related to their rushed and hurried culture. Breen (2004:67) has made an observation on impatience, particularly among males: "Korean organizations are full of impatient males who want things done 'yesterday' for results 'tomorrow,' irrespective of what may happen the day after." In reference to Korean impatience, there is the widely circulated cliché of a "thin frying-pan, which gets hot easily, and cools off quickly." Koreans can get mad and upset easily, but forget or forgive soon. In my own experience living in the United States, while Americans tend to wait in a long line dutifully and patiently without complaint, Koreans tend to be impatient while waiting in line, so they make every effort to keep lines short.

This impatience, coupled with their hurried culture, leads Koreans to show their feelings openly, while Westerners have learned to cover up or sublimate their emotions in order to be accepted in their own culture (Crane 1978:13). Breen (2004:35) quotes his Korean colleague on this matter:

> The language [Korean] lays itself open for such misinterpretation;

Koreans do not use language to convey literal meaning to the extent that we do. "If I say I'll kill you to a stranger in English, he might take pre-emptive action," said Shim Jae-hoon, a journalist fluent in English. "In Korea, you're just expressing a feeling. Korean is not a good language to argue in because there are so many shades of meaning. It is so easy to be misunderstood. English is a language for clarity and logic. It's a beautiful language to argue in.

According to Breen (2004:27), Koreans are not trained to think in a sufficiently rational and legalistic way: even "Korean negotiators in international forums make themselves look rather silly and end up making emotional appeals rather than reasoned arguments." Kwang-kyu Lee (2003:253) concurs with Breen, stating that "Koreans in general are better known as emotional rather than reasoning people." As Breen (2004:35) has pointed out, "Koreans can indeed explode in anger very easily." Breen (2004:8-9) sums up the Korean character as the "Irish of the East. ⋯ They are as vigorous in their character and the defense of their identity as the Israelis, and as chaotically attractive as the Italians ⋯ like the Irish, the Koreans are also a lyrical people, inclined to the spiritual, and exhibiting a warmth and hospitality that belies their violent image. They can be unrestrained in their passions, quick to cry and to laugh." One of the nicest aspects of Koreans is that they are not raised to feel that displays of emotion are a weakness. They push themselves to study and succeed. At the same time, they can be embarrassingly earthy and blunt.

According to Crane (1978:25), in expressing emotion as well as in interpersonal relationships, *gibun* (feelings or state of mind) is one of the most important factors influencing conduct and relations with others. "This rich word has no true English equivalent. 'Mood' may come close but much more is involved. When the *kibun* [*gibun*] is good, one 'feels like a million dollars,' when bad, one 'feels like eating worms'" (Crane 1978:25). One's bodily functions are largely dependent on the state of one's gibun. If the gibun is good, then one functions smoothly and with ease. If the *gibun* is upset, then functions may come to a complete halt. The way Koreans display emotion toward others in interpersonal relationships is governed by the state of the *gibun*.

Diminishing Traditional Patterns
Several traditional Korean patterns, once obvious and dominant, have begun to change in accordance with broad changes in Korea.

From Politeness and Humility to the "Can-do Spirit" of Self-Confidence
"Koreans are among the most naturally polite people one will meet when the proper rules of etiquette are followed," observed Crane (1978:51), "In the remotest mountain village, one will find gracious manners practiced unconsciously. Etiquette is observed in the humblest home as well as in the compounds of the great. The exquisite niceties of a cultured Korean make even an American Southern Gentleman 'seem crude and barbaric.'" According to Reed (1972:45), "Southerners will be polite until they're angry enough to kill you."

Koreans are known to be polite, kind, and humble to others. There is a Korean proverb about "three unworthy, uncivilized, and uncultured persons (*sambulchul*)," one who brags about himself, one who praises his children in front of others, and one who boasts about his wife. Even if one's accomplishments are outstanding, one has to show humility, which is regarded as a virtue and ideal pattern in traditional Korean society. Even at meals for guests, the host sits in the lowest place at the table, the farthest from the place of honor, and always states that he has "prepared nothing," even when the most lavish food he could afford sits on the table.

In the past, Koreans understood that if a person was worthy of recognition, people would agree by mutual understanding as documented in the case of Zuni Indians. Some seventy years ago, Chinese anthropologist Li An-che (1937:62-76) recognized that in the Zuni Indian tribe, where mutual give and take is harmoniously assumed, one might be "humble" and still be selected as a leader among men, if one merited it. In the same fashion, in Korea, an individual's merit has been naturally recognized by the mutual understanding of all. A humble attitude and humility were considered assets rather than liabilities.

These things are changing as Korea becomes a competitive society. As the Korean political system adopts a democratic electoral system, one has to run and promote oneself to become an elected official. Since Korea is no longer a small and mutually understanding society where everyone knows everyone else, someone who runs for election has to introduce himself or herself to the constituency as part of an emerging new culture. In this process, some tend to brag about themselves intentionally or unintentionally. This new pattern has been further reinforced by the "can do" spirit inspired by President Park Chung-hee, and the remarkable sense of self-confidence that has emerged as Korea has built one of the world's largest economies from the ashes of the destruction of the Korean War. These developments have further diminished the traditional pattern of fatalism.

From Inward Worldview to Outward Effort

The first Western anthropologist who conducted anthropological fieldwork in Korea, Cornelius Osgood (1951:331) observed that Koreans are passive and inner-directed (Kim 2000:17-21). Edward Poitras (1978:29-35) goes further in implying that such inner-directedness has encouraged Koreans to feel a strong attachment to their home country even after they emigrate, so they remain "aliens" rather than citizens of their new countries. Lee Gyutae (1981, I:297-338) agrees with these outsiders that inwardness is at the core of Korean cultural patterns. Such inwardness can even be seen in tool-making. While American-made hand-saws cut wood when one pushes outward, Korean-made hand-saws cut when one pulls inward, toward oneself. Koreans opt to use this metaphor: "The arms naturally bend inward" (*pareun aneuro gumneunda*).

Because of this inward thinking, Koreans are strongly attached to their hometowns. Until recently, Koreans rushed home during the holidays with the same intensity that American workers rush toward the parking lot after five o'clock. Furthermore, people like to be buried in some way in their hometown, even if it is nothing but a broken piece of tooth, a lock of hair, or a pair of shoes they once wore (Lee 1981, II:87-90). Horace H. Underwood (1978:89-93) points out that in Korea there are many songs and poems about hometowns and homesickness.

This characteristic of inwardness is also shared by China and Japan. Korea was forced to broaden its perspective when foreign attacks resulted in a Korean diaspora. Recently, however, Koreans have been expanding their sphere of interaction voluntarily toward the outside world through diplomatic missions, business expatriates, students, overseas missionaries, and by expanding FTAs with various countries. Perhaps Koreans, long characterized by inwardness, are on their way to becoming one of the most outward-looking people in the world.

From Prohibitive Norm-Oriented Patterns to Permissive Norm-Oriented Ones

Classic anthropological studies show that in a traditional society norms are prohibitive or constraining, but in a modern society they are permissive by providing alternatives (Redfield 1947:293-308). Some anthropologists understand this dichotomized explanation as too idyllic and simplified (Lewis 0 1966:51-64), but such a comparison does seem to hold in looking at how Korean society has evolved. Many Koreans of the old generation vividly remember that they were taught under the strict rule of prohibitive norms, such as "don't do this" or "that is not to be done." A child would be told not to dance on top of the dinner table, for instance, but would seldom have been told that he or she could dance on the floor. Such a child-rearing practice often resulted in blind obedience to parents, seniors, and superiors. "Obedience," Kwang-kyu Lee (2003:276) concurs, "is highly respected in the homogeneous society [Korea in the past]." Brandt (1971:173) has observed that when children are punished, beaten, or slapped, "it is usually for disobedience rather than wrongdoing." Brandt (1971:173) further elaborates on this point:

> In fact, most people are extraordinarily tolerant when a child causes trouble by breaking something, by making his younger brother cry, or through any other mischief. "He is only a child and doesn't know any better," is a phrase that is constantly heard. But once a command is given, strict compliance is required. Parents strike children for failing to obey such orders as, "Bring the dish," "Light the fire," "Carry the baby on your back," "Stop teasing the baby," "Don't eat that," and so on.

As Brandt (1971:173) has observed, "children are encouraged to be dependent, obedient, and cooperative," which differs from Euro-American norms. In America, most families enforce scheduled feeding and a fixed bedtime, but in Korea, children tend to stay up as late as they wish at night until they fall asleep from exhaustion. As a step toward becoming self-reliant, North American children sleep in separate rooms alone according to a bedtime schedule, so that they have to learn to cope with the tension arising from being left alone in the crib or bed. Korean children, however, go to bed with their parents. Such a practice might satisfy the children emotionally, but it promotes great dependency on the parents, the mother in particular, and inhibits the formation of self-reliance. On a social level, Korean children have been brought up to be so obedient that they are reluctant to speak their minds in front of their superiors in organizational life, which discourages feedback from subordinates.

Recently, however, this prohibitive norm is becoming more permissive. There are many plausible explanations for this change, but a major contributor is improvement in the Korean standard of living. A growing number of urban middle class people can afford to have a separate room for their child or children, in keeping with Western child-rearing practices. In such cases, while many parents still prefer to sleep on an *ondol* floor, almost all children sleep on beds.

Another factor contributing to the development of the permissive pattern is the small number of children in contemporary Korean families. Since Korea is a nation with one of the lowest birth rates in the world, children are considered extremely precious. Parents do not treat children the way the older generation did years ago in the days of overpopulation. Parents' obsessive and slavish concern for their children's welfare has turned them into dedicated "servants" of the children. Nowadays, it appears that Korean parents are less firm in disciplining their children than previous generations, and have instead become excessively protective and indulgent.

Many of today's Korean mothers tend to think that imposing prohibitive norms on their children would discourage their *gi* (exultant spirit). In the meantime, some children quickly learn that they can abuse permissive norms, taking advantage of them for their own self-interest. Contemporary Koreans seem to be even more permissive than their Western counterparts.

Persisting Patterns

While some traditional Korean patterns have been changed, somewhat altered, or replaced with emerging new ones, other traditional patterns still persist. These remaining Korean norms are an emphasis on education, a burning desire to release *han* (unfulfilled wishes and desires), the emotional display of *gibun* (feelings or state of mind), and the pattern of seeking to out-do one another ("one-upmanship").

Emphasis on Education

Although educational opportunities were once limited to certain privileged groups such as aristocratic families and the *yangban*, beginning in the Three Kingdoms period Koreans recognized the importance of education since it was the key to improving social and economic standing in society. The Korean emphasis on education and zeal for acquiring more and more of it have not diminished. Enough has been said on this topic, but a few words can be added here. The Korean respect for education has not simply persisted, but has actually intensified as Korea has become a key player in an increasingly globalizing world, undergoing a major transformation from a pre-industrial society to an ultra-modern one in the era of information technology.

A Burning Desire to Release "Han"

As mentioned above, an adequate translation of the word "*han*" into English is lacking, although "unfulfilled wishes and desires" comes close. The burning desire to release han *has* served as the major force driving Koreans to accomplish many things in many fields in a very short period of time. To maintain a decent way of life, persistent hunger and poverty have to be eliminated. The Korean pattern of *han* with respect to material goods has been released as Koreans have become better than ever at achieving economic success. Since national unification remains a *han* for Koreans, it might be released by the eventual unification of the two Koreas. This might not be a matter of "if" but "when," as long as this remains a *han* for Koreans. Despite the continuing importance of *han* for Korean culture, since *han* has been "released" or "fulfilled" to a certain extent nowadays, its function is diminishing.

Gibun

An adequate translation of *gibun* (feelings, mood, or state of mind) into English may be as difficult as that of *han*, but *gibun* is of prime importance in influencing conduct and relations with other people. If *gibun* is good, everything goes smoothly and easily, but if *gibun* is bad, even ordinary tasks become impossible. If one damages the *gibun* of others in personal relations, nothing can be accomplished. One American businessman told me that in dealing with the chairman of a large Korean business firm, he did not have to attend the second and third scheduled meetings, because the Korean chairman could foresee everything that was going to happen if his *gibun* was good, including the final outcome. Many subordinates in Korean organizations try to read the *gibun* of their superiors and often check with secretaries and chauffeurs who woul be the first to know if bosses are in good *gibun*. When one's *gibun* is bad, one is "justified in behaving badly, rejecting business proposals, barking at your wife and secretary" (Breen 2004:39).

Most of all, possessing good *gibun* gives one enormous power to drive forward beyond ordinary physical limits. Recent Korean economic prosperity has been accomplished so quickly because of the Korean drive to hurry supported by rising *gibun*. Indeed, according to Crane (1978:25), who is very perceptive about Korean patterns of *gibun*, "In interpersonal relationships, keeping the *gibun* in good order often takes precedence over other considerations."

"Out-doing" One Another (One-upmanship)

By examining Korean history, one can easily surmise that Koreans have been good students in learning foreign cultures and have also been good teachers. From the Three Kingdoms period, Koreans learned Chinese characters before they invented their own written language, *Hangeul*, in 1446, and they adopted the Chinese religions of Confucianism, Taoism, and Buddhism, which originated in India via China. Beginning in the late eighteenth century, in willy-nilly fashion Koreans adopted Christianity and some aspects of Japanese culture, even though it was forced.

After liberation, through intensive contacts with the United States, Koreans became knowledgeable in American political, academic, economic, business, and military affairs. For instance, Hyundai Construction Company, one of Korea's major conglomerates, became a world-class construction company by learning to win contracts for U.S. Army barracks construction, airport expansion projects and bridge-building projects during the war. Koreans then transferred the skills and knowledge they acquired from these projects to the Middle East and other parts of the world (Jones and Sakong 1980:356–358).

Not only have Koreans been good students of other cultures, but they have also been good teachers, transferring knowledge learned from other cultures to other countries. Japan has been a major beneficiary of Korean teaching on Buddhism and various arts associated with Buddhism and Neo-Confucianism. In early Japanese culture, "Chinese cultural influence had been imported by way of Korea for centuries and the Chinese script used for records from 400 onwards," writes Arthur Cotterell (1993:62). During the reign of Shotoku (574-622), who laid the foundations for the Japanese state, Japan adopted the rank system for Japanese court officials, modeling it after the "bone-rank" system of the Silla dynasty of Korea (Cotterell 1993:64).[18] Recently, rapid Korean economic progress and industrialization have served as a role model for Chinese economic development and industrialization. Recently, a growing number of developing countries have shown interest in learning about Korea's New Village Movement in order to vitalize their rural villages.

Once Koreans learn foreign religions and ideologies, they excel at proliferating the borrowed culture and often outdo its originators. Korean perpetuation and development of Confucianism, Buddhism, Christianity, Communism, and capitalism are among the most extreme and successful examples. Koreans have demonstrated that they have been more Confucian than the Chinese in their devotion to Confucianism, particularly with Neo-Confucianism (Janelli and Yim 1982:177; Osgood 1951:332; Peterson 1974:28). Korean has enthusiastically embraced Christianity when compared with traditionally Christian countries. With regards to Communism, North Korea remains one of very few countries that remain Communist (along with Cuba), even after the fall of the Soviet Union and Eastern European countries. South Korean capitalism can be seen as second to none.

Thus far, I have reviewed a few Korean national characteristics and patterns, some of which may no longer be relevant in a rapidly changing Korea. Max Weber (1970:45) wrote of the risk of becoming outdated in the face of new discoveries and change:

> In science, each of us knows that what he has accomplished will be antiquated in ten, twenty, fifty years. That is the fate to which science is subjected; it is the very meaning of scientific work, to which it is devoted in a quite specific sense, as compared with other

spheres of culture for which in general the same holds. Every scientific "fulfillment" raises new "questions;" it asks to be "surpassed" and out-dated. Whoever wishes to serve science has to resign himself to this fact. Scientific works certainly can last as "gratifications" because of their artistic quality, or they may remain important as a means of training. Yet they will be surpassed scientifically — let that be repeated — for it is our common fate and, more, our common goal.

I hope that this effort to identify and summarize Korean patterns and characteristics has in some way contributed to that common purpose.

CHAPTER 9

Economic Development, Industrialization, and Environmental Conservation

Economic Development and Industrialization

Background of the Study: A Personal Note

My interest in studying economic development, industry, and industrial workers predates my involvement in the field of business and industrial anthropology.[1] In the early 1960s, under the direction of Hahm Pyong-choon [Pyong-choon Hahm], my mentor and adviser at the Law School of Yonsei University, I studied labor law and trade unions in the Korean cigarette and tobacco industry (current KT&G) (Hahm, Yang, and Kim 1964). This was before the Korean economic "miracle" impinged on Western public consciousness. In the early 1970s after I was transplanted to America South, I did not know much about Korea's economic progress. Instead of having any interest in Korea, I conducted industrial ethnographic work[2] in the American South, and carried out a socioeconomic and demographic study of a native American tribe, the Choctaw, hoping to attract industrialists to harness the Choctaw labor force (Kim 1977; Spencer, Peterson, and Kim 1975).

A professor-turned-diplomat, Hahm, then the Korean ambassador to the United States, phoned me at the Choctaw tribal government headquarters to try to get me interested in an anthropological project on Korean industrialization. Despite the ambassador's hard sales pitch, however, I was unable to become as obsessed as he was with Korean industrialization. In the meantime, my Choctaw Indian project evolved into another project that kept me busily confined to the American South until the early 1980s.

When I completed the Choctaw Indian project in 1975, Hahm asked me to come to Washington, D.C. to discuss the possibility of my involvement in "salvage work" to document the remnants of *yangban* culture in Gyeongsangbuk-do province before some villages were buried forever because of a multiple-purpose dam being built on the upper section of the Nakdonggang. Knowing that I was not drawn to study Korean industrialization or the Korean economic miracle, Hahm instead induced me to study traditional Korean culture, focusing on villages in Gyeongsangbuk-do province since I am from that region. He told me that the Andong Dam would bury several traditional villages, including Dosan, the hometown of Yi Hwang.[3] This would be "salvage work" for cultural anthropologists, analogous to the work done by salvage archaeologists.[4]

Beginning the Korean Projects

Hahm realized that my lack of interest in studying Korea was the result of my prolonged absence from my home country, and that I still held in my mind images of Korea in the mid-1960s, unaware of all the change and progress that had been made since then. When he returned to Korea as a member of the Research Committee of the Institute of Foreign Affairs from 1980 and 1981, Hahm invited me to the Institute as a visiting professor in the summer of 1981. I returned to Korea for the first time since I had left in the mid-1960s, a visit that led me to document the tragedy of the dispersal of Korean families because of the Korean War.[5]

From Studying Traditional Korean Villages to Studying Korean Industry

My search for a suitable site for my study began with three possible villages: Dosan, home of Yi Hwang; Hahoe, where descendants of Yu

Seongryong(1542-1607), prime minister during the Joseon dynasty and student of Yi Hwang, still live; and if I could not arrange to do fieldwork in either of those villages, my own home village, Haejeo-ri, whose ancestor, Kim Seongil (1538-1593), had also been Yi Hwang's student. Neo-Confucianist Yi Hwang and his students were collectively called the Yeongnam School.

Dosan had to be ruled out because dam construction had already brought about major changes in the heartland of the Yeongnam School. A major village in Yi Hwang's home area had already been flooded and was completely under water. Dosan Seowon, sanctuary of zealous Confucianists in Gyeongsangbuk-do province, where Yi Hwang studied and taught, was protected by its elevation, but the remaining villages of Yi clan members scattered around Dosan were all submerged.

I was leaning toward Hahoe as a possible site. A compact village cloaked in the mysterious aura of ancient folk culture, Hahoe was designated a Korean folk village in 1972, and has aroused keen public interest.[6] I discussed with my sister and brother-in-law who happen to live in Hahoe the possibility of conducting fieldwork there. However, their answers to my questions were disappointing. They told me that most Yu clan members, especially the young ones, had left the village, although most still maintained houses there. Many were working for several large business conglomerates, or *jaebeol*, including one owned by one of their clan members. It turned out that Yu clan members who lived in Seoul outnumbered those who remained in the village. As evidence of the massive exodus of villagers to cities, the primary school had been closed permanently for lack of pupils.

While reevaluating Hahoe as a possible field site, I decided to study *yangban* and Confucianism in a business or industrial setting rather than a village setting. This would enable me to observe the relationship between traditional *yangban* villages and industry, and document the function of kinship among *yangban* in the management of modern Korean industry.[7]

Because most industrialists are reluctant to allow anthropologists to study their organizations intensively and extensively, I mobilized every available network to obtain permission from the industry. Finally, I was able to study Korea's largest non-steel metal industry and one of the top businesses, the thirtieth-ranking *jaebeol*, which was owned by a member of the Yu clan from Hahoe.

First Encounter with Korean Economic Development: A Personal Reaction

When I returned to Korea for the first time in the early 1980s, having been gone since the mid-1960s, I experienced all at once the results of years of economic development and industrialization, and as a result I had a real case of "future shock." The entire country seemed to be vibrating with economic progress.

Korean economic growth and industrialization may mean many different things to different Koreans. For Koreans of my generation and older who had experienced a marginal existence under Japanese rule and during the devastating Korean War, it has special meanings — a sense of pride, self-fulfillment, and also great relief. I remember that near the end of World War II, most Korean school children did not have decent shoes to wear because materials to make them had been confiscated by the Japanese for war supplies. During the Korean War, most Koreans were unable to eat three meals a day. Even a bowl of rice could hardly be found.[8]

Korea's economic accomplishment touched the emotions of many Koreans, especially the older generations. For instance, in 1987, when I saw a Korean-made Hyundai Excel parked in our university parking lot, I dashed over and touched its exterior. It was an emotional moment for me to see that a Korean-made automobile had come to a small, remote university town in Tennessee. Perhaps the younger generation of Koreans, who never had firsthand experience of the poverty, starvation, and massive destruction caused by war, would find it difficult to understand the sentiment of an older Korean. My friend once told me that when he was telling his children about his days of living on an empty stomach during the war, they commented, "Why didn't you take '*ramyeon*' (dried instant noodle), then?" It would be difficult for most young Koreans who are so used to affluence to even begin to comprehend the hardships endured by the older generations.

Record of Growth

Korea's economic growth has been phenomenal. From 1953 to 2004, the Korean domestic product (GDP) increased 523 times, and Korea now ranks as the tenth largest economy in the world,[9] averaging 6.9 percent growth annually, the fifth fastest pace among the thirty-member nations of the OECD. Korea's per capita income increased 211 times from $67 in 1953 to $14,162 in 2004 (The Bank of Korea: 2005:3-4).[10] By 2006, Korea's GNI was about $20,000. The total number of businesses and industrial firms jumped from 3,600 companies employing 240,000 workers in 1953 (Kim 1992:xiv) to over 3 million employing nearly 15 million workers in 2004.[11]

Korea ranked third in the world in terms of Internet use in 2003, trailing only behind Iceland and Sweden.[12] The number of Koreans who were connected to the Internet at home through broadband was nearly 12 million, and this figure increased three times in the four years after 2000 (The Bank of Korea, 2005:56). As Michael Breen (2004:250) has indicated, "South Korea is without a doubt the most wired-up nation in the galaxy. ⋯ Around 10 million Koreans chat online, 1 million use video chatting, 3.6 million have avatars — little thingies that represent you in chat rooms and e-mail."[13]

By November 1997, Korea's foreign currency reserves were nearly depleted at $20.4 billion (The Bank of Korea 2005:30, 70), when the nation was experiencing its worst economic crisis since Korean economic development had been implemented. Korea eventually sought a $58 billion emergency loan from the IMF to pay off short-term loans to avert bankruptcy. However, with a new reform policy initiated by the government and support from the Korean people, Korea was able to repay the loans from the IMF ahead of schedule, and Korean foreign currency reserves rose from $20.4 billion in 1997 to $205 billion in 2005 (The Bank of Korea 2005:30, 74). Korea now has the fourth largest foreign currency reserves, after Japan, China, and Taiwan.[14]

The expansion of Korean infrastructure has been remarkable. In 2004, the total length of roadway in Korea was four times what it had been in 1944. Nearly 3,000 kilometers of expressway have been built over twenty routes, a total increase of 34 times since the first expressway was built in 1968.[15] Beginning in 1990, the government constructed a high-speed railway between Seoul and Busan (412 kilometers), followed by the Seoul and Mokpo corridor (330 kilometers) (The Bank of Korea 2005:52; *Handbook of Korea*, 2003:300-301). In 1968, Korean Airlines (KAL) was established by privatizing the former state-owned Korean Airlines that had been launched in 1948. The civil aviation industry has grown rapidly. Due to increasing demand, another Korean flagship carrier, Asiana Airlines, was added in 1988. At the end of 2000, the newly built Incheon Airport handled nearly 27 million passengers and 1.7 million tons of air cargo annually, to serve forty large cities within three hours (*Handbook of Korea*, 2003:302-303).

Economic Growth by Export

In the early stages of its economic development, Korea focused on exporting labor-intensive and light industrial products such as textiles, wigs, leather and footwear, and plywood, which constituted 70 percent of Korea's export items.[16] Recently, however, major export items include consumer electronic products, semiconductors, automobiles, mobile phones, heavy petrochemical products, shipbuilding equipment, and steel, which all together constitute 82 percent of total export items. In this way, Korean exports increased more than 9,200 times from 1952 to 2004. In 2006, Korea ranked eleventh in the world in overseas shipment of goods according to the World Trade Organization.[17] Korea's world rank in export is almost identical with its work rank in GDP.

The most notable industries in Korea that have acquired a competitive edge globally include shipbuilding, automobiles, and electronic goods as well as the manufacturing of iron and steel.

A Shipyard of a Korean Shipbuilding Industry

Although the Korean shipbuilding industry only began in the 1970s, by 2005 it ranked first in the world in terms of market share.[18] Recently, the Korean shipbuilding industry has begun to focus on producing high-value-added ships: liquefied natural gas (LNG) carriers and floating production storage and offloading vessels, and luxurious cruise ships.[19] The Korean automotive industry was launched in the 1960s during the first five-year economic development plan, but it has excelled beginning in the early 2000s. By 2005, Korean automobile production topped 3.47 million units and made up 5.4 percent of the global total for that year, making Korea the world's sixth largest automobile producing nation.[20] Currently, there are five major automakers in Korea, including Hyundai Motor Co., Kia Motors Corporation, GM Daewoo Auto & Technology Co., Ssangyong Motor Co., and Renault Samsung Motors Co., Ltd. With respect to iron and steel, the state-owned POSCO, which was founded in 1968 and began production in 1973, is the major producer.[21] In 2004, POSCO produced 47,520 million tons of iron and steel, an increase of over 94 times from its output of 504 million tons in 1970.[22]

Also, Korea remained the fourth largest maker of electronic goods in 2004, producing $90.3 billion worth of products,[23] including semiconductors. Korea's semiconductor industry[24] has been bolstered by the Samsung Group, which has been recognized for its global leadership due to the outstanding performance of its flagship corporation, Samsung Electronics Co. As a Korean semiconductor maker, Samsung delivered the second best revenue growth among the top ten in the world in 2005 (total sales was $17.2 billion).[25] In the mobile phone market, *Anycall*, a Samsung brand, has led the U.S. premium market with its state-of-the-art mobile phone, including the world's first handset that converts voice calls to text, the U.S.'s first 2-megapixel camera phone, and the ultra-slim side phone.[26] Korean-made mobile phones are enjoying popularity in Europe as well.[27] Korean electronic companies are doing remarkably well in the liquid crystal display (LCD) market. LG Philips, a joint venture between LG and Philips, used to be the largest LCD maker in the world, but now as the result of a plant jointly owned by Samsung and Sony Corporation, Samsung has begun producing bigger and more profitable large LCD TVs from 40 to 46 inches, occupying the top of the LCD market.[28]

Scholarly Interest in Korean Development

The recent development of the Korean economy is indeed the tale of a "miracle"[29] for it is amazing that such a resource-poor country still bearing the scars of a devastating war has become an economic powerhouse in such a short period of time. As Richard Steers (1989) and his associates state, "It took the United States 100 years to move from an agrarian state to an industrialized economy, and it took Japan seventy years to make a similar adjustment, but it took Korea less than thirty years." Many scholars at home and abroad have been interested in knowing what has inspired Korea's impressive record of growth and development.

To answer this question, in the late 1970s a group of American and Korean scholars began to publish their findings on Korea's success.[30] Interest in Korean economic ascendancy encouraged the study of Korean management by scholars of business and management (Chung and Lee 1989; Steers et al. 1989; Yoo and Lee 1987). Some sociologists

(Kim E.M. 1997; Koo 1993) have discussed the dynamic relationship between the state and *jaebeol* in Korea. Still others (Kim SK 1977; Koo 1993) have studied the lives of factory workers and labor-union movements in the process of industrialization.

Except for a few studies by anthropologists (Janelli and Yim 1993; Kim 1992), most existing literature, by economists and scholars of management, has focused on highly aggregated and abstract economic analysis — capital accumulation, government policy, international trade flows.[31] An overzealous effort to generalize Korean economic success to build models or make theories applicable to other late industrializing societies might neglect local realities, and some social scientists have begun to question the merit of constructing theories designed to have universal applicability (Baker 1981:325-349; Booth 1984:761-787).

Also, the existing literature tends to treat Korean economic progress as if it were "ahistorical." Most literature on Korean economic progress and industrialization tends to focus on the period of manifest growth from the sixties on. Without a doubt, remarkable progress did take place after the 1960s. However, historians tell us that the national movement for Korean economic development, as well as nascent capitalism, began in the late nineteenth century (Eckert 1991, 1990:117; Eckert et al. 1990:388). The movement to raise the general level of national consciousness, education, and economic development was inaugurated by nationalists, especially cultural nationalists, in the early 1920s under colonial rule (Eckert et al. 1990:254-326; Robinson 1988). In those years, entrepreneurs and manufacturers were viewed as patriots, and such a perception still lingers in the minds of many Koreans.

The recent Korean economic take-off appears to be deeply indebted to unique Korean historical experiences. It is doubtful that any typology or model of Korean economic development and industrialization can be applicable to other late industrializing countries without taking into account the unique events of Korean history. In his well-received book on Japanese industry, sociologist

Robert Cole (1971:11) is equally skeptical about the possible application of Japanese experiences to developing countries, because "the historical period during which Japan industrialized had unique characteristics which can never be repeated for the benefit of presently industrializing countries."

Existing scholarship tends to overlook the feelings of the people — entrepreneurs, workers, managers, and government technocrats — who actually carried out the economic miracle. Perhaps foreign scholars, as outsiders, are unable to grasp the genuine feelings of natives toward their economic accomplishment in terms of their own native categories. Often the literature, especially the work of foreign scholars in English-language editions, romanticizes the Korean achievement too much to be reliable. Native scholars often take pains not to relate the inner feelings of the natives who contributed to the process, in order to avoid subjective biases. As a result, final reports tend to deal with statistics and policies, not people.

Possible Explanations for Korean Economic Growth and Industrialization

There are many plausible explanations for Korea's rapid economic growth and industrialization. Some scholars credit Korea's well-educated and disciplined workforce (Kim 1992:6); others point toward a government with a well-defined industrial plan and policy willingly followed by business and industry (Adelman 1969; Hasan 1976; Hasan and Rao 1979; Jones and Sakong 1980; Kim and Roemer 1979; Krueger 1979; Mason et al. 1980; Wade and Kim 1978; Westphal 1978). Still others cite the assistance of U.S. aid and foreign investment (Heo 1978:117; Koo 1987; Steinberg 1989).

Some sources have traced the infrastructure of Korean industrialization to the Japanese influence during the colonial era (Cumings 1984:20; Mason et al. 1980:75), while others (Heo 2005) strongly deny a positive Japanese role. Other scholars like to give credit to the various risk-taking activities of entrepreneurs (Kim 1986:51-64; Lim 1981:66-67), while still others believe that Korea's economic success has been accomplished by the exploitation of workers (Choi 1990). All causes that have been suggested may have played a role in Korea's rapid economic development and industrialization (Kim 1992:6).

Since the Korean economy remained "backward" before making great strides economically from the mid-1960s, the concept of the "privilege of backwardness" set forth by Leon Trotsky (n.d.:4-5), Alexander Gerschenkron (1962, 1968), and evolutionary-oriented anthropologists such as Marshall Sahlins and Elman Service (1960:93-122) has also been viewed as an explanation for Korea's rapid development. Nevertheless, some scholars remain skeptical about the role of backwardness in Korea's transformation.[32] The "privilege," according to these theories, is the ability to learn and borrow available technology from advanced countries rather quickly and inexpensively. As a late-industrializing country, Korea has taken advantage of advanced industrial technology from Japan and the West.

Along this line of thought, Alice Amsden (1989) has characterized Korean industrialization as "late industrialization" because of its practice of learning (or borrowing) foreign technology from industrialized countries rather than developing its own inventions or innovations.[33] She asserts that Korean industrialization is a classic model containing all the characteristic elements. She quite convincingly uses the example of POSCO to illustrate her argument.

Nevertheless, whether it is matter of learning or borrowing, Korea's exceptional learning ability as an "apprentice" has to be taken into account. In the case of POSCO, although over 500 engineers among over 23,200 employees and frontline supervisors had received overseas training prior to its opening: "when operations commenced in 1973, local engineers reached desired normal iron production level within eight days, an unprecedented record in the history of the industry" (Kim Linsu 1989:125). It appears that not all learners are able to digest with the same intensity all the technology that they wish to adopt (Kim 1992:7).

If one defines innovation as the refinement of existing cultural traits, e.g., industrial products, then in the process of Korean industrialization many indigenous innovations occurred. Also, efforts have been made to upgrade both products and the production process through "reverse engineering," that is, taking apart and reassembling available foreign products. Linsu Kim (1989:126) has witnessed this process of indigenous innovation by which a small and simple steel pipeline builder evolved into a world-ranking manufacturer of steel pipe machinery.

Motivating Forces of Korean Development: What Makes Korea Tick?

In tracing possible sources of the Korean drive and determination for economic development and industrialization, I have determined that several factors were key contributors to the process.

Historical Adversity

Koreans work hard to release *han*. The effects of pervasive poverty, loss of sovereignty due to foreign invasion, underdevelopment of science and technology, oppression in terms of educational opportunity and attainment have all persisted in the form of *han* for generations, and Koreans have long sought to get rid of these feelings.[34] The futurist Sha Seiki has pointed out that Korea's history of adversity motivates Koreans to work harder to succeed (Steers et al. 1989:135). So, perhaps the Korean work ethic and determination to achieve economic development germinated long before the 1960s (Kim 1992:5-6).

The Impact of the Korean and Vietnam Wars

Paradoxical though it may sound, the near total destruction of existing Korean industry by the war, often small and obsolete facilities inherited from the Japanese, allowed Koreans to build newer, larger, and more modern ones without being constrained by existing facilities. Almost all Korean industrial plants, ranging from the top-ranking steel plants to the gigantic shipbuilders, are newly built industrial sites (Amsden 1989:293).

During and after the war, some entrepreneurs, most obviously Jeong

Juyeong, founder of the Hyundai Group, actively participated in "repairing bridges, paving roads, and building army barracks, simple dams, and reservoirs, using 'appropriate technology' specified by the Army Corps of Engineers" (Amsden 1989:266). The skills and technologies acquired by Hyundai during the Korean War allowed the company to win bids for construction projects throughout the world, including bridge construction in Alaska.

It is an undeniable fact that the Vietnam War gave the Korean economy a boost when Korea dispatched thousands of troops to Vietnam. The total number of Korean troops in Vietnam from 1965 to 1973 was about 48,000. In spite of the human cost, in 1966 the war accounted for 40 percent of Korea's crucial foreign exchange receipts. Many Korean business firms, including Hanjin, the owner of KAL, and Hyundai received a tremendous economic boost from the war. Their wartime experience in construction paved the way for future construction projects in the Middle East (Kim 1992:20).

Confucianism's Unintended Consequence

The function of Confucianism and its impact on the Korean way of life, including rules for industrial relations, especially in terms of "harmony" (*inhwa* in Korean), have not yet been fully evaluated. However, Geert Hofstede and Michael H. Bond (1988:8) believe that the notion of harmony originated from Confucian thought. Some scholars, following Max Weber (1951) over a half century ago, viewed Confucianism as a hindrance to economic development. Some are very critical of its role as dysfunctional (Kim 2001). Young-iob Chung (1989:152) states that "Confucian teachings rejected training in economics for the pursuit of wealth and held business people in low esteem. The ruling elite, *yang-ban* [*yangban*], did not allow themselves to participate in profit-making enterprises." Kyuhan Bae (1987:79) has observed a similar view among Hyundai workers that Korean government and industry were taking advantage of Confucianism to exploit industrial workers. In other words, the early Korean industrialists were portrayed more as "developers" than "profit-makers." Roger Janelli with Dawnhee Yim (1993), on the basis of their anthropological fieldwork on a leading Korean business conglomerate, conclude that South Korean corporate culture is based on traditional family life in the village (see also Amsden 1995:452-455). Nevertheless, even Confucianism's critics do not deny that it has had some positive influence on Korean economic development, especially through its encouragement of education (Kim and Kim 1989:208; Steers et al. 1989:130). Even such critics as Young-iob Chung acknowledge some indirect benefit to economic development from Confucianism (Chung 1989:130).

Korea's Advantageous Location

There are many references to the importance of Korea's location in the middle of the Far East, where it is surrounded by bigger and sometimes hostile neighbors. If Korea had been located off the main continent of Asia, Koreans may have been spared invasions by their neighbors, just as Great Britain was set apart from the struggles in continental Europe. Now, as it becomes an industrialized nation, Korea has begun to capitalize on its location.

Because Korea is situated very close to two economic giants, Japan and China, it is convenient for Korea to engage in trade and commerce with them. Seoul can easily serve as the dispersal point for other major Asian cities, including Tokyo, Beijing, Osaka, Hong Kong, Singapore, and Shanghai. By air, only less than three hours separate Seoul from those cities, and Incheon-Seoul Airport provides this service. Seoul has great potential to serve as a center for commerce, transportation, and an international money market for Pacific Rim countries.

By normalizing relationships with Japan in 1965, Russia in 1990, and China in 1992, Korea is now on friendly terms with its former enemies. Because these three countries are located nearby, Korea recognized the potential to import ample natural resources such as coal, oil, natural gas, and timber at rather inexpensive prices from its northern neighbors. In turn, Korea now exports manufactured goods to them. Korea exported $62 billion in trade with China in 2005, which was 21.8 percent of total Korean exports that year, and imported $3,800 million in the same year, which is 1.4 percent of Korea's total annual volume of import in that year.[35]

Strong Leadership and A Feasible Development Plan

Proper credit has to be given to the leadership of President Park Chung-hee and his government's economic development program that was devised and carried out by many able, well-educated, and disciplined technocrats. Aside from his military-oriented autocratic rule, President Park initiated and ignited the sparks of Korea's economic modernization with the catch phrase "You can do it!" (Hussain 2006:31), bolstering an economic growth strategy by using social psychology. His basic goal was to create an economic base for industrialization and self-sustained growth.

The first five-year economic development plan was designed to attain an annual growth rate of 7.1 percent between 1962 and 1966, but this target was exceeded, with Korea achieving a higher growth rate beginning in 1963. Successive five-year economic development plans[36] contained specific goals and directions, but one consistent, basic policy has been an emphasis on export-oriented industrialization and growth. This fundamental policy goal remained unchanged even after Chun Doo-hwan's regime took over. In fact, when President Chun came to power after President Park's assassination, "Chun Doo-hwan called on the population to prepare for a 'second take-off'" (Woronoff 1983:35).

Motivated *Jaebeol* and Dedicated Workers

The *JoongAng Ilbo*, a daily Korean newspaper, reported the results of a national survey on 23 September 1987,[37] Koreans rated the top five factors contributing to Korea's economic success as having been brought about through the efforts of the Korean people.[38] W. Arthur Lewis (1966:270) is both perceptive and correct when he states that "the government can persuade, threaten, or induce, but in the last analysis it is the people who achieve." Indeed, the Korean people have worked hard in this endeavor, and they continue to do so. A recent survey reports that Koreans whose ages range from twenty to seventy-four work two hours longer per day than their American and German counterparts, while sleeping fifty minutes less per night.[39] Because of such single-minded willpower, Koreans have been able to accomplish their economic agenda. These include *jaebeol* groups and rank-and-file workers who are represented by labor unions.

The Role of *Jaebeol*

Although Korean *jaebeol* have been criticized, their contributions to Korean economic development have been indispensable. Ikeda Motohiro, the bureau chief of the Japanese newspaper *Nihonkeizai* in Seoul, states that "if Samsung were not in Korea, the Korean economy would have been at the same stage as that of the Philippines. ⋯ And, if Samsung management would be shaky, then the entire Korean economy would be shaky as well."[40] Ikeda's statement on Samsung may be no exaggeration.

Jaebeol is analogous to the Japanese zaibatsu. Although Chinese characters for *jaebeol* and *zaibatsu* are identical, and the two entities they refer to share many common characteristics, scholars familiar with both forms find they have some important differences (Hattori 1989). Sangjin Yoo and Sang M. Lee (1987) define a *jaebeol* as a business group consisting of large companies that are owned and managed by family members or relatives in many diversified business areas, commonly called a management of "octopus tentacles" (*muneobal*). A review of several available definitions and characteristic features of *jaebeol* (Lee 1989:182) seems to indicate that it has two major features: ownership by a family and a diversified business operation (Kim and Hahn 1989:52).

Notwithstanding their contributions to Korean economic development and industrialization, lately *jaebeol* groups have come to be viewed with great ambivalence and criticism by an increasing number of Koreans because of a poor system of corporate governance and bribery scandals. "The *jaebeol* are in some ways a visible and convenient target" (Hussain 2006:147). Perhaps, in this globalizing world, the *jaebeol* groups might seem to be outdated, for more than half the stock of these Korean companies is owned by foreign investors. Nevertheless, even though the chairmen own a very limited portion of their companies' stock, they control the *jaebeol* groups through a web of complicated shareholdings and a direct stake (Hussain 2006:125). Because of this structure, various irregularities are inevitable. Not many Korean *jaebeol* groups are free from charges of bribery, illegal wealth transfers, and slush funds.[41]

Without making their corporate finances transparent, it would be difficult for *jaebeol* groups to win the understanding and cooperation of strong and well-organized labor unions. It is a widely reported fact that the cost of labor in Korea's manufacturing industries has risen at a fast and perhaps excessive pace since the 1990s, becoming a major factor nibbling away at the country's competitiveness.[42]

Industrial Workers

Indeed, Korean industrial workers have worked hard, and they still do. Because of their single-minded willpower, Koreans have been able to accomplish an ambitious economic agenda. However, the confrontational behavior of Korean workers and their unions has been criticized, so some background information may be in order.

Labor Disputes and Workers' Demands

During my fieldwork on the Korean non-steel metal industry in the 1980s and early 1990s, I had the opportunity to witness the most furious labor unrest in Korean history. When I began my study, there was no organized labor union at the plant. There was no indication that Korea would see such an eruption of labor disputes. In fact, in the early 1980s, some scholars (Benjamin 1982; Chen 1981; Hofheiz and Cadler 1982; Winckler 1984) generalized about workers in newly industrializing countries in Asia, including Korea, portraying them as cheap, docile, loyal, and productive laborers because of their Confucian cultural heritage. Nevertheless, as evidenced by the recent rate of wage hikes and the prevalence of labor disputes, cheapness and docility are no longer traits of Korean workers, who may have appeared docile until 1987 because of strong control by the military-led government.

What had been a peaceful-looking Korean labor union movement in the early stages of my fieldwork suddenly faced a totally new situation when, in the midst of my study, the Chun Doo-hwan regime was brought to the brink of collapse by massive antigovernment demonstrations by students, workers, and intellectuals.[43] When Rho Tae-woo, then the ruling party's candidate for president, issued the "June 29 Proclamation," great labor unrest was touched off and there were widespread demonstrations and strikes. In 1987, the total number of labor disputes reached 3,749, the largest number in a single year in the entire history of the Korean labor movement.[44] Since 1987, labor disputes, strikes, and demonstrations have become a common occurrence in Korea.

Some labor disputes have been furious, explosive, and extreme at times. In the late 1980s, the streets of Seoul looked like a battlefield. In my fieldnotes I describe the setting (Kim 1992:186-187):

> Their slogans and wall posters became violent: "We are not afraid of dying." "500 percent wage increase, even if the company is bankrupted," "Poke out the eyes of reactionary union members (*bandong*)," and "Stop dictatorship over the workers." They poured waste oil and paint on the heads of employees at the management office and destroyed office furniture and equipment. They even made gallows labeled with the names of top executives in front of the storage facility where the most powerful explosives were stored [which was a munitions plant]. Striking workers threatened to blow up the plant by setting fire to 3,300 tons of explosives stored for the production of ammunition. They scattered waste oil and gasoline mixed with sawdust around the buildings to set them on fire. If the explosives had been set off, the impact would have been devastating. The explosives at the plant were 132 times more powerful than those at the Iri disaster.[45] The damage at An'gang could well have

reached the township of An'gang (near Kyŏngju, the ancient Silla capital) with its 34,031 inhabitants.

Some scholars are probably right when they assess that Korean labor-management relations reflect a confrontational mode rather than the cooperative mode manifested in Japan (Chung and Lie 1989:217; Deyo 1989:4, 139).

Since Koreans are paying such a high price for labor disputes, the frequent strikes and demonstrations have been criticized for being too confrontational, hostile, and expensive. In 2006, for instance, labor demonstrations cost at least $7.4 billion in taxpayers' money, equivalent to about 0.8 percent of Korea's GDP.[46] However, as long as some *jaebeol* groups are not free from charges of bribery, scandals, illegal wealth transfers, and slush funds, labor unions will push further for improved working conditions and demand even higher wages. Without *jaebeol* reform, the vicious cycle will continue.

However, there are some indications that the confrontational mode is changing toward a cooperative mode. It appears that both management and labor have begun working together for common goals as a consequence of foreign challenges.

Other Non-Economic Factors

There may be many other known and unknown reasons behind Korea's economic success. Seeing millions of Koreans cheering during the FIFA World Cup in 2002, I started to understand how they were able to accomplish such a formidable economic task. I also understood more when I heard (I was abroad at the time) how Koreans tried to recover from one of the worst financial crises, in 1997 and 1998, a time Koreans aptly call the "IMF" era, alluding to the loan that bailed them out.

This is what happened: "Tens of thousands got caught up in a gold-selling fever launched by KBS TV and the Korean Housing and Commercial Bank to raise dollars to help repay the IMF loans. People queued up to either donate or sell their gold after experts had announced there was an estimated $20 billion worth kept in Korean homes ⋯ young couples handing in their wedding rings and old ladies handing in items of tremendous personal significance with the feeling that they were helping save their country. ⋯ People stopped drinking coffee because it is imported (Breen 2004:159-160)." 3.49 million people participated in the three-month-long "gold collection campaign," and $2.17 billion (225 tons of gold) was collected.[47]

The Korean sentiment of "oneness" (*urineun hana*) appears to be a remarkable motivation for Koreans to work together toward a common goal if there is a clear-cut objective, national agenda, or moral cause to justify it. Such a motivational factor has contributed to Korea's accomplishment. Nevertheless, there are many differences and conflicts of interest among Koreans, and they cannot always reach a consensus as easily as they agreed upon victory in a soccer match or the repayment of IMF loans. Those differences include *jaebeol* versus labor union members, conservative versus liberal, rich versus poor, urban versus rural, pro-FTA versus anti-FTA, globalization versus localization, and Koreans versus non-Korean-foreigners, etc.

Rethinking the Anthropologist's Role in Economic Development Plans

As a business and industrial anthropologist, I have engaged in several projects focused on economic development, the Choctaw project being the most memorable and meaningful, for it served to bring industries to the reservation and provided employment opportunities for jobless Native Americans. In 1994, the tribe opened a Las Vegas–style casino that operated twenty-four hours a day. In 2000, when I visited the reservation before my return to Korea to say goodbye to the chief and other friends, I was overwhelmed by the evident cultural upheaval. The average annual income of Choctaws increased tenfold over the past quarter-century, and over 3,000 white people, who used to discriminate against Native Americans for several hundred years, are now working with them. After the North American Free Trade Agreement (NAFTA) in 1994, the Choctaws established a manufacturing plant in Sonora,

Mexico, the first Native American–owned company in the global market.

Before I left the reservation, I asked Chief Philip Martin about some of the negative impacts of economic development, such as crime, delinquency, fighting, gambling, mental disorders, etc. I felt I was one of the guilty parties for helping to bring about the development. Instead of just explaining it to me in words, he took me to a construction site and said, "This will be a new juvenile detention and rehabilitation center. People criticize me and say that because of sudden economic progress and the casino, youngsters are having all kinds of social problems. But, let me tell you, when we were poor as you witnessed in 1974, we had the same kinds of problems. I prefer to be economically well off and have some problems, rather than being poor and yet still having to force the same problems." As I listened to Martin's monologue concerning the morality of the Choctaws' casino, I felt I could never join the crowd of those who idealize a fantasy of "the noble savage" or "white man's Indian."

Certainly, Korean economic development, industrialization, and the taste of capitalism have also brought about some negative social problems in Korea. If I asked President Park Chung-hee, who persuaded Koreans to believe that economic development should be their utmost important priority for which they should sacrifice everything, would he offer the same explanation as the chief did? Or would he tell me that environmental protection and conservation must be as important as development? Economically well-off Koreans have now begun to think about the environment. Environmentalists would argue that even if we end up postponing some development projects, environmental issues have to be taken into consideration. In the remaining section of this chapter, I describe Korea's environmental problems and its conservation efforts.

Environmental Conservation

While Westerners tend to believe that human beings are the center of the universe and thus can control and challenge nature, up until recently Koreans have held a unitarian view of the universe in which human beings, nature, and god are equal, coexisting entities. Many Korean paintings, novels, and indigenous beliefs illustrate these views (Kim T.G. 1977).[48] This unitarian worldview stipulates that human beings essentially remain integrated with nature. Koreans must have been natural environmentalists and conservationists to keep a balanced ecosystem for so long.

The traditional Korean worldview began to change, however, with the wave of economic development and industrialization that began in the 1960s. Because of the priority given to "development for development's sake," everything else, including human rights, civil liberty, and environmental conservation, became secondary.

During the early stages of the economic development plan in Korea, even some informed citizens and intellectuals tended to think that Koreans had to accept the negative consequences of environmental problems as the price they had to pay for development. Air pollution was not even an issue until the 1970s. Because the entire country was so preoccupied by a process of economic development that was tightly controlled by the military-led government, the voices of the local people who would be most affected by major development projects such as the construction of dams and nuclear-generated power plants, both of which began in the early 1970s, were ignored.[49] The government simply picked the sites, and built the plants. Until very recently, local people had to "put up or shut up," so-to-speak. As a consequence, the Korean ecosystem has been altered and the environment damaged. Anyone who advocated for environmental protection and joined rallies against various development projects was labeled an anti-government activist. As a result, the Korean ecosystem was altered and the environment seriously damaged, in some cases irreparably.

As the Korean standard of living has improved, Koreans have become increasingly aware of environmental problems, and such an awareness is "better late than never," so-to-speak. Because of rapid industrialization and economic development, Koreans now have to deal with polluted air and water, toxic chemicals, the loss of wetlands, and the destruction of their country's beautiful mountain ranges. To improve environmental conservation, Korea has begun to take several measures, such as creating a government agency to regulate the environment at the ministerial level and enacting a series of environmental laws.[50]

Beginning in the 1980s, a civic environmental self-help movement sprang up to oppose reckless development projects throughout the nation. One example is what happened in Puan. In 2003 when the Korean government was seeking a repository site for nuclear waste, the county of Buan in Jeollanam-do province submitted a proposal to the central government to host its facility at Wido, a small island in the county. However, citizens of that county vehemently opposed the proposal and furious demonstrations raged on for months until the government finally cancelled the plan altogether.[51] The voices of local residents were heard loudly and clearly. Also, conservationists have sometimes been successful in stopping the government's plans to construct a dam, as was the case with the Yeongwol Dam on the Donggang.

In another case, a fifty-year-old Buddhist nun, Jo Gyeongsuk (Jiyul in her Buddhist name), was able to stop the Cheonseongsan tunnel construction for the KTX(Korea Train eXpress), the Korean version of a bullet trail, from Seoul to Busan by fasting. Construction was halted twice by her fasting after the project started in June 2002. If the KTX could not run through the planned tunnel, the train would have to detour, and the government would lose some 250 billion *won* (about $2.66 billion). President Roh Moo-hyun called for a detailed study, and construction was delayed for six months. Finally, the study concluded that the tunnel would not damage the environment as much as the protesters had claimed. Jiyul lost her court battle, and was sentenced to two years in prison and two years of probation. Construction resumed in November 2005. However, through protests, demonstrations, and court battles, Jiyul and her environmental supporters had been successful in bringing an environmental crusade to the attention of the public.

Before the general public became aware of the importance of conservation, in many instances the environment had already been damaged, people had been victimized and the ecosystem irrevocably altered. Nevertheless, eager restoration efforts are now being made. Non-governmental organizations (NGOs) for environmental conservation have become active. The activities of conservationists gained new life when the government announced a policy of leniency toward demonstrations and labor union activities via the "June 29 Proclamation" in 1987. Accordingly, Korea has signed a total of forty-four environmental conservation agreements, including the United Nations Framework Convention on Climate Change and the Montreal Protocol on Substances that Deplete the Ozone Layer. However, after the financial crisis in 1997 and 1998, economic development has once again taken precedence over conservation efforts, and several court decisions indicate this shift in priorities.

Environmental Alteration and the Restoration Movement

Environmental Disturbance

Mountain Ranges
The most visible environmental destruction has taken place in the Baekdudaegan (the Great Baekdu Mountain Range), which is the backbone of the Korean mountain range originating from Korea's tallest mountain, Baekdusan (2,750 meters). The steep, high mountain range and dense forests of the eastern slope sweep all the way down the peninsula to Jirisan (1,915 meters) in Gyeongsangnam-do and Jeollanam-do province. The entire length of the Baekdudaegan is about 1,494.3 kilometers. The others Korean mountains and their ranges connect to or branch out from the Baekdudaegan. While the less developed northern half of the range has been well preserved, the southern portion of the range below the DMZ has been badly

damaged by the construction of roads, dams, mining, hot springs, and the cultivation of vegetables that grow well in the cooler region of the highlands. For instance, Jabyeongsan in Gangwon-do province has had its height reduced by about 57 meters in the past twenty-seven years, from 872 meters when mining began in 1978 to 815 meters in 2005. The total number of sites destroyed in these mountain ranges is reported to be 10,255, an area covering 335.6 square kilometers.[52]

In order to prevent further destruction, the Korean government introduced a bill in December 2004. At the same time, the Ministry of Agriculture announced a plan to restore 215 damaged sites covering 3,688 hectares by planting trees until 2015. According to a report by Yonhap News' Wire Service dated 29 December 2004, while the Ministry of Environment and the Korea Forestry Service proposed to restore 535,918 hectares of the land, local governments included in the restoration plan demanded that this be reduced to 239,479 hectares (44.6 percent of the proposal). This is an indication that for local governments development still trumps conservation.

Dam Construction

Although there were several dam projects during the Japanese occupation,[53] construction of multi-purpose dams to control floods, supply water to industrial zones, and generate electric power was made as a part of Korea's economic development and industrialization. Most of those dams were constructed rather hastily without the benefit of environmental impact studies, feedback from the people who affected by them, or the input of local governments.

Although dams have made some positive contributions to the economy, they have also created environmental disasters. The Andong and Imha Dams in Gyeongsangbuk-do province, located only 3 kilometers from each other, are both situated on the upper part of the Nakdonggang (the longest river in South Korea at 506.17 kilometers). The two dams, covering 3,045 square kilometers combined, have created various environmental problems, altering the ecology of the surrounding regions. People who were forced to relocate, particularly those who did not receive any compensation from the government because they did not own any land, suffered hardships. The yield of major crops in the regions, such as rice, red peppers, and apples, was reduced largely because of a reduction in the number of sunny days; foggy days and unusual amounts of rain increased, and temperatures dropped. Rice production fell 10 percent after the construction of the dams.[54] Because of the changes in climate and weather conditions, the air in the surrounding area is badly polluted with sulfurous acid gas at a level of 0.073 ppm, which is much worse than that of Gumi, the largest industrial zone in the region. Many people suffer from upper respiratory diseases and complain of neuralgia.[55]

A variety of freshwater fish that were popular around the region have disappeared, replaced by new and unpopular varieties. A special variety of fish, *euneo* (sweetfish), which migrates from the warm ocean in winter to the fresh river in spring and is beloved by the Korean people, was almost exterminated because the dam blocked its migratory route between ocean and river.[56] Recognizing these environmental impacts, and faced with ever increasing demands by environmentalists and conservationists, in 1993 the Korean government introduced several laws that constrain indiscriminate dam construction to maintain a better balance between development and conservation.

Incidentally, one of Korea's largest dams, the Yeongwol Dam on the Donggang in Gangwon-do province, was planned by the Rho Tae-woo government after the worst Korean flood in 1990. In December 1995, a 130-meter-high, 333-meter-long dam project was announced, with a completion date set for 2001. The project faced strong challenges and vehement opposition from environmental activists, civic groups, local people, and anthropologists.[57] Aware of the adverse impacts the dam would have on the environment, on 5 June 2000 President Kim Dae-jung finally halted the project altogether.[58] It was a sweet victory for environmental conservationists because environmental concerns had finally outweighed the push for development. Instead of pursuing the dam project, the government allocated 18.5 billion *won* ($19,7 million) to preserve the ecology of the river region. Nonetheless, the river is still badly polluted by toxic water from abandoned mines on the Donggang.[59]

Disappearance of Wetlands through Land Reclamation
Korea's western shore has 1,980 square kilometers of tidal flats. Land-hungry Koreans have made efforts to expand arable land and industrial sites for the past fifteen years, and approximately 810 square kilometers (25 percent) of the tidal flats have been reclaimed for development. The reclamation has altered human lives in the area as well as natural habitats for migratory birds and marine species.

Sihwaho, a reclamation site located some 35 kilometers from Seoul, has been widely publicized for various environmental problems. The Sihwaho Project, started in June 1987 and completed in January 1994, required 50 billion *won* ($53.3 million) to create 169 square kilometers of new land to build a freshwater reservoir to irrigate farmland and accommodate an industrial site containing some 1,600 factories. This reclamation project has created nothing but a huge polluted reservoir, altering a once-balanced ecosystem in the surrounding area, destroying the environment, destroying precious wetlands, and deeply affecting the people of the region. It was one of the worst environmental disasters ever created by an overly zealous development effort. Several anthropologists led by Han Kyung Koo (Han et al. 1998) have written an ethnography of the human lives affected by this environmental alteration.

Learning from its mistakes and misjudgments, Korea ratified the Ramsar Convention on Wetlands of International Importance Especially as Waterfowl Habitat in 1997, followed by the Wetlands Reservation Act in 1999. The Wetlands Reservation Act entrusts the Ministry of Environment and the Ministry of Maritime Affairs and Fisheries to study the status of Korea's wetlands and to designate several sites as Wetlands Preservation Areas.[60]

Despite such preservation efforts, the map-altering Saemangeum Reclamation Project, which will be the world's longest seawall (33 kilometers long), has been launched. Costing 2.16 trillion *won* (about $2.8 billion), it is scheduled to be completed by 2011. The entire area it covers is 40,100 hectares, about two-thirds the size of Seoul, and more than six times the size of Manhattan. The project had been planned in 1987 by the Rho Tae-woo government and started in 1991, but it has faced severe opposition, including legal battles for three years between the government and environmentalists.

Both the Korean government and Jeollabuk-do province, where the project is taking place, claim that it is desperately needed to infuse life into a declining area. The project is aimed at increasing farmland and also parks that could help spur development in the region, which at the moment has no major industry and has been losing people to other parts of the nation. Conservationists, environmentalists, and over 3,000 local residents whose livelihood depends on digging for shellfish and farming fish and seaweed claim that the reclamation project will be a massive environmental disaster that will destroy fishing assets, kill rare migratory birds, and worsen the water quality of the rivers that feed into the tidal flat.

On 16 March 2006, the Korean Supreme Court ruled overwhelmingly in favor of the project by eleven to two votes. Perhaps this decision was influenced in part by the privileging of economic development over conservation after the financial crisis of the late 1990s. The court eventually valued development over environmental conservation so the project has a new life and is under way. Nevertheless, the resulting environmental impacts will reveal themselves in the years to come.

Restoration Projects

Korea has been polluted environmentally as it has gone through rapid industrialization and economic growth. Korea's air pollution in major cities, especially in Seoul, has been worsened by automobile exhaust resulting from the drastic increase in the number of automobiles from only 7,000 in 1945 to nearly 15 million in 2004. Another contribution to air pollution in Korea is the heavy yellow dust that blows in from China, especially Inner Mongolia, in spring and summer, worsening the quality of air in the peninsula. Korea's rivers and streams have also been polluted, largely by toxic industrial waste. The Hangang, which runs through Seoul and is a major source of water for the city, was once so polluted that no fish lived in its waters. Treatment of household waste for over 10 million Seoulites has been a major challenge for the City of Seoul.

As the problem of pollution reached an unbearable level, Korea began to adopt various measures to ease the situation. To improve air quality, various restrictions have been imposed on the manufacturing industry within city limits, and natural gas-operated automobiles, mostly taxicabs and city buses, have been encouraged. The Hangang has acquired a new life after a massive clean-up job before the city hosted the 1988 Summer Olympic Games. The 1999 enactment of the Water Resource Management in Hangang [the Han River] and Community Support Act has been instrumental in bringing about continuing improvement of the Hangang. Today, the river looks clean and attractive. At night colorful lights that decorate its twenty-seven bridges look marvelous and well-arranged, and the well-kept river banks are very appealing. Nonetheless, in the eyes of a naive anthropologist who used to live near the Mississippi River, the Hangang, with its banks and river basins that show heavy use of cement, looks very artificial. The river has lost its natural beauty as I remember it before I left Korea in the mid-1960s.

Also, realizing that there would be very limited landfill areas for household waste, the government launched the comprehensive Food Waste Reduction measure in 1996 to promote a more economical dining culture and maximize recycling.[61] The Ministry of Environment has been funding waste recycling facilities by investing many billions of *won*. These activities and measures are being spearheaded by a growing number of Koreans who are concerned about environmental conservation. In response to such concerns and inquiries, several restoration projects have been introduced. Two of these, the Cheonggyecheon restoration and the Nanjido transformation projects, are worth mentioning here.

Restoration of the Cheonggyecheon Stream

The 5.8 kilometer-long Cheonggyecheon stream runs through the heart of Seoul. It had been considered troublesome for more than half a millennium because of occasional floods, ever since the capital of the Joseon dynasty had been relocated in 1394 from Gaeseong, the old capital of the Goryeo dynasty, to Seoul. Several Joseon kings, notably Taejong (1400-1418), Sejong (1418-1450), Yeongjo (1724-1776), and Jeongjo (1776-1800), mobilized thousands and thousands of people to clean the stream and to dig its course more deeply to control flooding. As the stream became polluted, functioning as the city sewage system beginning in 1920 through the early 1940s, Japanese authorities planned to fill it in to make a new road, but the plan never materialized.[62] In 1958, the road project was resumed, and in 1963 as part of a government-led industrialization project, the stream was completely covered over with concrete. On top of the newly built concrete road, an overpass bridge was built.

In 1991, a small group of academics, environmentalists — especially Green Korea United — writers, and informed citizens, joined later by politicians, including then mayoral candidate Lee Myungbak, launched a methodical campaign to restore the stream by removing the concrete cover, including the overpass bridge. Despite opposition by shop owners and merchants in the surrounding area, on 1 July 2003, as Seoul's newly elected mayor, Lee Myungbak began the restoration project, with a budget of 3,600 billion *won* (about $3.8 billion). The project was finally completed on 1 October 2005, and included the construction of twenty-two bridges, a mixture of renovated originals and newly built replicas. The stream now looks attractive and charming. The trees planted alongside the dikes add an aesthetic beauty to the city.

The restoration not only attracts many tourists from Korea and abroad, but it also has brought back freshwater fish, frogs, and birds such as swallows, which were not found in Seoul recently due to

A scene of the Cheonggyecheon after the restoration

pollution. The temperature of the areas surrounding the restored stream has been found to be cooler than in other sections of the city.[63] Furthermore, the restoration boosted the business activities of the merchants who once opposed the project and increased the value of real estate in the surrounding areas. Mayor Lee, who actually carried out the project, sums it up: "the restoration of the environment, history, and cultural relic results in economic effects. The city has become livable for foreigners and friendly to foreign companies."[64]

The mayor attracted wide publicity not only from Seoulites but also from Koreans living elsewhere. Most mass media have made positive reports about the project. Hundreds and thousands of tourists from all over the country come to Seoul to see the "restored" stream. Because of the project's successful completion, the former mayor has become a front-runner for the forthcoming presidential election.

However, it now appears that this stream is quite costly: it takes 120,000 tons of water per day to keep it running continuously, water supplied from the Hangang (near *Jayang Chwisujang*) using four gigantic electric motors and over 30,000 kw/h of electricity a day, equivalent to that used by over 3,000 households daily. Keeping the Cheonggyecheon flowing costs about 1,800 million *won* (about $1.9 million) per year.[65]

As a naive anthropologist, my concern is not so much the expense of maintaining the present-day stream, but its aesthetic beauty compared to that of the original stream. Most of all, I wonder whether one can call this a "restoration project" *per se*, because the stream was really "recreated" to follow the course of the old stream. The present-day stream looks natural, but actually it has been built on top of a huge tray of cement lining the entire streambed. It looks so artificial that it reminds me of Japanese *bonsai* and *bonkei*.[66] If I did not have any memory of the stream of the past, I might find the newly created stream attractive. One might argue that before Koreans rebuilt the stream, before they covered it over with concrete, it had been so filthy, almost like a huge sewage and garbage dump, that a good many Koreans prefer the current one. I may well be in the minority because of my nostalgia for the past. Also, during the monsoon season, in the summer months, the stream has had a flooding problem since the time of the Joseon dynasty. Now, even after the renovation, continuous precautions must still be taken and warnings issued about possible flooding during the monsoon season. So what has really changed?

Regardless of what an anthropologist might think about all this, Gwangju, the most populous city in Jeollanam-do province, after witnessing the positive impact of the Cheonggyecheon restoration, is now planning to renovate Gwangjucheon (Gwangju Stream) that runs through that city by 2009.[67] Vietnam is now interested in developing the Hong River in Hanoi, emulating the Cheonggyecheon project. Indeed the city of Seoul is providing technical advice for the project.[68]

Nanjido Ecological Park

The transformation of the Nanjido Waste Repository into an ecological park is a meaningful success story from an ecological standpoint. The nearly 3 million square meters of Nanjido were created over a long period of time by the Hangang. Nanjido was an island that had drawn little attention except from some fishermen before it was designated as the major repository of the household waste of over 10 million Seoulites. From 1978 to 1993, when the site was completely closed

A scene of the Nanjido park after the transformation of the landfill to an ecological park

because it had been filled to capacity, 92 million cubic meters of waste from the Seoul Metropolitan area was deposited there.[69] The elevation of Nanjido was originally only 7 meters, but the accumulated waste raised it so it became a 100-meter high mountain. When the repository was in use, it created all sorts of environmental hazards, not to mention an unbearable stench. Winds often carried the odor to distant sections of the city. Because of the methane gas generated by the organic particles deposited in the lower layers, there have been 1,400 fires in the past fifteen years, some lasting for forty-five days.

The plan to transform the waste repository into an ecological park began in 1991, two years before the site was closed, and the restoration project was completed in 2001. The 942,000 square-meter waste site has now been transformed into an attractive ecological park. The site has became a sanctuary for over 400 species of plants and insects as well as over 9 million human visitors annually.

In 1998, the Sangam-dong Soccer Stadium, the largest and most modern soccer field in Korea, was built on this site. The stadium eventually hosted the 2002 FIFA World Cup Soccer Games. Furthermore, the city built parks, a golf course, and other sports and recreation facilities on the site; it also established the Digital Media City (DMC) there to lure high tech industries. Some reputable high tech industries have already moved in, and others are planning to build their facilities there. This is one of the world's most amazing projects that successfully transformed a waste repository into a man-made ecological park and complex.

DMZ as an Eco-Axe

The DMZ, which zigzags across the middle of the Korean peninsula, separates North and South Korea. It was established in 1953 when a ceasefire was declared in the Korean War to prevent inter-Korean acts of hostility. The DMZ runs along a line 248 kilometers (155 miles) long, 4 kilometers (1.25 miles) wide, and 2 kilometers on each side. The DMZ and the surrounding area within 5 to 10 kilometers south of the DMZ's southern boundary remains a heavily guarded no-man's land. The DMZ and its region provide habitats and migration routes for important aquatic birds and cranes.

Recently, for the first time, an ecological research team of South Koreans found eleven types of rare animals and 2,716 species of plants and animals in the DMZ area. Such ecological studies are expected to continue in the future.[70] The inaccessibility of the DMZ for more than half a century has allowed war-ravaged forests to return to their natural state and the DMZ and surrounding areas now serve as a sanctuary for many endangered species of plants and animals.

Covering 992 square kilometers, the DMZ includes mountains, fields, valleys, basins, and several rivers. Since the DMZ consists of mountains, inland marshes, freshwater and coastal ecosystems all existing together, it is a natural laboratory for environmentalists and ecologists to study. If North and South Korea could agree, both Koreas could create the world's most valuable ecological park and laboratory, which would attract many visitors from home and abroad to study ecosystems in action.

Conservation and Changes in Korean Burial Culture

Because Korea's population density is the second highest in the world (490.2 persons per square kilometers in 2003)[71] after Taiwan, excluding several city-states such as Singapore, and also because only 20 percent of Korean land is arable, the price of land in Korea is sky-high. Despite this scarcity, 1 percent of all the land in Korea is devoted to burials, and over 130,000 new burial mounds are erected yearly.[72] Anyone who has traveled in Korea, especially to the countryside, finds that the most attractive sites are occupied by burial mounds. Pungsu (wind and water), conventionally translated as "geomancy" in Western sources, used to discern "good" and "bad" grave locations, has contributed to the search for ideal burial sites.

Traditionally, even at present to a certain degree, people tend to believe that a grave site affects the welfare of descendants (see Janelli and Yim1982:71-85). Because of this, some wealthy families not only occupy good sites but also maintain sizable burial land surrounding a burial mound. As a consequence, living Koreans have to compete with the dead for land. A good many burial mounds not only take up a large amount of space, but they also disturb the environment.

In order to conserve Korea's available land and preserve its environment, the government and concerned citizens have launched a campaign to restrain the building of large burial mounds, suggesting cremation as an alternative. Traditionally, in Korean burial culture, cremation was not common, being limited to some Buddhists, including monks and nuns, and people who died of highly contagious diseases. However, since this campaign has begun, the rate of cremation of the dead has increased steadily from 5.8 percent in 1955, to 13.7 percent in 1981, and 17.8 percent in 1991. It then experienced a dramatic jump in 2005 to 52.6 percent. The Ministry of Health and Welfare predicts that the rate of cremation will reach over 70 percent by 2010.[73] Currently, in some cases funerals are delayed because of the long waiting list for cremations. Additional cremation facilities in Seoul are urgently needed, yet most Seoulites do not want them built near their homes.

After cremation, the ashes are usually stored in a pot, and placed in *napgoldang* (shrine-like facilities where the pots are stored along with the names of the dead persons for ancestor rites and family visits). However, such facilities also take up space. Nowadays, a good many people spread the ashes around in forest areas and bushes to become a part of nature. Koreans call such a burial *jayeonjang* (natural burial). Others bury the ashes under a designated tree, a burial called *sumokjang* (bury ashes under a tree). This newly emerging burial culture will be helpful in preserving the natural beauty of mountainous Korea since burials have long been concentrated in mountainous areas. Such a conservation effort is important because mountains and hills cover nearly 70 percent of the Korean peninsula.

Yellow Dust and Korean Air

Despite massive development activities in Korea over the past several decades, Korean air is cleaner now than it was in the 1970s thanks to conservation efforts. Nevertheless, Korea cannot control polluted air resulting from the yellow dust (*hwangsa*) that spreads over the peninsula beginning in early spring, carried from the Gobi desert by low atmospheric pressure moving eastward. Yellow dust clouds usually arrive more than ten times before disappearing in the summer. A strong yellow dust like this occurred on 30 March 2007, having a density of over 800 micrograms (microgram is one millionth of a gram) per cubic meter. The amount of dust on 30 March 2007 alone is estimated to have been from 46,000–86,000 tons, enough to fill four or five fifteen-ton dump trucks. On that day, downtown Seoul was nearly empty since citizens were unwilling to go outside, and many outdoor activities were either cancelled or restricted.

What can Korea do about this troublesome phenomenon other than issue warnings to alert its citizens? Many people aggravated by these dust clouds can only lament, "We pray that China reaches a mature stage of development soon, so it can make every effort to deal with environmental issues such as preserving clean air, as Koreans have done."

EPILOGUE

Korea's Place in the World: The "Hermit Kingdom" No More?

From "Mendicant" to Foreign Aid Donor

In 1964 when I was teaching assistant to Hahm Pyong-choon, Professor of Law at Yonsei University, Hahm asked me to read his manuscript entitled "Korea's 'Mendicant Mentality'?" before he submitted it to *Foreign Affairs* (1964:165-174). Hahm's article contained the following passage:

> Not long ago, at a social gathering, I overheard a high-ranking U.S. military officer berating the Korean people for their "mendicant mentality." He was deeply annoyed by the inability of Koreans to find a way to live independently, without always looking to the United States for financial help. He did not see how the American taxpayers could be made to carry indefinitely the burden of helping a poor nation that seems unable or unwilling to help itself. He cited the billions of dollars of American aid that have been poured into Korea since 1945. ⋯ The Koreans must be made to realize, he said, that they had to get onto their own feet very soon; otherwise continued American aid would only create what one American news magazine several years ago terms a "handout mentality."

The description was annoying, disturbing, and, most of all, it made me ashamed of Korea's reality. Nonetheless, I mailed the article to *Foreign Affairs* for Hahm.

David I. Steinberg,[1] who was in Korea as director of the Asia Foundation when Hahm was writing this article, also ruminates on the Korea of the past: "Per capita income for 1953 was only $67, ⋯ and one of the lowest in the world. ⋯ There was in Korea, moreover, a sense of despair and hopelessness, as well as a 'mendicant mentality,' a reliance on foreign patrons, especially the United States, for military, economic, and political support. Korea was at that time a U.S. client state" (Steinberg 1989:122). Assessing contemporary Korea in relation to the past, Steinberg says, "from the dark nadir of 1953, progress of this magnitude was virtually unthinkable; few Koreans radiated self-confidence; few foreigners realized Korea's potential" (Steinberg 1989:122).

Four decades later, on 2 April 2007, I became highly emotional watching TV as Koreans once labeled "mendicant" announcing a FTA between Korea and the United States in Seoul that had been achieved through tough talks and hard bargaining by two nations on an equal footing. This was by no means a "mendicant agreement." Still pending the congressional approval of both countries, the $29 billion accord is expected to boost Korean exports to the United States by $19 billion and U.S. exports to Korea by $10 billion. This agreement would be the biggest trade accord ever for Korea and the largest for the United States since NAFTA in 1993. It has symbolic meaning for Korea's ability to negotiate with a gigantic country like the United States, and it announces that Korea can make a fair deal.

By the way, the FTA between Korea and the United States has provided momentum for Korea to expand negotiations with twenty-seven members of the European Union (EU), which are expected to produce even bigger results: the average tariff rate imposed on Korean products imported by the EU is over 4 percent, compared with 3.5 percent for the United States; in 2006, the EU's gross domestic product stood at $13 trillion in 2006, higher than the United States' $12.5

trillion. In May 2007, Korea and the EU began to negotiate their first round of official free trade talks in Seoul. Now China also wants to have a FTA with Korea, although no specific plans have yet been made.

Korea, once the recipient of foreign aid from a variety of nations before, during, and after the Korean War, has now become a donor, assisting other countries. The government-sponsored Korea International Cooperation Agency (KOICA) has sent 3,003 volunteers, including physicians, city planners, and other professionals, to thirty-six developing countries, including India and China.[2] The program is growing yearly in the number of volunteers and countries included. Korea is indebted to Western missionaries for Korean modernization and the nation's independence. Now, the Korean Institute for Missions (KRIM) has sent many missionaries to various countries, and the number increased dramatically from ninety-three missionaries to twenty-six countries in 1979 to 12,874 missionaries to 160 countries by 2004.[3]

Military aid has also been expanded: during the Vietnam War from 1964 to 1973, nearly 50,000 Korean troops played a significant role assisting the United States. Since Korean and U.S. troops fought side by side in Vietnam, not to mention during the Korean War, Koreans often call the relationship between two countries *hyeolmaeng* (alliance through blood tie). As of 2007, about 2,519 Korean troops are stationed in thirteen different places around the world under the auspices of U.N. peace-keeping missions, including Iraq, Afghanistan, Lebanon, and ten other places.[4] It is now Korea's turn to render assistance to other U.N. member states just as Korea had been assisted by sixteen nations, most prominently America, during the Korean War.

The Challenge of Continuing Economic Development and Industrialization

Korean economic development and industrialization are the most remarkable phenomena in the contemporary world. Nevertheless, Korea is facing many new challenges and it can no longer rely upon the "privilege of historic backwardness" (Trotsky n.d:4-5) or the advantage of "late industrialization" (Amsden 1989). Perhaps Korea may even suffer "the penalty of taking the lead," as England did, becoming less efficient than Germany, a process described by Thorstein Veblen (1915) in his analysis of Imperial Germany during the Industrial Revolution.

Korea's Premature Mid-Life Crisis

According to an editorial in the *Financial Times* on 27 March 2007, the Korean economy, once held up as a model of development, is facing the crisis of "sinking into premature middle age," with an average of 4.2 percent annual growth in the past four years. Many Korea watchers at home and abroad characterize Korea's situation using a "sandwich or nutcracker" analogy — "a metaphor for Korea being squashed between low-cost China and high-tech Japan — and raise the spectre [specter] of a Japan or German-style 'hollowing out' of Korean industry."[5]

There have been many warnings and much advice that Korea has to generate a second wave of economic success. Tariq Hussain (2006:273-313), for one, offers eight agendas in his recent book, *Diamond Dilemma*, including reforming government, corporations, the labor market, universities, opening up the economy, harnessing the power of women, and budgeting social capital.

In this chapter, I will concentrate on the following reforms which I see as crucial for the future robustness of Korea's economy: redefining the role of *jaebeol* and reducing government regulations, creating an open policy to meet the challenges of globalization, preparing a future labor market in an increasingly aging society, and promoting the rejuvenation of the Korean spirit for a new leap forward toward further development.

Jaebeol Reform

The remarkable Korean economic advance of the last four decades has been led primarily by *jaebeol* groups. However, *jaebeol* have come under fire lately for their expansionist policy that created heavy debt in the late 1990s, a situation which contributed to the 1997 financial crisis. Also, the diversification of *jaebeol* groups hinders the creation of internationally competitive companies with an emphasis on research and development (R&D). Even Samsung, one of Korea's most successful companies, which has spearheaded Korea's technological advances as the largest R&D spender, has sixty-two subsidiaries. Among those, only Samsung Electronics has achieved a position of global leadership. In light of this situation, Hussain (2006:127) states that Korea might not need another *jaebeol* group like Samsung, but instead many more companies like Samsung Electronics. If Korean companies do not maintain a technological edge the way Samsung Electronics has, it will be difficult for them to remain competitive on a global scale. The existing *jaebeol*-centered model may no longer work for Korea.

Now is the time for Korean *jaebeol* groups to uphold business ethics, meeting global standards and improving corporate governance with transparency in management and accounting. It may be worthwhile for Korean *jaebeol* groups to heed the moral declaration made by the Knoxville Chamber of Commerce in Knoxville, Tennessee, in the early 1960s, that "what is morally right is economically sound" (Kim 1995:19). Such moral leadership has contributed a great deal to the reduction, if not elimination, of racial discrimination in the American South. This in turn has contributed to the transformation of the South from an agrarian, poverty-stricken, and racially discriminatory society into a dynamic, vibrant, and new industrial wonderland.

Without making their corporate finances transparent, *jaebeol* will not be able to gain the support of unionized workers. For instance, 4,200 Chinese employees (whose average age is 26) receive a base salary equivalent to $360 a month and belong to a workers' organization whose main task seems to be to encouraging greater effort rather than pushing for higher wages. By contrast, at Hyundai's Ulsan Plant in Korea, workers (whose average age is 41) earn $4,580 a month, and are heavily unionized. Consequently, in 2006, a twenty-five-day-long strike cost Hyundai about $127 million.[6] Indeed, the cost of labor in

Korea's manufacturing industries is high, perhaps even excessively high in some industries: the average annual income of Korea's POSCO workers ($66,000) is higher than the average salary of Japanese ($62,000) and American US Steel workers ($62,000).[7]

The high cost of wages in the manufacturing industry has become a major hindrance to the competitive edge of companies,[8] and has led *jaebeol* groups increasingly to invest abroad. *Jaebeol* groups must now redefine their previous role to leap forward with the changing times. This may be the most effective means of softening the confrontational mode of the labor unions. In 2007, for instance, as *jaebeol* groups began to reform, the number of labor strikes declined 41 percent from the previous year.[9] Korea faces the challenge of changing the fundamental attitudes of both workers and management toward labor unions, from the traditional view of confrontation and conflict to one of cooperation and reciprocity through collaboration and by establishing an exceptional rapport between management and labor union workers.

Reforming Government Regulations and Promoting FDI

Government and its bureaucratic machinery have to be ruthless about abolishing nonessential regulations. Korea is known to be a country in which business is overregulated. Up until 1970, for instance, exporting one single item required 120 documents. Although such burdensome regulations were reduced by more than 40 percent after the 1997 financial crisis, they are now increasing again (Hussain 2006:40). The Korea Development Institute (KDI) has reported that establishing a new company in Korea takes twelve stages and twenty-two days because of the many regulations, longer than it takes to establish a business in Mongolia and Vietnam.[10] If the boundary between two EU countries, Belgium and Luxemburg, divided an industrial plant in two, those nations would adjust their borders slightly to accommodate the factory. By contrast, Gwanghwamun Building in Gwanghwamun, a core section of downtown Seoul, is in two districts (*gu*), because the tenth floor and below belong to Jongno-gu, and the eleventh floor and above belong to Jung-gu. As a result, the building has ended up paying taxes to both districts since 1992.[11]

To achieve substantial growth, the Korean government has to open up the economy, and a starting point would be promoting more foreign direct investment (FDI), which is as important as export, if not more moreso. It is the government's responsibility to at least reduce, if not eliminate, the average Korean's fear that FDI might turn Korea into an "economic colony" for foreign investors. The *Financial Times* calls such an apprehension "economic nationalism."[12]

There are many instances in which FDI can make a positive contribution to the domestic economy. From the early 1970s, when a wave of Japanese and European FDI swept over the United States, particularly the American South, many patriotic Southerners were afraid of the foreign influence this would have on their economy.

However, American scholars and intellectuals have continuously sought to educate the public about the advantages of FDI. Robert Reich (1990:63), a political economist who became secretary of labor under President Bill Clinton, for one, advocates that Americans should "encourage, not discourage, foreign direct investment." His advice is pragmatic: foreign manufacturers, particularly the Japanese in Tennessee, have recently created more jobs in the United States than have American-owned manufacturing companies. "America's 500 largest industrial companies failed to create a single net new job between 1975 and 1990, their share of the civilian labor force dropping from 17 percent to less than 10 percent," Reich (1991:95) noted.[13]

Despite the initial fears of Southerners, knowing the advantages of FDI, the business communities in most southern states aggressively recruited investment from overseas, pointing out such attractive incentives as tax breaks and job training, infrastructure financing, low taxes, ample space, mild climate conditions, pro-business attitudes, good transportation systems, inexpensive living expenses, lower wages, and right-to-work laws (open-shop system). Because most southern states were successful in recruiting FDI — including the auto giant

Toyota in Kentucky and Nissan and the domestic GM's Saturn Plant in Tennessee — the traditionally agrarian states of the American South have been transformed into a new industrial wonderland, while the Detroit, once an automobile manufacturing Mecca, remains a "rust belt." After securing FDI, even during hard times when the U.S. economy was experiencing its worst recession, in the late 1980s and early 1990s, the "economic health"[14] of the southern states remained stronger than that of most non-southern states (Kim 1995).

A statement made by Reich (1990:50, 1991) persuasively illustrates the benefits of FDI. He says, "The typical argument suggests that a foreign-owned company might withdraw for either profit or foreign policy motives. But either way, the bricks and mortar would still be here. So would the equipment. So too would be the accumulated learning among American workers. … After all, the American government and the American people maintain jurisdiction — political control — over assets within the United States." According to the Korea Employers Federation (KEF), from 1995 to 2005, about 5,000 Korean firms have invested in China in the form of FDI, and created more than 1 million jobs there. As a result, some 210,000 manufacturing jobs in Korea have been lost. The KEF estimates that in the next ten years, an estimated 360,000 more jobs in Korea will be lost because of Korea's FDI in China.[15] It is reported that for every $1 million in FDI in Korea, about twenty well-paid new jobs for Koreans would be created (Hussain 2006:292).

The "Hermit Kingdom" No More

Outwardly Directed Koreans
To most Koreans, globalization means mainly outwardly directed activities. Korea now has diplomatic relations with 186 countries, the exceptions being Cuba, Syria, Macedonia, Monaco, and a few new nations. Nearly 1,000 diplomatic personnel are stationed in various overseas embassies. In order to promote Korean trade, business, and investment, the state-owned Korea Trade-Investment Promotion

Agency (KOTRA) has 102 branch offices in 74 countries. Nearly 13,000 Korean missionaries are in 160 countries, and over 3,000 KOICA volunteers are working in thirty-six countries. In the private sector, over 33,000 Korean firms are established in 158 countries, investing over $60 billion.[16]

Many Korean students study in various foreign countries. The total number of Koreans and their descendants dispersed throughout the world, in 174 countries, has been estimated to be over 6.6 million.[17] In addition, from 2001 to 2005, a total of over 5.5 million Koreans traveled overseas for various purposes.[18]

By the end of 2005, there were slightly over 18,000 foreign business firms in Korea, 15,000 less than the number of Korean firms that went overseas.[19] The number of foreign missionaries in Korea is fewer than their Korean counterparts overseas.[20] By the end of 2005, the total number of foreigners residing in Korea on a long-term basis was reported to be about 500,000 or about 1 percent of the total South Korean population.[21] The total number of foreign visitors who have traveled to Korea from 2001 to 2005 was over 4 million, 1.5 million less than the number of Koreans who went overseas.[22] The number of foreign students at all levels who were studying in Korea was reported to be less than 23,000 in 2005.[23] There are 8.5 times more Korean students studying in foreign countries than foreign students studying in Korea.

Well aware that recruiting FDI is no less important than exporting Korean products to other countries, Korean leadership is now making a deliberate effort to induce other countries to invest in Korea. It is not easy for Korea to compete with China in attracting FDI in the manufacturing sector because China's abundant supply of cheap and hard-working labor has given it the lead in manufacturing. Although both the Korean government and labor unions are keenly aware of the importance of FDI, the share of GDP, Korea's stock of the FDI in Korea, is relatively low, 8.1 percent compared with the world's average of 21.7 percent, making it 109th out of 140 countries.[24]

Recruiting FDI requires strong leadership. During my fieldwork on

Japanese industry in the American South, for instance, I witnessed the evolution of public opinion about Japanese investment in the region, beginning the late 1970s. Japanese foreign direct investment in the South has not always been met with open arms. Some Southerners viewed Japanese FDI in their region as a "threat" (Kim 1995:136).[25] Some worried that the intention behind heavy Japanese FDI could be interpreted as "buying into America" or the "Japanization" of the southern economy (Taira 1991:151–163). Other Southern responses to what was perceived as the Japanese challenge have been more explicit and direct. There was an incident of cross burning in the schoolyard of the Tennessee Meiji Gakuin School, which was established in the foothills of the Great Smoky Mountains to provide education for the children of Japanese expatriates in the United States (Kim 1995:136). When Nissan announced its decision to locate in Smyrna, Tennessee, Carl Montgomery, a patriotic Southerner and retired Air Force colonel from World War II, demanded that the County Commission rename the access to the plant "Pearl Harbor Boulevard" (Alexander 1986:152).[26]

In February 1981, when Nissan began building the Smyrna plant, Nissan hired a non-union construction company as general contractor. In response, a rowdy builders trade union demonstration marred the groundbreaking ceremonies at the Nissan plant. An airplane flew overhead trailing a banner reading "Boycott Datsun [Nissan]." And big burly men carried signs saying "Go home, Japs!" Local residents were so shocked by these antagonistic demonstrations that they heavily criticized the demonstrators. The next day the Tennessee legislature passed a resolution condemning the builders trade union. Later, the union apologized and ran full-page ads saying, "Hey, we apologize. We didn't really mean it. Things got out of hand" (Kim 1995:117–118). Ever since, American scholars and intellectuals have been continuously educating the public about the advantages of FDI.

There have recently been some positive developments in Korea with respect to FDI. For instance, on 18 April 2006, the Federation of Korean Trade Unions (FKTU) and the state-run Korea Trade Investment

Promotion Agency (KOTRA) signed an agreement to merge efforts to attract FDI and improve labor relations. This unusual move is part of the FKTU's call to shift the focus of the labor movement from antagonistic struggle to social dialogue and responsibility. "We are trying to open a new paradigm in the labor movement," said a spokesperson for the FKTU. "As well as calling for our rights, we will also take social responsibility."[27] In response to this, the government is planning to invite the president of the FKTU to join a promotional session to be held in the United States in the near future to explain FDI in Korea. This is a promising move for the government to seek the support and cooperation of unions.

In summary, a comparison of statistics concerning inwardly and outwardly directed activities gives the impression that Koreans tend to focus on outward efforts rather than on creating a favorable atmosphere to attract foreigners and foreign investment. Korea's export-oriented economy might contribute to this trend.

Addressing Nationalism Based on a Single Ethnic People
Gi-Wook Shin (2006:15) points out that "nationalism in itself is fairly harmless. Only when combined with other ideologies can its effect be felt ··· nationalism allows for chameleon-like permutations' because it can be combined with ideologies like liberalism, racism, and romanticism, which serve a variety of goals from democratic to authoritarian, divisive to unifying, modern to anti-modern." In the case of Korea, nationalism is sometime bound up with ethnicity.

It has been widely publicized and proudly proclaimed that Koreans are *danil minjok*, a single, homogeneous ethnic people with a common culture. Bruce Cumings (1997:434) states that "the perceived purity of the *minjok*, the ethnic people, gives them a long, continuous history, culture, and durability of which Koreans are deeply proud. At the same time this solid ethnic identity presents the non-Korean with an easy, superficial, seductive, and profoundly misleading sameness." No one knows for certain when Koreans started to use this term but it is assumed to have been in use since 1905 when Korea lost its sovereignty to Japan (Shmid

2002). The term connotes a combination of nation and race (Cumings 1997:207), and its use was further enhanced and reinforced during the years of Japanese domination, because when Korea lost its sovereignty as an independent nation, Koreans substituted "*minjok*" (ethnic people) for "nation" or "state."[28]

Nevertheless, the myth of a single ethnic people is just that — a myth — and the term is no longer applicable to the reality of contemporary Korea. As previously mentioned, beginning in 1990, a large number of rural Korean men married foreign women. A new and fashionable word, "multiculture," has been introduced to Koreans, but word and deed do not always coincide. There has been no systematic effort to enable those who have foreign-born family members to learn about other cultures. Nor has there been any bilingual program for children born to foreign women. Since Korea is new to multiculture, it may take an extra effort for it to build a truly multicultural society.

The visit of Hines Ward, who won the title of Most Valuable Player (MVP) in American football's Super Bowl XL in 2006, to Seoul in early April 2006 caused many Koreans to rethink their deeply rooted racial bias. Ward was born in Korea to a Korean woman and an African American ex-GI. He endured racial discrimination for being a "mixed-blood" half Korean until he left Korea in 1976 for the United States. Ward's highly publicized visit to Korea has generated many discussions about the unfair discrimination against mixed marriages and their offspring. In response to a public outcry against unfair treatment in the past, all political party leaders have promised to push for legislation to protect mixed-blood Koreans from discrimination in the workplace, schools, and other parts of Korean society. An article in the April 2006 the *Korea Herald* summarizes Korean sentiment about this issue: "Now we should break away from the prejudice of describing ourselves as a pure blood nation."[29]

Despite such an outcry, many Koreans even apply the notion of ethnicity to beef, pork, various vegetables, and other traditional Korean food. The phrase "*Sinto buri*" (body and soil are the same) is a prime example of this kind of thinking. According to Shin (2006:216), "*Sinto buri* claims that if a person has Korean blood, he or she is Korean, regardless of class background or place of residence. Therefore, it can be claimed that Koreans remain Korean because they share the same blood." As a result of this belief, some claim that it is better for Koreans to consume Korean-produced beef, rice, wheat, and many other native varieties. Using this catchphrase, Korean producers launch campaigns to capitalize upon their own domestic products by charging higher prices, sometimes even seven or eight times more than foreign-grown export products. In most Korean grocery stores, each item has to be identified by its place of origin. Perhaps even cow slaughtered in Tennessee and fish caught in the Atlantic Ocean have to carry passports to find a place on Korean grocery shelves. I am not able to discern the difference between the imported Chilean-grown grapes that appeared in the market after the FTA, and Korean-grown grapes. And *LA garbi* (beef ribs), as Koreans call it, is not necessarily poorer in quality than Korean *garbi*, and may even be better, but Korean consumers would rather pay higher prices for the Korean product. *Sinto buri* is no more than a promotional gimmick for native products, if not ethnocentrism. Shin (2006:216) comments on the connection between *Sinto buri* and commercialism: "it has transformed into the commercialization of the Korean culture and heritage. Food, drink, and other everyday commodities that incorporate traditional 'Korean' elements have become popular products in the Korean market. *Sikkye* (sweet rice juice) reportedly outsold Coca-Cola, that ultimate symbol of global commodities."

If one walks around Insa-dong and Samcheong-dong where many foreign visitors go, one sees many commodities with traditional Korean cultural elements, both material and non-material, on display and for sale. Many restaurants serve traditional Korean dishes. What they are doing is promoting the consumption of tradition for commercial purposes by appealing to nostalgia. Even now, as I write this passage, there is a big festival going on whose slogan is "Walk around the streets of Bukchon Hanok maeul [which literally means north of the Hangang, but specifically the vicinities of Insa-dong and Samcheong-dong], and feel for the life of the Joseon dynasty!"[30] Gwon Sugin (1998:186), quoted in Shin (2006:216), is right when he says, "National traditional culture is considered more than a product of the past or something to preserve and transmit. It has become an object to commodify to maximize its potential value."

Several popular TV soap operas such as *Daejanggeum* (Jewel in the Palace) and others set in various dynastic periods, especially the Joseon dynasty, as mentioned before, also appealed to Koreans' longing for traditional culture, and generated big profits as a result. Incidentally, such TV soap operas have also drawn a surprising amount of interest from people in China, Japan, and several Southeast Asian countries, as part of what was known as the *Hallyu* waves, of which "*Samulnori*" is one.[31] This traditional Korean farmers' outdoor musical performance was adapted in the 1970s for indoor performances of traditional culture. In the spring of 2004, a *samulnori* team organized and led by Kim Duksoo performed in ten U.S. cities and Canada to rave reviews.[32] The traditional vocal music of *pansori* is another popular-culture tradition that is regaining popularity.[33] Performed by a single vocalist who tells a long story, the music elicits many different emotions, ranging from sidesplitting laughter to profuse tears. Because it is a unique genre of traditional Korean music, *pansori* vocalists were invited to perform in Lyon, France, in April 2006.[34]

Regarding globalization and the Korean attitude toward it, Hussain (2007) comments that in Korea, "the hermit kingdom [a Korean epithet derived from the self-invoked international isolationist policy of the Joseon dynasty in the nineteenth century] may be gone, but the hermit spirit remains very much alive. Zealous government officials, radical labor unions and a deeply nationalistic mindset are holding back Korea's integration with the rest of the world. ⋯ Despite significant progress in recent years, Korea has a long way to go to truly open up: as a share of GDP, Korea's stock of foreign direct investment is lower than in any other OECD country except Japan. Korea, it seems, remains a hermit kingdom."[35]

Hussain's view may be too critical, but there is some truth to his observation. However, in considering Korea's behavior, we have to take into account the basic nature of globalization, which John Naisbitt (1994:24-26) characterizes in his popular book, *Global Paradox*: "The more universal we become, the more tribal we act." Therefore, we have to "Think locally, act globally." I hope that Korea is not thinking and talking globally, but acting locally. Any Korean action at odds with the trend toward globalization may be a manifestation of the Korean ethos of contradiction, in this case, between an effort to globalize by signing FTAs with various countries, and an attachment to *sinto puri*.

Preparing for the Labor Market of the Future

The birth rate among Korean women is one of the lowest in the world (1.08 in 2005), leading to projections that the population will decrease 13 percent by 2050. Korea's birth rate is nine per 1,000 and its death rate 5 percent per 1,000. The population mid-2006 was estimated at 45.8 million, but it was predicted to decrease to 42.3 million by 2050 after rising modestly to 49.8 million in 2025. Nineteen percent of the population is age fifteen or under, and 10 percent age sixty-five or older. The average life expectancy of South Koreans is seventy-seven —eighty-one for women and seventy-four for men.

Because of this demographic trend, in 2005 the proportion of the Korean population of working age (from fifteen to sixty-five) was 71.7 percent. However, it is estimated that this figure will decrease to only 53.7 percent in 2050, slightly more than half of the total population. This will create a huge shortfall of Korean workers in the very near future, and something has to be done about this looming problem. About half a million foreign workers now fill the vacuum created by the current shortage of Korean workers,[36] particularly in small — and medium — size manufacturing industries.

By far the most serious problem is that Korea as a nation is rapidly becoming an "aging society," in which the population sixty-five and older is 7 percent, if not an "aged society," in which those sixty-five and older comprise 14 percent of the population. Of 234 cities and counties (*gun*), with the except of greater metropolitan cities such as

Seoul, Busan, Daegu, and Gwangju, thirty-five (15 percent) actually belong to the category of a "super-aged society," in which those sixty-five and older age comprise more than 20 percent of the population, ninety (38 percent) to an aged society, and fifty-five (24 percent) to an aging society. Consequently, due to the increasing life expectancy of Koreans, a smaller number of young Koreans will end up supporting a growing number of older people. The Korean government and its policy makers have to come up with a long-range plan to address and manage the problems of an aging society.

Between Low-Cost China and High-Tech Japan

Many Korea watchers at home and abroad have expressed their concern that Korea is losing its dynamism in economic development, and the country has been pressured to come up with a new strategy — something only Korea can devise — in order to escape its uncomfortable position of being sandwiched between low-cost China and high-tech Japan. Nevertheless, Korean *jaebeol* groups are cautious about investing in large projects after experiencing the trauma of the financial crisis in 1997, so they remain conservative. Often striking union workers have been blamed for demanding higher wages, but wage hikes do not accomplish much because living expenses and prices of consumer goods outpace them.[37]

Given the current economic situation, Koreans are anxious to have a national leader who can provide a road map for their future destiny. In an editorial, the *Financial Times* blames the current Korean administration for a lack of leadership that "has both vision and political courage to pursue vigorous reforms."[38] Korea may need radical action to stimulate diversification, innovation, and enterprise by opening its economy to competition from newly industrialized competitors such as China and India. Certainly, the FTA with the United States and the forthcoming FTA with the EU could provide momentum for reforms and rejuvenation.

Improving the Quality of Life

In sum, despite what appears to be a temporary setback or stagnation, or whatever one might choose to call it, prospects for the future of Korea remain promising Nevertheless, an optimistic outlook depends on several "ifs." If the Korean government facilitates FDI by implementing reform policies that abolish nonessential regulations, if Korean *jaebeol* groups adopt a true, open, and transparent system of governance to meet global standards morally and ethically, and if Korean labor unions change their confrontational image into a cooperative one, then Korea will be able to leap forward toward further progress.[39] After all, Korea has a well-educated population, modern infrastructure, a high level of Internet penetration and an industrious workforce, strengths not many late industrializing countries have. If all goes well, Korea can look forward to becoming the financial hub of East Asia. In fact, on 12 April 2006, Alan Greenspan, former chairman of the U.S. Federal Reserve, in a speech at an international financial conference held by the London-based daily *Financial Times* in Seoul, alluded to this possibility if Korea can create an investment-friendly environment and appropriate financial infrastructure.[40] Kihwan Kim (2006:12), chairman of the Seoul Financial Forum, believes that Korea's chances of becoming the new international financial center of Northeast Asia are excellent.[41]

Korea may not yet be the financial hub of East Asia, but it is fast becoming an Asian hub for logistics in air, sea, and railway transportation of people and goods. Incheon International Airport, completed in 2000, handles 1.7 million tons of cargo along with 27 million passengers annually. When the final phase of the airport's construction is finished in 2020, it will handle 7.5 million tons of cargo in addition to 100 million passengers annually. The port of Busan, which is the largest in Korea and the fourth largest in the world, serves as a hub of Northeast Asia. In 2000, it hosted fifty major carriers from all over the world and handled 430 million tons of freight (*Handbook of Korea* 2003:302–306).

If the Trans-Korea Railway (TKR), which was cut off by the

partition of the peninsula and the introduction of the DMZ, is reopened, and the Trans-Asian Railway (TAR), which will span twenty-eight countries, connecting Korea with Europe via Manchuria, China, Mongolia, and Siberia, is completed, Korea could be a logistical hub of commerce and travel in Asia. By the way, on 17 May 2007, as a single-day event, trains from North and South Korea crossed the heavily fortified DMZ for the first time in more than fifty years. This could be a first step toward a long-range effort for the TKR, but the future is uncertain, although it was clearly a symbol of reconciliation. Given all these developments, Korea certainly has the potential to become *Asia's Next Giant* as Alice Amsden (1989) aptly entitled her book on Korea.

A New Need for the Humanities

Emphasis on the Humanities

Korea is the tenth or eleventh largest economy in the world, but according to British-based Mercer Human Resources Consulting, in 2007, quality of life in the capital city of Seoul rated eighty-seventh out of 215 cities in the world.[42] While quality of life cannot really be quantified objectively, this kind of ranking gives us some indication, and it appears that economic development and a high level of income do not necessarily mean a high quality of life.

As evidence, while it was difficult to find three meals a day during the Korean War when the per capita GNI was about $86, there were few suicides. Now, with a per capita GNI of around $20,000, more and more people are committing suicide. In fact, in 2005, Korea had the highest suicide rate — 24.7 out of every 100,000 people — among the thirty member countries of the OECD, followed by Hungary (22.6 people), Japan (20.3 people), and Belgium (18.4 people).[43] Relative deprivation, resulting from an income disparity between poor and rich and between rural and urban, is unsustainable in the long run, and must be reduced to ensure social justice and a peaceful society.

According to my experience living in Korea for the past six years, it appears that most Koreans are so preoccupied by economic development and meeting the goals set by government, business, and industry that everything else is secondary. Even the military dictatorship of the past tended to be excused, if not tolerated, for the sake of economic development; it was even called "*gaebal dokjae*" (dictatorship for economic development), as if it were unavoidable. If I may be allowed to say so, most Koreans are contaminated by a chronic social disease, obsessed with the notion of "better and more" economic progress with each year.

Recently, the *Korean Economic Daily* has published collateral reading material called "*Saenggeul Saenggeul*" to assist high school students in preparing for the essay part of the college entrance examination, and it has proven popular.[44] This manual promotes the principles of free enterprise and the positive role of enterprise in business. Recently, together with the Ministry of Education and Human Resources Development, the Federation of Korean Industries (FKI or Jeonguk Gyeongjein Yeonhaphoe or Jeongyeongnyeon) published *Gyeongje* (Economy), a textbook for use in high school and college freshmen classes. This book also promotes free enterprise and a pro-business attitude since it was published under the auspices of the FKI. It has been reported that the textbook appeals to students, and many schools have begun to adopt it.[45] There is also a movement underway to require students of law, medicine, and engineering to study business management.[46]

While a growing number of Korea's first tier universities are expanding their MBA programs since there is great demand, the popularity of liberal arts and the humanities — anthropology, history, literature, and philosophy — is fading away. Consequently, not many students wish to enroll in graduate programs in liberal arts and humanities. It seems to me that Korea as a society has to promote a liberal arts education with an emphasis on the humanities if Koreans wish to address some of the unethical and immoral conduct of businessmen, politicians, and many others, and to improve the quality of life. As everyone now realizes, a high GDP and GNI do not guarantee the happiness and well being of a society.

There was a time when Korea's GNI was less than $ 100 right after the Korean War, yet people were happy and appreciated the aesthetic values of their culture. A Korean intellectual and winner of a Guggenheim fellowship, Younghill Kang (1966:7-8), has depicted Koreans' appreciation of aesthetic value in his well received book, *Grass Roof* (Chodang):

> Our home was not exempted from this miserable dependence upon the elements, but my family did not seem to mind their helpless poverty, since most of them were indulging in the mystical doctrine of Buddhism, or in the classics of Confucius, who always advocated that a man should not be ashamed of coarse food, humble clothing, and modest dwelling, but should only be ashamed of not being cultivated in the perception of beauty. The sage said: "Living on coarse rice and water, with bent arm for pillow, mirth may yet be mine. Ill-gotten wealth and honors are like to floating clouds." A man has no place in society, Confucius teaches, unless he understands aesthetics.

Nevertheless, nowadays I may be in the minority for insisting upon the primacy of aesthetics over economic development. It is understandable that when Korea as a nation was below the absolute poverty line, people felt a strong drive toward economic betterment. Now that the Korean economy has achieved a certain standard of living, I wish that Koreans would sit back, relax, and once again appreciate aesthetic beauty. The capacity for such appreciation can be acquired by studying the humanities, music, and the arts. One does not have to be an economist and management expert to enjoy life. As Francis Hsu (1981:384) says, in reference to China and the Chinese, "we also cannot guess how many inefficient officials, unsuccessful scholars, and custom-bound teachers might have made China a better place in which to live and been happier themselves had the society been attuned to welcoming them as carpenters, scientists, novelists or entertainers." The same reasoning may apply to Korea and Koreans.

Despite an emphasis on economic or management-oriented

education, some university administrators such as Jung Chang Young, formerly the president of Yonsei University, are determined to advocate the teaching of arts and humanities. President Jung himself was trained in economics, but he sees the great value of the liberal arts and humanities in broadening the outlook of students. He says, "In this speedy time, technical skills and knowledge cannot last any longer than five years, but broadening the minds of students with humanities would last a lifetime."[47] I hope that many Korean educators will come to agree with President Jung.

Environmental Conservation
The most important challenge for the future of Korea will be preventing environmental crises, an urgent task which is far more important than economic development. A government report released on 6 April 2007 warned that plant and animal species in almost all forests on the Korean peninsula face the risk of extinction if the average temperature rises six degrees Celsius by the end of the century.[48] The report also offers a grim prediction of food shortages, torrid summer heat and rising oceans as a result of what it calls "the biggest threat to human beings for this century," global warming. The average temperature in Korea, which has been 13.5 degrees for the past thirty years, is expected to jump 1.2 degrees Celsius by 2020 and gradually increase five more degrees by 2080.

In other words, according to the government's forecast, in the years leading up to 2080, the average yearly temperature will increase by six degrees Celsius, endangering the forests on the peninsula. If this happens, the country's precious rice production will be reduced by 14.9 percent between 2081 and 2090, making the southwestern part of the country the most challenging area to grow rice plants. Given this dire scenario, environmental protection and conservation have to take priority over any other agenda.

Can an Anthropologist Go Home Again?
When I published an article, entitled "Can an Anthropologist Go

Home Again?" in *American Anthropologist* (Kim 1987), a friend of mine at the University of Tennessee told me, "You can go home, but you cannot go home, 'again'." While I was contemplating whether or not I should take an offer from Korea to assume the presidency of Korea Digital University in Seoul, this time the same anthropologist who had offered me his wisdom before, loaned me his copy of Salman Rushdie's book, *East, West, Stories* (1994). Of East Indian descent, Rushdie (1994:211) has the narrator in one of the stories soliloquize, "I, too, have ropes around my neck, I have them to this day, pulling me this way and that, East and West, the nooses tightening, commanding, choose, choose. I buck, I snort, I whinny, I rear, I kick. Ropes, I do not choose between you. Lassoes, lariats, I choose neither of you, and both. Do you hear? I refuse to choose."

In the same vein, it was difficult for me to choose between two worlds: Korea, which gave me birth; or the American South, where I have studied, lived, and created a wonderful family. Since I know the strengths as well as the weaknesses of both worlds, I cannot easily choose one of them over the other. When I lived in a small university town in Tennessee, my life was more tranquil than I liked, especially after my children left home, and I longed for the busy streets of Seoul, where one can observe the vibrant activities and struggle for existence characteristic of city life. But when I lived in Seoul for a few years, with all its hustle and bustle, I could not help longing for the tranquility of my little niche in a small southern town.

My eldest son and his wife have three children, two boys and a girl. As American expatriates working for an American investment firm, they live in Seoul. My younger son and his wife have two sons and live in Nashville, working for the state government of Tennessee. Despite Rushdie's suggestion to live in both worlds, I felt drawn to live near my eldest son — in Seoul, Korea. Despite all those years living in America, I must still be a strong believer in the traditional Korean family system. I regret that I was unable to bring the American South — hospitable people, great landscape, and wonderful weather — with me when I came to Korea.

Despite my prolonged absence from Korea physically, my adjustment to Seoul has been easier and faster than I anticipated. Emiko Ohnuki-Tierney (1984:11-12), a Japanese American anthropologist, admits that as soon as she resumed her work in Japan, her projects were completed more quickly. Indeed, being a native has many advantages.

Throughout this book, I have delineated many changing aspects of Korea. Nonetheless, the fundamental Korean culture faithfully persists. Changing patterns of behavior in Korea are analogous to change in the American South as described by W.J. Cash (1941:x), a Southern journalist: "The South, one might say, is a tree with many age rings, with its limbs and trunk bent and twisted by all the winds of the years, but with its taproot in the Old South." Likewise, it seems to me that the taproot of contemporary Korea remains Korea.

Notes

INTRODUCTION

1. M*A*S*H was a popular medical drama and black comedy in the 1970s, depicting the staff of a Korean War field hospital. It was produced by 20th Television Fox for CBS.

2. As the 25th king, Cheoljong (1849-1863) died without an apparent heir among Royal family members, the Royal Yi clan appointed Yi Haeung's second son, Yi Myeongbok as the 26th king, Gojong (1864-1907). The new king's father Heungseon Daewongun assumed control of the government, and ruled the monarchy as regent for the king as King Gojong was only twelve years old.

3. In the summer of 2005, for instance, American high school teachers who attended a summer lecture program in Korea under the auspices of the Korean Society in New York pointed out that the section on Korea in school textbooks is very brief compared with those on China and Japan. Their knowledge of Korea as teachers was so limited that they could not teach about Korea effectively.

4. David Steinberg (1989) himself wrote an introductory book on Korea, knowing that there are few scholarly publications on the subject.

5. George Kennan, "Korea: A Degenerate State," *Outlook*, 7 October 1905; George Kennan, "The Korean People: The Product of a Decayed Civilization," *Outlook*, 21 December 1905.

6. Kennan served as one of the most prominent apostles of Japanese imperialism. Before the Japanese Protectorate Treaty over Korea was signed on 17 November 1905, the United States in a secret agreement between Roosevelt and Katsura endorsed Japanese domination over Korea in exchange for a pledge that Japan would not harbor any aggressive designs on

the Philippines. The defeated Russian government in the Russo-Japanese War (1904-1905) recognized Japan's paramount political, military, and economic interest in the Korean peninsula. Later, the Korean people learned that George Kennan had played an important role in formulating the Taft-Katsura secret agreement on Korea (Choy 1979:143).

7_ While Koreans prefer to call it the "East Sea," using historical evidence in China since the period of the Spring and Autumn through the Warring States, and Russian usage up until the mid-nineteenth century, Japan insists on labeling it the "Sea of Japan" based on the frequency of usage in world maps. Koreans further argue that even Japan's own maps produced prior to the early nineteenth century designated it as the East Sea. Currently, its usage is in dispute, and the subject heightens nationalistic sentiments between the two countries.

8_ While South Koreans prefer to use "Hanguk", an abbreviation of "Daehanminguk (Republic of Korea)," which can be traced to "Daehanjeguk (Great Han Empire)," while North Koreans use "Joseon Minjujuui Inmin Gonghwaguk (Democratic People's Republic of Korea)" as the official names for their respective countries.

9_ Of the entire peninsula's area of 219,015 square kilometers, South Korea is 98,477 square kilometers, about 45 percent, including 3,579 islands, and excluding the 1,262 square kilometers of the Demilitarized Zone (DMZ). North Korea is 120,538 square kilometers, including islands and excluding the 1,262 square kilometers of the DMZ. The population of the two Koreas in 2003 was assumed to be over 70,447,000. According to the 2005 Korean Census, the total population of South Korea was 47,278,951(males 23,623,954; females 23,654,997) (*Summary of the 2005 Korean Census*, ROK, May 2006). No information on the population of North Korea in the comparable period is available.

10_ Since China, Korea, and Taiwan use the same Chinese characters to spell the word "*hallyu*", each country claims that they were the author of the word, but it is difficult to trace who used it first. Perhaps its usage developed spontaneously in each place.

11_ Internet edition of *Kyunghyang Shinmun*, 4 November 2005.

12_ Capitalizing on such popularity, beginning on 10 May 2006, Asiana Airlines, a Korean flagship carrier, covered its Boeing 767 jets that serve Asian countries with images from *Daejanggeum* and put close-up photos of Lee Youngae on the planes' tails.

13_ *Dong-A Ilbo*, 6 January 2004:C-5.

14_ According to James Fernandez (1982:xx), the works of Bronislaw Malinowski, Ruth Benedict, E.E. Evans-Pritchard, Marcel Griaule, and Clyde Kluckhohn are not considered "major 'point de répere' in anthropology," but because of their skillful presentation of local point of view.

15_ James W. Fernandez (1980:27-39) perceives reflexivity as the "sense of distancing from self" or "at least the sense of observing one's own body from a distance⋯. The way that we discover ourselves is precisely the way we discover others and these discoveries are in reflexive relationship."

16_ Abu-Lughold Lila (1988:139-161), Nina Kumar (1992), and Kirin Narayan (1993:676-686), just to name a few, have been most frank in discussing their personal backgrounds.

17_ I view ethnohistory as a process of reconstructing history using anthropological methods, such as collecting and interpreting the life history of an individual.

18_ Donald N. Clark (1997:1-2) reports on the genesis of the McCune-Reischauer System: "George M. McCune ⋯ the son of Presbyterian missionaries[in Korea]⋯ acquired a childhood command of colloquial Korean ⋯ One problem that often confronted them all was the lack of a consistent system for romanizing Korean. By contrast, Japan had the well-established Hepburn System, although the Japanese government had just decreed the use of a new system that made Korean Tyosen and the emperor's brother Prince Titibu ⋯ The same summer[1937], Edwin O. Reischauer and his wife Adrienne arrived in Seoul on their way to Peking, where he was to do his dissertation research on Ennin's travels in Tang China. He was the Japan-born son of the A.K. Reischauers, Presbyterian missionaries on the faculty of Meiji Gakuin in Tokyo. The 'China Incident' that same summer left them stranded in Seoul, where Reischauer spent his time helping McCune work out what came to be called the McCune-Reischauer System of Romanizing Korean ⋯ The work continued after the Reischauers got their clearance to proceed to Peking, and the results were published in the 1939 issue of the Transactions of the Korean Branch of the Royal Asiatic Society."

CHAPTER 1

1- Indirectly quoted from Wallace and Mangan(1996:17).

2- Sarah Nelson (1993:265-267) points out that "Other new traits might have resulted from the introduction into the population of just a few from other cultures. For example, the Kaya [Gaya] legend of a princess from India who arrived at Kimhae [Gimhae] in a boat with red sail, accompanied by rich marriage gifts and a retinue of servants and family, has possible archaeological corroboration. The legend relates that the princess, Yellow Jade, married King Suro and became the mother of all future kings of Kaya."

3- According to Hi-seung Lee's (1963:14) survey by examining six volumes of the Korean Dictionary (*keunsajeon*), 52 percent of the Korean vocabulary contained in the dictionary consists of Chinese loan words.

4- Harumi Befu (1971:17) reports that "Grammatical similarities between Japanese and Korean include (1) word order, (2) absence of noun inflection, and (3) lack of comparative in adjectives. Phonologically, both languages have what is called vowel harmony. ··· This vowel harmony is a characteristic feature of languages of the Altaic linguistic stock." Also, Sarah Nelson (1993:6) points out that "The differentiation of the Korean and Japanese languages from a common Altaic stem is believed to have occurred about four thousand years ago. An original homeland in the steppes, followed by a move to a region south of the Altai mountains, is believed to antedate the fragmentation into separate languages. Linguists place the Tungusic speakers in the Atlaic family tree, accounting for the ease with which the bronze-using inhabitants of Korea are pigeonholed as Tungusics."

5- Indirectly quoted from Nelson (1993:1).

6- The word "Asia" was originated from the Ancient Greek word $A\sigma ia$, first attributed to Herodotus (about 440 B.C.) in reference to Anatolia or, for the purposes of describing the Persian Wars, to the Persian Empire, in contrast to Greece and Egypt. Alternatively, the ultimate etymology of the term may be from the Akkadian word (w)*aṣû*(m), which means "to go out" or "to ascend," referring to the direction of the sun at sunrise in the Middle East, and also likely connected with Phoenician word *asa*, meaning east (Wikipedia Encyclopedia on-line: http: //en.wikipedia.org/wiki/Asia). As the world's largest and most populous continent, Asia covers 8.6 percent of the Earth's total surface area (or 29.4 percent of its land area), and is home to almost 4 billion people (about 60 percent of the world's current population).

Nevertheless, I was unable to identify when the Chinese used their own characters to describe the loan word "Asia."

7_ Period of the early Stone Age, when flint, stone, and bone tools were developed and hunting and gathering were the means of acquiring food (Ember and Ember 1996:580).

8_ Originally, Neolithic meant "the new stone age," but now it refers to the presence of domesticated plants and animals. The earliest evidence of domestication comes from the Near East at about 8000 B.C. (Ember and Ember 1996:580).

9_ The Mesolithic period is the archaeological period in the Old World beginning about 12000 B.C. Humans were starting to settle down in semi-permanent camps and villages, as people began to depend less on big game and more on relatively stationary food resources such as fish, shellfish, small game, and wild plants rich in carbohydrates, proteins, and oil (Ember and Ember 1996:580).

10_ The characteristics of civilization include the first inscriptions or writing; cities; many types of full-time specialists; monumental architecture; great differences in wealth and status; and the kind of strong, hierarchical, centralized political system we call the state.

11_ Carter J. Eckert (1990:9) and his associates consider that the Bronze Age in Korea lasted from about the ninth or eighth century B.C. until about the fourth century B.C.

12_ Around 1766–1120 B.C., the Shang dynasty had already invented a writing system, intensive agriculture, a highly developed bronze technology, and long-distance trade was well established (Chang 1986).

13_ Since rice is not native to Korea, it is reasonable to suppose that seeds were brought to Korea from China, possibly by way of Manchuria, for rice was cultivated in China at least by 5500 B.C. (Li 1983). Rice in Korea was originally dated about 1200 B.C. (Kim W.Y. 1982:513–518), but recently the dates are reported to be earlier than 2400 and 2100 B.C. (Choe 1991:38).

14_ Personal communication with Chong Pil Choe on 1 October 2005.

15_ The table-style (also called the northern style) was constructed by placing several upright stones in a rough square and covering them with a flat capstone, and its distribution has been found to be preponderantly north of the Hangang. The *baduk* (Japanese *gō*), known as the southern style, employed a large boulder as a capstone placed atop several smaller rocks, and it is most widespread in the area south of the Hangang (Lee 1984:12).

16_ Some archaeologists surmise that the stratification system during the Bronze Age in the Korean peninsula can aptly be described as a "rank society," not a society of class or caste. A rank society is characterized by social groups with unequal access to prestige or status, but not significantly unequal access to economic resources or power. In rank societies, chiefs are often treated differently than people of lower rank. In class societies, there is unequal access to prestige, but unlike rank societies, class societies are characterized by groups that have substantially greater or lesser access to economic resources and power.

17_ Korean bronze tools appear to have been locally manufactured. Also, Korean bronze is significantly different from Chinese bronze in chemical composition, containing a greater admixture of zinc (Nelson 1993:137–138).

18_ Before Ilyeon converted to Buddhism and became a monk, his real name was Kim Gyeonmyeong.

19_ There is another legend about Gija (*Chitzu* in Chinese), a nephew of the last king of the Shang dynasty of China. According to the tradition, Gija departed with a retinue of 5,000 people and went in exile to Korea, where he founded a state called Gija Joseon. Nevertheless, archaeologists have been unable to locate any evidence to prove the legend, for if the tradition were true, Gija as a Shang prince would have brought a few bronze vessels with him (Nelson 1993:156–157). Sarah M. Nelson does not believe Gija went to Korea (Personal communication with Nelson, 6 October 2005).

20_ In reconstructing prehistory, I can see that there are obvious differences in orientation between historians and anthropologists, including archaeologists. Even though some written documents exist from China beginning around the first century B.C. on Gojoseon and Wiman Joseon, anthropologists are skeptical about their reliability, because they were neither objective chronicles, nor meticulous ethnographies. "Chinese [historical] documents should be treated with caution for many reasons. Errors in transcription or translation have probably crept in; embroidering on facts by the Chinese for their own purposes (to point a moral, for example) may have occurred; and the original observers of the 'barbarians' might have misunderstood what they saw" (Nelson 1993:165; Gardiner 1969).

21_ In response to the Chinese Northeast Asia Project, on 1 March 2004, a group of Korean historians established the Goguryeo Research Foundation with the support of the Ministry of Education and Human Resources Development. In August 2006, the foundation merged with the Northeast Asian History Foundation, the Ministry of Foreign Affairs and Trade, ROK.

22_ Recently, an interesting proposition, if not a minority view, has been proposed. A Korean historian, Lee Jonguk (2006), who has also been trained in sociology, anthropology, and archaeology, insists that Goguryeo-centered Korean history has to be revised. Lee believes that the root and legitimacy of early Korean history has to begin with the Silla dynasty.

23_ Before the formation of the Three Kingdoms, the southern part of the Korean peninsula was inhabited by a number of distinctive but related tribes; Mahan was located in the region of modern Gyeonggi-do, Chungcheong-do, and Jeolla-do provinces, Jinhan, east of the Nakdonggang in Gyeongsang-do province, and Byeonhan, in Gyeonggi-do province the west of the Nakdonggang. "One modern view, however, places Chinhan in the Han river basin" (Lee 1984:26). In addition to these, small polities known collectively as Gaya existed alongside the Three Kingdoms. However, Gaya never joined the big three to become a true state. Gaya was caught between Silla and Baekje, and the struggle between those two kingdoms rendered it difficult for Gaya to achieve full political and societal development (Lee 1984:41).

24_ Bruce Cumings (1997:29-30) offers an explanation for the founding myth of North Koreat "North Korea utilized this mountain as part of its founding myth, and now Kim Jong Il is said to have been born on the slopes of Paektusan, in the desperate year of 1942. Unsurprisingly, it is also the Koguryŏ legacy that the Democratic People's Republic of Korea (DPRK) claims as the mainstream of Korea history. ⋯ North Korea's Kim Il Sung, also a sun-king, called himself by an Old Koguryŏ term meaning maximum leader (*suryŏng*) and privileged a direct line from that ancient kingdom through the Koryŏ dynasty and down to the present."

25_ Ironically, most surviving examples of Baekje art and architecture are to be found in Japan, and are carefully preserved as sacred relics. The temple foundations near Buyeo show that the layout was the same as that of early temples in Japan, where it was duplicated by Baekje architects.

26_ Although there are some debates on whether Cheomseongdae was an actual astronomical observatory, most Korean historians believe that basic astronomical observations were conducted in it by use of a sun-dial and other instruments (Lee 1984:85).

27₋ The five secular injunctions include loyalty to the king, filial love toward one's parents, fidelity in friendship, bravery in battle, and chivalry in warfare. They are characterized by mixture of Buddhism and Confucianism. There are many heroic tales of Hwarang like Kim Yusin.

28₋ Wang Geon's posthumous title is King Taejo (918–943).

29₋ The six Colleges of the Capital includes University College, High College, and Four Portals College to study the sources of the Chinese tradition, and the Law College, College of Calligraphy, and College of Accounting.

30₋ The original woodblocks for printing were burned during the Mongol invasion in the thirteenth century. That survives today at Haeinsa is a new edition, which was completed in 1251.

31₋ "According to Tosŏn, the natural features of a land area and their configuration deeply affect a country's or individual's fate" (Eckert et al. 1990:65).

32₋ *Waegu* is a derogatory term, which refers to the Japanese pirates who landed along the Goryeo coast and plundered the farming villages. The word, "*Wae* (*Wa* in Chinese)" came from China. According to a passage in the history of the T'ang dynasty, *Hsin T'ang Shu*, "Japanese were once called *Wa* ⋯ At this time (670) the Japanese who knew the Chinese tongue came to dislike the name *Wa* and changed it to Nippon. According to the Japanese ambassador, the new name was chosen because his country was so close to where the sun rises" (Cotterell 1993:62).

33₋ A rule of marriage that requires a person to take a spouse from within the local, kin, status, or other group to which the person belongs.

34₋ A marriage that involves more than two spouses.

35₋ All of these Joseon norms became the subjects of the aforementioned new reform of the contemporary Korean Civil Code.

36₋ As he was promulgating the *Hangeul*, King Sejong spelled out his philosophy as follows: "The sounds of our language differ from those of China and are not easily conveyed in Chinese writing. In consequence, though one among our ignorant subjects may wish to express his mind, in many cases he after all is unable to do so. Thinking of these, my people, with compassion, we have newly devised a script of twenty-eight letters, only that it become possible for anyone to readily learn it and use it to advantage in his everyday life" (The translation from Eckert et al. 1990:124).

37_ Beneath the freeman commoner class, there was a large lowborn population, predominantly comprised of slaves. In addition to the slaves, *baekjeong*, who hereditarily engaged in butchering and tanning. The *gisaeng*, female entertainers at male drinking parties, were assigned to duties in both the capital and local jurisdictions, and frequently became *yangban's* concubines or secondary wives.

38_ According to Edward W. Wagner (1974:1-8), "no less than 90 percent of those Koreans in the Joseon dynasty who reached the position of High State Councilor [a deliberate organ of the Joseon administration] had passed the *mungwa* [civil order] examination than the military one."

39_ The "turtle ship" was the world's first iron-clad ship, which precedes the ironclads "invented" by the Americans by 200 years. The ships invented by Yi averaged 100 feet in length and were propelled by oars. They were faster, and more maneuverable than the Japanese ships. An armored canopy studded with pointed objects made them in invincible to enemy projectiles as well as to enemy raiders trying to come aboard. The vessels were heavily gunned, and the bow of each ship was decorated with a large turtle's head that could emit sulphur fumes masking the movements of the fleet.

40_ The story of Sim Sugwan, a fourteenth-generation descendant of a Korean captive artisan in Japan relates the Sim family's poignant saga. Sim Sugwan's fourteenth great grandfather, Sim Danggil, was a Korean artisan who manufactured porcelain. Danggil was captured by the Hideyoshi forces in 1597 during the second invasion by Hideyoshi and was forcibly taken to Japan. He settled in Nawashiro, a village in Kagoshima in southern Japan, and worked as a manufacturer of porcelain. Nearly four centuries later his descendant, Sugwan, began searching for his identity. In 1964, Sugwan was able to trace Danggil back to Namwon in Jeollanam-do province in South Korea, where his ancestor had been captured by the Japanese. Finally, Sugwan was able to identify his genealogy. Subsequently, he found the original village of his ancestors. He often visits his ancestral land and has shared his kin relationships with his clan members (Kim 1988a:45-46). On 13 January 2005, when I visited Sims' porcelain manufacturing plant in Kagoshima, I was startled and touched by a hand-made Korean dictionary by the Sim family not to forget Korean language for the Sim descendants.

41_ The five basic relationships are ruler and subject, father and son, elder brother and younger brother, husband and wife, friend and friend. All of them except the last involve the authority of one person over another. The inferior owes loving responsibility to the superior person.

42_ Lee Ki-baik, "Gaehyeok Jajuui Daerip Han Segi[Conflict between reform and self- reliance for a century]," *Dong-A Ilbo*, 1 January 1994:10.

43_ The ideas of the School of Practical Learning took shape in the seventeenth and eighteenth centuries and displayed a broad and varied approach to the reform of Joseon dynasty institutions. As a pragmatic form of scholarship, this school of thought required a pragmatic methodology, and always sought explicit verification. The major goal of the Practical Learning scholars was to illuminate the history and contemporary workings of political, economic, and social institutions (Kim 1998:189 n.21).

CHAPTER 2

1_ Indirectly quoted from Hsu (1981:384-394).

2_ In an effort to characterize modernization, Émile Durkheim (1947), Robert Refield (1947), Ferdinand Tönnies (1963), and Max Weber (1957) attempted to define "modern" in contrast to "traditional" by dichotomizing and polarizing the two.

3_ On 3 October 2007, North Korea agreed to disable all of its nuclear facilities by the end of the year 2007. It was the first time North Korea set a specific timetable to disclose all its nuclear program and disable all facilities in return for 950,000 metric tons of fuel oil or its equivalent in economic aid. Also, the agreement calls on the United States to begin the process of removing North Korea from a United States terrorism list in parallel with the North Korea's actions.

4_ Itō Hirobumi, former prime minister of Japan, was known to Koreas as the principal instrument of Japanese aggression against Korea. His life was taken in 1909, one year before the formal annexation of Korea, by a bullet fired by An Junggeun.

5_ Cheondogyo evolved from Donghak (Eastern Learning), and originated in 1860 with Choe Jeu, who claimed to have received a vision from Heaven that instructed him to establish a religion based on faith in God and man to alleviate the sufferings of the people. Its members staged a rebellion against the ruling Joseon dynasty in 1894, and then participated in the Japanese occupation of 1910 to 1945.

6- These combined forces killed 7,509 Koreans. Additional 15,961 were wounded, and 47,000 were arrested (Steinberg 1989:43).

7- Korean historian Woo-keun Han (1981:476) provides some details of the casualties.

8- Leftist critics started to question the efficiency of establishing a university that would serve such a small segment (elite) of the population (Robinson 1988:88).

9- The dream of a Korean people's university never died for some cultural nationalists. Kim Seongsu, for one, made a faithful attempt to build a national university. Kim's drive was materialized in 1932, when he took over Boseong College and eventually expanded it to Korea University after Korea became independent from Japan after World War II (Kim 1998:105-106).

10- *Handbook of Korea* (2003:110).

11- The original writing on this was based on an interview with Yoshida Seiji, via MBC-TV (South Korean Broadcasting), 3 June 1984 (a complete transcript of the interview by Mun Suntae with Yoshida Seiji, a Japanese who was in charge of drafting Koreans in Gyeongsang-do, Jeolla-do, Jeju-do provinces, is in *Yeoseong Dong-A*, 246: 393-397(June 1984). When I revealed the poignant ordeal of the so-called "comfort women" in 1988, it went largely unnoticed (Kim 1988a:24, 153 n.38). But now it has become a revealing story as the victims started to speak out. Sympathetic demonstrations occur daily in front of the Japanese Embassy in Seoul, and some writers have discussed this topic in English (Cumings 1997: 179-180; Hicks 1995; Kim 1998:144, 203 n.22; Soh 1996:1226-1240). The exact number of the victims is yet unknown, because while Yoshida Seiji who actually was involved in the "women-hunting" confesses the incidence, the Japanese authorities who are supposed to have the necessary data are shy to admit the startling tragedy. Nevertheless, a Korean news network, MBC estimates the numbers were about 200,000, while Bruce Cumings (1997:179) estimates they were somewhere between 100,000 and 200,000, along with smaller numbers of Filipinos, Chinese, and a handful of Westerners.

12- According to Heo Suyeol's (2005:314-317) calculation, the total values of Japanese assets in Korea by August 1945 were only one seventh of the accumulated amounts of U.S. foreign aid given to Korea up to 1960.

13- According to David Steinberg (1989:46), "By 1930, 75 percent of farmers were in debt, and three-quarters of that debt was to Japanese financial institutions. Tenancy and partial tenancy became the norm; some 12 million people (2.3 million families) were tenants, paying exorbitant rents. There was migration out of rural areas; in 1925, 2.8 percent of such migrants went to Manchuria and Siberia, 16.9 percent to Japan, and 46.4 percent to Korean urban areas, where living standards were also low."

CHAPTER 3

1_ Historians do not agree on the exact date when World War II started. Some scholars believe that it started when the Japanese launched a full-scale assault on China in 1937, using the Marco Polo Bridge incidents outside Beijing as a pretext (Hsu 1970:60). Others date it from the German invasion of Poland on 1 September 1939 (Ropp 1976:381).

2_ The atomic bombs that fell on the Japanese cities of Hiroshima (6 August 1945) and Nagasaki (9 August 1945), produced over 132,000 victims, who were dead or missing. Among them, at least 10,000 Koreans, most of whom were dragooned for labor in war industries in Japan, were annihilated (Cumings 1997:183).

3_ Bruce Cumings (1981:70) reports that the colonial authorities approached Song Jinu on 9 August at an unidentified Japanese home.

4_ A list of those parties, organizations, and affiliated persons' names can be found in Kim C.S. (1998:130).

5_ Syngman Rhee as chairman; Yeo Unhyeong, vice chairman; Heo Heon, prime minister; Kim Seongsu, education; Kim Gu, interior; Kim Byeongro, justice; Kim Gyusik, foreign affairs; Ha Pilwon, economics; Jo Mansik, finance; Sin Ikhui, communication; Kim Wonbong, military; Choe Yongdal, security; Lee Gwansul, public relations; Gang Gideok, agriculture and forestry; and Lee Wisang, labor. Out of these, seven key members, including Syngman Rhee, Kim Gu, Kim Gyusik, Kim Wonbong, Jo Mansik, Kim Byeongro, and Kim Seongsu, were listed without their knowledge.

6_ About the KPA, Carter J. Eckert (1990:33) and his colleagues conclude "Scholars disagree about the political character and legitimacy of the KPR. Standard South Korean and American scholarship has tended to view the KPR as a communist front whose popularity was directly proportional to the degree it was able to camouflage its real intentions. ···Revisionist studies ··· have suggested that the KPR represented a genuine attempt at a leftist coalition government and that it had a strong popular backing. The communists must have been confident enough to allow the rightists a place in the new government for the sake of national unity."

7_ When the KDP leaders delivered some 9 million *won* for the living expenses of the KGP returnees, some KPG leaders, including Sin Ikhui refused to accept the money, saying "there would be some dirty money in the funds," and charged the association with collaborating: "How could you survive in Korea without being pro-Japanese?" (Go 1976:485).

8_ Bruce Cumings (1981:219) reports that Song was assassinated two hours after the meeting that lasted until 4:00 A.M.

9_ During the election, Communist disturbances were not minor: 846 people were killed, and 1,040 Communist terrorist acts and assaults were reported. Despite those disturbances, out of 8,300,000 eligible voters, 7,840,000 (96.4 percent) registered to vote, and 7,400,000 (95.5 percent) voted (Go 1976: 542-543).

10_ The general election resulted in the following distribution of the assembly seats: fifty-five members from Rhee's NSRRKI; twenty-nine from the KDP; twelve from Lee Cheongcheon's Great National Youth Corps (Daedong Cheongnyeondan); six from Lee Beomseok's Korean National Youth Corps (Joseon Minjok Cheongnyeondan); thirteen from several small social and political parties; and eighty-five from independents (*musosok*) (Kim C.S. 1998:14).

11_ According to the posthumously published memoirs of Lee Yunyeong, who was minister of the Ministry of Health and Welfare at the time of the war and later elevated to the position of deputy prime minister in the Rhee administration, President Rhee's optimism was wrongly inculcated by his defense minister, Shin Seongmo (*Sin Dong-A* 297[1984]:198-224).

12_ "The Soviet representative on the Security Council, having avoided the meetings which denounced the aggression in Korea, attempted to label the Security Council resolution illegal because of absence. However, since the Security Council had determined that mere absence did not constitute a veto, the North Korean regime and its communists accomplices stood accused before the bar of world opinion as aggressors" (U.S. Department of the Army 1952:11).

13_ At Daejeon prison, for instance, 1,724 people, including rightists and members of the South Korean military and police and their family members, were ruthlessly massacred 300 of them were later determined to have been buried alive. At Gwangju prison, 300 jailed anti-Communists were killed (Republic of Korea National Red Cross 1977:74-75).

14_ "The U.N. command estimated that about 486,000 enemy troops, or twenty-one Chinese and twelve North Korean divisions, were committed to the Korean front and that reserves totaling over one million men were stationed near the Yalu River, in Manchuria, or on the way to Manchuria" (Miller et al. 1956:4).

15_ During this retreat, the largest number of North Koreans to flee at one time also moved south. Koreans refer to this winter retreat as the *ilsa hutoe* or "January fourth retreat." However, the retreat actually took place in late November and early December of 1950, not on 4 January 1951, which was when Seoul was taken by the CPV.

16_ For further details on Gen. MacArthur's release, see Trumbull Higgins (1960) and Gunther (1950).

17_ This was after the United States had halted two large Communist attacks, and the ground war was experiencing a lull. On 30 May, Gen. Matthew Ridgway reported to Washington that the enemy had suffered heavy casualties. Ridgway believed the military situation in Korea would offer optimum advantages in support of diplomatic negotiation (Bernstein 1983:262-263).

18_ 111,000 South Koreans were dead, 106,000 wounded, and 57,000 missing. American casualties totaled 2,954 dead, 13,659 wounded, and 3,877 missing in action (Cumings 1997:276). In addition, the war created some 300,000 widows, 300,000 orphans, and 1 million tuberculosis cases (Kim C.S. 1988:3). Also, during the war, some 45 percent of industrial units were substantially damaged; in Seoul over 80 percent of public utilities and transport, three-quarters of the offices and more than half the dwellings (314,000 homes destroyed and 244,000 damaged) were in ruins (Mason et al. 1980:248-249). Exact North Korean casualty figures are unknown, but it is reasonable to assume that they are similar (Mason, et al. 1980:248-249).

19_ The total of 5 million was based on 3.5 million North Korean refugees who fled southward before the Korean War; 1 million North Koreans who fled southward during the war; 84,000 people kidnapped by North Koreans during and after the war; and 416,000 dispersed by other means. Koreans opted to call these *ilcheonman isangajok* or "10 million dispersed families."

20_ The first negotiations between North and South Korea for the repatriation of civilians kidnapped by the North during the war had begun under the auspices of the United Nations on 10 July 1951 and resumed in 1953. The negotiations continued through the 1960s, 1970s, 1980s, and 1990s.

21_ *Dong-A Ilbo*, 14 July 2005:6

22_ In the Geochang area of Gyeongsangnam-do province, Col. Kim Jongwon, one of Rhee's favorites, massacred some 500 innocent villagers for allegedly harboring Communist guerrillas. Despite having committed such a brutal crime, Kim was promoted by Rhee to the head of the National Police, and Kim even interfered with the National Assembly's investigation of the incident. Also, there was a scandal surrounding the National Guard (Bangwigun). Some high-ranking officers of the guard embezzled the supplies of the guard, but were left unpunished because they were favored by Rhee. Instead, only their subordinates were sentenced, and some were executed (Kim C.S. 1998:149).

23_ Park was a forty-three-year-old career officer from a provincial background when he led the coup. After he graduated from a pedagogical training school in Daegu, for a few years he taught elementary school in the rural part of Gyeongsangbuk-do province. Then he trained in Japanese military academies and served as a lieutenant in the Kwangtung Army in Manchuria during World War II. After the war, he joined the Korean Army. By 1960, he had risen to become deputy commander of the Second Army.

24_ *Yusin* is spelled with the same Chinese characters used in Japan for the Meiji Restoration in the late 1860s, which provided the occasion for Japan's rapid modernization. The word "Meiji" was coined on 23 October 1868, when the young emperor of Japan selected a slip of paper, which bore the two Chinese characters, "bright" and "rule," and thus gave the name "Meiji" to his reign.

25_ *Kukmin Ilbo*, 4 May 2005:15.

26_ *Dong-A Ilbo*, 4 November 2003:D-4.

27_ *Chosun Ilbo*, 26 August 2002:6.

28_ *Chosun Ilbo*, 27 August 2005:11.

29_ The government claimed the deaths of 200 people; the opposition estimated the number was 2,000.

30_ The Korean National Assembly is a unicameral body that was composed of 273 members until 29 May 2004. 227 were elected from single-member electoral districts and forty-six were shared by their parties in proportional representation. All members serve a four-year term. Since 29 May 2004, the membership has increased to 299, including fifty-six members elected through proportional representation.

31_ Characteristics of eight provinces delineated by Yi Hwang are translated and summarized by Paul S. Crane (1978:85–86).

32_ According to Paul S. Crane (1978:85), "The prejudice against certain provincial areas is so great that school children in Seoul often try to hide their home origins and assume Seoul customs, accent, and manners to avoid the provincial labels. When problems arise, these ancient prejudices are often received to justify the decisions made."

33_ *JoongAng Ilbo*, 1 January 1989:8.

34_ The Rohsamo [Nosamo] Fan Club was organized voluntarily and spontaneously by a group of people who loved Roh Moo-hyun and supported Roh's political career right after when Roh was defeated for a National Assembly seat in the 2000 general election. The club had some 13,000 members, mostly white-collar workers in their thirties (*Maeil Business Newspaper*, 17 March 2002:1). Its membership swelled to 100,000 during Roh's presidential campaign, but by 2007 it has declined to the same level when the club had started in 2000 as Roh was losing his popularity (*Hankyoreh Sinmun*, 20 February 2007:6). At any event, the club had been instrumental in electing Roh as the president in the 2002 presidential election.

35_ *Hankook Ilbo*, 15 April 2000:9; *Kukmin Ilbo*, 17 April 2004:6.

36_ The first negotiation between North and South Korea for the repatriation of civilians kidnapped by the North during the war had begun under the auspices of the United Nations on 10 July 1951, and resumed in 1953 (Kim C.S. 2002:219 n.10).

37_ The declaration included five points: (1) South and North, as masters of national unification, will join hands in efforts to resolve the issue of national unification independently of outside intervention; (2) Both parties acknowledged each others' respective formulas for reunification; (3) The South and North will exchange groups of dispersed family members and their relatives around 15 August, and, as soon as possible, resolve humanitarian issues, including repatriation of Communist prisoners who have completed their jail terms; (4) The South and North will pursue balanced development of their national economies and build mutual trust by accelerating exchanges in social, cultural, sports, health, and environmental fields; (5) In order to put these agreements into practice, the South and North will hold dialogues between government authorities at an early date. President Kim Dae-jung cordially invited National Defense Commission Chairman, Kim Jeongil to visit Seoul, and he agreed to do so at an appropriate time.

38₋ The gist of the agreement is as follows: 1) the two Koreas will actively implement the June 15 joint declaration; 2) the two Koreas will work for mutual respect and trust in order to overcome differences in ideology and systems; 3) the two Koreas will ease military tensions, and resolve disputes through dialogue and negotiations; 4) the two Koreas agree on the need to end the current armistice and establish a permanent peace; 5) the two Koreas will expand economic cooperation for balanced development and co-prosperity; 6) the two Koreas will develop cooperation in the history, language, education, technology, culture, sports and social sectors; 7) the two Koreas will actively push for humanitarian cooperation and the expansion of reunions of separated families; 8) the two Koreas will strengthen cooperation on the international stage for national interests and to benefit Korean residents abroad.

CHAPTER 4

1₋ According to a survey of 600 adult members in Seoul and its vicinities in Gyeonggi-do province, conducted by a marriage consulting center, Echorus, nine out of ten respondents were in favor of free choice marriage over arranged marriage (*Kyunghyang Sinmun*, 5 April 1999:18). However, it has been reported that "only 20 percent of people in South Korea marry just for love, said Lee Kwang-kyu, an anthropologist at Seoul National University [formerly]" (*Pittsburgh Post-Gazette*, 20 April 1997:A-4).

2₋ On 25 February 2007, a seventy-nine-year-old women who had lived with her husband for the previous sixty years sought divorce from him on the grounds of infidelity and physical abuse, a divorce which was granted by the family court of the Seoul District Court with a large sum of alimony

(*Chosun.Com*, 26 February 2007: n.p.)

3_ Kinship refers to a social relationship that connects people through genealogical lines, tracing the kinship relationship back to ancestors and forward to descendants.

4_ Hesung Chun Koh (1980) has provided a comprehensive guide to Korean kinship and family, with a special section on women (see also Kim 1968).

5_ There is a mathematical formula for defermining degree of relationship. The degree of relationship between husband and wife is 0 (no degree); one generation is counted as 1 degree, and the relationship between siblings is counted as 2 degrees. On the basis of this, for instance, the distance of a cousin from Ego (focal point person) can be calculated as follow:

$$\frac{1 \text{ degree}}{\text{(from Ego's generation to his father)}} + \frac{1 \text{ degree}}{\text{(from Ego's cousin's generation to his father)}} + \frac{2 \text{ degrees}}{\text{(from Ego's father to his brother)}} = 4 \text{ degrees}$$

This "4-degree" relationship can be translated as *sachon* (a Chinese loan word), meaning "cousin" in English kinship terms. Koreans use this as a kinship term for addressing someone as well as a reference kinship term. All kin members can be calculated on the basis of this formula (Kim 1968:24).

6_ Several theories have been proposed to explain the incest taboo. Some scholars explain that persons who have been closely associated with each other since earliest childhood, such as siblings, are not sexually attracted to each other. Therefore, they would avoid marriage with each other (Westermark 1894). Others see that without the incest taboo, sexual competition among family members would create so much rivalry and tension that the family could not function as an effective unit (Malinowski 1927). Still others explain that the value of the incest taboo is in promoting cooperation among family groups and that this helps communities to survive (White 1949).

7_ In 1274 during the reign of King Wonjong (1259-1274) of the Goryeo dynasty, the Goryeo court was forced by Yüan to send 140 Goryeo women, mostly widows, divorcées, and wives of traitors, to be married the Sung's (960-1279) surrenders to Yüan (Lee 1983:227). In this case, even if it was forced, the Goryeo court played the de facto matchmaker.

8_ There are some reports that conglomerate families tend to choose spouses from other conglomerate families. In a doctoral dissertation, Gong Jeongja (1989) made a survey based on 100 big business families selected randomly out of the membership firms who belong to the Federation of Korean

Industries (FKI), and found that 124 sons and 83 daughters of the 100 families married with offspring of other big businesses families. Nevertheless, according to another sociological study, of the 393 children from fifty-two prominent businesses families, only 20 people (5.1 percent) married offspring of other prominent businesses families. (Song n.d.).

9. *Seoul Economic Daily*, 13 April 2006:B-3.

10. Laurel Kendall (1996:133 n.10) reports on a newspaper clipping regarding Madam *Ttu*: "In 1980, after Chun Doo-hwan's coup, the new government identified illegal matchmakers as 'elements corrupting society' and began a major crackdown. ⋯ Seoul gossip held that the list of marriage prospects carried by a Madam *Ttu* brought to judgment included the names of the unmarried judge who presided at her trial. The Madam *Ttu* has, by all accounts, continued to flourish." Kendall elaborates further on the Madam *Ttu* phenomenon(*ibid.* 133-135).

11. *Seoul Economic Daily*, 13 April 2006:B-3.

12. *Segye Ilbo*, 17 October 2006:10.

13. *Seoul Economic Daily*, 13 April 2006:B-3.

14. *JoongAng Ilbo*, 22 July 2005:1; *JoongAng Week*, 22 July 2005:W1-W2.

15. *JoongAng Ilbo*, 18 March 2005:5.

16. Between 16 and 19 March 2005, in a survey of 298 students (153 females and 145 males) randomly selected from the student body, 32.7 percent of female respondents said that they did not plan to marry at all (compared with only 15.2 percent of male students) (*Yonsei Chunchu*, 21 March 2005:6).

17. *Yonsei Chunchu*, 21 March 2005:6.

18. *JoongAng Ilbo*, 20 July 2005:1.

19. The rate of increase has been phenomenal: 1.2 percent in 1990, 3.4 percent in 1995, 4.8 percent in 2001, 5.2 percent in 2002, 8.4 percent in 2003, 11.4 percent in 2004, and 13.6 percent in 2005 (*Yonhap News*, 6 June 2006:n.p.).

20. In 2006 alone, for instance, 4,278 international marriages ended in divorce, a whopping 15.8 percent increase compared with 2005 (*Chosun.com*, English edition, 21 September 2006:n.p.).

21. *Dong-A Ilbo*, 7 June 2006:8.

22. *Korean Economic Daily*, 23 November 2005:A-11.

23_ China had the same institution as Korea: the system of *t'ung yang-hsi* is a semiadoption of a girl as a later bride for the son; *chui-fu* is an adoption of a boy as a future husband for a girl when there is no male heir (Goode 1970:276).

24_ Laurel Kendall (1996:204) states that "Antique wooden ham, made of light paulownia wood and decorated with iron or brass fittings, are standard items on the Seoul antique market. Those who can afford display buy modern reproductions made of exquisitely carpentered wood or lacquered and inlaid with mother-of pearl."

25_ The exchange rate between the U.S. dollar and Korean *won* differs from the current rate.

26_ *Korean Economic Daily*, 6 September 2004:1.

27_ *Dong-A Ilbo*, 4 July 2005:35.

28_ In addition to the nuclear family, anthropologists have introduced the term "elementary family," which consists of a man, his wife, and their child or children. A childless couple would not constitute an elementary family.

29_ Data from the Korea National Statistical Office, ROK, 13 March 2007.

30_ Data from the Korea National Statistical Office, ROK, 5 May 2005.

31_ The accounts of filial piety in Korean society can be easily found in folktales about the feeding and care of aged parents (Choi 1979:163–166; Janelli and Yim 1982:50).

32_ *Chosun Ilbo*, 16 May 2005:A-10.

33_ The Korean divorce rate, which is calculated using the total number of divorces during a year, divided by the total population of the country in the middle of the year, and then multiplied by 1,000, has been rising constantly: 0.4 percent in 1970; 0.6 percent in 1980; 1.1 percent in 1990; 1.5 percent in 1995; 2.5 percent in 2000; 3.5 percent in 2003, and 2.9 percent in 2004 (Data from Korea National Statistical Office, 2005; see also *Dong-A Ilbo*, 22 July 2005:56; *Segye Ilbo*, 28 May 2005:21; *Munhwa Ilbo*, 29 December 2003:28; *Munhwa Ilbo*, 30 June 2005:6).

34_ *Chosun Ilbo*, 12 July 2000:26.

35_ *JoongAng Ilbo*, 1 July 2005:8.

36_ Data from the Korea National Statistical Office, ROK, 13 March 2007.

37_ *Kyunghyang Sinmun*, 22 February 2007:21.

³⁸⁻ *Maeil Business Newspaper*, 12 January 2006:A-39; *Kyunghyang Sinmun*, 22 February 2007:21.

³⁹⁻ *Dong-A Ilbo*, 4 March 2005:5.

⁴⁰⁻ *Dong-A Ilbo*, 1 July 2005:A-9.

⁴¹⁻ Sarah Soh (1993:2) has made a comprehensive analysis of women in Korean politics: "The membership of the first National Assembly (1948-1950) consisted of 199 men and 1 woman. The fourteenth National Assembly, which convened in 1992, has 295 men and 4 women. A total of 46 women found their way into the National Assembly between 1948 and 1992, and 14 of them have served for more than one term."

⁴²⁻ *Dong-A Ilbo*, 17 March 2006:1, 3.

⁴³⁻ There are two sets of kinship terms: term of reference, used in speaking about a relative; and terms of address, used when speaking to or addressing a relative. Regarding addressing terms, some anthropologists use cousin terms — how ego (a male) addresses his cousins — in classifying the kinship system of the world into six types, including Eskimo, Hawaii, Omaha, Crow, Iroquois, and Sudanese (Schusky 1965). It is difficult for any one to classify the Korean system into one of these types, particularly among *yangban* because of the heavy influence of Chinese loan-words on Korean kinship terms (Kim 1968).

⁴⁴⁻ In earlier times, Korean adoption was not so rigidly agnatic. A sister's sons, daughter's sons, wives' natal kin, and even non-kin were adopted heirs. But a strict agnatic rule became established over the last few hundred years (Lee 1982:328; Peterson 1974:28-35).

⁴⁵⁻ In Japan, for instance, if there was no son, a son-in-law could be technically adopted into the family at marriage. "If a family had a daughter she ordinarily would take over the family name and continue the *ie* [household]" (Vogel 1965:288).

⁴⁶⁻ Edward W. Wagner (1971:141-252; 1983:23-32) has studied Korean genealogy extensively.

⁴⁷⁻ The rule of inheritance in Korea has changed over a long period of time. Following the rule of primogeniture, the eldest or firstborn son normally assumes the headship of the family and inherits his parents' property. Prior to the 1600s, however, the rule allowed sons and daughters to inherit equally, without any discrimination by sex as was the case in China. After the 1600s, Korean law began favoring sons and discriminating against

daughters. Since the 1800s, the eldest son has been favored, to form a classic primogeniture system, which is the ideal of Korean inheritance. But, ultimogeniture, a system in which the youngest son inherits the family's estate, is not uncommon among people who have only a marginal livelihood and in some remote mountain villages (Han 1977:55).

[48] *Korea Herald*, 22 July 2005:4.

[49] In his psychocultural attributes of kinship hypothesis, Francis L.K. Hsu (1965:638-661, 1971, 1975:208-238, 1983:217-247, 1983:332-356; Serrie 1976, 1986) characterizes "continuity, inclusiveness, authority, and asexuality."

CHAPTER 5

[1] Although there are several other words for village in the Korean language, including *chollak*, *dongne*, or *burak* (the same as *buraku* in Japan, written using the same Chinese characters), all of thenm are Chinese loan-words (Gungnip gugeo yeonguwon 1999). Korean *maeul* is equivalent to *mura* in Japan (Befu 1971:67). *Buraku* in Japan has a negative connotation, referring to an outcast group at the bottom of the social order in Japan which has been discriminated against since the Tokugawa period of the seventeenth century. The *Burangmin* are similar to the *chonmin* (lowest or outcast) in the Joseon class system. Thomas P. Rohlen (1983:113) indicates this group is similar to lower castes in India: "this group was socially isolated and given the lowest forms of work for centuries prior to their legal emancipation in the Meiji period. Today they number between two and three million, or less than 3 percent of the population. Some *Burakuin* continue to reside in particular neighborhoods and to identify publicly with their own minority, but many have 'passed' by changing residence and identity."

[2] Personal communication with the Korea National Statistical Office, 16 March 2007.

[3] Data from Korea's Rural Development Administration, ROK, 2005.

[4] According to a document, *Ogat'ongsarok*, written in 1675 in the Joseon dynasty, village size was classified into three categories on the basis of the number of households: small-size village (*so-ri*, 25 to 50 households); middle-size village (*jung-ri*, 55 to 100 households); and large-size village

(*dae-ri*, 105-150 households) (Lee 1996:51). Kim Taik-kyoo (1986:v) assumes that the origins of Korean villages was in the settlement of small-scale kin groups — an extended family or a minimal lineage, but not a clan.

5_ According to Vincent S.R. Brandt (1971:179 n.), "Geomancy, an import from China, was enthusiastically adopted in Korea, where it underwent additional refinement and development. It is based on the belief that if tomb and house sites are properly chosen with respect to wind, water, compass direction, and topographic land features, good fortune and prosperity will result."

6_ *Jugan Dong-A*, 7 August 2003:91.

7_ Data from the Korea National Statistical Office, ROK, February 2006.

8_ The terms "clan" (or "sib") and "lineage" need to be distinguished. While lineage is defined "as a set of kin whose members trace descent from a common ancestor through known links," clan refers to "a set of kin whose members believe themselves to be descended from a common ancestor or ancestress but cannot specify the links back to that founder, often designated by a totem" (Ember and Ember 1996:576, 579).

9_ "Lineage villages are not necessarily centered around an upper class lineage, but there is a tendency for them to be upper class lineage whether their status is recognized on a local level or national level" (Lee 2003:151).

10_ *Dure* emerged in the seventeenth and eighteenth century spontaneously throughout all rural Korean villages as an effort to counteract the control of the *yangban* and land-owning villagers and landlords for the exchange of labor (*pumasi*) without payment in money or kind (Lee 1996:111).

11_ The label of peasant has carried a negative connotation for so long that the public of the state of Georgia even became angry over Arthur Raper's use of the word "peasant" instead of "tenant" or "sharecropper" in his book of *Preface to Peasantry* (1936).

12_ Several prominent Neo-Confucian scholars, notably Yu Seongryong, Kim Seongil (1538-1593), and Jeong Gu (1543-1620), all of whom had been taught by Yi Hwang, and who were of Yeongnam [Gyeongsang-do province] origins, have been called collectively the scholars of the Yeongnam School of Thought.

13_ Since there is no longer any institutionalized class system in Korea, the term "mixed villages" that Kwang-kyu Lee (2003:151) refers to, may be appropriate in order to reduce any negative connotations of such villages.

14_ This peasant revolt flared in Sangju at first, but erupted spontaneously and sporadically in unending successions across the country, including Wonju, Juksan, and Jeongju. A large force of peasant brigades, called the Red Trousered Bandits (*Jeokgojeok*) and "grass brigands (*chojeok*)," seized the southwest region of the capital. Government forces had to be sent to suppress these peasant brigands (Lee 1984:97-98). The use of "*jeok*," a derogatory term that is an abbreviation of "*dojeok*," which means "thief," reflects public disapproval of the rebellion.

15_ The Donghak peasant armies fought driectly against the economic aggression of the Japanese. Nevertheless, the peasant armies lacked the strength to successfully confront the modern weapons and training of the Japanese troops (Lee 1984:283-290).

16_ *Korea Herald*, 15 December 2005:2; *Korea Herald*, 19 December 2005:1; *Korea Herald*, 20 December 2005:1.

17_ *Korea Herald*, 5 June 2006:3, 6.

18_ Not only farming but also the overall annual economic growth between 1911 and 1938, for example, averaged 3.5 percent compared to 3.4 percent in Japan (Steinberg 1989:45).

19_ Ki-baik Lee (1984:357-358) reports that Korean migrants to Manchuria numbered 560,000 in 1927, 800,000 in 1931, and 1,450,000 by 1940. There had been less than 250 Korean residents in Japan in 1910, but the figure for 1930 was 419,000 and by 1941 it had swollen to 1,469,000.

20_ "The installment land payments, in the form of bonds, were too small to be of use: furthermore, the payments were spread over five years. Even those were suspended when the Korean War broke out in June 1950. The South Korean government defaulted on payments to landlords whose land had been transferred to the tenants under the reform law. Worst of all was the rate of inflation during the war years. In 1950, the rate of inflation was 374.5 percent. Most landlords were unable to cash their bonds for their transferred land until 1956. For the eight years from 1949 to 1956, total accumulated inflation was 848.6 percent" (Kim 2002:6).

21_ As evidence of his zeal, President Park Chung-hee made numerous visits to many rural villages. From 1970 to 1979, for instance, the president allocated about 9 percent of total speech time, including in New Year's press conferences and annual budget speeches, to rural problems. In order to upgrade the movement, the president appointed a vice minister to administer the movement, the president himself personally made speeches at the annual conference of movement leaders, and he personally awarded prizes to the best leaders (Whang 1981:44-45).

[22] Detailed information on the socio-economic backgrounds of the New Village Movement leaders can be found in I. J. Whang (1981:61-72).

[23] "In addition, there are 14 other central-level and 10 provincial-level training institutions which provide training modeled after the Suwon Institute. As a supplement, various types of training are provided at the village level on Saemaeul spirit, scientific farming, agricultural machinery, health, housekeeping and family planning. In total, 158 high schools (one in each county) provided Saemaeul classes for local leaders (200 persons in each school, or 31,600 in total in 1978), and a Saemaeul Adult Course was established in 9,300 primary and secondary schools throughout the country" (Whang 1981:165).

[24] Whang (1981:32-33) reports that "the total investment in the Saemaeul Undong during the whole period of 1971-1978 amounted to 1,991 billion won of which 28 percent (or 55.2 billion won) was invested by the rural people and the remaining 1.0 percent (or 19.1 billion won) was raised by donations from non-village individuals or private organizations. Of the total 12.2 billion won invested during 1971, the government contribution was 4.2 billion won (34 percent), while the rural populace contributed 8.1 billion won (66 percent)." David Steinberg (1989:149) updates the figure: "By 1986, $9.3 billion had been spent on it since its inception; of this amount, $5.5 billion [59.1 percent] came from government, the remainder [40.8 percent] from the villagers."

[25] "Zaytun" is an Arabic word, meaning "olive", which symbolizes peace. Since Koreans consider the mission of the troops stationed in Iraq to be peace-keeping and reconstruction, they named their troops in this way.

[26] *JoongAng Ilbo*, 1 August 2006:12. I.J. Whang (1981:256-268) discusses the also possibility of and preconditions for transferring the Korean model of the New Village Movement to other places.

[27] *JoongAng Ilbo*, 14 February 2006:1. Even before China expressed its genuine interest in learning about the Korean New Village Movement, in July 1996 China invited the former chairman of the Central Training Institute of the movement, Jeong Gyogwan, to advocate the New Village Movement in China. Since April 2001, Jeong, with an assistant, has provided 31 training sessions for 7,700 Chinese civil servants and farmers (*JoongAng Ilbo*, 8 March

2006:28).

28_ David Steinberg's (1989:153) figure was not based on the urban population as a whole. High-level civil servants, professionals, business peoples, and academicians were not included.

29_ Data from the Korea National Statistical Office, ROK, 2005.

30_ Data from Korea's Rural Development Administration, ROK, 2005.

31_ *Korea Herald*, 8 November 2005:5.

32_ Data from Korea's Rural Development Administration, ROK, 2005.

33_ Data from the Korea National Statistical Office, ROK, 2005.

34_ *Kangwon Ilbo*, 26 October 2005:1.

35_ *Hankyoreh Sinmun*, 16 April 2005:10.

36_ Data from the Korea National Statistical Office, ROK, 2005. There is no specific limit for child-bearing age. Nevertheless, the Korean Statistical Office provides data on child-bearing ages ranging from 15 to 49 years old.

37_ *Dong-A Ilbo*, 10 October 2005:A-13.

38_ Information obtained from the Ministry of Agriculture and Forestry, ROK, dated 6 May 2006.

39_ The mid-term effect of the FTA between Korea and Chile shows that the value of trade between the two countries has increased after the FTA. The export of Korean manufacturing goods, such as automobiles, wireless phones, TVs and video cameras has sharply increased through the effects of tariff elimination whereas the import of Chilean agricultural products such as wine, pork, kiwi, and prepared fruit has increased. Nevertheless, the import of Chilean fresh fruit such as grapes and peaches has not dramatically increased as anticipated (Im 2004:81-96).

40_ *Dong-A Ilbo*, 15 August 2005:6; *Saejeonbuk Sinmun*, 21 February 2005:1.

41_ Data from the Ministry of Agriculture and Forestry, ROK, May 2006.

42_ *JoongAng Ilbo*, 21 March 2007:E-1.

43_ January is the coldest month in Korea with the mean temperature ranging from 17.6 degrees to 44.6 degrees Fahrenheit, except in Jeju-do, which has a mean temperature above 41 degrees Fahrenheit even in January.

44_ On the basis of this fieldwork conducted in a rural village near Daegu, capital of Gyeongsangbuk-do province, Yunshik Chang (1989:236-251) argues that contrary to what has been predicted by the Marxist and substantivist prospective, market penetration into the small South Korean farming community did not destroy its cooperative unity.

45– *JoongAng Ilbo*, 27 December 2000:23.

46– *JoonAang Ilbo*, 9 July 2001:49.

47– Data from the Ministry of Government Administration and Home Affairs, May 2006.

48– *JoongAng Ilbo*, 9 December 2004:15.

49– *Korean Economic Daily*, 11 October 2005:A-14.

50– *Kyunghyang Sinmun*, 23 August 2005:1, 3.

CHAPTER 6

1– Animism is a belief in the dual existence of all things, which includes a physical, visible body, and a psychic, invisible soul.

2– Polytheistic religion recognizes many important gods, no one of which is supreme.

3– Although monotheism means one god in principle, most monotheistic religions actually include more than one supernatural being, such as demons, angels, and the Devil.

4– *Summary of the 2005 Korean Census*, 26 May 2006:32.

5– In his psychocultural attributes of kinship hypothesis, Francis L.K. Hsu (1965:638–661, 1971, 1983:217–247) has suggested that the religious inclusiveness of China, Japan, and Korea can trace its origin to the family and kinship system (Hsu 1975:208–238, 1983:362–356; Serrie 1976, 1986; Kim 1989:309–325).

6– *Summary of the 2005 Korean Census*, 26 May 2006:32.

7– The "jar of ancestors" (*josangdanji*) has various names in different regions of Korea. In some regions, it is called "grandmother," and is related to the fertility of the house (Lee 2003:216).

8– Shintō is a Japanese traditional belief, which is a composite of indigenous beliefs grouped under the name of Shintō or "Way of the Gods," and a number of foreign ideologies of which Taoism and Buddhism are the most important. It has been in existence for a long time in Japan, but it was only in the eighth century that Shintō beliefs and observances were put into writing. In 1882, Shintō was divided into State Shintō (or Shrine Shintō) and Sect Shintō, the traditional native religious belief. State Shitō was the official cult sponsored by the government for the purpose of inspiring in the Japanese single-minded obedience and loyalty to the emperor and, through him, to the state. "Until the end of World War II, State Shintōism played an indispensable role in unifying the nation and bolstering Japan's nationalism. The emperor was officially regarded as semi-divine and as the direct and lineal descendant of the Sun Goddess, who, in the legend of Kojiki, the oldest document in the Japanese language, created the heaven and the earth out of chaos (Befu 1971:96-97).

9_ Such negative images have been manifested by several Christian communities. For instance, in 1996 at Gwangju, Jeollanam-do province, a wall painting, which depicts an image of Shamanism had to be repainted because of protests by the local Christian community; in 1997, a plan to invite shamans to a folk festival in Daejeon was cancelled due to the opposition of a local Christian organization; in 1997, a hospital in the city of Taebaek, Gangwon-do province had planned to have a gut for the victims of industrial disasters, but because of a vehement opposition from a local Christian community the name "*gut*" had to be deleted (Cho 1998:107-108).

10_ Jo Seongyun (1998:99) has reported about much unfair treatments of shamans.

11_ The Chinese character "*jen*" (Koreans pronounce it as "*in*") is a combined symbol of two characters with "human" and "two," which conveys the idea of a relationship between persons.

12_ The University based its teaching on the *Five Classics* (*Book Poetry*, *Classic of Song*, *Book of Documents*, *Book of History*, and *Book of Change*), and *Four Books* (*Analects*, *Mencius*, *Great Learning*, and *Doctrines of the Mean*).

13_ Edward Y.J. Chung (1995) has studied these two leading thinkers of Neo-Confucianism, and compared them by drawing out the practical implications of their positions on ethics and spiritual cultivation.

14_ The philosophy of Taoism takes its name from the Chinese word *tao*, meaning "the way." Lao Tzu, the founder of Taoism, was an older contemporary of Confucius. It was introduced in 624 during the Goguryeo dynasty (others such as Song [1994:480] believe it was introduced during the Baekje dynasty around 346-374) teaching "naturalness," "spontaneity," and "simplicity." According to Hang-nyong Song (1994:483), "Although Taoism was received as the state rituals for Heaven in the Koryŏ and Chosŏn dynasties, it was merely ceremonial, no longer to be seen as a living religious manifestation."

15_ *Analects* is one of the *Four Books* of the Confucian canon, and is sometimes known as *Sayings* or *Conversations of Confucius*. It is mostly a record of Confucius' responses to a variety of questions put to him by his disciples on a variety of subjects.

16_ Heaven is generally interpreted to be an impersonal force. With this interpretation of heaven, a Confucian could be an agnostic, and even an atheist (Welty 1984:171).

17_ Personal communication with an official in *Yurim* in 12 December, 2005.

18_ *Summary of the 2005 Korean Census*, 26 May 2006:32.

19_ The *Four Noble Causes of Truth* includes the following tenets: (1) existing is suffering; (2) suffering is due to selfish desires; (3) the cure for suffering is to destroy selfish desire; (4) the cure can be accomplished by practicing the eight-fold path. The *Eight-fold Path* consists of (1) right belief; (2) right thought; (3) right speech; (4) right action; (5) right means of livelihood; (6) right exertion; (7) right remembrance; (8) right meditation.

20_ These prayers are also common and popular among Chinese Buddhists (Hsu 1981:254-255).

21_ In China, Buddhism was popular and diffused rapidly among the common people, because the prevailing Confucianism and Taoism generally did not deal with life after death (Welty 1984:163). In contrast, in the Three Kingdoms of Korea, Buddhism was patronized by the royal courts and the ruling elite.

22_ The *hwarang* warrior youth honored the "five secular injunctions": (1) to serve the king with loyalty, (2) to serve one's parents with filiality, (3) to practice fidelity in friendship, (4) to never retreat in battle, and (5) to refrain from wanton killing (Lee 1984:55).

23_ The Seon or Contemplative School was introduced to Korea in the seventh century, and argued that faith could not be grounded in the written word. Instead it emphasized getting away from the complexities of doctrine by cultivating the spiritual essence of the human mind. "The method of this path of sudden enlightenment is Seon, or meditation" (Lee 1984:107), which is known as Zen in Japan.

24_ *Summary of the 2005 Korean Census*, 26 May 2006:32.

25_ An Junggeun who shot Itō Hirobumi to death in 1909, and who was the first Japanese Resident-General and chief architect of the Protectorate Treaty, was a member of the Catholic church (Yun et al. 1994:183).

26_ *Summary of the 2005 Korean Census*, 26 May 2006:32.

27_ Gwanghyewon eventually became a medical school, merging in 1957, with Yeonhui University (formerly Joseon Christian College) established by Horace G. Underwood in 1915, and eventually becoming the medical school attached to Yonsei University.

28_ *Kukmin Ilbo*, 16 December 2005:6.

29_ *Summary of the 2005 Korean Census*, 26 May 2006:32.

30_ Korea's first Bible was published in 1887, not in Chinese characters but in *Hangeul*, so that most ordinary people could easily read and comprehend it. This also turned out to be a great promotion for *Hangeul* during the Japanese colonial period, via the Bible.

31_ While Sangjin Choi (2003) says the first Korean church was founded in 1903, Elaine H. Kim and Eui-Young Yu (1996:377 n.28) identify the San Francisco Korean Methodist Church as the oldest church, established in 1905.

32_ Figures about the new religions are estimated differently by different sources. While Kwang-kyu Lee (2003:247) estimates that there are about 250 different new religions, including 1.6 million believers, Jo Heung-yun (1994:212) estimates there are about 300 new religions.

33_ *Summary of the 2005 Korean Census*, 26 May 2006:32.

CHAPTER 7

1_ Unlike Indo-European languages, the Korean language, like the Japanese language, has a grade (class) of expression with "honorific" and non-honorific words as well as conjugation. Honorific expressions may vary by age and social status or class: younger people should use honorifics in addressing older people, and people lower in social class use honorific expressions in addressing people who have higher status or social class. Most of the time, age and social status overlap, but in the given example, social class takes precedence over age.

2— Some historians translate *seonggol* as "hollowed-bone" (Lee 1984:49), and others translate it "sacred-bone" (Lee 2003:28).

3— Kwang-gyu Lee (2003:29) elaborates that "Among the 17 grades, the first five grades were restricted to the royal clan. Grades 6 to 9 were for the men of the sixth class. The men of the fifth class occupied 10 and 11 grades. Below the 4th class were commoners who could not participate in government, but were distinguished from 12 to 17 grades."

4— A list of those lineages is in Lee (1984:111).

5— During the Goryeo period, the term *Baekjeong* referred to freeborn peasants, while in the Joseon dynasty it mean "butcher" as an outcast.

6— The examination given by the Joseon court was in three categories: one for literature, to become literati *yangban*; the second for military science, to become military officers; and the third miscellaneous, including miscellaneous subjects.

7— Ki-baik Lee (1984:251) reports that "The number of slaves on the government's rosters had fallen from 350,000 in the fifteenth century to less than 200,000 by the seventeenth century. This decrease was caused in part by the destruction of slave records and scattering of the slave population during the Hideyosi invasion ···."

8— According to the university's public relations department, "the neologism 'Womans' in the university name was made deliberately to emphasize and respect the uniqueness individuality of each of Ewha's students.

9— Japanese also have rated university professors at the top in both a 1955 and 1964 survey (Befu 1971:128). One can wonder whether that has anything to do with the Confucian tradition that respects literati (or scholar-bureaucrats). However, a study on occupational prestige by Donald Treiman (1977), known as the Standard International Occupational Prestige Scale (SIOPS), also indicates that the prestige of university professor has been rated third highest out of 33 listed occupations.

10— American anthropologists W. Lloyd Warner and Paul Lunt (1941) made a comprehensive study of a shoe-manufacturing town in New England, called *Yankee City*, utilizing all sorts of variables that determine an individual's class affiliation, and recognized six different classes, which include upper upper class (1.4 percent), lower upper class (1.6 percent), upper middle class (10.2 percent), lower middle class (28.1 percent), upper lower class (32.6 percent), and lower lower class (25.2 percent). By consolidating two classes in each category, three informal class divisions have been created that have been used widely, such as upper class (3.0 percent), middle class (38.3 percent), and lower class (57.8 percent). These distributions form a triangle-like shape.

11_ Figures in the *JoongAng Ilbo* (2 January 2006:4) show that from 1997 to 2004, while the proportion of upper class remains about the same from 21.8 percent in 1997 to 22.5 percent in 2004, lower class slightly increased from 9.7 percent to 13.6 percent in 2004, and middle class decreased 5 percent point during for the past seven years.

12_ *JoongAng Ilbo*, 2 January 2006:1.

13_ *Kyunghyang Shinmun*, 6 October 2005:80; *JoongAng Ilbo*, 2 January 2006:1, 5-6. Sociologist Hong Dooseung (2005) characterizes the Korean middle class, which includes Koreans whose education consists of two-year college and four-year university and above, and whose monthly income is about 2,792,400 *won* (about $2,800) for those living in cities. These would own their own houses whose average is 66 square meters (20 pyeong or about 711.66 square feet) (Hong 2005). Kwang-kyu Lee (2003:288-289) indicates that most middle class Koreans are paid employees, white-collar workers working for medium and large-size enterprises in urban areas, and most are apartment dwellers.

14_ *Korea Herald*, 19 March 2007:1.

15_ *Korea Herald*, 19 March 2007:1.

16_ *Kyunghyang Shinmun*, 6 October 2005:8.

17_ *JoongAng Ilbo*, 2 January 2006:4.

18_ The National University contained Six Colleges in the capital, including University College, High College, Four Portal College, Law College, Calligraphy College, and Accounting College. Under King Injong (1122-1146), along with the establishment of the Six Colleges of the Capital, schools were set up in rural areas to educate local youth (Lee 1984:119-120).

19_ The word *seowon* in Chinese characters was originated in T'ang China. *Seowon* were introduced into Korea in the form of private academies in the sixteenth century (*Sosu seowon* was the first royally chartered private academy in 1543). However, *seowon* became not merely halls of learning but seedbeds of patrician disputation. Because of this, as a part of his reform policy, Daewongun closed down *seowon*, and in 1864 he banned the rebuilding or unauthorized construction of *seowon*.

20_ In the early 1900s, Korean scholars formed education associations (*hakhoe*) to promote education in provincial areas, including North and West Educational Association (Seobuk Hakhoe), Gyeonggi-Chungcheong Educational Association (Giho Heung Hakhoe), Jeolla Educational Association (Honam Hakhoe), Society for the Fostering of Activists (Heungsadan), Korean Educational Association (Daedong Hakhoe), Gyeongsang Educational Association (Yeongnam Hakhoe), and Gangwon Educational Association (Gwandong Hakhoe). Some of these educational associations eventually established schools (Kim 1998:41-42).

21_ The Educational Ordinance for Joseon [Korea] summarizes its intent: "Common education shall pay special attention to the engendering of national [Japanese] characteristics and the spread of the national language; the essential principles of education in Chōsen shall be the making of loyal and good subjects by giving instruction on the basis of the Imperial Rescript concerning education" (Eckert et al. 1990:262).

22_ "There were two sets of schools in Korea, one set for Koreans, another for Japanese. These separate and unequal systems were differentiated by quality of instruction, facilities, and curriculum" (Eckert et al. 1990:263).

23_ Some scholars such as Michael Robinson (1988:86) translate the Minnip Daehak as the "National University." However, such a translation may cause confusion with the current national universities such as Seoul National University, which is the Korean government-run university. In order to avoid such confusion, I have translated it as the "Korean People's University."

24_ The radical critics of the cultural nationalists questioned the efficacy of establishing a university that would serve such a small segment of the population. Nevertheless, they agreed that higher education would be a key to future Korea's success (Kim 1998:85-86; Robinson 1988:6).

25_ Toward the end of World War II, the Japanese authorities squeezed those colleges. For instance, in March 1944, the Japanese authorities closed the law and liberal arts programs at the all junior colleges in Korea, and converted Boseong Junior College to Seoul Colonial Junior College for Vocation and Economics; and the name of Yeonhui College was changed to Seoul Junior College for Industries and Management.

26_ Former colleges, such as Yeonhui, Boseong, and Ewha, were elevated to integrated four-year universities, and added several new academic departments.

27_ Of the nine former Korean presidents since the birth of the republic in 1948, only three graduated from a regular four-year college or university: the other six graduated from military academies, a special teacher-training school, or vocational high school for commerce. Among large business conglomerates, former chairman and founder of Hyundai Corporation Jeong Juyeong attended a traditional Confucian tutorial school (*seodang*), but his formal education was curtailed at the primary school level (Jones and Sakong 1980:349-358; Kim 1992:63).

28_ *Korean Economic Daily*, 7 January 2006:A-2.

29_ Along with the Open University (Bangsong Tongsin Daehak) that was opened in 1972, seventeen 100 percent on-line colleges and universities were founded beginning in the early 2000s due to the development of information technology based on a well-developed infrastructure that operates the Internet throughout the country, including the remote regions inland and the coastal islands. Over 10 million Koreans are connected through the broadband Internet network.

30_ Data from the Ministry of Education and Human Resources Development, ROK, 2005.

31_ Data from the Ministry of Education and Human Resources Development, ROK, 2005.

32_ Data from the Ministry of Education and Human Resources Development, ROK, 2005.

33_ *Chosun Ilbo*, 12 January 2006:A-6.

34_ In addition to the central government budget allocated for education, local government education funds are spent to support primary and secondary school education. The total revenue for the sixteen provincial and metropolitan education authorities in 2002 was 23.42 billion *won* (about $2.3 million) (*Handbook of Korea*, 2003:338).

35_ Data from the Ministry of Planning & Budget, ROK, 2006.

36_ Data from the Ministry of Education and Human Resources Development, ROK, 30 March 2007.

37_ In 1980, only 23.7 percent of students who graduated from high schools enrolled in colleges and universities, and that figure increased to 68.0 percent in 2000, and it was further increased to 82.1 percent in 2005 (*Maeil Business Newspaper*, 7 January 2006:A-2, A-4; *Dong-A Ilbo*, 16 August 2005:A-5).

38_ *Maeil Business Newspaper*, 7 January 2006:A-4.

39_ Data from the National Center for High Education Management System; Common Core Data, Private High School Survey, Fall Residency and Migration Survey, 30 March 2007.

40_ To prepare for this plan, the Seoul Metropolitan Office of Education announced that it would recruit 920 native English-speaking teachers by 2009 to cover all primary and junior high schools in Seoul. The teaching of English by native English-speaking teachers will eventually diffuse widely throughout the entire country (*Korea Herald*, 29 March 2005:3; *Chosun Ilbo*, 12 January 2006:1).

41_ The Uruguay Round (UR), named after the 1986 negotiation site in Punta del Este, Uruguay, is the world's largest trading system. Since its formation in 1993 UR reached an agreement for negotiations on market access for goods and services. In April 1994, the deal was signed by ministers from 123 participating governments at a meeting in Marrakesh, Morocco.

42_ There is still a large gap between the number of Korean students who go abroad to study and the number of foreign students who come to Korean universities. The ratio between the number of outgoing Korean students and incoming foreign students is about 22 to 1 (*Dong-A Ilbo*, 7 February 2005:2).

43_ Those numbers were based on the reports made by each individual to the foundation. Some might not report the receipt of their degrees to the foundation because they did not feel the necessity of doing so, particularly for those who would be working in the U.S. or elsewhere.

44_ *Korea Herald*, 6 April 2007:1.

45_ *Dong-A Ilbo*, 4 January 2006:A-8.

46_ Restrictions on overseas study still remain in *de jure*, but in *de facto* the restrictions are hardly enforced.

47_ India is second largest with 77,220 (12.1 percent); China the third with 59,343 (9.3 percent); Japan fourth with 54,816 (8.6 percent), and Taiwan fifth with 36,091 (5.6 percent) (*JoongAng Ilbo*, 27 April 2006:2.).

48_ *Korea Herald*, 6 April 2007:1.

49_ Students take the CSAT test, which consists of 230 multiple-choice questions, and each question has four obvious wrong answers and one correct one, during the final year of high school.

50_ *Korean Herald*, 24 November 2005:3.

51_ *Korean Herald*, 24 November 2005:3; *Hankook Ilbo*, 7 October 2005:B-9.

52_ *Dong-A Ilbo*, 11 July 2005:11.

53_ *Dong-A Ilbo*, October 4, 2004:A-30.

54_ Phuong Ly, "A Wrenching Choice," The *Washington Post*, 9 January 2005: A01.

55_ It has been reported that Korea has the highest suicide rate among the 30 countries of the OECD (*Dong-A Ilbo*, 1 October 2005:31). In March 2005, a fifty-two-year-old building designer committed suicide after he sent off his wife, a son and a daughter to Canada for study; and in April, 2005, a highly paid bank manager was unable to cope with his lonely life while his wife and a son were staying in the United States for study, and eventually committed suicide. Both men's deaths were discovered several days after they had committed suicide (*Kukmin Ilbo*, 20 October 2005:8).

56_ *Korea Herald*, 4 October 2005:1.

57_ The civil service examination system in T'ang Chinese might have been an open system. According to Ki-baik Lee's (1984:90) report, "A large number of Balhae students were sent to T'ang to study and, as the case with Silla, many of them passed the T'ang civil service examinations."

58_ Such an examination was unnecessary because national compulsory education extended to middle school.

59_ *Korea Herald*, 24 March 2007:2.

60_ *Korea Herald*, 24 March 2007:2.

61_ *Korean Economic Daily*, 22 March 2005:A-39.

62_ Data from the Ministry of Planning & Budget, ROK, 2006.

63_ *Kangwon Ilbo*, 29 October 2005:3.

64_ Between 1953 and 1995, Korea's GNP grew at an average annual rate of 7.6 percent. The GDP growth rate in 1995 was 8.9 percent, 6.8 percent in 1996, 5.0 percent in 1997, -6.7 percent in 1998, 10.9 percent in 1999, 9.3 percent in 2000, 3.0 percent in 2001, 6.3 percent in 2002, 3.1 percent in 2003, 4.7 percent in 2004, and 4.0 percent in 2005.

65_ The number of unemployed totaled 887,000 in 2005, up 27,000 from 2004. The unemployment rate of 3.7 percent was the same as that of 2004, implying that no improvement was made on the job front (*Korea Herald*, 13

January 2006:1).

[66] Data from the Korea National Statistical Office, ROK, 2005.

[67] *Chosun Ilbo*, 26 November 2005:3; *Chosun Ilbo*, 14 December 2005:12; *Segye Ilbo*, 19 November 2005:2.

[68] *Chosun Ilbo*, 26 March 2005:A-3.

[69] *Chosun Ilbo*, 20 January 2006:A-4.

CHAPTER 8

[1] Indirectly quoted from Martin E. Marty (1977:134).

[2] Indirect quotation from Francis L.K. Hsu (1979:528).

[3] Data obtained from the Korea National Statistical Office, ROK, 5 April 2007.

[4] A complete list of those traits summarized and translated into English is appended to Han Kyung-Koo's article on "Koreanness" (Han 2003:16, 27).

[5] Unlike radical nationalists who advocated social revolution and overt resistance to Japanese imperialism, moderate nationalists (or cultural nationalists) advocated gradual solutions to the problem of independence, emphasizing education, and development of industry (Kim 1998:12–17; Robinson 1988).

[6] The Korean nationalist movement during the Japanese domination, by and large, was polarized and divided into two different groups of nationalists, moderate nationalists (cultural nationalists) and radical nationalists who advocated social revolution and overt resistance to Japanese colonialism (Kim 1998:1).

[7] The label "orange tribe" (*orange jok*) refered to young people of the late nineteenth-eighties and early nineties who indulged in spending and pleasure-seeking in a few lavish sections of Seoul using their parents' money. "They tended to avoid seriousness and liked soft, bright, and light things; hence the term 'orange'" (Han 2003:20 n.16).

[8] This word was originated in 1281 when a combined armada from Korea and southern China was about to start on the shore, and a typhoons suddenly destroyed much of the Mongol fleet. It was believed to have been sent by the sun goddess Amataerasu at the behest of the throne.

9 _Dong-A Ilbo_, 18 December 2002:49.

10 John Shelton Reed, in an interview with The _New York Times_, suggested that Clinton-watchers needed to check out Choong Soon Kim's book [_An Asian Anthropologist in the South_], which might help them to understand why southerners avoid straightforward expressions if possible (Peter Applebome, "Lamentations of a Good Old Rebel: The South is Losing Its Accent," The _New York Times_, 24 January 1993:18).

11 In Korea, there were 137 accidents per 10,000 cars in 2003, which is the highest accident rate in the world, and the total expenses involved in car accidents in 2004 were estimated to be over 8.6 trillion _won_ (about $916 million) (_Dong-A Ilbo_, 20 January 2006:12; _Kyunghyang Shinmun_, 13 January 2006:1).

12 _Chosun Ilbo_, 21 March 2006:1.

13 I am not so certain about the reliability of these claims, but according to Guk (1986:117–119), an average European walks 25 steps per minute, an American 27 steps, a Russian 30 steps, 38 steps for a Japanese, while the slowest walking Korean takes 45 to 55 steps on average. Most Koreans walk 70 steps per minute, which is almost three times faster than the average European.

14 _JoongAng Ilbo_, 8 February 2006:E-4.

15 _Korean Economic Daily_, 3 February 2006:B-6.

16 16 Fictional kinship is the socially defined equivalent of affinal (marital) or consanguine (blood) ties. For instance, adoption, godparent-hood, and blood-hood are common fictional ties (Keesing and Keesing 1971:151; Schusky 1965:76).

17 _Chosun Ilbo_, 27 May 2003:A-18.

18 Arthur Cotterell (1993:64) says, "That something akin to the Korean nobility should exist in early Japan is likely, considering the close relations between them. Nearly a third of the Japanese nobility had ancestors who were originally refugees from Korean states."

CHAPTER 9

1 Business and industrial anthropology is "anthropological practice that applies

the theories and methods of the discipline to problem-solving activity in private sector organizations, especially industrial firms" and the term industrial anthropology "is used in reference to anthropological research focusing on the industrial domain" (Baba 1986:1).

2_ Industrial ethnography is anthropological case studies of whole industrial cultures found in a single business enterprise or permeating a given industry (Baba 1986:1).

3_ The Andong Dam project began in 1971 and was completed in 1976.

4_ The ambassador told me that even a Tokyo University research team participated in the salvage research. Nevertheless, I was unable to accept his inducement because of my prior commitment to conduct an adult education project for American Indians who lived in twenty-two states east of the Mississippi River beginning in 1978.

5_ Unfortunately, however, when I completed my initial fieldwork on the dispersed Korean families, and was about ready to prepare for a study on the *yangban* village, the ambassador died on 9 October 1983 in a North Korean terrorist bombing in Rangoon, Myanmar (formerly Burma), while accompanying the president on a state visit.

6_ It received intensive international media exposure when Her Majesty Queen Elizabeth II of Great Britain visited on 21 April 1999.

7_ In fact, according to a survey made in 1980s by Leroy Jones and Il Sakong (1980:229), very few entrepreneurs have risen from the poor masses represented by tenant farmers and rural and urban laborers. Fathers of the entrepreneurs' tended to be landowners, and most of them were of *yangban* origin (47 percent). The breakdown of other occupations was as follows: merchants (19 percent), factory owners (16 percent), civil servants (6 percent), teachers (4 percent), and other professionals (7 percent).

8_ Nowadays, however, even if the farming population has decreased every year, rice production has steadily increased since 1970. By 2004, the surplus of rice was over 1 million tons according to the Ministry of Agriculture and Forestry, ROK, dated 6 May 2006.

9_ Recent devaluation of the U.S. dollar against the Korean *won* elevated Korea's GDP ranking to tenth largest economy in the world (*Maeil Business Newspaper*, 27 April 2006:1).

10_ *Korean Herald*, 11 August 2005:6; *Korea Herald*, 23 March 2006:1; *Dong-A Ilbo*, 16 August 2005: A-4. North Korean per capita income in 2004 was reported to be $914 (*Dong-A Ilbo*, 16 December 2005:A-35). The Bank of Korea has made an optimistic prediction that by the year 2040, Korea's per capita income would reach $45,000, roughly two-thirds of that of the United States (*Korea Herald*, 27 September 2006:5). Jim O'Neal, London-based head of global economic research at Goldman Sachs concurs with the Bank of Korea's hopeful estimate (*Korean Economic Daily*, 14 December 2005:A-24).

[11] Data from the Korea National Statistical Office, ROK, March 2006. Its ranking went up to eleventh in 2006 (*Korea Herald*, 13 April 2007:8).

[12] *Korea Herald*, 11 August 2005:6.

[13] An association of psychologists specializing in Internet addiction surmises that 40 percent of teenagers and 10 percent of the general population of Koreans are addicted to the Internet (Breen 2004:250).

[14] *Korean Herald*, 11 August 2005:6. Furthermore, the volume of Korea export has steadily increased annually. By November 2005, Korea's trade volume had reached $481.2 billion, of which the export volume was $250.5 billion, and import volume was 230.7 billion. By the end of 2005, Korea's trade volume had reached $500 billion, which is comparable to the total trade volume of 38 Latin American countries, except Mexico, with $513 billion, and exceeded the total of 53 African countries with $443.5 billion (*Dong-A Ilbo*, 24 November 2005:1).

[15] The expansion of roads and highways happened simultaneously with the increase in individual motor vehicles. In 1945, there were only 7,000 automobiles in Korea, but the number has swelled to nearly 15 million in 2004, an increase of 2,132.8 times, at an annual rate of 12.3 percent.

[16] In 1986, for instance, Korea was the world's largest exporter of footwear ($1.1 billion) and leatherwear ($69 million) (Kim 1992:xiv).

[17] *Korea Herald*, 13 April 2007:8.

[18] According to a study by Lloyd's, a British survey group specializing in the shipbuilding and marine industry, Korea shipbuilders received orders for 11.5 million compensated gross tons (CGT), which is a measurement of ship category, accounting for 39.6 percent of total orders worldwide in the first nine months of 2005; Japan came in second with 5.9 million CGT, the European Union came in third with 5.1 million CGT, and China had 3.8 million CGT (*JoongAng Daily*, English edition, 4 January 2006:n.d.).

[19] Hyundai as the top shipbuilder in Korea holds 15 percent of the world

market share. However, other Korean shipbuilders are moving forward fast as well. For instance, it has been reported that Daewoo Shipping & Marine Engineering Co. (DMHI) delivered the first three vessels built at its eastern Romanian shipyard in Magalia. Currently, DMHI is building 18 container carriers, including a 4,860 TEU (20-foot equivalent unit) vessel for Germany. The DMHI hopes to receive orders worth $1 billion by 2008 and reach an annual sales of $500 million by 2010 (*Korea Herald*, 26 March 2006:5).

[20] *Korea Herald*, 11 August 2005:6.

[21] After being turned down for World Bank and US EX-Im Bank loans to finance the mill (Breen 2004:151), President Park Chung-hee with the assistance of single-minded Park Taejun, used all the available financial resources, including a $300 million direct grant from Japan for normalization of the Korea-Japan relationship, $200 million in loans, and $300 million from private firms (Cumings 1997:321).

[22] The Bank of Korea, 2005:25.

[23] *Korea Herald*, 11 August 2005:6.

[24] "Semiconductors include discretes and integrated circuits. Discretes perform a single electronic function acting as a diode or a transistor. Integrated circuits (ICs) incorporate thousands or millions of microscopic transistors and other functional components to form complex electronic circuits on the surface of a rigid substrate such as a 'chip' of silicon; thus, they are sometimes called computer chips" (*Handbook of Korea*, 2003:258).

[25] A report from the public relations office of iSuppli Corporation in El Segundo, California, 17 May 2006.

[26] *Chosun Ilbo*, English edition, 5 January 2006:n.d.

[27] *Chosun Ilbo*, 28 November 2005:B-4.

[28] *Korea Herald*, 25 August 2005:6.

[29] Regarding Korean economic success, scholars and critics from at home and abroad have lionized the country's performance with terms such as "miracle" or "man-made miracle" (Cho and Eckert 2005; Jones and Sakong 1980:3; Kim E.M. 1997:xii; Woronoff 1983) and "Asia's next giant" (Amsden 1989), to name just a few.

[30] The most notable of these studies have been conducted by the joint program of the Korea Development Institute (KDI) and the Harvard Institute for

International Development (Jones and Sakong 1980; Kim and Roemer 1979; Krueger 1979; Mason et al. 1980) and by the World Bank (Hasan 1976; Hasan and Rao 1979; Wade and Kim 1976; Westphal 1978).

31_ As Gary Hamilton and Narco Orru (1989:39-47) have warned us, aggregate economic data are often misleading and cannot be interpreted.

32_ "Even so, many underdeveloped nations in Latin America and Africa today exhibit these same features yet remain locked in poverty with little sustained economic growth" (Steers et al. 1989:13).

33_ Preoccupation with Korea's late industrialization by learning rather than by either invention or innovation might deter a researcher from seeking out the inventive side of Koreans. Korea's history, however, offers plenty of examples of innovative (Steers et al. 1989:129).

34_ Some scholars claim that the Japanese did remake the face of old Korea by laying railways, building parts, and installing modern factories (Cumings 1984:20). Nevertheless, the perceptions of native Koreans about the role of the Japanese in Korean industrialization are decidedly negative. The installation of modern industry was concentrated in North Korea and can hardly be said to have influenced recent South Korean industrialization. Most of those installations were destroyed or too damaged during the Korean War to affect recent development. Instead of seeing this as a positive influence for economic development, it should be seen as exploitation (Heo 2005; Kim 1992:17).

35_ Data from the Korea International Trade Association (KITA), April 2006.

36_ Successive five-year economic development plans include the first (1962-1966), second (1967-1971), third (1972-1976), fourth (1977-1981), and fifth (1982-1986).

37_ Quoted indirectly from Mary Ann von Glinow and Byung Jae Chung (1989:34).

38_ Among them were the cooperation of all the Korean people (46.8 percent), hardworking wage earners (18.5 percent), the leadership of the president of Korea (11.4 percent), the efforts of businessmen (7.7 percent), and the efforts of government officials and technocrats (5.4 percent).

39_ *Dong-A Ilbo*, 28 December 2005:A-2; *JoongAng Ilbo*, 28 December 2005:2.

40_ Indirectly quoted from The *Korean Economic Daily*, 13 April 2006:A-2. While the total sales volume of Samsung in 2004 was $91.8 billion, the Philippines' GDP in the same year was reported to be $85.1 billion (*Dong-*

A Ilbo, 31 March 2006:D-2), and average annual economic growth rate since 1961 was 3.93 percent (*Dong-A Ilbo*, 16 August 2005:A-5).

41_ Recently, a Korean civic group filed complaints against various *jaebeol* groups for their irregularities (*Korea Herald*, 12 April 2006:3).

42_ *Korea Herald*, 13 April 2006:6.

43_ Most notable supporting groups include the Urban Industrial Mission (UIM) sponsored by the Protestant church, and the Young Catholic Workers' Organizations, sponsored by the Roman Catholic Church organizations.

44_ Before the June Proclamation, there had been some labor disputes, 'wildcat" revolts, but such occurrences were limited in number compared with those in the post-proclamation years: there were 105 in 1979, and 848 in 1980, for instance (Kim 1992:177).

45_ In November 1977, in Iri, Jeollabuk-do province, 25 tons of similar explosives were touched off; 59 people near the site were killed, and 1,343 people were injured.

46_ *Korea Herald*, 2 February 2007:2.

47_ *Chosun Ilbo*, 12 January 2006:A-6.

48_ There are remarkable similarities between Chinese and Korean arts. While in Western arts the focus is on human beings, the emphasis in Chinese art is on the individual's place in the external scheme of things. "Even when Chinese artists do portray the human form, they either treat it as a minute dot in a vast landscape" (Hsu 1970:20).

49_ The first nuclear power plant began to be built in 1971 in Gori, Busan-si, Gyeongsangnam-do province, and began operation in 1978. By 2005, there were four sites with over twenty nuclear power reactors, generating over 17 million kilowatt (gross) of electricity, which is sixth largest among all nations, following the U.S., France, Japan, Russia, and Germany.

50_ In order to uphold the environmental goal of creating a "symbiotic community of all living organisms," in 1994 the Korean government promoted the Environmental Agency to ministry status accountable to the Ministry of Environment, and promulgated 33 environmental laws as of 2002 under the directive of the Ministry of Environment.

51_ In November 2005, the city of Kyeongju won the bid to host the depository site with an overwhelming majority of its citizens (89.5 percent) approving.

52_ *Chosun Ilbo*, 27 January 2005:1.

53_ Most of them were constructed during the Japanese occupation, except the Goesan Dam in 1957. They include the Bulgapje Dam in 1926, Cheongpyeong Dam in 1943, Tapjeongje Dam in 1944, and Hwacheon Dam in 1944.

54_ *Chosun Ilbo*, 2 December 1993:25.

55_ *Kyunghyang Shinmun*, 29 September 1997:26.

56_ *Hankyoreh Sinmun*, 21 April 1995:11.

57_ Several anthropologists, such as Kim Byeongmo (archaeologist), Han Kyoung Koo (socio-cultural anthropologist), and others have made several reports on the cultural impact of the dam project. Among various other things, they have pointed out that the Donggang region around the dam site contains many Paleolithic archeological sites and preserves rich material cultural remains. Their estimate was that it would take at least ten or fifteen years to excavate and remove the artifacts before they would be buried permanently by the dam water (Unpublished research reports made in spring, 2000).

58_ *Kukmin Ilbo*, 3 June 2000:18.

59_ *Chosun Ilbo*, 22 March 2006:3.

60_ The Korean government designated five sites (44.3 square kilometers) as Wetland Reservation Areas, two of which, Yong Neup (Marsh) at Daeamsan and Upo Neup (Swamp) in Changnyeong County, are registered as Ramsar Sites (*Handbook of Korea*, 2003:363).

61_ "The amount of total waste generated in Korea has been decreasing since 1993. Household waste significantly dropped in the 1990s, and daily waste volume per person, which stood at 1.3 kg in 1994, dropped to 1.01 kg in 2001" (*Handbook of Korea* 2003:367).

62_ A detailed history of the Cheonggyecheon from 1394 to the date of its recent restoration has been documented by Jo Gwanggwon (2005).

63_ At two o'clock in the afternoon on 27 July 2005, about three months before the completion of the project as the fresh water started to run into the stream, temperature of the surrounding area was 32.7 degrees Celsius while other section of the city was 36.3 degrees Celsius (*Dong-A Ilbo*, 12 August 2005:1).

64_ *Korea Herald*, 4 October 2005:3.

65₋ *Financial News*, 10 April 2007:20.

66₋ *Bonsai* are Japanese miniature potted trees and plants, and *bonkei* can be translated literally as a "landscape on a tray."

67₋ *Chosun Ilbo*, 22 March 2006:A-12.

68₋ *Dong-A Ilbo*, 18 April 2006:A-14.

69₋ As the Nanjido Repository was closed, the city of Seoul acquired a new landfill, Gimpo Sudogwon Maeripji (Gimpo Repository of the Greater Capital City), which is located in a part of the cities of Gimpo and Incheon. It covers an area of about 20.7 square kilometers, and takes 20,000 tons of waste every day. A project is now underway to transform this site using the Nanjido project as a model (*Hankyoreh Sinmun*, 6 January 2006:12).

70₋ *Korea Herald*, 1 May 2006:2.

71₋ In 2003, for instance, South Korean population density (per square kilometers) was the highest in the world after Taiwan and small city-states, including Macao (17,118), Hong Kong (6,190), Singapore (6,128), and Taiwan (624.6) Data from the Korea National Statistical Office, ROK, 26 April 2007.

72₋ Data from the Ministry of Health and Welfare, ROK, 24 April 2007.

73₋ Data from the Ministry of Health and Welfare, ROK, 24 April 2007.

EPILOGUE

1₋ Incidentally, as a director of the Asia Foundation, Steinberg awarded us a research grant in 1963. Hahm was director and I served as a research associate at the Social Science Research Institute, Yonsei University, studying Korean people's attitude toward law. It was the first nation-wide survey research.

2₋ KOICA was officially established in 1991, although its operation had started in 1990, in order to seek international cooperation, exchange, and assistance for socio-economic development with developing countries, similar to the Peace Corps in the United States.

3₋ Data from the Korean Institute for Missions, May 2006.

4₋ Data from the Ministry of National Defense, ROK, 26 April 2007.

5_ *Financial Times*, 19 March 2007:11.

6_ *Financial Times*, 19 March 2007:11.

7_ *Maeil Business Newspaper*, 16 April 2007:A-15.

8_ *Korea Herald*, 13 April 2006:6.

9_ *Maeil Business Newspaper*, 16 April 2007:A-2.

10_ *Maeil Business Newspaper*, 24 March 2006:A-2.

11_ *Chosun Ilbo*, 16 April 2007:A-14.

12_ *Financial Times*, 19 March 2007:11.

13_ Robert Reich (1990:54-55) reports that "Forty percent of IBM's world employees are foreign. ⋯ IBM Japan boasts 18,000 Japanese employees.⋯ Whirlpool now employs 43,500 people around the world in 45 countries — most of them non-Americans. TI employs over 5,000 people in Japan alone. ⋯ American corporations now employ 11 percent of the industrial work force of Northern Island. ⋯ More than 100,000 Singaporeans work for more than 200 U.S. corporations. ⋯ More than one-thirds of Taiwan's notorious trade surplus with the United States comes from U.S. corporations making or buying things there, then selling or using them back in the United States."

14_ "Economic health" has been measured on the basis of five economic variables, including the rates of income growth, employment growth, unemployment decline, home price increase, and business bankruptcy (Kim 1995:140-142).

15_ *Dong-A Ilbo*, 27 April 2006:1. Cf. Hussain (2006:67) who estimates that the number of jobs lost in Korea was 770,000.

16_ Data from the Export-Import Bank of Korea, March 2006.

17_ Of which the greatest number lived in China (2,439,395), followed by the United States (2,087,496), and then Japan (901,284). Data from the Ministry of Foreign Affairs and Trade, ROK, May 2006.

18_ Data from the Korea Tourism Organization, May 2006.

19_ Data from the Ministry of Commerce, Industry and Energy, May 2006.

20_ Perhaps because foreign mission work in Korea is no longer necessary. However, in 2002 about 1,020 foreign missionaries were still to be found in Korea. Data from the Ministry of Culture and Tourism, ROK, 2002.

21_ The absolute numbers of foreigners may be lower than in some other OECD countries, but the rate of increase is reported to be faster than any other OECD country. In fact, it has increased 10 times over the past 13 years from 1992 to 2005 (*Chosun Ilbo*, 8 April 2006:1).

22_ Data from the Korea Tourism Organization, May 2006.

23_ Of them, Russian students comprised the largest group with 13,091 (58.1 percent), followed by Japanese at 2,789 (12.4 percent), Americans at 892 (4.0 percent), and various others at 3,712 (16.5 percent). Data from the Ministry of Education and Human Resources Development, ROK, May 2006.

24_ *JoongAng Ilbo*, 3 February 2006:25.

25_ "Given the size of the trade imbalances, Japan's competitiveness in high technology fields, and anxiety that the ANIEs [Asian Newly Industrializing Economies] are catching up technologically, it is understandable that the United States might view Asian economic growth as a threat." And, according to a U.S. public opinion survey in October 1989, 33 percent of the people who were asked, "Which do you think is a greater threat to the United States?" opted for the Soviet Union's military strength [before the U.S.S.R was divided into several republics], while 52 percent cited Japanese economic strength (Okita 1991:31).

26_ Displays of antagonism and hostility at times against Japanese investment were not solely a Southern phenomenon, but part of a general sentiment of Japan-bashing throughout the United States. In January 1992, in Michigan, where antagonism rand deep among auto-workers, UAW Local 900 in Wayne County pushed foreign cars to a back parking lot at a local Ford plant (Kim 1995:9). Also in Wayne County, a former auto-plant foreman at Chrysler who mistook a Chinese-American for a Japanese bludgeoned him to death with a baseball bat (Gelsanliter 1990:143). In reporting Sony's acquisition of Columbia Pictures Entertainment for $3.4 billion, *TIME* wrote, "Some entertainment-industry observers suggested that Congress should challenge the Sony deal as well. For one thing, entertainment is the second largest U.S. export industry (aerospace is first)" (Castro 1989:70).

27_ *Korean Herald*, 19 April 2006:1.

28_ *Dong-A Ilbo*, 8 April 2006:4.

29_ *Korea Herald*, 6 April 2006:2.

30_ Ki-Wook Shin (2006:215-216) reports that "The Korean government has supported such folk festivals both directly and indirectly. The Ministry of

Culture and Tourism issues a recommended list of folk festivals for tourists. The seventeen festivals that the ministry recommended for the second half of 2002, for instance, featured *kimch'i*, ginseng, ceramics, the mask dance, martial arts, and traditional music, all supposedly representing Korea's cultural heritage and tradition."

31_ "*Samul*" means "four" while "nori" refers to "play or performance," which means that it is performed using four instruments, including small and large gongs made of bronze and leather, a double-headed hourglass and barrel drums. The instruments are distinctly different in terms of musical range, timbre and resonance, yet their sounds are brought together to form harmonious whole.

32_ *Maeil Business Newspaper*, 5 February 2004:1.

33_ The songs of the *Pansori* tend to be very long, some of them taking more than eight hours to perform. The *Pansori* alternates between a slow and fast tempo, quick and dramatic passages, and melodic passages and passages rendered in every speech.

34_ *Chosun Ilbo*, 21 April 2006:A-31.

35_ This quotation is from an excerpt of Hussain's writing in English, which was published in the *Korea Herald* (30 March 2006:7) as a part of a 14-part series.

36_ By 2005, the number of foreign workers was estimated to be 485,144, in accordance with figures from the Korea National Statistical Office, ROK. However, it is difficult to estimate the exact number of foreign workers, because there are so many undocumented workers. Some estimate that the number might be nearly 1 million, including illegal workers.

37_ *JoongAng Ilbo*, 16 April 2007:2.

38_ *Financial Times*, 27 March 2007:10.

39_ Hussain (2006:265-313) has proposed eight agendas for change.

40_ *Korea Herald*, 13 April 2006:1.

41_ A full page of article by Kihwan Kim, entitled "Korea's Prospects as Global Financial Hub Bright," was published in the *Korea Herald*, 8 May 2006:12.

42_ The quality of living index is based on several criteria such as politics and society, economic environment, heath and sanitation, public service, recreation, consumer goods, housing and natural environment, used to judge whether an expatriate is entitled to a hardship allowance (*Korea Times*, 4

April 2007:n.p.).

[43] *Korea Herald*, 25 April 2007:3. It also reports that, according to a survey conducted by the student counseling center at Sogang University, in November 2006, of 620 university students, more than half felt the urge to commit suicide, and 12 percent said they felt the desire to kill themselves at least once a month.

[44] *Korean Economic Daily*, 4 June 2007:A-14, and its editorial of the same newspaper, 5 June 2007:A-39.

[45] *Dong-A Ilbo*, 12 June 2007:1.

[46] *Maeil Business Newspaper*, 11 June 2007:A-15.

[47] *Korean Economic Daily*, 7 June 2007:A-10.

[48] *Korea Herald*, 7 April 2007:1.

Selected Bibliography Cited*

Abe Yoshio, *Nihon shushigaku to Chōsen* [Japanese Neo-Confucianism and Korea], Tokyo: Tokyo University Press, 1965.

_____, "Nihon jukono hatten to Yi T'oegye [The development of Confucianism in Japan and Yi T'oegye]," *Han* 1:3-27, 1972.

Abelmann, Nancy, *Echoes of the Past, Epics of Dissent: A South Korean Social Movement*, Berkeley: University of California Press, 1996.

Adelman, Irma, ed., *Practical Approaches to Development Planning: Korea's Second Five-Year Plan*, Baltimore: Johns Hopkins University Press, 1969.

Akiba, Takashi, "Study on Korean Folkways," *Folklore Studies* 14:1-106, 1957.

Alexander, Lamar, *Friends: Japanese and Tennesseans*, New York: Kodansha International, 1986.

Amsden, Alice, *Asia's Next Giant: South Korea and Late Industrialization*, New York: Oxford University Press, 1989.

_____, "Review of 'Making Capitalism: The Social and Cultural Construction of a South Korean Conglomerate' by Roger L. Janelli with Dawnhee Yim Janelli; and 'The Culture of Korean Industry: An Ethnography of Poongsan Corporation' by Choong Soon Kim," *Economic Development and Culture Change* 43:452-455, 1995.

Bae Gidong, "Jeongongni guseokgi yujeogui josagwajeongui munjejeom [Jeongongni Paleolithic Site, Current Understanding]," Paper presented at the International Seminar in Memory of the Excavation of Paleolithic Site, 3 May 2002, Yeoncheon, Korea, 2002.

Bae, Kyuhan, *Automobile Workers in Korea*, Seoul: Seoul National University Press, 1987.

---

* Daily, weekly, and monthly newspapers and magazines are not included.

Baek Nakjun (George Paik), "Inchon Kim Seongsuwa minjok gyoyuk [Kim Seongsu and national education]," *Inchon Kim Seongsuui aejok sasanggwa geu silcheon* [The patriotism of Kim Seongsu in thought and deed], ed. Kwon Ogi, pp. 207-220, Seoul: The Tong-A Ilbosa, 1982.

Baker, Christopher, "Economic Reorganization and the Slump in South and South-East Asia," *Comparative Studies in Society and History* 23:325-349, 1981.

Barnes, G.L., *China, Korea, and Japan: The Rise of Civilization in East Asia*, London: Thomas and Hudson, 1993.

Bateson, Mary Catherine, *With a Daughter's Eye: A Memoir of Margaret Mead and Gregory Bateson*, New York: William Morrow, 1984.

Befu, Harumi, *Japan: An Anthropological Introduction*, New York: Thomas Y. Crowell, 1971.

Benedict, Ruth, *The Chrysanthemum and the Sword*, Boston: Houghton Mifflin, 1946.

Benjamin, Roger, "Political Economy of Korea," *Asian Survey* 22:1105-1116, 1982.

Berger, Carl, *The Korean Knot: A Military-Political History*, Philadelphia: University of Pennsylvania Press, 1957.

Bernstein, Barton J., "The Struggle over the Korean Armistice: Prisoners of Repatriation," *Child of Conflict: The Korean American Relationship, 1943-1953*, ed. Bruce Cumings, pp. 261-307, Seattle: University of Washington Press, 1983.

Biesanz, Marvis H., and John Biesanz, *Introduction to Sociology*, Englewood Cliffs: Prentice-Hall, 1973.

Booth, David, "Marxism and Development Sociology: Interpreting the Impasse," *World Development* 13:761-787, 1984.

Brandt, Vincent S. R., *A Korean Village: Between Farm and Sea*, Cambridge: Harvard University Press, 1971.

Breen, Michael, *The Koreans: Who They Are, What They Want, Where Their Future Lies*, New York: Thomas Dunne Books of St. Martin's Griffin, 2004.

Cash, W.T., *The Mind of the South*, New York: Knopf, 1941.

Chang, Kwang-chih, *The Archaeology of Ancient China*, 4th ed, New Haven:

Yale University Press, 1986.

Chang, Yunshik, "Peasants Go to Town: The Rise of Commercial Farming in Korea," *Human Organization* 48:236-251, 1989.

Chen, Yu-his, Dependent Development and Its Sociopolitical Consequences: A Case Study of Taiwan. Ph.D. dissertation, University of Hawaii, 1981.

Choe Chong Pil, "Illyuhak sangeuro bon hanminjok giwon nyeongue daehan bipanjeok geomto [A critical review of research on the origins of Koreans and their culture]," *Hanguk Sanggosa Hakbo*[Journal of Early History of Korea] 8:7-43, 1991.

Choe Chong Pil, and Martin T. Bale, "Current Perspectives on Settlement, Subsistence, and Cultivation in Prehistoric Korea," *Artic Anthropology* 39:95-121, 2002.

Choe Taeryong, *Hanguk sahoegwahak gyeongu* [Studies on Korean social sciences] 7:143-163, 1983.

──────, "Jigeop wisinui byeonhwa [Change of occupational prestige]," *Jigeopgwa nodongui segye* [The world of job and labor], ed. The Committee for honoring retirement of Professor Kim Gyeongdong, pp. 29-86, Seoul:Bagyeongsa, 2002.

Choi, Hochin, *The Economic History of Korea*, Seoul: The Freedom Library, 1971.

Choi, Inhak, *A Type of Index of Korean Folktales*, Seoul: Myong Ji University Press, 1979.

Choi, Jaeseuk, *Hanguk gajok yeongu* [A study of the Korean family], Seoul: Minjung-seogwan, 1966.

Choi, Jang Jip, *Labor and the Authoritarian State: Labor Unions in South Korean Manufacturing Industries, 1961-1980*, Seoul: Korea University Press, 1990.

Choi, Sangji, "Korean American Immigrants & Religious Peace Movement," Paper presented at the Korean American Centennial Commemoration Seminar, the Smithsonian Institution, Washington, D.C., 15 August 2003.

Choy, Bong-youn, *Koreans in America*, Chicago: Nelson-Hall, 1979.

Chung, David, and Kang-Nam Oh, *Syncretism: The Religious Context of*

Chung, Edward Young-iob, "The Impact of Chinese Culture on Korea's Economic Development," *Confucian and Economic Development: An Oriental Alternative?*, ed. Hung-chao Tai, pp. 149-165, Washington, DC: The Washington Institute for Values and Public Policy, 1989.

_____, *The Korean Neo-Confucianism of Yi T'oegye and Yi Yulgok: A eappraisal of the "Four-Seven Thesis" and Its Implications for Self-Cultivation*, Albany:State University of New York Press, 1995.

Chung, Kae H., "An Overview of Korean Management," *Korean Managerial Dynamics*, eds. Kae H. Chung and Hak Chong Lee, pp. 1-8, New York: Praeger, 1989.

Chung, Kae H., and Hak Chong Lee, eds., *Korean Management Dynamics*, New York: Prager, 1989.

Chung, Kae H., and Hary K. Lie, "Labor-Management Relations in Korea," *Korean Managerial Dynamics*, eds. Kae H. Chung and Hak Chong Lee, pp. 217-231, New York: Praeger, 1989.

Clark, Charles Allen, *Religions of Old Korea*, Seoul: The Christian Literature Society of Korea, 1961.

Clark, Donald, "How the McCune System Got Started," *Korea Studies Newsletter*, no. 62:1-2, 1997.

_____, *Christianity in Modern Korea*, New York: University Press of America, 1986.

Cole, Robert E., *Japanese Blue Color: The Changing Tradition*, Berkeley: University of California Press, 1971.

Collins, J. Lawton, *War in Peacetime: The History and Lessons of Korea*, Boston: Houghton Mifflin, Co., 1969.

Cotterell, Arthur, *East Asia: From Chinese Predominance to the Rise of the Pacific Rim*, New York: Oxford University Press, 1993.

Crane, Paul S., *Korean Patterns*, Seoul: Royal Asiatic Society, Korea Branch, 1978 (orig. 1967).

Cumings, Bruce, *The Origins of the Korean War: Liberation and the Emergence of Separate Regimes, 1945-1947*, Princeton: Princeton University Press, 1981.

———, *The Two Koreas*, Headline Series no. 269, New York: Foreign Policy Association, 1984.

———, "The Origins and Development of the Northeast Asian Political Economy: Industrial Sectors, Product Cycles, and Political Consequences," *The Political Economy of the New Asian Industrialism*, ed. Frederic C. Deyo, pp. 44–83, Ithaca: Cornell University Press, 1987.

———, *Korea's Place in the Sun: A Modern History*, New York: W.W. Norton & Co, 1997.

Deuchler, Martina, *Confucian Gentlemen and Barbarian Envoys: The Opening of Korea, 1875–1885*, Seattle: University of Washington Press, 1977a.

———, "The Tradition: Women during the Yi Dynasty [Joseon]," *Virtues in Conflict: Tradition and the Korean Woman Today*, ed. Sandra Mattielli, pp. 1–47, Seoul: The Royal Asiatic Society, Korea Branch, 1977b.

———, *The Confucian Transformation of Korea: A Study of Society and Ideology*, Cambridge: The Council on East Asian Studies, Harvard University, 1992.

Deyo, Frederic C., *Beneath the Miracle: Labor Subordination in the New Asian Industrialism*, Berkeley: University of California Press, 1989.

Dix, Griffin M., "The Place of the Almanac in Korean Folk Religion," *Journal of Korean Studies* 2:47–70, 1980.

Durkheim, Émile, *The Division of Labor in Society*, Glencoe: Free Press, 1947.

Eckert, Carter J., "The South Korean Bourgeoisie: A Class in Search of Hegemony," *Journal of Korean Studies* 7:115–148, 1990.

———, *Offspring of Empire: The Koch'ang Kims and the Colonial Origins of Korean Capitalism, 1876–1945*, Seattle: University of Washington Press, 1991.

Eckert, Carter J., et al., *Korea Old and New: A History*, Seoul: Ilchokak, 1990.

Ember, Carol R., and Melvin Ember, *Anthropology*, Upper Saddle River, NJ: Prentice-Hall, 1996.

Fairbank, John K., Edwin O. Reischauer, and Albert M. Craig, *East Asia: The Modern Transformation: A History of East Asian Civilization*, vol. 2, Boston: Houghton Mifflin, 1965.

Fallers, Lloyd, "Are African Cultivators to be Called Peasant?" *Current Anthropology* 2:108-110, 1961.

Farnsworth, Paul, "Identity through Beer," *Anthropology News*, February 2000:18, 2000.

Fernandez, James W., "Reflections on Looking into Mirrors," *Semiotica* 30:27-39, 1980.

_____, *Bwiti: An Ethnography of the Religious Imagination in Africa*, Princeton: Princeton University Press, 1982.

Ferraro, Gary P., *The Cultural Dimension of International Business*, 3rd ed., Upper Saddle River: Prentice-Hall, 1998.

Gardiner, Kenneth Herbert James, *The Early History of Korea*, Honolulu: University of Hawaii Press, 1969.

Geertz, Clifford, *After the Fact: Two Countries, Four Decades, One Anthropologist*, Cambridge: Harvard University Press, 1995.

Gelsanliter, David, *Jump Start: Japan Comes to the Heartland*, New York: Farrar, Straus & Giroux, 1990.

Gerschenkron, Alexander, *Economic Backwardness in Historical Perspective*, Cambridge: Harvard University Press, 1962.

_____, *Continuity in History and Other Essays*, Cambridge: Harvard University Press, 1968.

Gibson, John, "Done neomu jipchakhanda [Too much concern about money]," *Hangugineun nuguinga: Oegugini bon uriui uisik gujo* [Who are the Koreans: Structure of the Korean thought patterns seen by foreigners], ed. Sin Dongho, pp. 269-274, Seoul: Chosun Ilbosa, 1978.

Go Jaeuk, ed., *Inchon Kim Seongsu-jeon* [The biography of Kim Seongsu], Seoul: Inchon Ginyeomhoe, 1976.

Goha seonsaeng jeongi pyeonchan wiwonhoe, *Dongnibeul hyanghan jimnyeom: Goha Song Jinu jeongi* [The will to national liberation: A portrait of Song Jinu], Seoul: Dong-A Ilbosa, 1990.

Gong Jeongja, Hanguk daegieopga gajogui honmaege gwanhan yeongu [The families of Korean big businessmen and their marriage networks], Unpublished Ph.D. dissertation, Ehwa Womans University, 1989.

Goode, William J., *World Revolution and Family Patterns*, New York: The Free Press, 1970.

Gorer, Geoffrey, "Themes in Japanese Culture," *Transactions of the New York Academy of Science*, series 2, 5:106-124, 1943.

Grajdanzev, Andrew J., *Modern Korea*, New York: Institute of Pacific Relations, 1944.

Guk Heungju, "hangugineun wae seodureuneunga [Why do Koreans so hurry?]," *Hangugin hangukbyeong* [Koreans and their illness], eds. Lee Gyutae, et al., pp. 111-119, Seoul: Illyeom, 1986.

Gunther, John, *The Riddle of MacArthur*, New York: Harper and Brothers, 1950.

Hahm, Pyong-choon, "Korea's 'Mendicant Mentality?'" *Foreign Affairs* 43:165-174, 1964.

Hahm, Hanhee, "Rice and Koreans: Three Identities and Meanings," *Korea Journal* 45:89-106, 2005.

Hahm, Pyong-choon, Yang Seung Doo, and Kim Choong Soon, "Hanguk nodong johabui hyeonsilgwa nodongbeop [Labor law and the reality of the trade unionism in Korea]," *Yonsei Nonchong* 3:213-250, 1964.

Hall, David L., and Roger T. Ames, *Thinking through Confucius*, Albany: State University of New York Press, 1987.

Hamilton, Gray G., and Narco Orru, "Organizational Structure of East Asian Companies," *Korean Management Dynamics*, eds. Kae H. Chung and Hak Chong Lee, pp. 39-47, New York: Praeger, 1989.

Han Kyung-Koo, "The Politics of Network and Social Trust: A Case Study in the Organizational Culture of Korean Venture Industry," *Korea Journal* 40:353-365, 2000a.

_____, "Wigi inseonggwa 21segi hanguk sahoe [Crisis-ridden personality and Korean society in the 21st century]," *20segi ditgo neomgi* [Jump over by stepping on the 20th century], ed. hwangyeong undong yeonhap 21segi wiwonhoe, pp. 289-303, Seoul: Nanam, 2002b.

Han, Kyung-Koo, "The Anthropology of the Discourse on the Koreanness of Koreans," *Korea Journal* 43:5-31, 2003.

Han Kyung-Koo, et al., *sihwaho saramdeureun eotteoke dwaeseulkka : munhwa illyu hakjadeurui hyeonjang bogo* [What happened to the people of Sihwa Lake: A field report by cultural anthropologists], Seoul: Sol Publisher, 1998.

Han, Sang-bok, *Korean Fisherman: Ecological Adaptation in Three Communities*, Seoul: Seoul National University Press, 1977.

Han, Woo-keun, *The History of Korea*, Seoul: Eul-Yoo, 1981.

Harvey, Youngsook Kim, *Six Korean Women: The Socialization of Shamans*, St. Paul: West Publishing Co., 1979.

_____, "*Minmyŏnuri*: The Daughter-in-Law Who Comes of Age in Her Mother-in-Law's Household," *Korean Women: A View from the Inner Room*, eds. Laurel L. Kendall and M. Peterson, pp. 45-61, New Haven: East Rock Press, 1983.

Hasan, Parvez, *Korea: Problems and Issues in a Rapidly Growing Economy*, Baltimore: Johns Hopkins University Press, 1976.

Hasan, Parvez, and D.C. Rao, *Korea: Policy Issues for Long-Term Development: Report of a Mission Sent to the Republic of Korea by the World Bank*, Baltimore: Johns Hopkins University Press, 1979.

Hatada, Takashi, *A History of Korea*, trans. by Warren W. Smith Jr., and Benjamin H. Hazard, Santa Barbara: Chio Press, 1969.

Henderson, Gregory, *Korea: The Politics of the Vortex*, Cambridge: Harvard University Press, 1968.

Heo Suyeol, *Gaebal eomneun gaebal : Ilje Joseon gaebarui hyeonsanggwa bonjil* [Development without development: Reality and essence of Korean economic development under the Japanese colonial period], Seoul: Eunhaengnamu, 2005.

Hicks, George, *The Comfort Women*, St. Leonard, Australia: Allen and Unwin, 1995.

Higgins, Trumbull, *Korea and the Fall of MacArthur: A Précis in Limited War*, NY: Oxford University Press, 1960.

Ho, Samuel P. S., *Economic Development of Taiwan, 1860-1970*, New Haven: Yale University Press, 1978.

Hoebel, E. Adamson, *Anthropology: The Study of Man*, New York: McGraw-Hill, 1958.

Hofheiz, Ray, Jr., and Kent E. Calder, *The Eastasia Edge*, New York: Basic Books, 1982.

Hofstede, Geert, and Michael Harris Bond, "The Confucius Connection: From Cultural Roots to Economic Growth," *Organizational Dynamics*

Spring:5-21, 1988.

Holzberg, Carol S., and Maureen J. Giovannini, "Anthropology and Industry: Reappraisal and New Directions," *Annual Review of Anthropology* 10:317-360, 1981.

Hong Duseung, *Hangugui jungsancheung* [The middle classes in Korea], Seoul: Seoul National University Press, 2005.

Hong Uiseop, *Hanguk jeongsinsa seoseol* [Introduction to history of the Korean thoughts], Seoul: Yonsei University Press, 1975.

Hsu, Francis L.K., "The Effect of Dominant Kinship Relationships on Kin and Non-kin Behavior," *American Anthropologist* 67:638-661, 1965.

_____, *Americans and Chinese: Purpose and Fulfillment in Great Civilizations*, Garden City, NY: Natural History Press, 1970.

_____, *Kinship and Culture*, Chicago: Aldine, 1971.

_____, *Iemoto: The Heart of Japan*, Cambridge, MA: Schenkman, 1975.

_____, "Intercultural Understanding: Genuine and Spurious," *Anthropology & Education Quarterly* 8:202-209, 1977.

_____, "The Cultural Problem of the Cultural Anthropologist," *American Anthropologist* 81:517-532, 1979.

_____, *Americans & Chinese: Passage to Differences*, 3rd ed, Honolulu: University of Hawaii Press, 1981 (orig. 1953).

_____, *Rugged Individualism Reconsidered: Essays in Psychological Anthropology*, Knoxville: University of Tennessee Press, 1983.

Hurh, Won Moo, and Kwang Chung Kim, *Korean Immigrants in America: A Structural Analysis of Ethnic Confinement and Adhesive Adaptation*, Cranbury, NJ: Associated University Presses, 1984.

Hussain, Tariq, trans. Sae-min Lee, *Diamond Dilemma*. Seoul: Random House JoongAng (in Korean), 2006.

Im Jeongbin, "Han · Chile FTA hyeopsang balpyo ihu urinaraui nongsanmul gyoyeok donghyanggwa sisajeom [Trend and problem of the trades of Korean industrial and agricultural products from the FTA between Korea and Chile]," *Nongchon Gyeongje* [Rural Economy] 4:81-96, 2004.

Janelli, Roger, and Dawnhee Yim, *Ancestor worship and Korean Society*. Stanford: Stanford University Press, 1982.

―――――, *Making Capitalism: The Social and Cultural Construction of a South Korean Conglomerate*, Stanford: Stanford University Press, 1993.

Jo Ganghui, "Yeongnam jibangui honban nyeongu : Jinseong Yissi Toegye jongsoneul jungsimeuro [The marriage network in the Gyeongsang-do province: Focusing on the main heir of the Chinseong Yi clan]," *Minjok munhwa nonchong* [The Journal of the Institute for Korean Culture] 6:79-121, 1984.

Jo Gwanggwon, *Cheonggyecheoneseo yeoksawa jeongchireul bonda* [Ruminating history and politics from Cheonggyecheon], Seoul: Yeoseong Sinmunsa, 2005.

Jo Heungyun, "sinheung jonggyo [New Religion]," *Hanguginui jonggyo* [Korean religion], eds. Yun Yiheum, et al., pp. 205-231, Seoul: Mundeok-sa, 1994.

Jo Ijae, and Carter J. Eckert, *Hanguk geundaehwa: Gijeogui gwajeong* [Modernization of the Republic of Korea: A miraculous achievement], Seoul: Wolgan Chosun, 2005.

Jo Seongyun, "Saneop sahoeui mudang [Shamans in industrial societies]," *Jeontonggwa Hyeondae* 6:94-133, 1998.

Jones, Leroy P., and Il Sakong, *Government, Business, and Entrepreneurship in Economic Development: The Korean Case*, Cambridge: Council on East Asian Studies, Harvard University, 1980.

Kang, Younghill, *The Grass Roof*, New York: Follett Publishing Co, 1966.

Keesing, Roger M., and Felix M. Keesing, *New Perspectives in Cultural Anthropology*, New York: Holt, Rinehart and Winston, 1971.

Keidel, Albert, "Regional Agricultural Production and Income," *Rural Development*, eds. Sunghwan Ban, Pal Yong Moon, and Dwight H. Perkins, pp. 112-159, Studies in the Modernization of the Republic of Korea, Cambridge: Council on East Asian Studies, Harvard University, 1980.

Kendall, Laurel, "Caught Between Ancestors and Spirits: A Korean Mansin's Healing *Kut*," *Korean Journal* 17:8-23, 1977.

―――――, "Korean Ancestors: From the Women's Side," *Korean Women: View from the Inner Room*, eds. Laurel Kendall and Mark Peterson, pp. 97-112, New Haven: East Rock Press, 1983.

―――――, *Shamans, Housewives, and Other Restless Spirits*, Honolulu:

University of Hawaii Press, 1985a.

_____, "Ritual Skills and Kowtow Money: The Bride as Daughter-in-law in Korean Wedding Rituals," *Ethnology* 24:253-267, 1985b.

_____, *The Life and Hard Times of a Korean Shaman: Of Tales and the Telling of Tales*, Honolulu: University of Hawaii Press, 1988.

_____, *Getting Married in Korea: Of Gender, Morality, and Modernity*, Berkeley: University of California Press, 1996a.

_____, "Korean Shamans and the Spirits of Capitalism," *American Anthropologist* 98:512-538, 1996b.

Keyes, Charles F., "Peasant Strategies in Asian Societies: Moral and Rational Economic Approach — A Symposium," *Journal of Asian Studies* 42: 753-768, 1983.

Kim, Choong Soon, "Functional Analysis of Korean Kinship System," Unpublished Mater's thesis, Emory University, 1968.

_____, "The Yŏnjul-hon or Chain-string Form of Marriage Arrangement in Korea," *Journal of Marriage and the Family* 36:575-579, 1974.

_____, *An Asian Anthropologist in the South: Field Experiences with Blacks, Indians, and Whites*, Knoxville: University of Tennessee Press, 1977.

_____, "The Korean value System as Reflected in a Fortune-telling Book," Paper presented at the annual meetings of American Anthropological Association, 16-20 November 1983, Chicago, Illinois, 1983.

_____, "Can an Anthropologist Go Home Again?" *American Anthropologist* 89:943-946, 1987.

_____, *Faithful Endurance: An Ethnography of Korean Family Dispersal*, Tucson: University of Arizona Press, 1988a.

_____, "An Anthropological Perspective on Filial Piety versus Social Security," *Between Kinship and the State: Social Security and Law in Developing Countries*, eds. Von Benda-Beckmann, et al., pp. 125-135, Dordrect, Holand: Foris Publications, 1988b.

_____, "The Olympic Games as a Force of Cultural Exchange," *The Olympics and East West and South North Cultural Exchange*, eds.

Shinpyo Kang, John MacAloon, and Roberto DaMatta, pp. 191–206. Seoul: The Institute for Ethnological Studies, Hanyang University, 1988c.

———, "Attribute of 'Asexuality' in Korean Kinship and Sundered Koreans during the Korean War," *Journal of Comparative Family Studies* 20:309–325, 1989.

———, "The Role of the Non-Western Anthropologist Reconsidered: Illusion versus Reality," *Current Anthropology* 31:196–201, 1990.

———, *The Culture of Korean Industry: An Ethnography of Poongsan Corporation*, Tucson: University of Arizona Press, 1992.

———, "Koreans," *Encyclopedia of World Cultures*, vol. 5: East and Southeast Asia, ed. Paul Hockings, pp. 144–149, Boston: G.K. Hall & Co, 1993.

———, *Japanese Industry in the American South*, New York: Routledge, 1995.

———, "Applaudir d'une seule main: pour un renouveau de la tradition anthropologique occidental, Special issue," *Les cahiers Ethnologiques: Histories et Culture* Nr 18:29–47, Bordeaux, France, 1996.

———, *A Korean Nationalist Entrepreneur: A Life History of Kim Sŏngsu, 1891–1955*, Albany: State University of New York Press, 1998.

———, *Anthropological Studies of Korea by Westerners*, Institute for Modern Korean Studies Series, no. 5, Seoul: Yonsei University Press, 2000.

———, *One Anthropologist, Two Worlds: Three Decades of Reflexive Fieldwork in North America and Asia*, Knoxville: University of Tennessee Press, 2002.

Kim, Dong Ki, and Chong W. Kim, "Korean Value Systems and Managerial Practices," *Korean Managerial Dynamics*, eds. Kae H. Chung and Hak Chong Lee, pp. 207–216, New York: Praeger, 1989.

Kim, Duck Choong, "Role of Entrepreneurs in Korea," *Toward Higher Productivity*, ed. D.K. Kim, pp. 51–64, Tokyo: Asian Productivity Center, 1986.

Kim, Elaine H., and Eui-Young Yu, eds., *East to America: Korean American Life Stories*, New York: New Press, 1996.

Kim, Eun Mee, *Big Business, Strong State: Collusion and Conflict in South Korean Development, 1960-1990*, Albany: State University of New York Press, 1997.

Kim Gyeongdong, "Jigeop pyeonggae uihan gihoe gujoui insik [Understanding of opportunistic structure by evaluating one's vocation]," *Sahoegwahakgwa Jeongchaek Yeongu* [Social sciences and policy studies] 1:63-76, 1979.

Kim Gyeongil, *gongjaga jugeoya naraga sanda* [Country can servive when Confucius dies], Seoul: bada chulpansa, 2001.

Kim Hakjun, *Goha songjinu pyeongjeon: Minjokjuuieonnonin:Jeongchigaui saengae* [A critical biography of Song Jinu: A journalist and a statesman: The life and times of a Korean nationalist democrat], Seoul: The Tong-A Ilbosa, 1990.

Kim Inhoe, *Hanguginui gachigwan* [Korean value system], Seoul: Muneumsa, 1980.

Kim, Inhoe, et al., *Hanguk musok yeongu* [History of the studies of Korean shamanism], Seoul: Institute of Korean Culture, Korea University, 1982.

Kim Jaedeuk, et al., *Cheonjugyowa hanguk geunhyeondaeui sahoe munhwajeok byeondong* [A study on the socio-cultural influences of Korean Catholic church during the 20th century: Final report of questionnaire survey for evaluation and vision of Catholic church], Seoul: Hanul Academy, 2004.

Kim Jusu, *Chinjok sangsokbeop* [Kinship and inheritance laws], Seoul: Beobmunsa, 1983.

Kim, Kwang-Ok, "The Communal Ideology and Its Reality: With Reference to the Emergence of Neo-Tribalism," *Korean Journal* 38:5-44, 1998.

Kim, Kwang Suk, and Michael Roemer, *Growth and Structural Transformation*, Cambridge: Council on East Asian Studies, Harvard University, 1979.

Kim, Linsu, "Technological Transformation of Korean Firms," *Korean Managerial Dynamics*, eds. Kae H. Chung and Hak Chong Lee, pp. 113-129, New York: Praeger, 1989.

Kim Seong-Nae, "Hanguk mugyoui jeongcheseonggwa jonggyoseong: Jaengjeom bunseok [Identity and importance of Korean shamanism: Analysis of the debating Issues]," *Shamanism Yeongu* [Studies of shamanism] 4:359-394, 2002.

Kim Seong-Nae, et al., "Hanguk mugyo yeonguui yeoksajeok gochal," *Hanguk jonggyo munhwa yeongu 100nyeon* [One hundred year's studies of Korean religious culture], eds. Kim Seong-Nae, et al., pp. 139-207, Seoul: Cheongnyeonsa, 1999.

Kim, Seung-Kyung, *Class Struggle or Family Struggle?: The Lives of Women Factory Workers in South Korea*, New York: Cambridge University Press, 1997.

Kim Taegil, *Soseol munhage natanan hanguginui gachigwan* [Korean value systems reflected in Korean novels], Seoul: Iljisa, 1977.

Kim Taek-kyoo, *Dongjok burak yeongu* [The cultural structure of a Consanguineous village], Daegu: Cheonggu University Press, 1964.

―――, *Ssijok buragui yeongu* [Study on a consanguineous village], Seoul: Ilchokak, 1986 (orig. 1979).

Kim, Won-yong, "Discoveries of Rice in Prehistoric Sites in Korea," *Journal of Asian Studies* 41:513-518, 1982.

Kitano, Harry H.L., and Roger Daniels, *Asian Americans: Emerging Minorities*, Englewood Cliffs, NJ: Pretice Hall, 1995.

Koh, Hesung Chun, *Korean Family and Kinship Studies Guide*. New Haven: Human Relations Area Files, 1980.

―――, "Korean Women, Conflict, and Change: An Approach to Development Planning," *Korean Women: View from the Inner Room*, eds. Laurel Kendall and Mark Peterson, pp. 159-174, New Haven: East Rock Press, 1983.

Koo, Hagen, "The Interplay of State, Social Class, and World System in East Asian Development: The Cases of South Korea and Taiwan," *Political Economy of the New Asian Industrialism*, ed. Frederic C. Deyo, pp. 165-181, Ithaca: Cornell University Press, 1987.

Krueger, Anne O., *The Developmental Role of the Foreign Sector and Aid*, Cambridge: Council on East Asian Studies, Harvard University, 1979.

Kumar, Nita, *Friends, Brothers, and Informants: Fieldwork Memoirs of Banaras*, Berkeley: University of California Press, 1992.

Kwon, Yi-gu, "The Population of Ancient Korea in Physical Anthropological Perspective," *Korea Journal* 30:4-12, 1990.

Langness, L.L., *The Life History in Anthropological Science*, New York: Holt, Rinehart and Winston, 1965.

Lee, Changsoo, and George De Vos, *Koreans in Japan: Ethnic Conflict and Accommodation*, Berkeley: University of California Press, 1981.

Lee Gwangsu, "Minjok gaejoron [Reconstructing the nation]," *Gaebyeok* [Creation] 23:18-72, 1922.

Lee Gyutae, Hanguginui uisik gujo [Structure of the Korean thought patterns], 2 vols., Seoul: Munrisa, 1981.

Lee Haejun, *Joseon sigi chollak sahoesa* [History of village during the Joseon Dynasty], Seoul: Minjok munhwasa, 1996.

Lee Haeyeong, and Kim Gyeongdong, sireop gyoyukgwa jigeop [Vocational education and occupation], Seoul: Population and Development Institute, Seoul National University, 1970.

Lee, Hak Chong, "Managerial Characteristics of Korean Firms," *Korean Managerial Dynamics*, eds. Kae H. Chung and Hak Chong Lee, pp. 147-162, New York: Praeger, 1989.

Lee, Hi-seung, "Characteristics of Korean Culture," *Korea Journal* 3:13-16, 1963.

Lee Jangu, and Lee Minhwa, *Han gyeongyeong* [Han management], Seoul: gimmyoungsa, 2000 (orig. 1994).

Lee Jonguk, *Minjoginga, gukgainga?* [Nation, state?], Seoul: Sonamu, 2006.

Lee, Ki-baik, *A New History of Korea*, trans. Edward W. Wagner with Edward J. Schultz, Cambridge: Harvard University Press, 1984.

Lee Kwang-kyu, "Dongjok jipdangwa josang sungbae [Descent group and ancestor worship]," *Hanguk munhwa illyuhak* [Korean cultural anthropology] 9:1-24, 1977.

_____, *Hanguk gajogui gujo bunseok* [A structural analysis of the Korean family], Seoul: Ilchisa, 1982.

_____, *Hanguk gajogui sajeok yeongu* [A historical study of the Korean family], Seoul: Ilchisa, 1983.

Lee, Kwang-Kyu, ed. Joseph P. Linskey, *Korean Traditional Culture*, Korean Studies Series no. 25, Seoul: Jimundang, 2003.

Lee Man-gab, *Hanguk nongchonui sahoe gujo* [The social structure of Korean farming villages], Seoul: Korean Research Center, 1960.

Lee Mangyu, *Yeo Unhyeong seonsaeng tujaengsa* [History of Yeo Unhyeong's struggles], Seoul: Minju munhwasa, 1946.

Lee Taekhwi, "Bulgapihan seontaek: jeongchi jidojaui gil [Unavoidable choice: The way of a political leader]," *Pyeongjeon Inchon Kim Seongsu* [A critical biography of Kim Seongsu], ed. Sin Ilcheol, pp. 339–421, Seoul: Dong-A Ilbosa, 1991.

Lee Taeyeong, *Hanguk gihon jedo yeongu* [A study of divorce in Korea], Seoul: Yeoseong munje yeonguwon, 1957.

Lessa, William A., and Evon Z. Vogt, eds., *Reader in Comparative Religion: An Anthropological Approach*, 4th ed, New York: Harper & Row, 1979.

Levy, Marion J., Jr., *Modernization and Structure of Society*, Princeton: Princeton University Press, 1966.

Lew Young Ick, "The *Kabo* Reform Movement: Korean and Japanese Reform Efforts in Korea," Unpublished Ph.D. dissertation, Harvard University, 1972.

_____, *Gabo gyeongjang yeongu* [Studies on the *Gabo* reform movement], Seoul: Ilchokak, 1990.

Lewis, Oscar, "Tepozlan Revisited," *Readings in Modern Sociology*, ed. Alex Inkeles, pp. 51-64, Englewood Cliffs: Prentice-Hall, 1966.

Lewis, W. Arthur, *Development Planning: The Essentials of Economic Policy*, New York: Harper and Row, 1966.

Li An-che, "Zuni: Some Observations and Queries," *American Anthropologist* 39:62–76, 1937.

Li, Hui-Lin, "The Domestication of Plants in China: Ecogeographical Considerations," *The Origins of Chinese Civilization*, ed. D.N. Keightley, pp. 21-64, Berkelely: University of California Press, 1983.

Lila, Abu-Lughod, "Fieldwork of a Dutiful Daughter," *Arab Women in the Field*, eds. S. Altorki and C. Fawzi El-Solh, pp. 139-61, Syracuse: Syracuse University Press, 1988.

Lim, Youngil, *Government Policy and Private Enterprise: Korean Experience in Industrialization*, Berkeley: Institute of East Asian Studies, University of California, 1981.

Lindstrom, Lamont, and Peter Stromberg, "Beyond the 'Savage Slot,'" *Anthropology News Letter* 40:9-10, 1999.

Lowell, Percival, *Chosŏn: The Land of Morning Calm*, Boston: Ticknor, 1888.

Malinowski, Bronislaw, *Sex and Repression in Savage Society*, London: Kegan Paul, Trench, Trubner, 1927.

Maruyama, Magorah, "Epistemology of Social Science Research: Explorations in Intercultural Research," *Dialectica* 23:229-280, 1969.

Mason, Edward S., et al., *The Economic and Social Modernization of the Republic of Korea*, Cambridge: Council on East Asian Studies, Harvard University, 1980.

McCune, Shannon, *Korea: The Land of Broken Calm*, New York: D. Van Nostrand, 1966.

_____, "Geographical Observations on Korea," *Bulletin of the Korean Research Center, Journal of Social Sciences and Humanities* 44:1-19, 1976.

_____, *Views of the Geography of Korea, 1935-1960*, Seoul: The Korean Research Center, 1980.

Mead, Margaret, "The Study of National Character," *The Policy Sciences*, eds. D. Lerner and H.D. Haswell, pp. 70-85, Stanford: Stanford University Press, 1951.

_____, "National Character," *Anthropology Today*, ed. A.L. Kroeber, pp. 642-647, Chicago: University of Chicago Press, 1953.

_____, "Review of National Character and National Stereotypes: A Trend Report Prepared for the International Union of Scientific Philosophy by H.J.C. Duiker and N.H. Frijda," *American Anthropologist* 64:688-690, 1962.

_____, *Blackberry Winter: My Earlier Years*, New York: Morrow, 1972.

Mead, Margaret, and R. Metraux, eds., *The Study of Culture at a Distance*, Chicago: University of Chicago Press, 1953.

Middleton, Harry J., *The Compact History of the Korean War*, NewYork: Hawthorn Books, 1965.

Middleton, Russell, Brother-Sister and Father-Daughter Marriage in Ancient Egypt, *American Sociological Review* 27:603-611, 1962.

Miller, John, Jr., Owen J. Carroll, and Margaret E. Tackley, *Korea, 1951-1953*, Washington, D.C.: U.S. Government Printing Office, 1956.

Miller, Roy Andrew, *Origins of the Japanese Language*, Seattle: University of

Washington Press, 1980.

Na, Se-jin, "Physical Characteristics of Korean Nation," *Korea Journal* 3:9-29, 1963.

Narayan, Kirin, "How Native Is the 'Native' Anthropologist?," *American Anthropologist* 95:676-686, 1993.

Nelson, Sarah M., "Korean Archaeological Sequences from the First Ceramics to the Introduction of Iron," *Chronologies in Old World Arachaeology*, 3rd ed. R. W. Ehrich, vol. 1 pp. 430-438; vol. 2 pp. 417-424, Chicago: University of Chicago Press, 1992.

_____, *The Archaeology of Korea*, New York: Cambridge University Press, 1993.

Neufeldt, Victoria, and David B. Guraluik, eds., *Webster's New World Dictionary of Ameriucan English*, 3rd. ed., New York: Simon & Schuster, 1988.

Okita, Saburo, "Japan's Role in Asia-Pacific Cooperation," *The Annals of the American Academy of Political and Social Science* 513:25-37, 1991.

Ohnuki-Tierney, Emiko, *Illness and Culture in Contemporary Japan*, New York: Cambridge University Press, 1984.

Osgood, Cornelius, *The Koreans and Their Culture*, New York: The Ronald Press, 1951.

Park Myung-Lim, *Hanguk jeonjaengui balbalgwa giwon* [The Korean War: The outbreak and its origins], 2 vols., Seoul: Nanam, 1996.

Pelto, Pertti, *Anthropological Research: The Structural Inquiry*, New York: Harper & Row, 1970.

Perkins, Dwight H., *China: Asia's Next Economic Giant?*, Seattle: University of Washington Press, 1986.

Peterson, Mark, "Adoption in Korean Genealogies: Continuation of Lineage," *Korea Journal* 14:28-35, 1974.

_____, "Women without Sons: A Measure of Social Change in Yi Dynasty Korea," *Korean Women: View from the Inner Room*, eds. Laurel Kendall and Mark Peterson, pp. 33-44, New Haven: East Rock Press, 1983

Poitras, Edward W., "Maredo seoyeori itda [There is an order even in speech]," *Hangugineun nuguinga: Oegugini bon uriui uisik gujo* [Who are the

Koreans: Structure of the Korean thought patterns seen by foreigners], ed. Sin Dongho, pp. 29-35, Seoul: Chosun Ilbosa, 1978.

Queen, Stuart A., and Robert W. Habestein, *The Family in Various Cultures*, New York: J.B. Lippincott Co., 1974.

Raper, Arthur F., *Preface to Peasantry: A Tale of Two Black Belt Counties*, Chapel Hill: University of North Carolina Press, 1936.

Redfield, Robert, "The Folk Society," *American Journal of Sociology* 52:293-308, 1947.

_____, *Peasant Society and Culture and the Little Community*, Chicago: University of Chicago Press, 1960.

Reed, John Shelton, *The Enduring South: Subcultural Persistence in Mass Society*, Chapel Hill: University of North Carolina Press, 1972.

Reeves-Elington, Richard, "From Command to Demand Economies: Bulgarian Organizational Value Orientations," *Practicing Anthropology* 21:5-13, 1999.

Reich, Robert B., "Who is Us?," *Harvard Business Review*, January-February: 53-64, 1990.

_____, *The Work of Nations: Preparing Our-selves for 21st-Century Capitalism*, New York: Knopf, 1991.

Reischauer, Edwin O., and John K. Fairbank, *East Asia: The Great Tradition*, Boston: Houghton Mifflin, 1960.

Republic of Korea National Red Cross, *The Dispersed Families in Korea*, Seoul: Republic of Korea National Red Cross, 1977.

Richardson, Miles, "Anthropologist: The Myth Teller," *American Ethnologist* 2: 517-533, 1975.

_____, "Comments on: Anthropological Studies in the South by Carole E. Hill," *Current Anthropology* 18:321, 1977.

Robinson, Michael E., *Cultural Nationalism in Colonial Korea, 1920-1925*, Seattle: University of Washington Press, 1988.

Rohlen, Thomas P., *Japan's High Schools*, Berkeley: University of California Press, 1983.

Ropp, Theodore, "World War II," *World Book Encyclopedia*, vol. 1 pp. 381, Chicago: Field Enterprises Educational Corporation, 1976.

Rushdie, Salman, *East, West, Stories*, New York: Pantheon Books, 1994.

Sahlins, Marchall D., and Elman R. Service, *Evolution and Culture*, Ann Arbor: University of Michigan Press, 1960.

Sayers, Robert, and Ralph Rinzler, *The Korean Onggi Potter*, Smithsonian Folklife Studies no. 5, Washington, D.C.: Smithsonian Institution Press, 1987.

Schmid, Andre, *Korea between Empires, 1895-1919*, New York: Columbia University Press, 2002.

Schusky, Ernest L., *Manual for Kinship Analysis*, New York: Holt, Rinehart and Winston, 1965.

Serrie, Hendrick, "Constancy and Variation in Chinese Culture: An Analysis of Fourteen Mainland, Offshore, and Overseas Communities in terms of the Hsu Attributes," Unpublished Ph.D. dissertation, Northwestern University, 1976.

_____, "Chinese Business Management Behavior and the Hsu Attributes: A Preliminary Inquiry," *Anthropology and International Business*, Studies in Third World Series, ed. Hendrick Serrie, no. 28 pp. 59-71, Williamsburg: Department of Anthropology, College of William and Mary, 1986.

_____, "Training Chinese Managers for Leadership: Six Cross-Cultural Principles," *Practicing Anthropology* 21:35-41, 1999.

Shin, Gi-Wook, *Peasant Protest and Social Change in Colonial Korea*, Seattle: University of Washington Press, 1997.

_____, *Ethnic Nationalism in Korea: Genealogy, Politics, and Legacy*, Stanford: Stanford University Press, 2006.

Smart, Clifford E. J., "Taineun modu jangaemul [Strangers are Impedimens]," *Hangugineun nuguinga: Oegugini bon uriui uisik gujo* [Who are the Koreans: Structure of the Korean thought patterns seen by foreigners], ed. Sin Dongho, pp. 117-123, Seoul: Chosun Ilbosa, 1978.

Soh, Chunghee Sarah, *Women in Korean Politics*, Boulder: Westview Press, 1993.

_____, "The Korean 'Comfort Women': Movement for Redress." *Asian Survey* 36:1226-1240, 1996.

Song Bok, *Hanguk sangcheungui sahoejeok guseonggwa teukseonge gwanhan yeongu* [A study on the social structure and characteristics of Korean upper class people], A research report, n.d.

Song, Hangnyong, "A Short History of Taoism in Korea," *Dogyowa hanguk sasang* [Taoism and Korean thoughts], ed. Hanguk dogyo sasang yeongu [Association for the Studies of Korean Taoism], pp. 479-484, Seoul: Asia Munhwasa, 1994.

Sorensen, Clark W., "Women, Men: Inside, Outside: The Division of Labor in Rural Central Korea," *Korean Women: View from the Inner Room*, eds. Laurel Kendall and Mark Peterson, pp. 63-78, New Haven: East Rock Press, 1983.

_____, *Over the Mountains Are Mountains: Korean Peasant Households and Their Adaptations to Rapid Industrialization*, Seattle: University of Washington Press, 1988.

Spencer, Barbara, John H. Peterson, Jr., and Choong Soon Kim, *Choctaw Manpower and Demographic Survey*, Philadelphia, Miss.: Mississippi Band of Chocaw Indians, 1976.

Steers, Richard M., et al., *The Chaebol: Korea's Need Industrial Might*, New York: Harper & Row, 1989.

Steinberg, David I., *The Republic of Korea: Economic Transformation and Social Change*, Boulder: Westview Press, 1989.

Stern, Curt, *Principles of Human Genetics*, 3rd. ed., San Francisco: W. H. Freeman, 1973.

Stone, I. F., *The Hidden History of the Korean War*, New York: Monthly Review Press, 1953.

Suh, Dae-sook, *The Korean Communist Movement, 1918-1948*, Princeton: Princeton University Press, 1967.

Taira, Koji, "Japan, An Imminent Hegemon?," *The Annals of the American Academy of Political and Social Science* 513:151-163, 1991.

The Korean Overseas Information Service, *Handbook of Korea*, Seoul: The Korea Overseas Information Service, 1983.

_____, *Handbook of Korea*, Seoul: The Korean Overseas Information Service, 2003.

The Ministry of Culture and Tourism, *Hangugui jonggyo hyeonhwang* [A current report on Korean religion], Seoul: The Ministry of Culture and Tourism, 2002.

The World Almanac, *The World Almanac and Book of Fact*, New York: World

Almanac Books, 2004.

Ti, Uting, "Sihaeng chagowa nakgwanjuui [Trial and error, and optimism]," *Hangugineun nuguinga: Oegugini bon uriui uisik gujo* [Who are the Koreans: Structure of the Korean thought patterns seen by foreigners], ed. Sin Dongho, pp. 241-247, Seoul: Chosun Ilbosa, 1978.

Tönnies, Ferdinand, *Community and Society*, ed. & trans. Charles P. Loomis, New York: Harper Torchbooks, 1963.

Treiman, Donald, *Occupational Prestige in Comparative Perspective*, New York: Academic Press, 1977.

Trotsky, Leon, *The History of the Russian Revolution*, Ann Arbor: University of Michigan Press, n.d.

Tu, Wei-ming, *Confucian Ethics Today: The Singapore Challenge*, Singapore: Federal Publications, 1984.

_____, "Confucius and Confucianism," *Confucianism and the Family*, eds. Walter H. Slote and George A. DeVos, pp. 3-36, Albany: State University of New York Press, 1998.

Tweddell, Colin E., and Linda Amy Kimball, *Introduction to the Peoples and Cultures of Asia*, Englewood Cliffs: Pretice-Hall, 1985.

U.S. Department of the Army, *Korea-1950*, Washington, D.C.: U.S. Government Printing Office, 1952.

Underwood, Horace H., "Gipeun gajok yudaegam [Deep rooted family ties]," *Hangugineun nuguinga: Oegugini bon uriui uisik gujo* [Who are the Koreans: Structure of the Korean thought patterns seen by foreigners], ed. Sin Dongho, pp. 89-93, Seoul: Chosun Ilbosa, 1978.

Veblen, Thorstein, *Imperial Germany and in the Industrial Revolution*, New York: MacMillan, 1915.

Vogel, Ezra F., "The Japanese Family," *Comparative Family System*, ed. M.F. Nimkoff, pp. 287-300, Boston: Houghton Mifflin, 1965.

_____, *Japan as Number One: Lessons fro America*, New York: Harper Colophon, 1979.

von Glinow, Mary Ann, and Byung Jae Chung, "Korean Chaebols and the Changing Business Environment," *KoreanManagerial Dynamics*, eds. Kae H. Chung and Hak Chong Lee, pp. 27-38, New York: Prager, 1989.

Wade, Larry L., and Bong-Sik Kim, *Economic Development of South Korea: The Political Economy of Success*, New York: Praeger, 1978.

Wagner, Edward W., "The Korean Chokpo as a Historical Source," *Studies on Asian Genealogy*, ed. S. J. Palmer, pp. 141-252, Provo: Brigham Young University Press, 1971.

_____, "The Ladder of Success in Yi Dynasty Korea," *Occasional Papers on Korea*, no.1:1-8, 1974.

_____, "Two Genealogies and Women's Status in Early Yi Dynasty Korea," *Korean Women: View from the Inner Room*, eds. Laurel Kendall and Mark Peterson, pp. 23-32, New Haven: East Rock Press, 1983.

Wallace, Anthony F.C., "Review of: The Revolution in Anthropology by I.C. Javie," *American Anthropologist* 68:1254-1255, 1966.

Wallace, Jonathan, and Mark Mangan, *Sex, Laws, and Cyberspace*, New York: Henry Holt, 1996.

Warner, W. Lloyd, and Paul S. Lunt, *The Social Life of a Modern Community*, New Haven: Yale University Press, 1941.

Weber, Max, *The Religion of China*, New York: The Free Press, 1951.

_____, *The Theory of Social and Economic Organization*, trans. A. H. Henderson and Talcott Parsons, New York: Free Press of Glencoe, 1957.

_____, "Science as a Vocation," *The Relevance of Sociology*, ed. Jack D. Douglas, pp. 45-63, New York: Appleton, 1970.

Welty, Thomas, *The Asians: The Evolving Heritage*, 6th ed., New York: Harper & Row, 1984.

Westermark, Edward, *The History of Human Marriage*, London: Macmillan, 1894.

Westphal, Larry E., "The Republic of Korea's Experience with Export-Led Industrial Development," *World Development* 6:347-382, 1978.

Whang, In-Joung, *Management of Rural Change in Korea: The Saemaul Undong*, Korea Studies Series no. 5, Seoul: Seoul National University Press, 1981.

White, Leslie A., *The Science of Culture: A Study of Man and Civilization*, New York: Farrar, Straus, & Cudahy, 1949.

Whiting, Allen S., *China Crosses the Yalu: The Decision to Enter the Korean*

War, Stanford: Stanford University Press, 1960.

Wilk, Richard R., "'Real Belizean Food': Building Local Identity in the Transnational Caribbean," *American Anthropologist* 101:244-255, 1999.

Wilkie, Laurie A., and Paul Farnsworth, "Trade and the Construction of Bahamian Identity: A Multi-Scalar Exploration," *International Journal of Historical Archaeology* 3:283-320, 1999.

Woronoff, Jon, *Korea's Economy: Man-Made Miracle*, Seoul: The Sisayeongeosa, 1983.

Yang, Key P., and Gregory Henderson, "An Outline History of Korean Confucianism," *Journal of Asian Studies* 43:81-101, 1958.

Yee, gaeyeol, "The Social Networks of Koreans," *Korea gournal* 40:325-352, 2000.

Yim, Seock Jae, *Roofs and Lines: A Study of Korean Architecture*, trans. Jean Young Lee, Seoul: Ewha Womans University Press, 2005.

Yoo, Sangjin, and Sang M. Lee, "Management Style and Practice of Korean Chaebols," *California Management Review* Summer:95-110, 1987.

Yoshino, Kosaku, *Cultural Nationalism in Contemporary Japan: A Sociological Inquiry*, London: Routledge, 1992.

Young, John, "Situation and Time: Observations on the Chinese Way of Doing Business," *Practicing Anthropology* 22:13-17, 2000.

Yu Jino, *Yanghogi* [Teaching at Korea University], Seoul: Korea University Press, 1977.

Yun Hyeongsuk, "Gukje gyeolhon baeujaui galdeunggwa jeogeung [Conflict and adjustment of spouses of international marriages]," *Hangugui sosuja, siltaewa jeonmang* [Minority in Korea: Past and Future], eds. Choe Hyeop, et al., pp. 321-349, Seoul: Hanul Academy, 2004.

Yun Iheum, et al., *Hanguginui jonggyo* [Korean religion], Seoul: Mundeoksa, 1994.

Yun Taekrim, *Uisik gujosangeuro bon hangugin* [Koreans in terms of their thought patterns], Seoul: Hyeonamsa, 1971.

Zenshō Eisuke, *Chōsen-no-syōroku* [Korean villages], Seoul: Chōsen Sōtokufu [Japanese Government-General in Korea], 1935.

List of Abbreviations

ACT: American College Test
AKS: Anthropologists for Korean Studies
APEC: Asia-Pacific Economic Cooperation
ASEAN: Association of Southeast Asian Nations
CGT: Compensated Gross Ton
CICI: Corea[Korea] Image Communication Institute
CPKI: Committee for the Preparation of Korean Independence
CPV: Chinese People's Volunteer
CSAT: College Scholastic Ability Test
DJP: Democratic Justice Party
DMC: Digital Media City
DMZ: Demilitarized Zone
DPR: Democratic Republican Party
DPRK: Democratic People's Republic of Korea
EU: European Union
FDI: Foreign Direct Investment
FIFA: Fédération Internationale de Football Association
FKI: Federation of Korean Industries
FKTU: Federation of Korean Trade Union
FTA: Free Trade Agreement
IMF: International Monetary Fund
IT: Information Technology
KAIST: Korea Advanced Institute of Science and Technology
KAL: Korean Airline
KBS: Korean Broadcasting System

KCIA: Korean Central Intelligence Agency
KDI: Korea Development Institute
KDP: Korean Democratic Party
KEDI: Korean Educational Development Institute
KEF: Korea Employers Federation
KOICA: Korea International Cooperation Agency
KOTRA: Korea Trade-Investment Promotion Agency
KPG: Korean Provisional Government
KPR: Korean People's Republic
KRIM: Korean Institute for Missions
LCD: Liquid Crystal Display
LNG: Liquefied Natural Gas
NAFTA: North American Free Trade Agreement
NGO: Non-Governmental Organization
NSRRKI: National Society for the Rapid Realization of Korean Independence
OECD: Organization for Economic Cooperation and Development
POSCO: Pohang Iron and Steel Company
R&D: Research and Development
ROK: Republic of Korea
SAT: Scholastic Aptitude Test
SERI: Samsung Economic Research Institute
SWNCC: United States' State-War-Navy Coordinating Committee
TAR: Trans-Asian Railway
TKR: Trans-Korea Railway
TSR: Trans-Siberian Railway
UNESCO: United Nations Educational, Scientific, and Cultural Organization
UR: Uruguay Round Agreement
USAFIK: United States Armed Forces in Korea
USAMGIK: United States Army Military Government in Korea.
WTO: World Trade Organization

Index

Abelmann, Nancy 158
Amsden, Alice 291~294, 334
Ancestor Worship 183, 184
April 19 Student Revolution 75, 91
Aquaculture 148, 173

Baekje 27, 29~33, 112, 199, 220
    Latter Baekje 35
Balhae 25, 33
Befu, Harumi 182, 267
Brandt, Vincent S.R. 147, 259
Breen, Michael 1, 230, 256, 285
Bronze Age 19, 21, 22, 220
Buddhism 8, 29, 30, 32, 34, 36, 38, 40, 182, 190, 191, 193, 197~204, 212, 214, 215, 277, 278, 336
    cultural contribution 204
    introduction to Korea 199
    membership of 203
    spreading to Japan 199
Bulguksa 32, 199, 200
Business and industrial anthropology 281
Buyeo 22, 27~29

Carter, Jimmy (James Earl) 96
Catholicism (see also Christianity) 45, 52, 55, 204~207, 213
    as sanctuary to dissidents 206
    as Western learning 204
    introduced to Korea 204
    martyrdom of 205
Cheondogyo (see also Donghak) 8, 60, 180, 194, 213, 214
Chinese People's Volunteers (CPV) 86
Choe Jeu 55, 213
Choe Namseon 253, 258
Choe Si-hyeong 213
Choe, Chong Pil 16, 21, 22
Choi Kyu-hah 94
Christianity (see also Protestantism and Catholicism) 8, 34, 77, 179, 188, 190, 193, 208, 210, 216, 223, 277, 278
    contributions made by 206
    population of 210
Chu Hsi 191, 192
Chun Doo-hwan 95, 100, 101, 141, 164, 295, 298
Chuseok (the Harvest Festival) 181
Cold War 2, 106
Confucianism (see also Neo-Confucianism) 26, 34~36, 40, 41, 132, 183, 184, 190~196, 213~215, 226, 256, 263, 276, 278, 283, 293, 294
    basic tenet of 190
    contribution to 196
    in economic development 194
    introduction to Korea 191
    number of devotees 196
    religiousness of 193
Crane, Paul 100, 260
Cultural nationalists 57, 59, 63, 65, 289
Cumings, Bruce 30, 35, 77, 78, 327

Dangun 23, 183, 185, 187, 215

Demilitarized Zone (DMZ) 9, 51, 87, 304, 314, 334
    as eco-Axe 314
Deuchler, Martina 50, 113
Discrimination 41, 95, 100, 133, 134, 136, 139, 188, 267, 321, 328
    against interracial marriage 267
    against mixed-race 267
Dispersed Korean family 76, 90
Donghak (Eastern Learning; see also Cheondogyo) 157, 182, 213–214
    membership of 214
    peasant army 214
    peasant rebellion 214
Dongnip sinmun (*Independence*) 56, 62

"Early Villages" period inhabitants 18
Eckert, Carter J. 196
Education 2, 8, 9, 42, 50, 54, 56, 59, 63–65, 100, 110, 118, 119, 138, 163, 165, 168, 170, 176, 177, 194–196, 219, 220, 226, 228–234, 236–247
    as *han* 230
    college entrance examination 237
    financial burden for parents 243
    for upward mobility 230
    for overseas studies 236
    impact of Confucianism 226
    in acquiring desirable marriage partner 231
    role of missionaries 228
Enlightenment Thought (*Gaehwa sasang*) 45, 52–54
Environmental conservation 203, 281, 301–304, 306, 308, 309
    activities of conservationists 304
    changing burial culture 314
    participation of anthropologists 306
    restoration of Cheonggyecheon 309–312
    transformation of Nanjido 309, 312, 313

Ethos (see also national character and pattern) 9, 249, 250, 252–257, 260
    defined as 250
    in conceptualizing 250

Family reunion 90
Family 8, 9, 13, 26, 35, 38, 54, 76, 85, 87–90, 105, 106, 109–111, 114, 115, 117, 120–122, 124, 125, 127, 129–132, 134, 137, 138, 140
    extended family 131
    nuclear family 131, 132
    stem family 131, 132
Federation of Korean Industries (FKI) 335
Federation of Korean Trade Unions (FKTU) 326, 327
FIFA World Cup, 2002 6, 9, 258, 259, 262, 299, 313
Five-Year Economic Development Plan 70, 144, 163, 168, 287, 295
Foreign Direct Investment (FDI) 322–327, 330, 333
Free Trade Agreement (FTA) 3, 158, 171, 172, 273, 300, 318, 319, 329, 331, 332

Gabo Reform (*Gabo gyeongjang*) 50, 54, 157, 219, 223
Gapsin jeongbyeon (the coup d'état) 54, 92
Generationalism 99, 102
    386 generation 103, 242, 255
Goguryeo (Koguryŏ) dynasty 24–33, 112, 137, 183, 191, 199, 220
    Latter Goguryeo 35
Gojoseon (Old Joseon) 5, 23, 215
Goryeo (Koryŏ) dynasty 5, 17, 34, 35, 113, 115, 119, 149, 201, 212, 221, 226, 310
    celadon of 36
    woodblock-printing in 36
Gwangju Rebellion 95

Hallyu 7, 25, 330
Han, Kyung-Koo (Han Kyung-Koo) 51, 103, 194, 254, 255
Han 230, 231, 246, 275, 276, 292
    original nuance of 230
Hangeul 39, 57, 63, 64, 277, 210
Hermit Kingdom 2, 317, 324
Heungseon Daewongun (Daewongun or Yi Haeung) 2, 52
High civil service examination (*gwageo*) 153, 241
Hodge, John Reed 79
Hsu, Francis L.K. 12, 15, 109, 181, 251
Hussain, Tariq 247, 320, 330
Hwarang ("flower of youth") 31, 34, 200, 201
Hyundai 2, 136, 143, 195, 277, 284, 287, 293, 321

Identity creation (*changssi*) 64, 160, 161
Independence Club 54, 56, 57
Indigenous innovation 292
Information technology (IT) 49, 174~177, 276
    applied to farming 174
    cyber village 174, 175
Inter-Korean dialogue 105
International Monetary Fund (IMF) 97, 176, 225, 285, 299, 300
    aid and intervention of 97
Internet 12, 102, 174, 175, 285, 333

Jaebeol (*Chaebŏl*, big business conglomerate) 231, 260, 283, 284, 289, 295~297, 299, 300, 320~322, 332, 333
    characteristic features of 253, 296
    of octopus tentacles 296
    role of 254, 291, 296, 320, 335
Janelli, Dawnhee Yim 132, 133, 150, 187, 294
Janelli, Roger M. 132, 133, 150, 187, 294
Jang Myeon (John M. Chang) 70, 92
Japanese invasion 8, 42, 43, 51, 149, 151, 153, 201, 268
    Hideyoshi invasion 42, 52
Japanese mobilization 65, 66
    comfort women 67, 160
    National Manpower Mobilization Act 66
    Special Volunteer Army Act 66
    Women's Volunteer Workers Corps 66
Jeon Bongjun 157, 214
Joseon dynasty (Yi dynasty) 11, 25, 34, 38, 40, 44, 45, 52, 53, 61, 113, 116, 117, 120, 126, 134, 137, 140, 145, 149, 151, 153, 156, 157, 161, 184, 185, 188, 191, 192, 195, 201, 202, 221~225, 241, 256, 261, 263, 269, 283, 310, 312, 330
    Yi Seonggye (King Taejo) 38, 40, 42, 113, 185, 201
June 29 Proclamation 298, 304

Kendall, Laurel 110, 188, 230
Kennan, George 3, 253
Kim Dae-jung 89, 95~97, 101, 102, 106, 207, 306
    sunshine policy of 98, 106
Kim Gu 80~83, 94
Kim Ilseong 83, 140
Kim Jeongil 97, 106, 108, 140
Kim Seong-Nae 182, 186
Kim Young-sam 95, 97, 101, 235
Kimchi 18, 130, 264
Kinship system 112, 134, 137~139
    clan (sib) 112~117, 134, 137~140
    fictional kinship 140
    lineage 111~113, 133, 137~139
Korea Development Institute (KDI) 322
Korea Employers Federation (KEF) 324
Korea International Cooperation Agency (KOICA) 319, 325
Korea Trade Investment Promotion

Agency (KOTRA) 325~327
Korean Central Intelligence Agency (KCIA) 94
Korean Church in the U.S. 211
   functions of churches 211
Korean Democratic Party (KDP, Hanguk Minjudang) 80, 81, 83, 162
Korean ethnicity 16, 17
   cultural origin of 8, 19
   identity of 17
   racial origin of 16
Korean Provisional Government (KPG or Daehanminguk Imsi Jeongbu) 62, 74, 77, 80, 81
Korean War 3, 5, 8, 11, 51, 71, 74, 75, 84, 85, 87, 88, 90, 126, 202, 209, 212, 234, 254, 268, 272, 282, 284, 293, 314, 319, 334, 336
   casualties of 8, 9, 15~17, 19, 84
   cease-fire 87, 88
   impact of 46, 175, 191, 200, 226, 242, 292, 312

Labor (Trade) Union 96, 207, 281, 296~300, 304, 322, 325, 326, 330, 333
   controlled by the military-led government 302
   confrontational mode of 322
   number of labor strikes 322
Lee, Ki-baik 156, 159, 220, 223
Lee, Kwang-kyu (Lee Kwang-kyu) 120, 145, 146, 148, 204, 215, 260, 266, 270, 273
LG 2, 136, 143, 288

MacArthur, Douglas 75, 84, 85
March First Movement (*Samil Undong*): 60~63, 257
   declaration of independence 60, 208, 214
Marriage 8, 9, 35, 38, 40, 107~120
   age of 121

arranged marriage 109~111, 115, 116, 118, 119, 124, 125
free choice 109, 111, 112, 119, 124
marriage consulting center (*gyeolhon jeongbo hoesa*) 117~119, 130
marrying foreign women 122, 170
monogamy 119
polygamy 38
system of matchmaker 118
remarriage 38, 118
McCune-Reischauer system 13
Mead, Margaret 10
Meiji Restoration, Japan 49, 54, 93
Mesolithic (broad spectrum food collecting) 19, 20
Mongolian invasion 32

National character (see also ethos and pattern) 249~251, 253, 255, 263, 278
   new urgency for 251
Nationalism 58, 59, 250, 257, 258, 323, 327
   on single ethnic people (minjok) 327, 328
Nelson, Sarah M. 2, 16, 183
Neo-Confucianism (see also Confucianism) 40, 43, 191, 192, 278
   influence in Japan 192, 194
Neolithic inhabitants 16, 21
New Village Movement (*Saemaeul Undong*) 8, 71, 163~167, 185, 188, 278
   as a role model to 167
   beginning in 164
   objectives of 164
North American Free Trade Agreement (NAFTA) 301

Oriental Development Company 58, 159
Osgood, Cornelius 272
Paleolithic foragers 16
Panmunjeom 87, 89

Park Chung-hee 69, 92, 93, 100, 105, 162, 206, 207, 265, 272, 295, 301
Pattern (see also ethos and national character) 41, 131, 132, 135, 157, 263, 265, 269, 271, 272, 275, 276
    diminishing traditional ones 259, 271
Peasant rebellion 54~56, 156, 214
POSCO 123, 264, 287, 291, 322
Practical Learning (*Silhak*) 45, 52, 222
Protectorate Treaty, 1905 53
Protestantism (see also Christianity) 207, 209, 210
    growth in 210
    introduced to Korea 207
    members of 207, 209, 210
    role of early missionaries 208
    role in the March First Movement 208, 257

Radical nationalists 59, 65, 229, 253
Reagan, Ronald 96
Regionalism 99~102
Reich, Robert 323, 324
Religious syncretism 182
Reunion telethon, KBS 76, 88, 89, 141, 299
Revitalizing reform (*yusin*) 93, 95, 206, 207
    Yusin Constitution 93, 95, 207
Rho Tae-woo 97, 100, 141, 165, 298, 306, 308
Rice 22, 63, 107, 130, 145~147, 153, 157, 158, 160, 162, 165, 167, 171, 172, 177, 182, 250, 284, 306, 329, 336, 337
    commercialization of farming 173
    consumption of 171, 172
    culture of 171
    farmers' sentimentality to 171~173
    market liberalization on 171
Robinson, Michael 59
Roh Moo-hyun 98, 102, 106, 108, 237, 241, 242, 247, 303

Roosevelt, Franklin D. 69
Roosevelt, Theodore 3, 53
Rural village 8, 135, 143~145, 148, 153, 155, 156, 163~165, 167, 168, 170, 171, 176, 189, 278
    changing paradigm of 171
    massive exodus of 176, 283
    origins of 144
    social structure of 148
    types of 145, 146, 148
Russo-Japanese War 2, 51, 53

Samguksagi 22, 24
Samgungnyusa 22, 24
Samhan (Three Han) 23
Samsung 2, 136, 143, 258, 287, 288, 296, 321
Segyehwa 235
Seo Jaepil 56
Shamanism 8, 34, 182, 186~189, 194, 199, 210, 269
    discrimination against 188
    functions of 186
    gut (shaman ritual) 186, 188, 189
    members of devotees 188, 189
Shin, Gi-wook 158, 327
Silla 18, 25, 27, 29, 31~35, 51, 112, 113, 137, 156, 191, 198~201, 220, 225, 241, 278, 299
    United Silla 32, 199, 201
Single ethnic people (*danil minjok*) 327, 328
Sino-Japanese War, 1937 44, 63
Six-party talk 52
    on nuclear weapons 52, 107
    U.N. Security Council's resolution 107
Social stratification 22, 31, 116, 220
    occupational prestige 222, 224, 225
    open-class system 222, 225
Song Jinu 77, 80, 81
Sorensen, Clark W. 133, 146

Steinberg, David 3, 49, 95, 160, 318
Summer Olympic Games, 1988 6, 9, 309
Syngman Rhee 13, 75, 80~85, 90, 94, 208, 209

Taft-Katsura Agreement 53
Taoism 8, 36, 40, 191, 193, 213, 215, 277
Thirty-eighth parallel 5, 78, 84~88
Three Kingdoms (see also Goguryeo, Silla, and Baekje): 18, 24~27, 32, 33, 99
   cultural legacy of 33, 34
   gender equality of 34
Tripitaka Koreana 201
Truman, Harry S. 85
Tu, Wei-ming 190, 192

U.S. State-War-Navy Coordinating Committee (SWNCC) 78
Uibyeong (Righteous armies) 43, 54
Unification Church (Tongilgyo) 216
United States Armed Forces in Korea (USAFIK) 79
United States Army Military Government in Korea (USAMGIK) 79
Uruguay Round Agreement (UR) 171

Vietnam War 71, 292, 293, 319

Wedding 124~129, 300
   ceremony 129
   costs of 129
   gifts 129
   jurye 129
Western Learning (*Seohak*) (see also Catholicism) 45, 52, 55, 204~207, 213
Wonbullgyo (Won Buddhism) 214
World Trade Organization (WTO) 158, 286
World War II 2, 3, 8, 34, 66, 70, 71, 73, 76, 152, 161, 188, 209, 235, 251, 254, 284, 326

Xenophobia 267

Yangban 11, 40~42, 44, 54, 55, 110, 113, 116, 117, 119, 120, 124, 126, 134, 143, 148~150, 152, 153, 155~158, 161, 163, 184, 194, 204, 205, 214, 219, 221~223, 225~227, 241, 242, 261~263, 275, 282, 283, 293
Yeo Unhyeong 77, 80
Yi dynasty (see also Joseon dynasty) 38, 192
Yi Gwangsu 253, 255
Yi Hwang 100, 143, 153, 191, 192, 282, 283
Yi Sunsin 43, 94
Yu Seongryong 149, 153, 282
Yun Po-sun 92, 93